4/96

Rogers Hornsby

Also by Charles C. Alexander

Crusade for Conformity:
The Ku Klux Klan in Texas, 1920–1929

The Ku Klux Klan in the Southwest

This New Ocean: A History of Project Mercury

Nationalism in American Thought, 1930–1945

Holding the Line: The Eisenhower Era, 1952–1961

Here the Country Lies:
Nationalism and the Arts in Twentieth-Century America

Ty Cobb

John McGraw

Our Game: An American Baseball History

Rogers Hornsby

...

A Biography

Charles C. Alexander

HENRY HOLT AND COMPANY
NEW YORK

Henry Holt and Company, Inc.
Publishers since 1866
115 West 18th Street
New York, New York 10011

Henry Holt® is a registered
trademark of Henry Holt and Company, Inc.

Published in Canada by Fitzhenry & Whiteside Ltd.,
195 Allstate Parkway, Markham, Ontario L3R 4T8.

Library of Congress Cataloging-in-Publication Data
Alexander, Charles C.
Rogers Hornsby: a biography / Charles C. Alexander.—1st ed.
p.   cm.
Includes bibliographical references and index.
1. Hornsby, Rogers, 1896–1963.   2. Baseball players—United
States—Biography.   I. Title.
GV865.H6A32   1995
796.357′092—dc20   95-3841
[B]   CIP

ISBN 0-8050-2002-0

Henry Holt books are available for special promotions and
premiums. For details contact: Director, Special Markets.

First Edition—1995

Designed by Brian Mulligan

Printed in the United States of America
All first editions are printed on acid-free paper.∞

1   3   5   7   9   10   8   6   4   2

Frontispiece: Rogers Hornsby in 1921.
(National Baseball Library and Archive, Cooperstown, N.Y.)

*For Don and Mary Jo Pickens and
Joanne Smith, and to the memory of
Eugene C. Murdock (1921–1992)*

Contents

• • •

Acknowledgments

· · ·

Of the many people in different parts of the United States who helped me in my efforts to discover and understand Rogers Hornsby, I wish especially to thank the staffs of the National Baseball Library, Cooperstown, New York; *Sporting News* Archives, St. Louis, Missouri; Austin History Center, Austin, Texas; Office of Records of the Clerk of the Circuit Courts, City of St. Louis, Missouri; County Clerk's Office, Runnels County, Ballinger, Texas; and Library of Congress, Washington, D.C. Brad H. Hornsby, Murfreesboro, Tennessee; Ann Hornsby Rice, McLean, Virginia; Rogers Hornsby III, Denison, Texas; Fred Graham of the Texas Sports Hall of Fame, Dallas, Texas; Thomas H. Smith, historian of the Texas Rangers baseball franchise, Arlington, Texas; George Parkinson, chief, Archives-Library Division, Ohio Historical Society, Columbus, Ohio; and Fred Schuld, Macedonia, Ohio, also provided important assistance. A number of others who were kind enough to share their time and memories of Hornsby are cited in the notes and bibliography; I thank them here collectively.

ACKNOWLEDGMENTS

As always, Warren F. Kimball, Robert Treat Professor of History, Rutgers University, and one of my oldest friends, was willing to read my work cheerfully and perceptively. Steven F. Gietschier, Director of Research for the *Sporting News,* and William M. Kimok of Ohio University also gave the manuscript close and constructive readings. William B. Strachan of Henry Holt and Company has been both a professional associate and a friend, and so has Gerard F. McCauley, my longtime literary agent.

Finally, my daughter, Rachel C. Alexander, D.V.M., continues to bring joy into my life, as does her mother, the altogether remarkable JoAnn Erwin Alexander.

Athens, Ohio
November 1994

Rogers
Hornsby

I have never been a yes man.

—Rogers Hornsby, 1950

Prologue

· · ·

Beaumont,

Texas,

Summer

1950

At the bottom half of each inning, the stout, silver-haired manager of the Beaumont Roughnecks would emerge from the first-base dugout, trundle across the diamond, take his place in the third-base coaching box, and ritually clap his hands to exhort the leadoff Roughneck batter. Of course I knew *who* he was. The name Rogers Hornsby was a familiar one for anybody who followed baseball closely; as a fourteen-year-old who scanned box scores in the local daily newspapers, absorbed the weekly contents of the *Sporting News,* and studied how-to-play books in an effort to improve my own decidedly limited skills, I knew about all the sport's great men. I could quote career and season statistics for contemporaries such as DiMaggio, Musial, Williams, Kiner, and Feller, as well as for Cobb, Ruth, Young, Johnson, Wagner, Gehrig, and other past heroes.

Rogers Hornsby's achievements were among the most familiar and imposing: a .358 lifetime batting average (second only to Cobb's) in twenty-three major-league seasons (1915–37); a .424 average in 1924

1

(highest for the twentieth century); two other .400-plus seasons; seven National League batting titles; player-manager of the St. Louis Cardinals in 1926 when they defeated Babe Ruth and the New York Yankees in a legendary World Series. By nearly everybody's estimation, Hornsby was the foremost right-handed hitter over the first century of American baseball.

Studying him from the grandstand behind third base, where I sat with my parents through something like twenty-five games that summer, I couldn't figure *why* this famous person had ended up back in his native Texas, managing at Beaumont, of all places. With a population of about 100,000, Beaumont was the smallest city in the Texas League—a Class AA circuit two levels below the majors. After all the glory Hornsby had gained and all the money he must have earned in baseball, what circumstances could possibly have led him to Beaumont?

Not that we weren't delighted to have Hornsby managing the local team. After last-place finishes for three straight seasons, we'd come to expect little from the players the New York Yankees assigned to their Beaumont farm club. Yet in August and early September, Hornsby's Roughnecks astonished everyone by surging into first place and staying there, finishing in front of the Fort Worth Cats—a perennial powerhouse stocked with talented youngsters from the Brooklyn Dodgers' farm system. It was enough to make the summer of 1950 one of the best times of my life.

When the pennant was almost clinched, local business and civic leaders organized a Rogers Hornsby Day, with appropriate ceremonies to take place before that night's game. A crowd of 6,259, close to capacity, was present at Beaumont's Stuart Stadium as Mayor Otho Plummer thanked Hornsby on behalf of the city and then presented a Texas Stetson and the keys to a new black Cadillac sedan. Hornsby took the hat (but wouldn't put it on), glanced at the Cadillac, and then grunted into the microphone, "It's nice. Now get it outta here so we can start the game."[1]

A barely audible reaction—a mixture of surprise, disappointment, and dismay—moved through the crowd. My parents, who always put considerable store in appearances, simply didn't know what to make of Hornsby's graceless response to a genuine, openhanded expression of civic gratitude.

Apart from what could be learned in official baseball records, we knew little about Hornsby—little about the succession of trades and dismissals that marked his career and what in effect was a thirteen-year exile from the major leagues. Had we known Hornsby as many people in the little universe of Organized Baseball knew him, we might have expected just about what we all got that night in Beaumont.

More than twenty years earlier, the venerable St. Louis sportswriter John B. Sheridan observed that Hornsby "is, as the French say, deficient in the social relation. . . . Hornsby can be cold, indifferent, even rude." "As cold as tempered steel" was the way another acquaintance described him. "He cares little for what anyone says, and still less for what they think." Travis Jackson, Hornsby's teammate on the 1927 New York Giants, remembered that "he had a good way of making everybody irritated," while Les Tietje, who pitched briefly for the St. Louis Browns when Hornsby managed them in the mid-1930s, was rather more explicit: "Rogers Hornsby. Now there was a real p-r-i-c-k."[2]

Cold, gruff, aloof, loner—such adjectives show up with remarkable frequency in contemporary recollections of Hornsby. Acquaintances also noted his extraordinarily clear, blue eyes: "steel blue," said most people; "large tawny eyes, not unlike a mountain lion's," recalled a former teammate; "go to hell eyes," in the journalist Westbrook Pegler's phrase.[3] Hornsby was also, by his own admission and nearly everybody else's account, bluntly honest and utterly lacking in tact.

"I have never been a yes man," he declared during spring training with his 1950 Beaumont team. "When a man asks me a question I believe he wants me to give him an honest answer no matter who it hurts. But some of the owners don't want that. They want the answer that they want to hear. But that's not the way I was brought up." "More than all my honors in 48 years of baseball," he insisted less than a year before he died, "I'm proudest of the fact that I am not a baseball hypocrite. . . . I've never taken back anything I ever said and I've never failed to say exactly—and I mean exactly—what I was thinking. To everybody—from the owner to the bat boy." Hornsby, a longtime friend believed, "was as addicted to the truth as a drunk was to his bottle."[4]

Plenty of people—especially teammates, players on teams he managed, club owners who employed him, and no doubt his first two wives—found his tactlessness insufferable. But for baseball writers covering his career over the decades, his candor was his most attractive feature. Usually a good interview subject, Hornsby boasted of never saying anything off the record. "The most personable thing about Hornsby," enthused Bozeman Bulger of the *New York World* in 1927, "is his frankness. He says what he thinks without any thought of what effect his words will have. . . . If he believes a thing, he says it."[5] Bulger might have added that whatever Hornsby had to say was usually punctuated with profanity and scatology.

When Hornsby talked, moreover, he rarely talked anything but baseball. Not only was baseball his professional livelihood; it was central to his understanding of American society as well as the only organized athletic competition worth doing. Although he played a little football before he dropped out of high school, later on he had no use for that or any other sport besides baseball. In 1953, on the eve of the annual preseason game at Chicago's Soldier Field between the College All-Stars and the reigning professional champions, he remarked to a group of visiting sportswriters, "You fellers are up here for the football game—that's a goddamn lousy sport." And when he asked his grandson about his favorite sport and the boy replied that he preferred football, Hornsby professed to be "flabbergasted."[6]

Hornsby sometimes went bird hunting in late autumn, but unlike many ballplayers, he never took up golf and dismissed card playing as a waste of time. He read little and, at least during the baseball season, avoided motion pictures, convinced that both activities were bad for a hitter's precious eyesight. That he'd never tasted liquor or tobacco was one of the best-known facts about him.

J. Roy Stockton of the *St. Louis Post-Dispatch* once contrasted Hornsby's personality and habits to those of Frank Frisch, the brilliant second baseman for whom Hornsby was traded in 1926, in what was probably the most sensational player exchange in baseball history up to then. Frisch, a Fordham University graduate, smoked, danced, liked to read and garden, and could play the guitar. He kept a decent stock of wine, enjoyed travel, and went in for photography and amateur movie-making. "Hornsby," Stockton said, "never read a book in his life and doesn't even read the daily newspaper, except perhaps the headlines and the baseball columns." Hornsby had never held a camera or a musical instrument, never spaded a flower garden, never smoked or chewed tobacco. For Hornsby, the chief value of travel was "to get from one baseball town to another." He didn't dance, "and his comment on music was 'How the devil can a fellow talk baseball with those fellers makin' all that racket with them instruments.' "[7]

Stockton exaggerated, though not by much. It's notable that Hornsby never took issue with Stockton's less-than-flattering characterization; the two remained on good terms for the half century they knew each other.

One who likes to judge people by stereotypes might explain Hornsby as basically a Texan—born in 1896 on the state's semiarid plains, raised mostly in Fort Worth, and buried in the family plot in a cemetery near Austin. Although he lived outside the state most of his adult life, he started out in professional baseball in Texas, kept up his contacts with a considerable number of Texan relatives and acquaintances, and managed teams in two Texas cities.

Hornsby might fit the image of the Texas plainsman—laconic, hard-bitten, no-nonsense, straight-from-the-shoulder—except for the fact that from the age of six he lived in an urban industrial environment. Besides, the gallery of American stereotypes offers an equally familiar Texan: the swaggering, loud-mouthed braggart and bullshitter.

If stereotypes rarely explain much of anything, caricatures, particularly self-caricatures, sometimes reveal more. Over the years Hornsby created a kind of self-caricature, which his contemporaries in the press

5

and baseball came to accept as representing the whole truth. When he was a boy, Hornsby often said, his mother taught him not only to shun alcohol and tobacco but "above everything to always tell the truth."[8]

Of course Hornsby didn't always do so. Like the rest of us, he sometimes dissembled, backtracked, contradicted himself—and outright lied. Contrary to what he let people believe, he didn't always get along with umpires; he was ejected from games on a number of occasions and drew several fines and suspensions. While he possessed the finest batting eye in the game, sometimes he swung at pitches outside the strike zone; sometimes he even looked at called third strikes. Despite his reputation for never praising his players when they did well—"Why should I? That's what they're being paid to do," he said repeatedly—he often spoke warmly of men he managed.[9]

Hornsby insisted that he always gave his best on the ballfield, and as a manager he demanded the same from his players. They owed that not to him but to the club that paid their salaries, to the fans who paid to see them play, and most of all to themselves as professionals. Yet at least twice during his own playing career—in episodes that were well publicized at the time but subsequently overlooked by Hornsby and everybody else—he deliberately slacked off because he was unhappy with his team's management.

Although Hornsby had little contact with his older son after the breakup of his first marriage, he seems to have been a reasonably good father to his son by his second wife—at least while the boy was growing up. He generally enjoyed the company of young people, and in the many baseball schools and clinics with which he was associated, beginning in 1933, he worked to teach tens of thousands of boys the basics of the game.

Regarding the one nonbaseball activity that held his attention—betting on horse races—Hornsby was particularly plainspoken. While other kinds of gambling failed to interest him, he belonged to the legion of ballplayers who liked to bet on horses. Hornsby, unlike most of his peers, bet excessively and often profligately; although he won big on a few occasions, his losses kept him in financial straits for much of his life. Especially in the 1920s and 1930s, with the cloud of the 1919 World Series scandal still hanging over professional baseball, Hornsby's gambling habits vexed the sport's officialdom and repeatedly put him at odds with the people he worked for.

Hornsby never tried to conceal his fondness for putting money on a horse's nose. Over and over he insisted that betting on a race was his only real enjoyment away from baseball, that what he did with his own money hurt nobody but himself, and that what financiers did with other people's money in the stock market was much worse.

Yet Hornsby refused to recognize that those who employed him as player and manager and those responsible for trying to keep baseball honest might plausibly object to his piling up gambling debts and possibly making himself vulnerable to pressure from big-time operators seeking a sure thing. Nor would Hornsby concede that his gambling took a toll on his finances and family life, although that was obvious to people who knew him well.

Limited in formal education and outlook, Rogers Hornsby seemed a simple person. In a sense, baseball *was* his whole life, both on and off the playing field. It was a life full of conflict, complications, and frustration. Hornsby's is the story of a determined, difficult man who, for all his fabled franknesss, wouldn't acknowledge his own conspicuous shortcomings. Hornsby never seemed to understand that by itself brilliance in his chosen field just wasn't enough. To survive, prosper, and keep others' respect, he would also have to accommodate himself to what others thought and felt.

"You gotta go along to get along" goes an old Texas saying, but Hornsby more nearly fit John Dos Passos's characterization of Thorstein Veblen, who "couldn't get his mouth round the essential yes."[10] Although it's improbable that Hornsby ever heard of Veblen (or vice versa), both men paid a heavy price for being independent in ways that really didn't make them independent.

In his fine biography of Babe Ruth, the late Marshall Smelser noted that, unlike writers, politicians, warriors, and saints, people who are "known mostly for performance"—such as actors, musicians, and ath-

7

letes—usually leave little in the way of written materials bearing on their lives. Late in his life Hornsby collaborated with journalists on two books about himself that, while useful for events in his career and his opinions on baseball matters, reveal little about his nonbaseball existence. A person who lived by deeds, not words, he left behind no collection of letters, no diary or journal.

To piece together Hornsby's life, I've had to rely mostly on contemporary press coverage, surviving anecdotes and yarns, recollections of people who knew him, and of course the precise records of his prowess as a ballplayer. "The job of writing the life of such a person," observed biographer Smelser, "is to try to combine these hard-to-mix parts into a narrative which makes sense."[11]

That I've tried to do with Rogers Hornsby—not just the baseball man but the fellow human being.

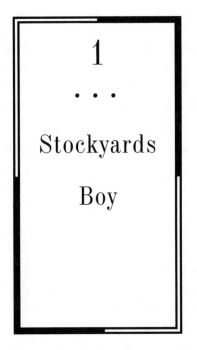

1

. . .

Stockyards

Boy

If there had been any baseball connections in his ancestry, Rogers
Hornsby might have talked quite a lot about his numerous forebears.
Since there weren't any, he ignored everybody named Hornsby before
his parents' generation.

In fact, Hornsby's family line was long, well documented, and if not
truly distinguished, at least distinctive—as well as thoroughly Texan.
Early in the eighteenth century, English-born Leonard Hornsby settled
in Wales, where he married and raised a large family. Four of his sons
migrated to the colony of Virginia, then went their separate ways.
Moses Hornsby, born in 1759 and apparently the youngest of the
brothers, moved to northwestern Georgia shortly after the end of the
Revolutionary War and married Katherine Watts, who bore six sons. All
except one (who settled in Louisiana) ended up in Texas.

Reuben Hornsby, born near Rome, Georgia, in 1793, first moved to
the rich delta country of Mississippi, where he married Sarah Morrison.
Eight children were born to them during their stay in Mississippi; two,

both sons, died in infancy. In 1830, wittingly or not, Reuben Hornsby's family became an instrument in what would soon be proclaimed the American people's "manifest destiny" to acquire everything that lay between them and the Pacific Ocean. Along with thousands of other Anglo-Americans (including, sooner or later, four other sons of Moses and Katherine Watts Hornsby), Reuben and Sarah Morrison Hornsby sought the cheap land being offered by the Republic of Mexico between the Trinity and Colorado Rivers, in the Mexican state of Coahuila and Texas.

Landing at Matagorda Bay on the Gulf of Mexico, the Hornsbys followed the Colorado River to the northwest, first locating at the settlement called Mina (later Bastrop), where Sarah Hornsby bore the last two of her ten children—of whom five sons and two daughters survived to adulthood. In 1832 Reuben Hornsby explored still farther upriver, finally deciding on an enormous tract of land—some 4,700 acres in all—about twelve miles from Mina, in a horseshoe bend in the Colorado. With title secured from the Mexican government, the Hornsbys built a cabin overlooking an expanse of tall grass stretching along the river and started clearing and cultivating what travelers soon called Hornsby's Bend.

The Hornsbys were the first Anglo family in what was to become Travis County, Texas. The area was rugged, remote, and frequently menaced by roving bands of American Indians, particularly the fierce and fearless Comanches. Reuben Hornsby took no active part in the rebellion against Mexican rule that flared in the winter of 1835–36, although he and his family joined thousands of others who fled east during the Runaway Scrape precipitated by the annihilation of the Texan garrison at the Alamo.

After Sam Houston's hastily gathered forces routed the Mexican army at San Jacinto and won independence for the Republic of Texas, the family returned to Hornsby's Bend, again to encounter deadly Indian sorties. Two young Kentucky natives, recruits of the newly formed Texas Rangers, were killed by Comanches as they worked in a field in sight of the Hornsby cabin; they became the first persons buried at

Hornsby's Bend, in a grove where generations of Hornsbys would subsequently come to rest, about seventy-five yards from the original
homesite.

For more than a decade, life remained precarious for the Hornsbys
and the growing number of other families in the area. Hornsby's Bend
became a semimilitary post with a fortified stockade, and Reuben
Hornsby sometimes served as a guide for expeditions of Rangers. Nineteen-year-old Daniel Hornsby, Reuben and Sarah's seventh born, died
in an Indian fight in 1845, and his older brothers William and Malcolm
took part in several bloody raids on the Comanches.

By the late 1840s the relentless efforts of the Rangers and local
militia units had virtually ended Indian resistance in east-central Texas.
The county of Travis had been organized, and about twelve miles
northwest of Hornsby's Bend, the little frontier outpost of Austin, the
republic's seat of government from 1839 to 1845, had become the
capital of the new state of Texas.

Reuben Hornsby outlived his wife and all but one of his children,
dying in 1879 at the age of eighty-six. By that time scores of Hornsbys
and Hornsby relatives lived in Travis and neighboring counties. In his
old age Reuben Hornsby presided over Sunday afternoon gatherings at
which aunts, uncles, nieces, nephews, and cousins picnicked, visited,
and tended graves in the steadily populating family cemetery.

The one offspring who survived him was the veteran Indian fighter
William Watts Hornsby. Born in Mississippi in 1817, Billy, as family
members called him, married Lucinda Burleson in 1839 and fathered
eight children—four boys, four girls. The next-to-last of their offspring
was Aaron Edward (known as Ed), who on March 25, 1882, at the age
of twenty-four, married Mary Dallas Rogers, from the nearby commu-
nity of Rogers Hill. One of eight offspring herself, she wasn't quite
eighteen.

Although their first child died at birth late in 1882, within seven
years Ed and Mary Rogers Hornsby had four more children: Everett in
1884, Emory the next year, William Wallace in 1887, and Margaret in
1889. By then, Travis County had become relatively crowded, at least

for young people seeking affordable and fertile farmland. Then, too, with railroads being built farther and farther west, cattle-raising seemed to offer more opportunity than the cotton cultivation that dominated the eastern half of Texas, especially when agricultural prices fell sharply beginning in 1893. The days of the open range were over, but good grazing country, they'd heard, was still available in western Texas.

Ed Hornsby's older brother Daniel already owned a section of land (640 acres) in Runnels County—a couple of hundred miles northwest from Hornsby's Bend and some forty miles south of the bustling cattle town of Abilene. In the spring of 1894 Daniel Hornsby deeded the land to his younger brother for $1,000 in cash and Ed's promise to meet four notes of $604 each at 10 percent interest. That autumn Ed and Mary Hornsby and their four children arrived in Runnels County and occupied their new homesite—a cabin with outbuildings on a rise about two miles northwest of a little settlement called Winters.

For the next four years the Hornsbys raised a few cattle and a little wheat and corn, and struggled to make a life for themselves on the windswept, thin-topsoiled plain that was broken only occasionally by stands of squat trees and distant mesas.

On April 27, 1896, still another Hornsby came into the world: a boy they named Rogers, after his mother's family. He possessed blue eyes and light brown hair that would darken as he grew older. One day, two and a half years later, the little boy was called in from playing in the yard and told to say good-bye to his father. Of causes apparently never recorded, Aaron Edward Hornsby died on December 17, 1898, at the age of forty-one.

Left with five children, of whom the oldest was only fourteen, and far from family and friends, Mary Rogers Hornsby did about the only thing she could. After burying her husband in the family cemetery at Hornsby's Bend, she resettled in Travis County. During the next four years, while Everett, Emory, and William grew big enough to start earning a living, the six Hornsbys resided with Mary's parents on a farm about nine miles outside Austin.

Frequently they joined the Sunday afternoon picnics and cemetery work parties at Hornsby's Bend; long afterward, a few elderly members of the vast Hornsby clan remembered how the young people would play baseball on the bottomland near the river until it was too dark to see. Some even remembered Rogers Hornsby—a little boy in overalls with a bandana hanging from his rear pocket—who insisted on being allowed to play with the big kids. "As I look back to my youngest days," he recalled more than half a century later, "I can't remember anything that happened before I had a baseball in my hand."[1]

Sometime in the winter of 1902–3, Mary Hornsby and her daughter and four sons put themselves and a trunkload of personal belongings aboard a train at Austin and headed for the little city of Fort Worth, 200 miles to the north. The Hornsbys' decision to move—the transforming event in the life of six-year-old Rogers Hornsby—was a consequence of recent events that proved transforming for Fort Worth, Texas, as well.

Fort Worth had hitherto been a shipping point for West Texas cattle bound for the slaughter pens and packinghouses of Kansas City, Chicago, and St. Louis. Now it was about to become the greatest meat-processing center in the Southwest. In the fall of 1902, local citizens promised to build a bank, an exchange building, and a stockyards rail line; to concede two-thirds ownership of the stockyards facilities; to incorporate the stockyards area into the separate municipality of North Fort Worth; and to do whatever else was needed to induce the giant Swift and Armour corporations to establish packing plants there.

The quickly spreading news that "the packers" were coming to Fort Worth convinced the Hornsbys that they should abandon their rural roots and become city folks. Together, Everett, Emory, and William could earn enough at the packing plants to support the family in reasonable comfort. So the Hornsbys joined the millions of Americans leaving farms and villages to work for wages in industrial towns and cities—an historic migration that, both in numbers and consequences, matched the massive immigration from Europe of the late nineteenth and early twentieth centuries.

Centered on Exchange Avenue and Main Street and bounded by

Grand Avenue to the west, the Santa Fe railroad tracks to the east, Marine Creek to the north, and the winding Trinity River to the south, North Fort Worth quickly grew to about 5,000 people and employed twice as many men, women, and children as Fort Worth itself, which numbered close to 27,000 in the 1900 census. Most people worked in the stockyards and packing plants (and the canneries added in 1906); others made a living from the hotels, cafés, saloons, and whorehouses that lined Exchange Avenue. Every morning at 5:30, North Fort Worth residents awoke to the whistle signaling the change of shifts at the packing plants.

The Hornsbys moved into a little rental house across Marine Creek from the meatpacking complex. While the three older Hornsby males went to work, Rogers Hornsby attended elementary school and played with neighborhood children—always baseball, if his memory is to be believed. By the time he was nine, he was the leader of a semiorganized local team whose uniforms (complete with removable sliding pads) were sewn by Mary Hornsby. Wearing their blue flannels, Hornsby and pals sometimes traveled to their games by trolley; usually they walked to play against boys in outlying areas such as Diamond Hill and Rosen Heights.

Young Hornsby was hardly exceptional in having a passion for baseball, ambitions to make it a profession, or dreams of being like Ty Cobb or Honus Wagner. It was a time when baseball, in numbers of both spectators and participants, was virtually unchallenged as the nation's foremost sports activity. All over the United States—on school playgrounds and vacant lots, on college campuses and military posts, in small-town "semipro" competition and municipal and company-sponsored industrial and commercial leagues—millions of boys and men played baseball, not only for the sheer love of it but sometimes with visions of professional careers. Especially for working-class youths such as Rogers Hornsby, baseball might be a route to something better —if not to riches and fame, then at least to more money and some kind of recognition.

What made Hornsby exceptional was the natural coordination he

14

exhibited even at that early age. At ten, when he went to work after school and during the summer months as a messenger boy at the Swift and Company plant, he first looked after bats and balls and then served as substitute infielder for one of the several teams made up of stockyards and packing-plant workers. Right-handed all the way, he couldn't hit much as yet, but he held his own anywhere in the field.

By the time he was fifteen, he was good enough to play with grown men on the North Side Athletics in the Fort Worth city league, as well as occasionally to hire out to other teams in the area. In 1911, for example, he played twelve games for a team at Granbury, southwest of Fort Worth, receiving two dollars per game plus rail fare and room and board. Thirty years later H. L. Warlick, who managed the Granbury outfit, remembered Hornsby as a cocky kid. When Warlick praised his second-base play after a victory at Weatherford, Hornsby replied, "Yeah, and there are eight other positions I can play just as good."[2]

The next year a promoter named Logan J. Galbreath brought to Dallas his Boston Bloomer Girls—one of several touring women's baseball teams of that period. Finding himself shorthanded, Galbreath advertised in local newspapers for two players under the age of eighteen—sex unspecified. Hornsby and a friend caught the interurban electric train over to Dallas and looked up Galbreath, only to learn that they were expected to wear wigs and bloomers and pretend to be female. Apparently any chance to play ball and make a little extra money was worth taking, so the two lads acted their parts as Bloomer Girls while the team met its Dallas dates, then appeared in towns along the rail line north. When the team reached the Red River, they collected their pay—seventy-eight cents apiece after expenses—and headed home.

Baseball teams multiplied in and around Fort Worth at about the same rate as the city's growth. Boosted by the annexation of North Fort Worth in 1909, Fort Worth became Texas's fourth largest city (behind San Antonio, Dallas, and Houston), with an officially reported 1910 population of 73,312. Although the remaining wooden structures on Main Street had been condemned and torn down, most Fort Worth streets were still unpaved, as was the road to Dallas thirty-five miles to the east. Travelers to Dallas usually took the interurban railway, although in 1904 three intrepid Fort Worthians made the trip by automobile in a remarkable one hour and thirty-five minutes.

By 1910 Fort Worth registered 959 automobiles and enforced a ten-mile-per-hour speed limit, as well as an ordinance requiring motorists to sound their horns at least 100 feet from street crossings. Theodore Roosevelt visited the city in 1905 as president and again in 1911, the year before his unsuccessful effort to regain the White House. Most Fort Worthians saw their first powered aircraft early in 1913, when touring Swiss and French aviators gave a flying exhibition on the western outskirts of the city.

If any of the Hornsbys were among the estimated 15,000 at the air show, it would have been a rare occasion when they mingled with the elite families of bankers, merchants, and cattlemen concentrated on Quality Hill, at Lancaster Street and Summit Avenue. At the other end of the social scale were Fort Worth's black inhabitants (18 percent of the local population in 1910) and the smaller numbers of Mexican-Americans, Bohemians, Poles, Serbs, and Slovaks who came looking for work in the packing plants. As native-born whites—Texans of Deep South ancestry—the Hornsbys absorbed and sustained the racial and ethnic prejudices that were an elementary feature of American life.

In 1909 Rogers Hornsby entered recently constructed North Side High School, where he played on both its baseball and football teams. Like many other city schools, North Side High had already succumbed to the football fever that would sweep the whole of Texas within a couple more decades. North Side's football coach was Robert L. Myers; his star player was Alvin "Bo" McMillin, who in 1921, having been recruited to little Centre College in Kentucky by athletic director Myers, would lead the "praying Colonels" to a legendary victory over mighty Harvard University. (From Centre, McMillin would go on to a career as a professional football player and college and professional coach.)

Hornsby later said that he played in the same backfield with McMillin; if so, it wasn't for long. Perhaps because baseball was his first love and North Side emphasized football, because he needed to start earning a full-time income to support his mother and sister, or because he just had had enough of school, he dropped out after two years and got a job as office boy for J. P. Elder, superintendent of the Swift and Company plant.

Spending nearly all his working time around Elder, Hornsby came to know the day-to-day operations of the stockyards, packinghouses, and canneries. "I could run a packing plant today," he bragged in 1926. "I could go back and get a job anytime with Elder and believe me I could run the whole works. But I'd rather play baseball than run a packing plant and I guess that's why I'm here instead of on my way to the presidency of a big packing company."[3]

For all his baseball determination, Hornsby hadn't awed anybody with his talent in stockyards, city league, high school, or any other baseball venue. By the age of seventeen, he'd grown almost to his full height—a half inch under six feet—but he still weighed no more than 135 pounds. "I had trouble swinging the bat," he recalled. "But I could field. . . . I always could field."[4]

Rogers and Margaret, the two youngest Hornsbys, still lived at home with their mother. Although the family's religious heritage was Presbyterian and Mary Hornsby appears to have been fairly pious herself, little religious feeling manifested itself in her offspring, least of all her youngest. In every other respect, though, the relationship between Mary Hornsby and her "baby" seems to have been especially close. She not only made his boyhood baseball uniforms but encouraged him to play as often as he could and made no effort to stifle his professional ambitions.

Besides, her oldest son was already making a career in professional baseball. Twelve years older than Rogers, Everett Hornsby was a stocky pitcher who relied mainly on a spitball—a perfectly legal pitch before 1920. Nicknamed "Pep" by his baseball peers, Everett played seven years in the Class B Texas League and made it to the top of the minor leagues one season (1913) with the Kansas City Blues in the American Association.

17

Everett Hornsby played for Waco, Shreveport, Houston, and Dallas in the Texas League, though never for the local Fort Worth Panthers. In 1909, when Everett pitched for Houston, he and his regular battery-mate, Michigander Bill Killefer, often came to the Hornsby home for fried chicken, with Killefer bringing along discarded baseballs and broken bats for baseball-crazy Rogers Hornsby.

In the spring of 1914 Everett Hornsby, now a thirty-year-old minor-league journeyman, found himself on the roster of the Dallas Steers. His kid brother talked him into arranging a professional tryout, which amounted to little more than taking infield and batting practice with the Dallas players. The youngster apparently made something of an impression, because the Dallas management signed him to a contract. But when the season started, he sat on the bench game after game, waiting for a chance to play that never came; after two weeks he was handed his release.

Resolved to play professionally somewhere, Hornsby traveled to Hugo, Oklahoma, a new member of the Class D Texas-Oklahoma League, at the bottom of Organized Baseball.[5] He tried out, made the team as its shortstop, and signed for seventy-five dollars a month. When the Hugo franchise folded about a third of the way into the season, his contract was sold to Denison, Texas, in the same league, for $125.

Denison was a thriving little city of about 15,000 whose livelihood was built on its huge locomotive maintenance shops. It was a good baseball town, but its Railroaders could do no better than third place among the four teams finishing the 1914 Texas-Oklahoma League season. Playing on the league's rocky and skinned diamonds, eighteen-year-old Hornsby committed forty-five errors in 113 games and batted an uninspiring .232. Herb Hunter, his teammate that year and a future major-league player, minor-league manager, and baseball scout and promoter, remembered the youngster pleading, "Won't somebody teach me how to hit?"[6]

After another winter at J. P. Elder's elbow, Hornsby again reported to Denison, which for the 1915 season had affiliated with the Western Association—still at Class D. His pay soared to $90 per month, in a league that imposed a $1,200 per-club monthly salary cap and limited rosters to thirteen men.

That spring the St. Louis Cardinals of the National League did their spring training at Hot Wells, Texas, on the southern outskirts of San Antonio. One of the poorest franchises in the major leagues, the Cardinals were owned by Helene Robison Britton, who inherited the franchise from her father and uncle. Her husband, Schuyler Britton, served as club president.

Since joining the National League in 1892, St. Louis had never won a pennant. The 1914 club, led by diminutive manager–second baseman Miller Huggins, climbed to third place but still ran a substantial deficit because both the Cardinals and the American League's Browns split local baseball patronage with the St. Louis Terriers, an entry in a third major-league venture called the Federal League.

Late in the 1914 season, Huggins told Bob Connery, the Cardinals' only scout, that given the ballclub's financial condition, it was a waste of time for Connery to look at players in the upper minor leagues. "Even if you like a certain player," said Huggins, "we can't afford his price tag. How about looking over some of the smaller leagues? You might find a kid who might help us."[7]

The next spring Huggins split his players into two squads. While the regulars, under his direction, kept exhibition dates at Houston, Dallas, and Fort Worth as they made their way back to St. Louis, Connery took charge of the rookies and substitutes for a series of exhibitions in smaller places, including a three-game set at Denison with the local Railroaders.

It was only St. Louis's second team, and several of the players wouldn't be around once the season got under way. Still, Rogers Hornsby got the chance to play against "what I thought was a big-league team. It was my big break." Holding his bat at the end and taking full swings, Hornsby didn't hit much. Yet as Connery remembered long afterward, "The more I looked at the kid, the better I liked him. He was green and awkward, but possessed a great pair of hands. He fielded bad hoppers neatly and got the ball away quickly."[8] Noticing the boy's cheap glove and playing shoes, Connery bought him new equipment out of his own pocket.

The 1915 Western Association season was a good one all around for a teenager who loved to play baseball, loved to win, and desperately sought to accomplish more as a professional than he had so far. At season's end, manager "Babe" Peebles's Denison Railroaders led the rest of the league with a record of 76–54, four and one-half games better than runner-up Oklahoma City. Hornsby played in 119 games and—in a league that produced only four .300 hitters—boosted his batting average to .277, with seventy-five runs scored and twenty-four stolen bases.[9] Along with that offensive improvement, though, went fifty-eight errors.

Fewer than a dozen Western Association players showed any major-league potential, wrote a Paris, Texas, correspondent for the *Sporting News,* baseball's leading trade weekly. One of them was Denison's shortstop Hornsby, "who is only a kid yet, and may need a little more seasoning."[10]

With the Western Association season almost over, Roy Finley, who doubled as Grayson County prosecuting attorney and president of the Denison franchise, took Hornsby aside to tell him that Bob Connery had recommended his purchase by the St. Louis Cardinals, and that Finley had just sold his contract—for $600, Hornsby later learned. He was to join the ballclub in Cincinnati for the remaining month of the National League season.

The September 9, 1915, issue of the *Sporting News* carried a final Western Association report, out of Fort Smith, Arkansas: "Roger [*sic*] Hornsby, the star shortstop of the Denison pennant winners, goes to the St. Louis Cardinals."[11]

2

. . .

Making

It

R ogers Hornsby found himself with the St. Louis Cardinals early
in September 1915 because of unique circumstances throughout
baseball that year, especially for indigent franchises such as the Cardinals. Menaced by the Federal League, which in 1914 had proclaimed
itself a major circuit and gone after players wherever they might be
available, both the National and American League teams struggled to
keep their rosters intact. While baseball's top performers—Ty Cobb,
Walter Johnson, Christy Mathewson, Tris Speaker, Grover Cleveland
Alexander, and Eddie Collins, among others—stayed put under multi-
year contracts providing hefty pay raises, a considerable number of sec-
ond- and third-level major-leaguers, as well as players in the upper
minors, cast their lots with the Federals.

The talent-depleting effect of the Federal League and the lean finances of the St. Louis Cardinals created an opening for a nineteen-
year-old with two seasons of undistinguished Class D experience to
jump all the way to the top of Organized Baseball. Without the "Fed-

eral League war," as baseball people came to call it, Hornsby wouldn't have been in Cincinnati on September 3, 1915.

"The St. Louis Cardinals have a new player on trial in the person of Dick Hornsby, a product of the lots of Fort Worth, where he began with a team made up of stockyards huskies," reported the *Sporting News* in its weekly National League Notes.[1] (For nearly a year, the press around the league would continue to get the youngster's name wrong, until he explained to everybody that he was named "Rogers," after his mother's family.) Hornsby joined the Cardinals after a two-day train trip from Denison to Fort Worth to Cincinnati, traveling the entire 1,200 miles by day coach.

The ballclub with which he signed a contract (for $200 for the rest of the season) had made a good showing into July, then, as usual, faded from contention. When Hornsby joined them, the 1915 Cardinals rested in fourth place with a 63–66 record. Near the end of his playing career but still at second base most days, Cardinals manager Miller Huggins directed a few solid major-leaguers—but only a few.

Frank Snyder was a fine young catcher, and outfielder–first baseman Jack Miller had been a steady performer since his rookie season in 1909 with the world's champion Pittsburgh Pirates. Spitballer Bill Doak, a twenty-game winner in 1914, and Harry "Slim" Sallee, a tall left-hander who'd posted eighteen wins in each of the two previous seasons, were Huggins's pitching mainstays, while Lee Meadows, the only be-spectacled player in the majors, was on his way to a 13–11 record in his rookie year.

Otherwise, the Cardinals consisted of players who would never amount to much, plus dimming former stars such as Bob Bescher, once a champion base stealer with Cincinnati; Owen "Chief" Wilson, who'd hit a record thirty-six triples (with Pittsburgh) three seasons earlier; and Leon "Red" Ames, formerly a mound stalwart for John McGraw's New York Giants.

At a time when television was a fantasy and the sixteen National and American League teams were all located in the northeastern quadrant of the United States, it wasn't unusual for ballplayers to take part in the first major-league game they ever saw. For Rogers Hornsby, who'd never before traveled north of Tulsa, Oklahoma, it was a matter of donning a gray, red-trimmed visitors' uniform and then watching from the dugout as Meadows outpitched the Reds' Pete Schneider for a 3–1 win.

After that the Cardinals returned to St. Louis to begin a home stand that would last almost to the end of the season. Light-hitting Artie Butler remained at shortstop; Hornsby remained on the bench. Meanwhile Hornsby moved into a boardinghouse where several other Cardinals bachelors resided, on St. Louis's north side near Robison Field, the team's home ballpark.

In that thriving Mississippi River city of more than 700,000—the United States' fifth most populous in the 1910 federal census—young Hornsby repeatedly got lost, even in the immediate area where he lived. It was a strange environment in many ways, not only in its size and complexity but also in its diverse population, which included many "foreigners" speaking with peculiar accents, if they spoke English at all. Since the middle of the previous century, St. Louis's population had been substantially German-American; among the various European peoples arriving in recent decades, Italians predominated.

Yet unlike what Georgian Ty Cobb, for example, had encountered when he arrived in Detroit ten years earlier, Hornsby found St. Louis's racial mores little different from what he was used to in Texas and neighboring states. In matters of race and in many other respects, St. Louis (as well as East St. Louis, Illinois, a city of some 60,000 across the river) remained decidedly southern. By Missouri law, municipal ordinance, and ingrained custom, the 50,000 or so black St. Louisians were segregated in everything from housing, transportation, and entertainment to worship, schooling, and burial practices.

Athletically, whites competed in their own spheres in high schools, at St. Louis and Washington Universities, on sandlot and municipal baseball teams, and in professional baseball. White sports fans knew scarcely more of the St. Louis Giants, a professional baseball club with a dedicated following among local black residents, than of the athletes performing at Sumner and Vashon, the city's black high schools.

In the major leagues (including the short-lived Federal League) and the whole of Organized Baseball, "for whites only" was the ruling policy—even if that policy was never officially acknowledged. So, although the young white ballplayer from Texas encountered black St. Louisians on the streets, at trolley stops, and even at Robison Field (where they sat in a separate section of the bleachers), for the most part he lived and worked in a white world, mingling with but generally ignoring "colored people."

Situated at the intersection of Vandeventer Avenue and Natural Bridge Road and across from the fairgrounds, Robison Field was six blocks from Sportsman's Park, home of the American League Browns, and not far from the Federal League Terriers' home base. Named for owner Helene Robison Britton's father, Robison Field was one of only two surviving American or National League facilities constructed entirely of wood.[2] Though far bigger, structurally it wasn't much of an improvement over the ballparks Hornsby had known in the minors— certainly not the equal of Cincinnati's steel-and-concrete Redland Field, the first big-league facility he saw. Occupied by the St. Louis National Leaguers since 1893, Robison Field could accommodate about 15,000 customers (on seats that usually needed a coat of paint) in its single-deck grandstand and its bleachers in left and right field. The distance down the right-field foul line was 320 feet; the closest point in left field was 380 feet away; and dead center field was 435 feet from home plate. With the plate set 120 feet from the grandstand backstop, Robison Field offered plenty of room in foul territory for catchers and first and third basemen. It was a pitcher's park even by the standards of the first two decades of the century, when pitchers generally held the upper hand.

Hornsby arrived, remembered Dick Farrington of the *St. Louis Globe-Democrat,* "with a badger haircut, a carpetbag, and $2.85 in a three-compartment pocketbook." John B. Sheridan, another longtime St. Louis sportswriter, recalled rookie Hornsby as a scrawny, "hollow chested, large footed, gangling boy," yet also noted his "good forehead, straight nose, firm mouth and chin and particularly level, determined eyebrows."[3] Deeply dimpled and slightly buck-toothed, he possessed a fresh-faced, wholesome look, even if he wasn't a particularly handsome youngster.

Hornsby also wasn't "soiled by being half-educated," as Sheridan remembered him, which was probably a polite way of saying that the Texan was, in the Victorian phrase, a "callow youth"—raw, ill-mannered, generally innocent of the world.[4] He spoke with a high-pitched, thwangy north Texas accent; his grammar would have dismayed his third-grade teacher, and so would the pungent vocabulary he'd learned working around stockyards people.

At five-foot-eleven-and-a-half and 135 pounds, Hornsby was an inch or so taller but also lighter by about forty pounds than the typical major-league ballplayer. "As a hitter," Sheridan recalled, "he looked especially impotent."[5] Still holding his bat at the end and taking full swings, the youngster soon found that he couldn't handle big-league pitching. Both manager Huggins and Bob Connery worked with him after games, getting him to crowd the plate and choke up on a thick-handled bat—the accepted style at a time when the "dead ball" made free-swinging generally ineffective.

Huggins finally put him into a game on Friday, September 10. With the Cardinals trailing Cincinnati 7–0 after six innings, much of the crowd of 2,000 or so had left by the time Hornsby took over for Butler at shortstop. Nothing much happened the rest of the way, except that the home team managed one run in the eighth inning. Hornsby had no chances in the field and went hitless in two times at bat against rookie right-hander Charles "King" Lear. Except for listing him in the box score, local accounts of the game ignored Hornsby in favor of pitcher Fred Lamline, newly arrived from the Three-I League, who relieved Meadows and held the Reds scoreless over the final three innings.

Hornsby sat out the games versus Brooklyn on Saturday and Sunday, then discovered his name penciled into the starting lineup when he got to Robison Field on Monday. Jack Coombs, onetime American League star, held the rookie hitless in beating St. Louis 6–2. The next day (September 14) Hornsby recorded his first big-league base hit: a single off Brooklyn's Richard "Rube" Marquard, a tall left-hander who'd posted nineteen straight victories for the New York Giants three years earlier.

Huggins gave the kid a pretty thorough looking-over, keeping him at shortstop for all of the Cardinals' remaining fifteen games. Always hitting eighth in the batting order and gripping the bat about six inches from the handle, he punched and chopped at pitches, seldom striking out but also seldom hitting the ball hard. He did manage a double—his first extra-base hit—off Grover Cleveland Alexander of pennant-bound Philadelphia, and in his first meeting with the illustrious John McGraw and his last-place New York Giants, he touched burly Charles "Jeff" Tesreau for two singles.[6]

All told, he made fourteen hits in fifty-seven official times at bat, for a batting average of .246. All his hits were singles except for two doubles, and he drove in only four runs and scored five. At shortstop he continued to show the same faults—overanxiousness and an erratic throwing arm—that had plagued him at Denison, and he erred at about the same rate (eight errors in eighteen games). Teammates became impatient with his rookie mistakes; when he covered second base on a steal attempt and dropped Frank Snyder's throw, Snyder gave him a thorough chewing-out in the dugout.

Finishing in sixth place with a record of 72–81 (with one lost rain-out in the 154-game schedule), the Cardinals obviously needed help. But Hornsby's dreary showing in the six games of the annual post-season "city series" with the Browns—two hits in twenty at bats and four errors—did nothing to convince Huggins that the nineteen-year-old from Class D would be of much use to him in 1916. When Hornsby came to Huggins after the Cardinals finished the season and asked about his prospects, the manager replied, "Kid, you're a little light, but you got the makings. I think I'll farm you out for a year."[7]

As implausible as it may seem, Hornsby completely mistook Huggins's meaning—that the Cardinals would probably assign him to a minor-league club for 1916 and let him get more experience. Hornsby thought Huggins was telling him to spend the off-season on a farm, which is exactly what he proceeded to do. "I was just a country boy, with only three or four weeks in the big cities," Hornsby remembered, "so I took him at his word." Instead of moving back in with his mother in North Fort Worth, he went to his uncle H. T. Rainey's farm at Lockhart, south of Austin. There he spent the fall and winter months helping out with chores, tramping the woods with a shotgun in search of game birds, sleeping twelve hours a night, and consuming steak and fried chicken and "all the milk I could hold."[8]

Meanwhile the Cardinals secured an option to buy a flashy shortstop named Roy Corhan from San Francisco of the Pacific Coast League, and Huggins predicted that Corhan would be his regular at the position in 1916. According to what one local sportswriter later claimed, the Cardinals offered to sell Hornsby to Little Rock of the Class A Southern Association for $500. Although that was $100 less than what they'd paid Denison for Hornsby's contract, the price was still too steep for the Little Rock ownership!

If young Hornsby's baseball future seemed less than promising that winter, the outlook for the St. Louis Cardinals and Browns and the National and American Leagues as a whole brightened considerably. After two years of heavy financial losses, the Federal League promoters agreed to disband in exchange for generous compensation from the established leagues. Part of the settlement allowed Charles Weeghman, owner of the Chicago Federal League franchise, to purchase the National League Chicago Cubs, and Philip deCatesby Ball, who owned the St. Louis Terriers, bought the Browns from Robert Lee Hedges. As Weeghman did at Chicago, Ball amalgamated players from his former and his new teams. Ball also bought Sportsman's Park from Hedges, whereas Weeghman moved the Cubs into the modern ballpark on Chicago's North Side built for his Federal League Whales.

The Baltimore Federal League group sought to buy the Cardinals with the intent of moving them to Baltimore but were closed out of the settlement. So the Cardinals remained in St. Louis, where at least they wouldn't have to compete with a Federal League entry that almost won a pennant in 1915 and outdrew both the Cardinals and the Browns.[9]

Hornsby received his 1916 contract at his uncle's farm at Lockhart. It specified a season's salary of $2,000—$333.33 per month, figured the way he'd reckoned his pay in Class D. Without delay, he signed the contract and put it in the return mail. Not only was he being offered a healthy wage by prevailing workforce standards (if, that is, he survived the roster cut at the start of the season), but in the retrenching aftermath of the costly Federal League war, it was as much as a nominal rookie could expect.

Besides, neither Hornsby nor anybody else within Organized Baseball had any alternative but to sign the contracts offered them. Under the reserve clause, initially adopted by the National League back in 1879, a franchise possessed exclusive rights to resign a particular player for the coming season, unless it sold, traded, or released him. A player might grumble about his salary and delay signing, or even refuse to play and hold out for more, but if he wanted to continue to earn a living within Organized Baseball, he eventually must come to terms with the franchise holding him under reserve.

The necessarily tightfisted Cardinals management again scheduled spring training for Hot Wells, Texas. Located on the southern outskirts of San Antonio, Hot Wells was a village that included a seedy hotel (the Terrell) and a mineral springs catering to people who sought the restorative and curative benefits of the waters but couldn't afford the more famous spa at Hot Springs, Arkansas.

Hot Wells's baseball facilities consisted of an unfenced field next to the hotel. No diamond had been laid out, so the ballplayers stepped off the distances themselves and put down bases. They dressed at the hotel and, at the end of practice, returned for showers and soaks in tanks full of mineral water. Only twenty-eight men were on hand, both because the ballclub couldn't cover food and lodging for a larger number and because, under the roster limitation imposed during the Federal League war, only twenty-one places were available anyway.

Citizens from the San Antonio area south and west to the Rio

Grande were in a jittery mood that spring. On March 18, 1916, President Woodrow Wilson ordered a U.S. Army expedition led by General John J. Pershing into northern Mexico in an effort to apprehend the bandit caudillo Francisco "Pancho" Villa, whose followers had raided trains and towns along the U.S.-Mexico border and killed a number of U.S. citizens. Pershing's force marched 300 miles into Mexico, and while it never caught up with the wily Villa, its operations brought the Wilson administration into conflict with the revolutionary government of Venustiano Carranza in Mexico City—and perilously close to outright war.

Little of that or anything else except baseball concerned young Rogers Hornsby as he packed his bag, said good-bye to his Lockhart relatives, and caught a train for San Antonio, about seventy-five miles away. His determination to build himself up physically had paid off; he reported to Huggins about thirty pounds heavier and, as he later put it, "I had the power." Wrote one observer, "Hornsby was hardly recognized when he appeared. He has grown from a gangling boy into a well-developed physical specimen." "It's all good, solid weight, too," enthused another at the scene. "The additional poundage has made him much stronger."[10]

Huggins was also in for a surprise when Hornsby first took batting practice. Instead of standing close to home plate, crouching, and choking the bat, he returned to the batting style he'd used at Denison. Taking his position in the batter's box as far back and away from the plate as he could, he stood nearly upright with feet about eighteen inches apart, held the bat well away from his body, and gripped it at the very end. To be able to cover the strike zone from that stance, he stood with his left foot a little closer to the plate than his back foot, stepped into the pitch at a forty-five-degree angle to the pitcher, and took a full swing using a thirty-six-inch, thirty-eight- to forty-ounce bat with a relatively thin handle.

As Hornsby slammed line drives to all parts of the field, Huggins, Connery, and everybody else stopped to watch. He also impressed observers as "a real hustler, always on the jump"; like his brother Everett, he quickly acquired the nickname "Pep." Although Huggins was skeptical about his future at shortstop, he did acknowledge, "Hornsby gives great promise for a third baseman." Twelve years later, John B. Sheridan recalled the Hornsby of 1916 as having undergone "what appeared to be a spiritual and physical metamorphosis."[11]

Hornsby roomed with Roy Corhan, the man he needed to beat out for a place on the team.[12] In mid-March Corhan hurt his shoulder and couldn't get the ball across the infield, but Artie Butler played shortstop in early exhibition games against the Texas League San Antonio Broncos. Although Hornsby finally got into the lineup on March 18, doubling and driving in a run against the Broncos, when the team broke camp a few days later, Butler accompanied the regulars for stops at Houston and other cities on the way to St. Louis. Hornsby traveled with the second squad for games at Sherman and Denison (where his appearance as a former Railroader occasioned mild applause).

With everybody reassembled in St. Louis, Huggins put Hornsby at shortstop for the traditional preseason series with the Browns. Although "Roger" (as his name was still being rendered) missed two games of the seven-game set with an outbreak of neck boils, he proceeded to solidify his place on the team by making five singles and three doubles in five games, erring but once, and generally impressing the fans at Sportsman's Park and Robison Field with his hustling style. "Hornsby cannot be denied," wrote the *St. Louis Post-Dispatch*'s W. J. O'Connor, "and regardless of Roy Corhan's condition, the milk-fed fiend will desport himself at short."[13]

Still a few weeks shy of his twentieth birthday, Hornsby appeared extraordinarily glib and self-confident, which must have struck Cardinals veterans as decidedly unrookie-like. "I never touched beer in my life and as far as I know, whisky is a hair tonic," he bragged to O'Connor (or so O'Connor quoted him). "Lady Nicotine and I never mix, so I'm a second edition of the ideal boy." When Hornsby threw high to first base in one of the games with the Browns and Jack Smith speared it, trotted into the infield, and yelled encouragingly, "Nice play, Pep. I made it look a little hard," Hornsby yelled back, "Never mind that, Jack. Just stick around that bag and I'll make a first baseman out of you." Added O'Connor, "What colossal nerve! But it wins."[14]

Partly nerve but mostly his newfound batting prowess put Hornsby in the lineup at shortstop on April 12, when the Cardinals opened the season at home versus Pittsburgh. His counterpart at shortshop for the Pirates was forty-two-year-old Honus Wagner, one of the Texan's boy-hood idols. Whatever meaning that may have had for the cocky young Texan was never recorded, but the box score showed that Hornsby, seventh in Huggins's batting order, drove in both runs with two singles, as "Spittin' Bill" Doak pitched a six-hit, 2–1 victory.

Obviously Huggins had a real prospect on his hands, and so Hornsby stayed in the lineup as both Roy Corhan and Artie Butler spent most of their time on the bench. A month into the season, Hornsby was being described as "about the most popular athlete that ever wore a Cardinal uniform." Although he was still shaky in the field and, by one account, "a weird base runner[,] and the coacher has yet to be sent to the lines who can aid him apparently," long-suffering St. Louis fans, who appreciated ability and allowed for youth, made him one of their favorites.[15]

The 1916 Cardinals were a bad team, falling out of contention early and finishing in a tie with Cincinnati for seventh place—more than thirty games behind first-place Brooklyn. At season's end, one of the few consolations for die-hard Cardinals fans was the showing of Rogers (as he was finally being called by late summer) Hornsby, who'd estab-lished himself as one of baseball's outstanding young players.

On May 14, at Robison Field, Hornsby recorded his first major-league home run (his eighth in Organized Baseball). Hit off Brooklyn's Edward "Jeff" Pfeffer, it was a freak blow that landed behind third base, skipped into foul territory, and then bounced into the stands—a homer by pre-1931 rules. His first "legitimate" home run came nine days later, when he drove the ball over Boston center fielder Fred Snodgrass's head and outran the relay throw to score standing up. Longtime Robison Field fans agreed it was one of the longest hits ever made on the home grounds. On June 28 he pushed his batting average to .300 by registering two singles, two triples, and a home run in a victory at Cincinnati that closed a long road trip. "Hornsby is the 'find' of 1916," announced O'Connor.[16]

As the team's leading hitter, Hornsby moved up in the batting order—to fifth and then fourth place. He also moved all over the diamond, playing every infield position at one time or another and making forty-five errors. For most of the last half of the season, Huggins put him at third base; in an interview with a writer for *Baseball Magazine,* Hornsby agreed that third might be his natural position.

Voicing a view he would reiterate in coming decades, he said it was easier to hit in the major leagues than in the minors, mainly because big-league pitchers possessed better control and a hitter could usually expect to get at least one pitch to his liking. As for his own style, swinging from the end of the bat, he declared, had always been "my natural bent."[17]

In July the *Sporting News* captioned Hornsby's photograph "best youngster in National [League]" and "a star of the first water." Local baseball writers and knowledgeable fans compared his versatile talents with those of the Browns' George Sisler, whose strong batting and adroit first-base play in his second year in the majors had about persuaded manager Fielder Jones to forget Sisler's pitching potential. Miller Huggins called Hornsby "the greatest free-swinging hitter in baseball," while an unnamed veteran pitcher was impressed by the youngster's ability to wait for a good pitch, terming him "as cold as ice." "The fellow hits the hardest ball I have ever seen," enthused Brooklyn manager Wilbert Robinson, who'd been in baseball since 1885. "He gets distance because of a perfect stride. . . . he doesn't seem to swing hard. He strides into the ball perfectly; he's never off balance." Queried about how he came by his ability with the bat, Hornsby replied (as his accent was rendered), "I simplay cain't help it."[18]

In mid-August Charles Weeghman telegraphed the Brittons an offer to buy Hornsby for his Chicago Cubs (for an unpublicized sum), and Brooklyn put out feelers about a deal that would send shortstop Ollie O'Mara and outfielder Charles Dillon "Casey" Stengel to St. Louis for

Hornsby and $20,000. Thus began a long series of efforts by other National League clubs to obtain Hornsby's services. Refusing cash they needed badly, the Brittons announced that while they might trade Hornsby or other sought-after Cardinals such as Lee Meadows and Frank Snyder for comparable players, they wouldn't sell anybody outright.

Hornsby missed eleven games in late August and early September after he sprained an ankle sliding into home plate. Although the Cardinals lost their last twelve games of the season (all away from home), he kept registering base hits and ended with a .313 average. That was sixty-six points above the average for the National League as a whole and fourth in the league behind batting champion Hal Chase of Cincinnati (who hit .339), Pittsburgh's Bill Hinchman, and Brooklyn's Jake Daubert. Hornsby led his teammates with six home runs (Philadelphia's Clifford "Gavvy" Cravath hit twelve), thirteen triples (third in the league), and sixty runs driven in (twenty-three less than the league's best). Although he wasn't and never would be a daring base runner, he also stole seventeen bases.

The Browns bested the Cardinals four games to one in a desultory city series that drew only about 14,000. Hornsby headed home with his loser's share of forty dollars and what was left of his season's salary, after he'd paid his own expenses and mailed part of each paycheck to his mother. With no off-season weight-gain program scheduled, he settled in with his mother in North Fort Worth and went to work at Swift and Company as a checker on the loading docks. He could look forward to next spring with his place on the Cardinals secure; Roy Corhan would again be playing in the Pacific Coast League, and Artie Butler had received his outright release.

Meanwhile the Brittons' marriage fell apart; Miller Huggins ended up having to return to St. Louis from his home in Cincinnati to testify in the divorce proceeding. Helene Robison Britton declared herself president of the Cardinals; anybody on her ballclub, she declared, was for sale or trade—except Rogers Hornsby.

When Weeghman renewed his efforts to acquire Hornsby, she declared that she wouldn't exchange him for the whole Chicago Cubs roster. That was so much bravado; although she rejected Weeghman's offer of $75,000 cash, indications are that she and Huggins would have been ready to deal Hornsby for Jim "Hippo" Vaughn and another frontline pitcher—plus cash—had Weeghman been so inclined.

But what she really wanted, now that she was ridding herself of Schuyler Britton, was also to be free of the bothersome and unprofitable baseball franchise she inherited. As the Cardinals players again began gathering at what a local writer called "the hard-boiled, wind-swept plateau which has been dignified by the name of Hot Wells," a syndicate of 110 St. Louis businessmen and civic leaders, headed by James C. Jones, paid her $25,000 for a sixty-day option to buy the ballclub for $250,000.[19] Two weeks later Jones signed a purchase agreement on behalf of the syndicate and made an initial $75,000 down payment.

To direct their new property as franchise president, Jones and his associates signed Wesley Branch Rickey to a three-year contract at $15,000 per year. A thirty-five-year-old native of Stockdale, Ohio, Rickey had managed the Browns from 1913 through 1915 and then, the past year, moved into the front office as Browns vice president and business manager. A pious Methodist who wouldn't go to the ballpark on Sunday (but assiduously counted gate receipts on Monday morning), Rickey was also a relentlessly determined man who'd played briefly in the American League (as a light-hitting catcher), coached baseball and other sports to pay his way through Ohio Wesleyan College and the University of Michigan law school, and then fought off tuberculosis.

Robert Lee Hedges, the Browns' owner until 1916, liked and admired Rickey, especially after Rickey maneuvered the University of Michigan's George Sisler away from the Pittsburgh Pirates. But Rickey's relationship with Phil Ball, who bought the Browns as part of the Federal League settlement, was an unhappy one. Rickey didn't like being kicked upstairs in favor of Fielder Jones, Ball's Federal League manager; and Ball didn't appreciate Rickey's penchant for quoting the Bible and launching into long-winded, polysyllabic discourses on baseball, among many other subjects. For Ball, a sparsely educated, self-made millionaire, Rickey was a pretentious know-it-all whose services he could do without.

Although nobody realized it at the time, Branch Rickey's arrival as president of the St. Louis Cardinals in the spring of 1917 would profoundly alter the history not only of that franchise but of all Organized Baseball. It was an event that also critically affected the future of young Rogers Hornsby. For the next two decades the professional lives of Rickey and Hornsby would be closely—yet ambivalently—intertwined.

3

. . .

Toward

Stardom

W hile Branch Rickey hustled Cardinals stock to as many St. Louisians as he could persuade to invest in the franchise (and bought
200 shares at five dollars each for himself), Miller Huggins traveled to
Texas to prepare for another spring training. Still unable to afford the
comforts of San Antonio, the Cardinals again trained at Hot Wells.

Worry about a war with Mexico had passed by the time the earliest
arrivals began throwing baseballs around; late in January 1917 General
Pershing's "punitive expedition" began its withdrawal, having failed to
come within shooting distance of Pancho Villa but having shot at—and
been shot at by—plenty of other Mexicans.

Now a much bigger international crisis was at hand: the Wilson
administration's dogged insistence on respect for U.S. neutral rights by
the belligerents in the war convulsing Europe since 1914 had failed
to preserve peace. Since January, when the Imperial German high
command resumed unlimited submarine warfare in the north Atlantic,
American shipping had been under attack and a growing number of

American citizens had lost their lives. With U.S.-German diplomatic relations officially broken, events moved the two countries steadily toward war.

That spring, at the behest of league president Ban Johnson, American League players performed military drills at their training sites under the direction of army officers detailed from nearby posts. President John Tener of the National League apparently thought such a show of "preparedness" unnecessary for his league, so the Cardinals and other teams in the "senior circuit" were spared the daily regimen of shouldering their bats and marching to and fro across the diamond.

With the May–September player limit raised to twenty-two per club, Rickey worked to trim salary fat. As he sought to dispose of Bob Bescher and the $4,500 salary Bescher had received since the Federal League war, Rickey told Cincinnati president August "Garry" Herrmann that he was "positive the St. Louis club will not be a contender for the pennant this year." The Cardinals were trying to "rebuil[d] along economic lines, and therefore with young material."[1]

The principal figure in Rickey's reconstruction wasn't cooperating with his efforts to do things "along economic lines." Although Rogers Hornsby possessed only seven months of big-league experience, he knew he was the top player on a poor ballclub. He wanted $4,000, twice his rookie pay, and at the beginning of spring practice he remained unsigned. Huggins thought he'd settled matters by telephone, only to learn, when Hornsby arrived at Hot Wells on March 5, that the young man still wasn't happy.

A couple of days around the ballfield, though, worked the same effect on Hornsby it usually did on recalcitrants. On the seventh he agreed to a one-year salary of $3,000. It wasn't a lot of money compared to the $15,000–$20,000 commanded by such reigning stars as Ty Cobb, Eddie Collins, Tris Speaker, and Walter Johnson (all American Leaguers), but for a second-year player who still hadn't attained legal manhood, a 50 percent raise wasn't bad.

When the Cardinals left Hot Wells and started north on the spring exhibition trail, Hornsby accompanied the second team to Denison, where he was honored at home plate by local people who remembered his Denison Railroader exploits and his stopover as an unproven rookie a year earlier. They greeted him now as an established star. After rejoining Huggins and the regulars for a game at Fort Worth, he was again honored, this time as a native son who brought pride and recognition to his hometown.

Back in St. Louis, the Cardinals discovered that Robison Field's seating capacity had shrunk by about 1,500 because the city building commissioner decided that the top part of the left-field bleachers was unsafe and ordered several rows sawed off. Although the lost space wasn't missed, more of the remaining seats would be filled in the coming season than had been in several years; by the end of June some 168,000 fans had paid to see the Cardinals at home. Huggins's 1917 squad didn't come close to a pennant, but they offered local National League fans a surprisingly good brand of team baseball, as well as the opportunity to watch the ripening of one of the sport's greatest individual talents.

On April 12, ten days after President Wilson addressed a joint session of the Congress and asked for a declaration of formal hostilities against Imperial Germany, the Cardinals opened the National League schedule by losing at Cincinnati before a near-capacity crowd of 24,000. Eight days later, a standing-room-only turnout greeted them when they opened at Robison Field with a 5–1 victory over the Reds, behind Bill Doak.

Actually the war affected baseball relatively little in 1917. Total major-league attendance—though still a couple million below the figure for 1913 (the last season before the Federal League war)—about equaled that for 1916. Mobilization of people and resources went forward deliberately; the Congress took a month to establish a military conscription system, registration for the draft didn't commence until June 6, and it was December before the first round of call-ups took place. For more than a year, the United States' participation in the war was of little direct military significance. Great Britain and France continued to expend huge numbers of men in an effort to break the stalemate on the western front, while Imperial Germany used the time to prepare a victory offensive before American power could alter the strategic balance.

Boston catcher Hank Gowdy, star of the Braves' four-game sweep of the heavily favored Philadelphia Athletics in the 1914 World Series, became another kind of hero as the first major-leaguer to enlist for military service. But the great majority of others throughout Organized Baseball, wanting nothing more than to proceed with their professional and personal lives, showed little enthusiasm for rushing into a war that had already killed several million Europeans.

Other matters besides the prospect of military service intruded on young Rogers Hornsby's efforts to concentrate on baseball. On Tuesday evening, May 29, his family wired that thirty-year-old William W. Hornsby had been shot and killed in an argument with a bartender in a Fort Worth saloon. The teetotaling younger brother caught a night train, arrived home the next day, attended the funeral on June 1, hurried to another train as soon as the interment services concluded, and was back in the lineup at Robison Field against the New York Giants on June 3. Eleven days later he broke out of a mild slump with a single, double, and bases-loaded home run in an 8–7 victory over Boston.

Two weeks after that, the Cardinals closed their home stand and began a road trip in Chicago. While they were away, the century's worst race riot up to then erupted across the river in East St. Louis, Illinois. That city had absorbed a heavy influx of mostly southern black people, attracted by the St. Louis area's booming wartime economy and seeking affordable (and permissible) places to live. On July 2, 1917, mutual anger and resentment erupted into pitched battles in which at least eight whites and thirty-nine blacks died before fifteen companies of the Illinois National Guard occupied the city. For days, smoke from burning black-occupied residences and businesses rose above East St. Louis.

Bob Connery—who was probably as little interested in the East St. Louis horrors as was Rogers Hornsby—now spoke proudly of his "discovery": "That kid is playing short[stop] in a manner far beyond our wildest dreams."[2] Connery's encomiums aside, Hornsby was far from being a polished infielder. Spending the entire season at shortstop, he participated in eighty-two double plays (second best in the major leagues), but he also committed the third-highest number of errors (fifty-two).

Most of the customers at Robison Field liked Hornsby and usually overlooked his inconsistent efforts afield, but in mid-August, when he dropped a pop fly that center fielder Jack Smith could have caught, the outfield bleacherites gave out with a barrage of catcalls. One foghorn-voiced occupant of the right-field stands was so abusive that, as one witness put it, "the milkfed young man got sore . . . and called the police."[3] (What Hornsby actually did was call time and ask a park policeman to quiet the heckler—a tactic that only encouraged more jeers.)

If Hornsby appeared a bit thin-skinned that day, maybe it was because he was worrying about his mother, whose poor state of health had recently caused him to be away from the team for some thirty-six hectic, sleepless hours en route to and from Fort Worth. It was the beginning of nine years of chronic illness for Mary Rogers Hornsby— as well as nine years of periodic trips to her bedside by her favorite offspring.

Yet however troubled he may have been by matters at home, the young Texan remained on top of his game when he took a bat in his hands. In 145 of his team's 152 games (with two rain-outs), Hornsby improved over his previous year's batting mark by fourteen points (to .327), besides hitting eight home runs (only four fewer than the league's best), driving in sixty-six runs, and again stealing seventeen bases. As evidence of his status as a hard hitter, he led the National League with 253 total bases.

The Cardinals finished the season in third place—three games above the .500 mark and sixteen games behind the pennant-winning New York Giants. Home attendance held up well for most of the season, so that Rickey was able to declare a $20,000 profit and a small dividend for the franchise's stockholders.

The National Leaguers won four of six decisions in the postseason series with the Browns (seventh-place finishers in the American League) and gained an extra $109 per man. "Pep" Hornsby, as some of his teammates still called him, drove home to Fort Worth in his first automobile, a new Buick roadster, stopping in Denison to see Sarah Elizabeth Martin, whom he'd known since his stay with the Railroaders. Still in her teens, a brown-haired, sweet-faced young woman, Sarah was no doubt much taken by the courtship of somebody who almost overnight, it seemed, had become a famous baseball player.

But baseball came first for Hornsby—as it always would. That October, while the Giants fell to the Chicago White Sox six games to two in the World Series, he toured the middle part of the country with a group of major-leaguers that included the Browns' George Sisler as well as Walter Johnson, the American League's best pitcher, and Grover Cleveland Alexander, fresh from his third-straight thirty-win season for the Philadelphia Phillies. War or no war, the touring ballplayers drew good crowds and nicely supplemented their regular-season salaries.

Meanwhile Miller Huggins decided to seek greener fields. Unhappy since the sale of the Cardinals franchise and Rickey's elevation over him in player-disposition matters (at a bigger salary), Huggins turned down a $10,000 offer and went over to the American League, signing a two-year contract with the lackluster New York Yankees for $12,500 per year and taking ace scout Bob Connery with him. Rickey quickly offered the manager's job to Jack Hendricks, who in 1917 managed Indianapolis to both a pennant in the American Association and a post-season "Little World Series" victory over Toronto of the International League.

Over the winter Chicago Cubs owner Charles Weeghman renewed his efforts to buy Hornsby. After paying Philadelphia $60,000 for the illustrious battery of Alexander and Bill Killefer, Weeghman came to St. Louis, lunched with Rickey, and offered a flat $75,000 for Hornsby. Sorely tempted, Rickey finally decided that he wouldn't be "the goat of Mr. Weeghman's publicity game." It wasn't a game, as well-publicized overtures from the New York Giants and various other clubs confirmed. "Rogers Hornsby," said a local sportswriter, "is now enjoying the . . .

glory of being . . . the most sought after player in the National League."[4] For reasons of his own, the shrewd Rickey thought better of giving up his best player solely for cash.

In January, Hornsby wrote Rickey the good news that his local draft board in Fort Worth had placed him in Class 3—deferment status—because he provided sole support for his mother and his sister, Margaret, who put off marriage to remain at home and care for Mary Hornsby. Three weeks later Rickey received a less-agreeable communication: Hornsby had received his contract for 1918 and didn't like it. He wanted $7,000, a demand that prompted the St. Louis Post-Dispatch's John E. Wray to remark upon the young man's "elephantiasis of the cranium."[5]

Although he made the usual front-office claim that fans turned out to see a winning team regardless of particular performers, Rickey knew he had to deal with the young man. While manager Hendricks made a futile trip to Fort Worth to try to talk Hornsby into signing, Wray (who like most sportswriters tended to side with management in contract disputes) suggested that "[Hornsby] sit on the bench until he wakes up to a realization that the European war is on and the Federal war is off."[6]

Finally Rickey himself went to Fort Worth and spent two days talking with Hornsby and his mother. In the end Hornsby agreed to a two-year contract at $4,000 per year—the salary he sought and failed to get a year earlier—and Rickey consented to a clause that prohibited Hornsby's sale or trade without his concurrence. The player was signed, Rickey wired back to St. Louis, and "mighty glad he was not traded to Chicago."[7]

Fearing losses of players to military service and the effects of unsettled wartime conditions, American and National League presidents and club owners decided to save a few thousand dollars apiece by halving the time spent at spring training—at the same time that they scheduled the standard 154-game season. So on March 20 Hornsby arrived at Hot Wells to start his third full big-league season weighing a robust 183 pounds (about eight more than his usual midseason weight), claiming to be fully satisfied with his contract, and saying nice things about club president Rickey.

When the Cardinals stopped at Fort Worth, on their way north, for a game with the Panthers, Hornsby was again called to home plate before the game and lauded and applauded. The ballclub proceeded to Kansas City, while Hornsby received Rickey's permission to stay behind for a few days because his mother had suffered another relapse. He arrived in St. Louis in time for the preseason series with the Browns, but he might as well have lingered in Texas; the weather was foul, the teams played only four of seven scheduled games (all won by the American Leaguers), and Hornsby failed to hit at all. It was a dreary preview to what became an unhappy season for Hornsby, the St. Louis Cardinals, and all baseball.

Only 8,000 were on hand for the season opener at what was now called Cardinal Field. A year earlier the war in Europe had still seemed far away, but now the setting was decidedly martial. One difference was that, while the starting time for local home games remained at 3:15, the sun would set an hour later under wartime daylight-savings time. Before the game the crowd was serenaded by the Great Lakes Naval Training Station band, exhorted by Liberty Loan speakers, and entertained by a pantomime at home plate called "Swatting the Kaiser," in which "Uncle Sam" pummeled a spike-helmeted representation of the German monarch.

When the game finally got under way, Grover Cleveland Alexander pitched for the first time as a Chicago Cub, yielding a triple to Hornsby and eight other hits, and losing to Lee Meadows, 4–2. Ten days later, at Chicago, Alexander again faced St. Louis in his last game before entering the army. The Cubs won a 3–2 thriller in the ninth inning.

Although Hornsby made two hits in Alexander's farewell appearance, for most of the year he struggled both at bat and afield in the worst full-season performance of his major-league career. Partly Hornsby's poor showing was a matter of injuries: a groin pull sustained in mid-May, later a sore shoulder and a spike wound in his right thumb.

Mostly, though, it had to do with his acute personal dislike for manager Jack Hendricks.

A high-school dropout, Hornsby generally had no use for "college boys." He made an exception for Miller Huggins—a graduate of the University of Cincinnati law school and a licensed attorney—not only because Huggins had given the youngster a fair chance to prove himself but also because Huggins was an honest, plainspoken, down-to-earth fellow who wore his formal learning lightly.

Hendricks, on the other hand, never gained Hornsby's trust. That Hendricks was a graduate of Northwestern University may have appealed to Rickey, who enjoyed the company of educated people, but he impressed Hornsby only as an incompetent "bush leaguer."[8] Lacking confidence in whatever Hendricks might be trying to do with the ballclub, Hornsby generally played for himself. For his part, Hendricks resented the way Hornsby had practically brushed him off in February when he visited Fort Worth to talk contract terms, and he became convinced that Hornsby was a "malingerer" whose groin pull and other physical complaints were excuses for not playing as hard and as often as he should.

Of course it didn't help poor Hendricks that, as the 1918 season wore along, he lost player after player either to the military draft or to some kind of civilian employment deemed an "essential occupation," which usually meant signing on with shipyards, munitions plants, or steel mills and playing for company baseball teams in highly competitive semipro leagues. By June 19, when the Cardinals returned home, only Hornsby and three others from the opening-day lineup were still with the club, and forty-four-year-old Bobby Wallace, an outstanding shortstop for many years who joined the Cardinals as a coach in 1917, had been pressed into service.

Ten new players—replacements assembled from wherever Rickey could find them in the collapsing minor leagues—were waiting in St. Louis. (Of the ten minor leagues starting the 1918 season, only one—the Class AA International League—completed a full schedule.)[9] Among the newcomers were Austin McHenry, a tough-looking, hard-hitting outfielder from southern Ohio, acquired from Milwaukee of the American Association, and Charlie Grimm, a St. Louis native who'd been playing first base for Little Rock in the Southern Association.

Early in July, Hornsby received notification from his draft board in Fort Worth that he was now in Class 1, subject to the draft. Shortly after that, his board ordered him either to "engage in an essential wartime occupation" or prepare to enter military service.[10] He thus became the first major-league player to be so ordered under the War Department's recently issued "Work or Fight" directive, which now became an added woe for ballclubs struggling to keep competent players on the field—in front of the smallest crowds so far in the century.

Meanwhile rumblings of friction between Hornsby and Hendricks became increasingly audible in the St. Louis press. Some local writers went so far as to suggest that in view of Hornsby's lackluster showing, Branch Rickey might be sorry he hadn't taken one of Charles Weeghman's offers.

On July 8 Hornsby departed for Fort Worth, amid speculations that he was on the outs with Hendricks and his teammates, that his mother was ill again, or that he wanted to talk with his local draft board. In fact he did seek reclassification as "the sole support of an invalid mother and a sister."[11] After his board reaffirmed his Class 1 status and gave him until August 1 to obtain a war-essential job, Hornsby returned to St. Louis and told Rickey he intended to go to work in a shipyards, either at Bethlehem, Pennsylvania, or Wilmington, Delaware. Both places had sought his skills—not for making ships, of course, but for sparking their companies' baseball teams.

Rickey now publicly acknowledged that, while he and Hornsby remained "the best of friends," the Texan wasn't on speaking terms with Hendricks or several teammates. Loquacious as always, Rickey couldn't resist expanding on what the trouble was. Hornsby possessed "a peculiar character," said Rickey, and one couldn't understand him "unless one is intimately associated with him." An "egotistical" young man, Hornsby not only thought of himself as baseball's greatest player but "must be made to believe it if his club is to realize to the maximum of his ability." That was the way he had to be "handled." No, Rickey had no regrets about refusing offers for Hornsby; in fact, he said, "I continue to bless that day." And once the war ended and Hornsby came back to baseball, "he'll be able to show his former admirers who apparently have deserted him that he still is one of the greatest players who ever wore a uniform. I know he can do that."[12]

Even at that early date, as Rickey described him, Hornsby was basically a loner. At the boardinghouse where he lived with other players, he had little to say on any subject except baseball. He didn't take part in after-dinner card games, didn't go out with teammates for a couple of beers, and was in bed by ten or eleven o'clock. Generally he kept to himself, as well as kept his mind on the business at hand: the next baseball game.

As things turned out, Hornsby was able to remain with the Cardinals until the end of the season, under a dispensation granted by the War Department whereby what remained of Organized Baseball was allowed to carry on through the traditional Labor Day doubleheaders and play the World Series immediately thereafter. Club presidents officially notified their players and managers that salaries would stop as of September 2. Meanwhile Rickey secured a major's commission in the U.S. Army and showed up at his office in uniform.

By batting .342 (twenty-four hits for seventy at bats) during an eighteen-game road trip, Hornsby raised his average to a respectable level, but the team stayed in last place. A three-game series with Cincinnati in mid-August didn't sell enough tickets to cover the Reds' hotel bills from the visitors' share of the receipts.

On August 26, after New York swept a doubleheader at Cardinal Field, Hendricks went to Rickey and asked that Hornsby be fined fifty dollars for taking a called third strike early in the first game and then wrangling at such length with umpire Pete Harrison that Harrison ejected him. Convinced that Hornsby deliberately got himself kicked out, Hendricks complained to Rickey that all season long Hornsby had been a "bad actor" (in baseball parlance, a player hard to deal with). A few days earlier, when he failed to slide and was tagged out at home plate, Hornsby told his teammates, "I'm too good a ball player to be sliding for a tailend team."[13]

When Rickey notified Hornsby of the fifty-dollar fine, the angry ballplayer invited Sid Keener, a young sportswriter for the *St. Louis Star,* to have dinner with him. Later that evening, related Keener many years later, the two went to a gambling joint outside the city on Easton Avenue owned by an ex-convict named Tony Foley. There Hornsby exchanged fifty dollars in Federal Reserve notes for the same amount in silver dollars, which he carried home in a cloth sack. The next afternoon he walked into the Cardinals dressing room, went over to Hendricks, said "Here!" and threw the sackful of silver at the manager's feet. "He just thought it would be funny to pay Jack off that way," explained Keener.[14]

Hornsby also sounded off publicly, describing Hendricks as "a boob manager" and his teammates as "stool pigeons."[15] In Pittsburgh a few days later, no doubt at Rickey's urging, Hendricks sought out the young malcontent and agreed to remit the fifty-dollar fine.

Nothing more was said on the matter for what remained of the shortest professional baseball season since the 1880s. For the Cardinals it ended at Cincinnati, where they lost both Labor Day games to finish last at 51–78, thirty-three games behind first-place Chicago. Hornsby batted only .281 and made forty-six errors in 115 games, all but two of which he played at shortstop.

As soon as he got back to St. Louis, he announced to any and all concerned that he would never again play for Jack Hendricks. Then he made preparations to leave for Wilmington, Delaware, where he would work for the Harlan Shipyards as a steel plate-setter at $400 per month—and play for the shipyards' baseball team.

Hendricks, himself about to depart for overseas work in the Knights of Columbus athletic program, exhibited a petition of support signed by sixteen Cardinals, and reminded everybody that his contract still had a year to run. Rickey, complained Hendricks, gave in to Hornsby before the season on salary, during the season when he left the team and spent a leisurely period in Texas, and then later when Hornsby's fine was rescinded.

Major Rickey, also bound for Europe, lamented the whole business. "Each [man]," he said, "had a poor opinion of the other and the result was disastrous." Yet Rickey remained convinced that Hornsby, "under handling that will humor his own notion that he is one of the greatest diamond stars that ever put on a spiked shoe, and at the same time keep the proper reign [sic] on him," would become "one of the game's wonders."[16]

So while Hornsby went to Harlan Shipyards and Rickey, Hendricks, and a number of other baseball notables (including Miller Huggins, Ty Cobb, George Sisler, and Christy Mathewson) went to France, James C. Jones acknowledged that the franchise had lost upwards of $30,000 during the past season and worried about how to meet the $210,000 balance on its indebtedness.

As soon as he was settled at Wilmington, Hornsby sent for Sarah Martin, his fiancée since the previous summer. After two days aboard a train, she arrived in Philadelphia, where Hornsby was waiting with a wedding ring. They married in a civil ceremony on September 23 and honeymooned for a couple days in Philadelphia and Wilmington before Hornsby returned to work—nominally as a plate-setter, mostly as a ballplayer.

The war ended much more quickly than anybody had anticipated. The arrival in France of the American Expeditionary Force in ever-increasing numbers finally turned the battle against the Germans. Early in November, with his armies in retreat, Kaiser Wilhelm II fled to the neutral Netherlands, and the leadership of the new German republic asked for an armistice, which went into effect on November 11.

Meanwhile the newlyweds stayed on at Wilmington only long enough for Hornsby to play a couple more chilly ball games and collect his last paycheck at the end of November. He could look forward to more agreeable off-season employment at his first white-collar job: traveling from town to town and using his baseball name and connections to arrange a string of Texas automobile dealerships.

When Hornsby and his bride stopped over in St. Louis on their way home, Cardinals secretary-treasurer Hiram W. Mason cautioned him against talking with newsmen, but Hornsby was more than willing to air his discontents. "I'm not trying to stir up trouble on the club," he said. "But it might as well be understood that Jack Hendricks and I cannot be friends." When teammates had asked him to sign the pro-Hendricks petition, he couldn't "bring myself to do it." Yes, he had a poor season, "but after Hendricks 'got on' me I just lost heart." If Hendricks returned for 1919, he wanted to be traded; but if Rickey took over the team, "I'll be out there giving the best that's in me."[17]

Asked about Hornsby upon his return from France at the end of the year, Hendricks was conciliatory: "I'm sorry he says he doesn't like me. I have no personal dislike for him."[18] Obviously trying to save his job, Hendricks went on to say that nobody on his ballclub had tried any harder in 1918 than Hornsby and Doug Baird, an infielder who also publicly criticized the manager. (Within three weeks Baird was gone, traded to Philadelphia with two third-rate pitchers for infielder Milton Stock, another pitcher, and a third-rate catcher.)

On January 26, 1919, the Cardinals' board of directors met at chairman Jones's office and voted to pay off Hendricks for an undisclosed portion of the balance of his contract. Rickey, just home from the wars, was invited to become Cardinals manager. Jones convinced the other directors that combining the positions of president and field manager would save $10,000 a year, as well as make it easier for Rickey to find and develop young players. With genuine reluctance, Rickey agreed to take on both jobs—at the same $15,000 salary but with a three-year contract extension and a share of whatever profits the franchise might make.

Trying to operate in a wartime season that was abbreviated by a full month, every major-league franchise—even the pennant-winning Chicago Cubs and Boston Red Sox—lost money in 1918. Bewailing their financial reverses, the club owners voted for a twenty-one-player June–September roster and a 140-game regular season—two weeks shorter than the schedule in place since 1903. Thus spring training for 1919 wouldn't commence until the last week in March. As things turned out, the money the owners saved on two weeks' worth of salaries didn't equal what they lost in two weeks' lost gate receipts, as crowds returned to the National Pastime in numbers equaling or exceeding prewar days.

The St. Louis Cardinals, one of the neediest franchises to begin with, came out of the war in particularly bad shape. Seeking to save wherever he could, Rickey decided not to order new uniforms for 1919 but to have last year's repaired and saved for the season's opener. During spring practice the players would wear spare uniform parts gathered from wherever they could be had, even from high school and semipro teams. Moreover, the Cardinals wouldn't train at Hot Wells, Texas, or anywhere warmer than St. Louis. Rickey arranged with Washington University for the use of Francis Field, the facility that served both football and baseball teams. If it was too wet and cold outside, the players would move into the university's field house. With as many as four players sharing a room, they would lodge at the Hamilton Hotel in the western part of the city.

Hornsby stayed at the hotel with the other players, although once the season began, Sarah joined him in a furnished apartment at 5455 Delmar Boulevard, in the western part of the St. Louis city limits, near Forest Park. (They still listed their home address as 1304 Commerce Street, North Fort Worth.)

Spring training for the 1919 Cardinals commenced at 9:30 on the morning of March 26, when some twenty-five men alighted from a streetcar and strolled onto Francis Field, an unfenced expanse of tall, dead grass except for a skinned diamond. It soon began to rain, so the first day's workout consisted of playing catch indoors and attending the first of countless blackboard-diagrammed strategy lectures Rickey would give his Cardinals teams over the next six years.

Manager Rickey was all over the place that spring, instructing, exhorting, and encouraging everybody. He drilled his men in complicated signals and insisted that they look sharp and do what he told them. "We had more signals than a freight yard," one Cardinal recalled.

"Some of the boys thought they had to raise their hands to go to first base."[19]

Over the winter Rickey had picked up two American League castoffs, each for the $2,500 waiver price: Burt Shotton, a ten-year veteran outfielder, and shortstop John Lavan (called "Doc" because he was a medical student at the University of Michigan). Shotton became Rickey's "Sunday manager" and close personal friend; Lavan, Rickey was convinced, could be a first-class shortstop.

So the Cardinals' resourceful manager decided to make Hornsby into a second baseman. Patiently and at length, Rickey drilled Hornsby on play around the "keystone," concentrating on the intricacies of the double play from the right side of the infield: coming across the base, taking the throw from the shortstop while hitting the bag with the instep of his left foot, and then snapping the ball across his chest to first. Although Hornsby had played only one major-league game at second (in 1916), he respected Rickey's baseball knowledge and, after some preliminary grumbling, took readily to his coaching.

Following a minimal exhibition schedule—games with Kansas City and Indianapolis of the American Association and Evansville of the Three-I League—the Cardinals met the Browns in the spring city series. Physically trim and still not needing eyeglasses (as opposed to the portly, bespectacled baseball mogul familiar to a later generation), Rickey was in uniform to meet at home plate with Browns manager Jimmy Burke and the two umpires before the opening game at Sportsman's Park. In exceptionally agreeable weather, the teams drew good turnouts in both ballparks for a projected five-of-nine-games set, which the Browns won in eight.

On April 23 an overflow opening-day crowd at Redland Field, Cincinnati, saw the Reds beat the Cardinals 6–2 behind Adolfo Luque, a clever Cuban right-hander and one of the earliest Caribbean-area players in the majors. In the next day's game (also won by the Reds, 3–1), Hornsby smashed a long drive and dashed around first base, only to be called out for passing rookie Cliff Heathcote, who, fooled by the second baseman's pantomime catch, had headed back to first. Rickey allowed that although he wasn't a swearing man, he could see the satisfactions one could sometimes get from it.

Had he been so inclined, Rickey would have sworn plentifully that season—it was another unhappy year for St. Louis National League fans. After losing twenty-two of their first thirty-two games, the Cardinals won the next seven straight, but it took another small spurt in September to keep them out of the league cellar. They finished seventh with a record of 54–83.

Baseball's general attendance recovery helped the Cardinals in terms of their portion of receipts on the road, but at home they could attract only 173,604 paying spectators. With his ballclub going nowhere in the pennant race and the franchise constantly short of funds, Rickey irked Cardinals loyalists when he sent Walton Cruise, one of his more consistent hitters, to Boston for cash and traded Lee Meadows and Frank Snyder, two of the club's mainstays. For Meadows, Philadelphia returned Doug Baird plus two nobodies; for Snyder, New York exchanged sore-armed left-hander Ferdie Schupp and an estimated $15,000.

For all the time Rickey spent coaching him in the spring, Hornsby was at second base in only twenty-seven of the 138 games in which he appeared. He played third base most of the time, although he also handled first and shortstop. At bat he got off to a slow start, but by June he was pushing his average up week by week. He finished at .318, with eight home runs (the league's fourth best) and seventy-one runs batted in (tied for second). Although some unofficial tabulations listed Hornsby as the National League's batting leader, official statistics released early in December certified that Edd Roush, Cincinnati's superb center fielder, had beaten him out by three percentage points.

Hornsby intended to spend the whole off-season at Fort Worth, but he ended up traveling back and forth to St. Louis several times, as the defendant in the first of a long succession of legal controversies that would plague him over the decades.

On the morning of the previous June 17, Hornsby had driven his Buick roadster out of the driveway on Clara Avenue, turned west onto

Delmar Boulevard, and struck and knocked over an elderly local citizen named Frank G. Rowe. Five weeks later, claiming to be suffering from a variety of serious injuries, including a permanently crippled right arm, Rowe brought suit against Hornsby in city circuit court, seeking $15,000 in damages. Hornsby, according to Rowe's petition, "was driving carelessly and negligently operating . . . his said automobile at a careless and reckless rate of speed: to-wit, in excess of fifteen miles per hour and with a reckless disregard of the life and limb of the plaintiff."[20]

In a deposition given at the end of September, at the office of Rowe's attorney, Hornsby maintained that he blew his horn at the intersection (as required by local traffic law) and Rowe suddenly stepped out in front of him. Rowe himself was to blame; he simply walked out into traffic.

Nearly five months later, after Rowe's attorney filed various amended petitions and Hornsby's filed various answers, Hornsby and Rowe agreed on a settlement. On March 20, 1920, Rowe and his attorney and Hornsby's two attorneys (signing in behalf of "Roger Hornsby") agreed to a stipulation for dismissal, "all of the matters and things in controversy . . . having been adjusted, compromised and finally settled." Besides assuming all court costs, as ordered by the judge, Hornsby undoubtedly made some kind of cash payment to Rowe, although the amount wasn't indicated in the records of the case.[21]

While the suit against Hornsby drifted along, Branch Rickey met with the Cardinals' board of directors and received another three-year extension on his contract as president and manager. Then, in January 1920, Sam Breadon, hitherto an obscure stockholder, loaned the Cardinals $18,000 on condition that he be elected president of the franchise. Chairman of the board Jones and the other directors complied with Breadon's terms, and Rickey suddenly found himself demoted to vice president yet also expected to continue managing the ballclub—a job he always claimed he hadn't wanted in the first place.

Forty-three years old, Breadon was a native of New York City who never finished grade school. He migrated to St. Louis in 1900 to take advantage of "more opportunity in the West," as he put it.[22] An early automobile entrepreneur (in partnership with Marion Lambert of Lambert Pharmaceuticals), he built a thriving business selling White Steamers and Pierce-Arrows. In 1917 James C. Jones talked him into buying fifty shares of Cardinals stock, and over the next two years he picked up others' shares as they became available. When he became president of the Cardinals franchise, he was just about to purchase what proved to be a highly profitable Ford agency; in the decade-long automobile boom just getting under way, he became one of the richest men in the city.

The relationship between Rickey and Breadon would be one of mutual respect but never affection; Rickey soon discovered that his new boss was an even tighter man with a dollar than he was. He had to plead with Breadon for $10,000 with which to purchase a right-handed pitcher named Jesse Haines, who won twenty-one games at Kansas City in 1919. And he had to convince Breadon that it was in the long-term interests of the ballclub to continue to resist offers for Rogers Hornsby, however enticing they might be.

Rumors that John McGraw's New York Giants were again in quest of Hornsby's services surfaced as early as December. "McGraw wanted Rogers Hornsby," Rickey recalled, "and I couldn't blame him, because I wanted to keep him just as badly."[23] Soon it became known that Jack Hendricks, Hornsby's onetime nemesis, was acting as agent for New York in negotiations for the Cardinals' star and was to receive a $10,000 commission. Hendricks acknowledged as much, adding that the Giants would give St. Louis $70,000 plus first baseman George Kelly, second baseman Larry Doyle, a substitute outfielder, and the pick of the Giants' catchers. Hendricks even offered to sweeten the deal with half of his commission, boosting the cash involved to $75,000. Breadon, according to Hendricks, was inclined to take the offer but deferred to Rickey's judgment.

Many years later, Rickey related how, in a meeting in New York City, John McGraw and Giants president Charles Stoneham pressured him hard, with McGraw going so far as to show him how he could use each new player in his lineup. Exasperated by Rickey's failure to do what was obviously in his own best interest, Stoneham starting talking straight cash: the Cardinals could have $300,000, keep Hornsby until the end of the 1920 season, and then receive another $50,000 if the Giants happened to win the pennant.

Rickey still wouldn't deal, although he did indicate an interest in some kind of arrangement if it included Frank Frisch, a twenty-one-year-old infielder who'd joined the Giants during the 1919 season out of Fordham University. As yet, few people had taken notice of Frisch, but both Rickey and McGraw, shrewd judges of baseball flesh, knew he was a great prospect. McGraw rejected Rickey's ploy out of hand, and the remarkable encounter broke up with the Cardinals vice president–manager trembling with apprehension at having turned down far more money than had ever been offered for a ballplayer.

"It is pleasing," Rickey told St. Louis newsmen, "that all the puffing and big offers for Hornsby cannot affect his playing. . . . All this talk about offers ranging upward to in the neighborhood of $100,000 have [*sic*] reached his ears, but he has no inflated ideas as to his value."[24] Apparently not, because at the end of January, on one of his various trips into St. Louis to confer with his attorneys about the Rowe suit, Hornsby met Rickey at his little downtown office, listened patiently to his lecture about the club's financial ills, and signed a one-year contract for $5,000, a raise of only $1,000.

In the years ahead, the young man wouldn't have to inflate his own sense of value as a baseball property, because others would do that for him. Already one of the National League's top players, he was about to emerge as its most renowned and highest paid as well—in a period when batting prowess surpassed pitching skills for the first time since the 1890s and attendance for baseball games reached unprecedented levels. Ahead lay what commentators were soon calling "the golden age of American sports."

4

. . .

Best

in His

League

In addition to the annual speculation about how particular ballclubs and ballplayers would perform in the coming season, baseball gossip over the winter of 1919–20 included rumors that something fishy had gone on in last autumn's World Series, which the underdog Cincinnati Reds won in eight games (of a projected five of nine) from a Chicago White Sox team many had called the greatest ever. Despite strong denials from baseball officials, leading sportswriters, and others presumably in a position to know about such matters, the whispers would persist through the spring and summer months.

Of more immediate consequence was the restored 154-game schedule, which meant that players would again be expected for spring training about March 1. The major-league club owners also voted to increase the June roster cutdown to twenty-three, so that two more positions would be open on each of the sixteen teams.

There was also considerable talk that a new-model baseball might be used in the 1920 season, one that was more lively than the ball previously in use throughout Organized Baseball. Over the winter, moreover, the club owners voted to outlaw the spitball and other trick deliveries. Except for seventeen designated spitballers (including the Cardinals' Bill Doak) who would be allowed to load up until their careers ended, nobody in the majors or anywhere else in Organized Baseball could legally moisten, scuff, cut, smear, or otherwise alter the surface of the ball.

Once the season got under way, it soon became apparent that pitchers had lost more than the prerogative of tampering with the ball. Hits traveled faster and farther off the bat than anybody could remember; measured against 1917 (the most recent 154-game season), offensive statistics rose markedly in every category. Gains in runs, batting averages, home runs, and other offensive figures were smaller in the National than in the American League, where Babe Ruth, playing his first season as a New York Yankee, hammered fifty-four home runs (15 percent of his league's total), but close observers in both leagues understood that something had happened to the ball itself. What they didn't realize was that power-oriented baseball—inspired by Ruth's home-run exploits and unprecedented earnings—would redefine play in the golden age ahead.

The Yankees bought Ruth, erstwhile Boston Red Sox left-handed pitching ace, following a season in which he hit twenty-nine home runs—a major-league record he proceeded to obliterate in 1920. Ruth came to New York for a record $125,000 in cash, plus a $300,000 loan secured against the Red Sox's ballpark.

Struggling to keep the Cardinals franchise solvent, Branch Rickey understood that (1) St. Louis was simply too small to support two major-league franchises and (2) the Cardinals would never enjoy the kind of wherewithal the Yankees or, in Rickey's own league, the New York Giants and Chicago Cubs could draw upon. Rickey coaxed enough money out of Sam Breadon to buy Jesse Haines, and he swapped three Cardinals-controlled minor-leaguers for Jacques Fournier, a former American League first baseman who'd batted well in the Pacific Coast League. For the long run, however, Rickey decided to build his ballclub with raw young prospects, signed for little or nothing and developed at minimal cost.

In the fall of 1919, at Cardinal Field, Rickey organized the first in what would become yearly tryouts for anybody who thought he might be good enough to play professionally. Out of that first tryout group of about 100 aspirants, Rickey signed some three dozen youngsters, including Jim Bottomley, a left-handed, nineteen-year-old first baseman from Nokomis, Illinois, and Ray Blades, a stocky outfielder whom Rickey had first observed the previous summer when the Cardinals played an exhibition game against a team from the streetcar factory at Mount Vernon, Illinois.

Rickey assigned his hopefuls to minor-league clubs, in exchange for his pick of whatever other players those clubs might want to sell at the end of the season. But his long-range design was far more ambitious. Subsequently (early in 1921) he persuaded Breadon to buy controlling interest in the Syracuse franchise of the International League. It was the beginning of Rickey's far-flung farm system, which by 1928 would number 203 players on eight Cardinals-owned minor-league teams, as well as a number of other teams with which Rickey formed working agreements. In the coming decade and for long afterward, Rickey's system provided a formula for consistent success on the playing field and—through the sale of surplus talent—steady fattening of the Cardinals' treasury.

But all that was far into the future. During the off-season of 1919–20, nobody paid much attention to what Rickey was doing; the Yankees' acquisition of Ruth dominated the sports pages in St. Louis and everywhere else. The Cardinals remained a down-and-out operation with only one outstanding player.

At the beginning of March, carrying a career batting average of .310 after four big-league seasons and a fraction of another, Rogers Hornsby left his newly pregnant wife in Fort Worth with his mother and sister and headed for another spring training. Although Hornsby's destination lay within his home state, it was almost as far away as the distance from Fort Worth to St. Louis. Rickey assembled his players at Brownsville, a town of 10,000 or so near the mouth of the Rio Grande—the farthest south any major-league team had trained up to then.

Workouts began on the military parade grounds at Fort Brown, about ten miles downriver, then transferred to a new baseball field just completed by the municipality. The Cardinals contingent needed all forty rooms of Brownsville's only decent hotel, because besides holdovers and off-season acquisitions, Rickey invited all his tryout-camp signees.

As of January 16, 1920, in accordance with the Eighteenth Amendment to the federal Constitution and the implementing Volstead Act, it became illegal to make, transport, sell, or consume alcoholic beverages anywhere in the United States. If the advent of prohibition as national policy bothered the abstemious Hornsby (and Rickey) not at all, neither did it present any great hardship for the tipplers among the Cardinals. Right across the Rio Grande in Matamoros, cantinas and gambling houses operated freely.

Once the players returned to St. Louis, they would discover that local criminal elements had already organized thriving bootlegging operations, and speakeasies could be found all over the city. Throughout the thirteen-year prohibition era, beer flowed freely for St. Louis's many German-Americans, while wine (mostly homemade) kept its sizable Italian-American population refreshed.

Hornsby settled at second base and appeared in all the spring exhibition games against Connie Mack's woefully weak Philadelphia Athletics, who trained at McAllen, farther up the valley. The two teams got to see such valley towns as Pharr, Mercedes, San Benito, and Donna before heading north and stopping at Bonham, College Station, and Checotah, Oklahoma. For more than a week, the players slept only in their Pullman berths. Back in St. Louis, the Cardinals dropped four of six games to the Browns in characteristically disagreeable weather.

About 10,000 people paid their way into Cardinal Field on April 13 for the 1920 season opener, which the home team lost to Pittsburgh. Hornsby was at second base, where he would remain for all 149 games he played that season. A good number of the male customers showed up in overalls—a briefly fashionable middle-class protest against rapidly rising clothing prices. Branch Rickey wasn't in overalls, but he wasn't in uniform, either, having decided (permanently, as it turned out) to stay off the coaching lines and manage exclusively from the bench in street clothes.

Hornsby hit safely in the first fourteen games of the season before Cincinnati stopped him on May 8. A month later, he and his teammates ended Grover Cleveland Alexander's eleven-game winning streak, Hornsby driving home two runs with two triples over the Chicago left fielder's head. Said Alexander afterward, "Hornsby is the greatest hitter I've ever had to face. I've tried to fool him every way possible, but it just cannot be done. Personally I don't think a more skillful man ever stepped up to the plate." John B. Sheridan added that while Hornsby wasn't particularly brainy and nothing exceptional afield or on the bases, "he can hit!"[1]

Hornsby's robust hitting, which stayed near the .400 mark most of the season, prompted the New York Giants to make still another bid for his services. In June, Rickey confirmed that John McGraw had recently offered $200,000 cash and two players for the Cardinals second baseman. Hornsby still wasn't for sale, said Rickey, not even for $1 million.

That was pure bluster on Rickey's part, but in fact Sam Breadon's emergence as the franchise's largest stockholder did provide an element of financial stability. In May the board of directors authorized a new issue of $100,000 in stock to pay off the $75,000 remaining on the debt undertaken when the ballclub was purchased from Helene Robison Britton. Breadon then announced that he'd reached an agreement with Browns president Phil Ball for the Cardinals to play their home games at Sportsman's Park, six blocks south and west of Cardinal Field, at Grand Boulevard and Dodier Street. Breadon signed a ten-year lease at an annual rental of $20,000, and he and Rickey moved into two small offices in the west wing of the ballpark.

On the last day of June, having won twelve of twenty-one games on the road and occupying third place, the Cardinals made their debut at

Sportsman's Park. Only 3,000 of the ballpark's 18,000 seats went unsold, as Mayor Henry Kiel and other dignitaries commemorated the event with home-plate ceremonies. Cardinals fans went home unhappy over the team's 6–2 defeat but at least were consoled by the fact that from here on they could watch their favorites in modern, well-built surroundings.

It was an opportune time for Hornsby to start playing half his games at Sportsman's Park, because the livelier ball, together with more agreeable distances than those at the old ballpark, made him a far more powerful hitter. Although the bleachers in center and left fields were 430 feet and 340 feet away, respectively, it was only 315 down the line to the bleachers in right, only 354 to right-center.

The team played poorly on that first home stand in their new environs and dropped to sixth place. Hornsby kept pounding out base hits, enjoying his first two-home-run game on July 30 in a losing effort at the Polo Grounds in New York. A heavy cold disabled him at the end of August and the beginning of September, but he was fully recovered when the Cardinals departed on their last road trip.

At Brooklyn, where Wilbert Robinson's club was fighting McGraw's Giants for the pennant, an incident occurred that was all too common under baseball's generally lax governance. A Brooklyn player told Hornsby that he and his teammates would contribute $750 for each game the Cardinals won from the Giants when they crossed the East River for a series at the Polo Grounds. Hornsby quickly reported the offer to Rickey, who disclosed it to the newspapers and supposedly squelched the thing. As it happened, though, St. Louis lost back-to-back doubleheaders at Brooklyn, then beat the Giants two games out of three in a series that effectively decided the race.

Brooklyn finished seven games ahead of New York and eighteen ahead of the Cardinals, who tied Chicago for fifth place with a 75–79 record, behind Cincinnati and Pittsburgh. At bat the 1920 Cardinals were potent; their .289 team average was the National League's highest in eight years. But their sloppy play in the field—256 errors (of which Hornsby committed thirty-four)—gave away many games. Among all major-league clubs, only the Philadelphia Athletics erred more frequently. Bill Doak won twenty games and Ferdie Schupp, supposedly washed up when Rickey traded for him, won sixteen; but Haines lost twenty, though yielding less than three earned runs per nine innings.

Rogers Hornsby made 218 base hits and won his first batting championship with a .370 average, nineteen points better than the Giants' Ross Youngs. Hornsby also topped his league in runs batted in (ninety-four), doubles (forty-four), and total bases (329), and he was second in triples (twenty). Although he hit only eight home runs, his .559 slugging average (total bases divided by times at bat) was the league's highest since 1913.

The Browns' followers also saw plenty of offense that year, because Jimmy Burke's fourth-place finishers led the majors in team batting (.308) and featured the stylish exploits of George Sisler, whose .407 average was the highest in either league since Ty Cobb's .410 eight years earlier. Sisler's nineteen home runs trailed Babe Ruth's total by thirty-five, but no American Leaguer besides Ruth had ever hit more.

While Hornsby took off-season employment as an agent for the Missouri State Life Insurance Company, most of the rest of the Cardinals, with Milton Stock serving as manager, made a little extra money from the receipts of a four-game split with the St. Louis Giants. The Giants had just completed the inaugural season of the Negro National League, an organization directed from Chicago by Andrew "Rube" Foster and based in six other midwestern cities besides Chicago and St. Louis. Although few white people who attended the Cardinals-Giants games at Kuebler's Park (North Broadway and Clarence) were familiar with the local black professionals, black fans knew pitcher-manager Bill Gatewood and star center fielder Oscar Charleston as well as St. Louis whites knew Rogers Hornsby and George Sisler.

During the World Series (which Brooklyn lost five games to three to Cleveland), more rumors of deals involving Hornsby were in the air, and at the end of the year Rickey confirmed that the New York Giants had again bid $200,000 plus four players. "Hornsby is absolutely not on the market," declared Rickey. An unnamed Cardinals official—either president Breadon, board chairman Jones, or Rickey himself—accused John McGraw of "working on" Hornsby during the past season, trying to turn him into a malcontent. Although that wasn't the first time McGraw had been so accused by National League colleagues, he indignantly answered, "It isn't our policy to keep driving after a man in a way to break up another owner's ball club."[2]

Even in St. Louis, such vivid off-season news yielded headlines to the stunning revelations coming out of Chicago, where an inquiry by the Cook County grand jury, begun the previous August, triggered admissions by various White Sox players that gamblers had bribed a third of the 1919 team to lose the World Series to Cincinnati.

The "Black Sox scandal" (as the press quickly named it), together with related disclosures of dishonesty involving other players, at other times, and on other ballclubs, provided the coup de grâce to the moribund National Commission—the three-member body that had tried to govern Organized Baseball since 1903.[3]

Fearing a massive loss of public confidence in their sport's integrity, the club owners surrendered much of their jealously held power over franchises and players and, scrapping the National Commission and subordinating the two league presidents to a single chief executive, created the office of Commissioner of Baseball. To clean up the mess—which meant eradicating not just outright dishonesty but also such suspicious practices as Brooklyn's offer of incentive payments to the Cardinals the previous September—the owners chose Kenesaw Mountain Landis, the florid, pugnacious judge of the federal district for northern Illinois in Chicago. Along with a salary of $50,000 a year, they gave Landis virtually dictatorial authority over the affairs of Organized Baseball.

Rogers Hornsby never had any use for politics, baseball or otherwise, and it's doubtful that he took much interest in the epochal changes occurring in the wake of the Black Sox revelations. He understood fully, though, that he'd become the National League's foremost player. He was also a new father, Rogers Hornsby Jr. having been born in November 1920. While his name and local notoriety brought him several nice commissions on insurance sales that winter, Hornsby wanted more money from the Cardinals—a lot more than they'd paid him so far.

Jack Ryan, a Cardinals scout in the 1920s and later Hornsby's associate in various ventures, dated from the early part of 1921 "what was to be, in some ways, a running feud" between Hornsby and Sam Breadon.[4] Breadon was now unquestionably the boss in the Cardinals organization, having sold most of the old Vandeventer and Natural Bridge Road ballpark property to the St. Louis Board of Education for $200,000 (to become the site of Beaumont High School), as well as a corner of the property to the local streetcar company for another $75,000. With that money, Breadon paid off the franchise's remaining debts and kept a sizable amount for Rickey's minor-league ventures.

When Hornsby asked for a three-year contract at $18,000 a year, the club president vetoed the proposal. The dispute simmered for two months, until, with Breadon ill in St. John's Hospital, Hornsby visited his bedside and agreed on a one-year contract for $11,000—a hefty $6,000 raise. Yet each man came away feeling that the other was unappreciative of his particular circumstances.

Maybe because vice had been so readily available a year earlier at Matamoros, Rickey thought better of returning to Brownsville and scheduled the Cardinals' 1921 spring training for Orange, Texas. The town was a small inland port, about the same size as Brownsville but nearly 500 miles up the Gulf Coast. Seeking to build upon the virtuousness supposedly gained from the legal prohibition of liquor, Rickey even banned cigarette smoking (while he continued to puff his cherished cigars). The smoking ban concerned Hornsby no more than liquor prohibition, but several Cardinals players insolently broke out pipes and still puffed away.

Hornsby arrived at Orange on March 5 and the next day played all nine innings of an exhibition game with the Athletics, who were training at Lake Charles, Louisiana. Eleven days later the Cardinals and the Yankees, based that spring at Shreveport, converged on Lake Charles for a much-touted exhibition encounter. On what the local chamber of commerce had proclaimed Ruth-Hornsby Day, an overflow crowd of 2,500, many of whom paid a dollar apiece for standing-room tickets, saw the Yankees win 14–5. Ruth obligingly homered over the short right-field fence; Hornsby managed only a single. George Toporcer, a bespectacled rookie dubbed "the four-eyed wonder" by a St. Louis writer, was the Cardinals' batting star with a homer and three singles.[5]

Branch Rickey once wrote that, as a player, Hornsby "did little to help other players" who might have learned from him. Yet Toporcer, fresh out of New York–area semipro ball, later remembered that spring as a time when "Hornsby singled me out for special attention almost immediately." As they walked from their hotel to the Orange High School athletic field, Hornsby, recalled Toporcer, "fell into step with me," "made me feel at ease in my new and strange surroundings," and later gave instructions on shortstop play. Toporcer could offer no explanation for Hornsby's solicitousness, except that maybe he "felt sorry for this skinny, eye-glassed, undernourished kid from the sandlots."[6] Originally scheduled for assignment to Syracuse, the young New Yorker hit and fielded so well that Rickey decided to keep him on his roster, which club owners had enlarged to twenty-five positions for the first time since 1914.

The biggest crowds in the history of the preseason St. Louis city series—about 74,000 in all—watched the Browns win four games to the Cardinals' three. Toporcer, stationed at third base in place of Milton Stock, who still hadn't signed a contract, dimmed Rickey's enthusiasm by hitting safely only three times in the series.

Finally signed, Stock was at third base when the Cardinals opened the season by losing to Grover Cleveland Alexander in Chicago before an overflow crowd of 20,000. Toporcer was at second and Lavan at shortstop, while Hornsby occupied left field in place of the injured Austin McHenry. After nine losses in the first ten games, Rickey benched the slump-ridden Toporcer (and eventually farmed him out to Syracuse) and, with McHenry healthy, sent Hornsby back to his accustomed second-base position.

As far as his batting was concerned, it mattered little where Hornsby played. Like many others that year, he hit the ball farther than he ever had. On June 10 his average was .426, and by midseason he'd already exceeded his previous season's high of eight home runs. Whereas in past years most of his homers had come on inside-the-park drives, now he nearly always cleared the fences.

Jesse Burkett, National League batting star in the 1890s and now a coach for John McGraw, was like most aging ballplayers in his belief that today's performers were inferior to those of his time. For Hornsby, though, Burkett had nothing but praise. "He . . . stands up there and bats sensibly," said Burkett. "That wonderful batting eye, combined with an ability to place a hit, will make a batting record for all time."[7]

Seventy-eight homers—double the total at the same point in 1920— were hit over the first twenty-one major-league playing dates; the seven games on Monday, June 6, produced eighty-five runs, 148 hits, and eleven homers. By that time the Cardinals had overcome their dreary start and, with McHenry, Fournier, and almost every nonpitcher joining Hornsby in the offensive surge, started to win more frequently than they lost.

By taking three games in a row at Pittsburgh at the beginning of September, St. Louis assumed a firm hold on third place and also reduced the Pirates' once-comfortable lead to a half-game over New York. A week later, while the Giants moved ahead of Pittsburgh, two losses at Cincinnati left the Cardinals seven and one-half games out of first place and ended whatever pennant fantasies they may have nurtured. They then killed off Pittsburgh by sweeping a doubleheader at Sportsman's Park on September 29.

The next day, a Friday, was Rogers Hornsby Day. With the grandstand decorated with flags and streamers, two brass quartets provided musical accompaniment for home-plate festivities in which acquaintances from the Junior Chamber of Commerce and the Masonic Order (which he'd joined in St. Louis back in 1918) bestowed on him a diamond ring, a diamond-studded Masonic watch fob, and $2,500 in Liberty Bonds. His teammates presented a bouquet of roses. The Cardi-

nals proceeded to pound the forlorn Pirates 12–4, with Hornsby bang-
ing a homer and two doubles.

Hitless in the final two games on Saturday and Sunday, Hornsby
missed the magical .400 mark by just three points. Still, it was the finest
season any National League hitter had enjoyed in the twentieth century.
Besides again finishing first in average (by a big margin over Edd
Roush), he led the league in base hits (235), runs batted in (126), runs
(131), doubles (forty-four), triples (eighteen), and slugging percentage
(.639). George Kelly of the Giants, with twenty-three home runs, beat
him out by two.

In rising to third place with an 87–66 record, the Cardinals batted a
lusty .308, again the best team mark in the league. Besides Hornsby's
.397 and Fournier's .343, all the outfielders topped .300, led by Mc-
Henry, whose .350 average, seventeen homers, and 102 runs driven in
forecast stardom for the Ohioan.

As compared with 1917, runs scored in 1921 increased by 28 percent in the National League, 38 percent in the American. In 1917, all
the players in the two leagues hit a total of 338 home runs; by 1921
they combined for an astonishing 937. In two years (1919–21) overall
batting averages jumped thirty-one points for National Leaguers,
twenty-four points in the American League, while pitchers' earned run
averages swelled proportionately.

Players, managers, sportswriters, and fans wondered what had happened. They performed weight and bounce tests with the baseballs and
sometimes tore them open, only to find that in composition nothing
had changed. Consisting of a cork center inside hard rubber, which in
turn was wrapped in woolen yarn and covered in two pieces of stitched
horsehide, it was the same ball that had been adopted a decade earlier.
Spokesmen for A. G. Spalding and Brothers, the firm that, under different labels, had manufactured balls for all of Organized Baseball since
the 1880s, would only acknowledge that Spalding was using a higher-
grade, tighter-winding yarn; otherwise, the manufacturer couldn't explain the ball's greater liveliness.[8]

Others, though, pointed out that the horsehide covers were also tighter and that the stitches were sewn flush with the cover (some insisted they were countersunk), both of which features especially handicapped curveball pitchers. Still others noted that the club owners were increasingly willing to let customers keep baseballs fouled into the stands (as opposed to the traditional practice of having such balls returned to play), and that, apparently at the direction of the league presidents, umpires now exchanged smudged and scuffed balls for fresh ones.

So from the early 1920s on, batters swung at whiter, cleaner, and apparently more solid, straighter-thrown baseballs, and generally regained the advantage they'd lost to the pitchers after 1900. To judge by the fattening attendance totals, fans everywhere loved the new power-oriented game.

Most of all, they loved what Babe Ruth did. As remarkable as were the 1921 batting feats of Hornsby and others, Ruth transcended everybody. Besides homering fifty-nine times to surpass his own record by five, he batted .378, drove in 171 runs, drew 144 walks, scored 177 times, and recorded a majestic slugging average of .846, topped only by his own previous record. Ruth's heroics pushed the Yankees to their first pennant since they joined the American League in 1903. Although the Giants triumphed in the World Series, Ruth more than earned his dazzling $52,000 salary.

Seeking to cash in on his drawing power, Ruth then took two teammates on an ill-advised exhibition tour and ended up being suspended for the first month of the next season by Commissioner Landis, who'd forbidden such barnstorming by World Series participants.

In St. Louis, Milton Stock arranged more modest postseason activity, starting with another series versus the local St. Louis Giants, to be played this time in Sportsman's Park. Criticized in the white press for renting the ballpark for such "bad stuff," Browns business manager Bob Quinn cut short the series after the Cardinals swept a Sunday doubleheader that was watched by a small crowd, consisting of whites on the third-base (home) side of the grandstand and blacks opposite them. Picking up $300 apiece from what one wit called "the grand

African show," Stock and his teammates then left on a barnstorming odyssey that took them from Wisconsin to southern Louisiana.[9]

Like Ruth, Hornsby had bigger off-season fish to fry. Sarah and Rogers Hornsby Jr. remained in St. Louis while he caught a train for the West Coast to play for the Los Angeles entry in the California State League—a four-club circuit operating on a ten-week, late-autumn schedule. Ty Cobb, now Detroit's player-manager, and Detroit's Harry Heilmann, the American League's batting leader, signed with two San Francisco teams; George Sisler appeared for an outfit representing the Los Angeles suburb of Vernon. Each was to serve as player-manager at a salary prorated on his season's earnings, which in Hornsby's case came out to a little more than $4,500.

Sisler's club finished first, Hornsby's third. Cobb beat out Hornsby in batting average, but the Cardinals star hit .390 in sixty-one games and led everybody with thirteen home runs. Made up mostly of Pacific Coast Leaguers who were often former big-leaguers, the four teams offered a good brand of baseball, but the costly venture—promoted in the expectation that people would flock to see big-league stars about whom they'd only heard and read—lost money and wouldn't be tried again.

Back in St. Louis by New Year's Eve, Hornsby said he would remain in the city to sell life insurance. Asked about his contract situation, he replied cheerily, "Mr. Rickey and Mr. Breadon are very fair and I want to be."[10]

What he thought fair was a three-year contract at $25,000 a year. Besides the size of his demand, the fact that he was being closely advised by Bob Newman, a former Washington University athletic star who owned part of Missouri Life, became a matter of annoyance for both Sam Breadon and John E. Wray, the *Post-Dispatch*'s senior sportswriter. If relations between Hornsby and the Cardinals management broke down, warned Wray, "the young insurance executive who advised Hornsby would probably be burdened by the painful thought that he had cost the local team and the St. Louis fans a pennant."[11]

Such dire speculation proved unwarranted, because Hornsby met with Breadon on Thursday evening, March 9, signed for $18,500 per year for three years, and hurried to catch a train for Fort Worth. He hadn't got as much as he wanted, but he was now the highest-paid player in National League history.

Two days later Hornsby said good-bye to his increasingly frail mother and drove to Dallas, where he stepped right into an exhibition game against the Cleveland Indians. From Dallas, he accompanied the ballclub to Orange, again the Cardinals' preseason base.

Breadon, having just bought the holdings of James C. Jones and several other stockholders and gained a two-thirds interest in the franchise, came down from St. Louis, donned an old uniform, and frisked around the diamond, enjoying his status as a rich and still-youthful baseball baron. Rickey, though, complained to J. Roy Stockton, a junior *Post-Dispatch* sports reporter, that his regulars were all "smug-faced," that the main threat ahead was "swell-headedness, unjustifiable swell-headedness."[12]

Some baseball pundits picked the Cardinals to finish first that year, and big things were also expected of the Browns, who under manager Lee Fohl had ended up third in 1921. Record numbers for the city series, including an overflow estimated at 29,000 for the last contest, paid to see the Browns take three games to their tenants' one. (Shirtfronts on the National Leaguers' new uniforms displayed two cardinals perched on either end of a bat—a logo that would become one of the best known in American sports.)

Except for the failure to produce a pennant winner, 1922 proved to be the best year up to then in the history of St. Louis professional baseball. With the defending-champion Yankees deprived of Babe Ruth until mid-May, the Browns battled New York all the way. They finished only a game behind the Yankees and played before 713,000 people at Sportsman's Park—the most they would draw in their fifty-two-year history. George Sisler batted .420, while outfielder Ken Williams displaced Ruth as home-run champion (thirty-nine) and led both leagues in runs batted in (155).

The Cardinals stayed in the race most of the season and set a new attendance record of their own—about 550,000. Despite a .301 team batting average (to which Toporcer, handling shortstop most of the time, contributed a surprising .324), they tied for third place, as the New York Giants took their second pennant in a row. For Rickey's men, the season's high point came on July 22, when they defeated the Boston Braves before 15,000 at Sportsman's Park—their twenty-third win in twenty-nine games—and moved a game and a half ahead of New York.

Within another month, though, the Cardinals, Cincinnati, and Pittsburgh had again given way to the Giants, who overcame a midseason disclosure that pitcher Phil Douglas had written St. Louis outfielder Les Mann offering to desert McGraw's team if the Cardinals would make it worth his while. Commissioner Landis immediately banished Douglas from Organized Baseball, but the Giants went on to take the pennant by a comfortable margin.

If Austin McHenry had remained healthy, St. Louis might have made it much tighter. As early as May it was apparent to Rickey that something was wrong with his hard-hitting left fielder. Complaining of blurred vision and having trouble judging fly balls, McHenry stayed behind when the Cardinals went on the road late in June, rejoined the team briefly in New York, then returned to St. Louis for tests at St. John's Hospital. Specialists there eventually decided that he had some kind of growth inside his skull; surgery, performed at Good Samaritan Hospital in Cincinnati, revealed a tumor wrapped almost entirely around the brain. The favorite of the "Knot Hole Gang" kids who sat in the bleachers free of charge on Fridays, and potentially one of the premier players of his time, McHenry died the following November at Mount Orab, Ohio, at the age of twenty-seven.

While McHenry's career ended suddenly and sadly, that of twenty-six-year-old Rogers Hornsby continued to brighten. Playing in all 154 games, Hornsby hammered the "jackrabbit" ball with greater authority than ever, and his, Sisler's, and Williams's batting feats prompted daily comparisons on the St. Louis sports pages.

Even though Hornsby had left Winters, Texas, as a two-year-old and hadn't been back since, the townspeople there now proclaimed him their own and eagerly awaited the Fort Worth *Star-Telegram* that arrived by train (three times a week) with news of his diamond deeds. The town drugstore installed a telegraph and began posting inning-by-inning accounts of the Cardinals' games. In Winters, according to one report, "Hornsby's name is on the lips of every person—man, woman, and child"; even the "Bohemian farmers" in the area had become his avid rooters.[13]

On July 20, at Sportsman's Park with two out in the ninth inning and the Cardinals behind Boston 6–4, the Winters native won the game by driving his twenty-fifth home run into the right-center-field bleachers with two men on base. That broke the "modern" (post-1900) National League record set by Philadelphia's Gavvy Cravath seven years earlier, and brought many in the crowd of 16,000 out of the stands to carry Hornsby from the field. Two weeks later he erased the all-time National League homer total of twenty-seven, set back in 1884 by Chicago's Ned Williamson.

"He's not the most showy or the noisiest player in the game," noted a *Sporting News* columnist, "but his quiet thoroughness can't be equaled anywhere."[14] Yet if thorough, he wasn't always so quiet. When he was called out at first base during the morning half of a July 4 doubleheader with Cincinnati at Sportsman's Park, he argued at length with rookie umpire Charles "Cy" Pfirman, wagging his finger under Pfirman's nose until he finally made contact, whereupon Pfirman used his own thumb to order him out of the game.

Such episodes were rare, though. As long as his team kept winning and his base hits kept coming, Hornsby paid little attention to umpires. In August and September, he batted safely in thirty-three consecutive games to set another modern National League mark before Brooklyn's Burleigh Grimes, an officially designated spitballer, stopped him at Ebbets Field.[15]

Shortly before the Cardinals took the field to close the season at Chicago, James M. Gould of the *St. Louis Post-Dispatch* told Hornsby that, according to his tabulations, he needed three base hits that day to finish at .400. Hornsby got his three hits and so ended the season at .401—250 hits in 623 official times at bat. His forty-two home runs were the third-most-prolific season's output ever (behind Ruth's fifty-four and fifty-nine in 1920 and 1921), and his 152 runs batted in and .722 slugging percentage were also new National League records.

Inasmuch as lucrative postseason play in California no longer beckoned, Hornsby headed up a group of National Leaguers who barnstormed around the Midwest, starting at Grand Rapids, Michigan. Meanwhile the "checkbook champions"—so derided in St. Louis because both the Giants and Yankees had purchased needed players in the midst of the pennant race—again met in the World Series, and again McGraw's splendid ballclub prevailed.[16]

Outwardly, Rogers Hornsby seemed to have his life well in hand. He was a three-time National League batting champion, well paid for his services, and on his way to becoming a national celebrity—if he wasn't one already. The father of a healthy little boy, he seemed contentedly married as well. Yet by the fall of 1922, Hornsby had become a distracted and very confused young man. If, in later years, he ever spoke about that difficult period in his life, nobody left a record of what he said. In fact, he found himself caught up in a messy extramarital affair that would wreck his own marriage and prove an embarrassment all around.

5

· · ·

Troubles

On an open date midway through the 1922 baseball season, Hornsby went to the dog-racing track on the other side of the Mississippi at Collinsville, Illinois, in the company of Eddie Ainsmith, a native New Englander, twelve-year major-leaguer, and the Cardinals' regular catcher that year. For some time—perhaps for the past three or four years—Hornsby had gambled regularly, never at cards or dice but occasionally on greyhounds and frequently on horses. He always said that he never really learned how to use a racing form, and that initially he depended on tips picked up from ballplayers, bookmakers, and other generally unreliable people. Eventually he would come to rely on professional handicappers, who studied daily racing entries and then advised Hornsby on how to make his bets.

At the Collinsville track that afternoon, Ainsmith introduced Hornsby to a shapely, strikingly pretty brunette who called herself Jeannette Pennington. Mutually attracted, she and Hornsby chatted awhile; then she went off with friends. On several occasions after that, he found her waiting at the Sportsman's Park pass gate following games. Although he later denied taking her to restaurants or anywhere else in St. Louis, both of them acknowledged meeting in New York late in August at the Pennsylvania Hotel where the Cardinals were staying—albeit in the company of her mother and Flavia Foley, wife of St. Louis gambler and speakeasy operator Tony Foley.

She would almost certainly have been aware that Hornsby was married, but he claimed to have known her originally only as Jeannette Pennington. Her full name was Mary Jeannette Pennington Hine, and not only had she been married for more than two years—to a traveling automobile-supply salesman named John Hine—but she also had a reputation around St. Louis as a flapper who loved the nightlife and enjoyed friends of questionable propriety. Although she told Hornsby and everybody else that she was only twenty-three, George H. Williams, a prominent local attorney, subsequently reported to Branch Rickey that, according to his information, "she is much older than she claims to be—older than Hornsby, even, and is a tout for Tony Foley's gambling place and has another married man on the string and is strictly a woman of the town and out for money."[1]

Until Hornsby met Jeannette Pennington Hine, Sarah Hornsby was likely the only woman he'd known sexually. Though hardly the romantic type, he quickly fell in love with someone who seemed to be just about everything his less glamorous, down-to-earth Texas wife wasn't. Hornsby, according to Sarah Hornsby's ensuing petition for divorce, became quarrelsome, faultfinding, and "cold and indifferent . . . manifesting by his actions that he [had] little or no affections for her." When she complained about living in furnished apartments and suggested they might be happier if they bought a place of their own, he suggested that "because of their apparent inability to get along together, he thought it best they should separate."[2]

Hornsby took to stopping at the downtown millinery where Jeannette Pennington clerked and inventing other ways to see her, such as coming by the apartment she and her husband occupied on Goodfellow Avenue, on the pretext of leaving a dozen quail he'd shot in rural

St. Louis County. Meanwhile the Hornsbys' marriage disintegrated. Sarah Hornsby hired private detectives to confirm her suspicions, and late in December, following various angry and futile calls to the other woman, she and Rogers Jr. left for Los Angeles to live with her widowed mother. Hornsby moved into the Jefferson Hotel in downtown St. Louis and kept up as much contact with his lover as was possible, given the delicate nature of their legal situations.

Apparently John Hine remained ignorant of the affair until the end of 1922. At a New Year's Eve party, Hine suddenly confronted his wife, slapped her face, and then got her to promise not to file for divorce. She filed anyway. Thus deceived (or so he claimed), Hine didn't appear for the hearing in circuit court, where, on February 2, 1923, Mary Jeannette Pennington Hine received a speedy divorce decree that included the restoration of her maiden name.

Maybe because he wanted to put the best face on things (or because he was weary of the ongoing angst in St. Louis), Hornsby decided to leave for spring training earlier than usual. After a final tryst at the Melbourne Hotel, he boarded a train in zero-degree weather in the company of Ainsmith and pitcher Bill Pertica, en route to Bradenton, Florida, a rapidly growing town on the southern shore of Tampa Bay. Besides upgraded hotel accommodations, Bradenton afforded the Cardinals a ballpark with a covered grandstand and grassy infield. On February 26 Hornsby was the first man onto the diamond to start spring practice.

In an ill-considered letter dated March 7 (obviously part of an ongoing exchange), Hornsby wrote Jeannette Pennington: "You ask in my letter whether my wife will come back to St. Louis. I am not sure, but it will be better for us two if she don't as you know the detectives were pretty hot on my trail." After a paragraph of endearments, he signed it, "Your loving sweetheart, Rog."[3]

Hine, who claimed that he repeatedly tried to reconcile with his wife, waited until she and her mother were absent from the apartment they shared at 1143 Union Boulevard, persuaded the janitor to let him in, went through her things, and found Hornsby's March 7 letter. He typed a copy, then rushed to his attorney's office to proclaim, "Rogers Hornsby has ruined my home."[4] Later, when Hine demanded an explanation from his ex-wife and ex-mother-in-law, they both scuffled with him in his automobile, and the original letter was torn to bits. Hine still retained his typewritten copy as principal evidence to support a motion he filed in circuit court on March 17, seeking to overturn Jeannette Pennington's divorce decree.

With his wife on the other side of the continent and the woman he loved halfway in between, Hornsby tried to get ready for another season of doing what he did best. That spring of 1923 the Cardinals toured with the International League's Rochester Rustlers, managed by George Stallings, who nine years earlier had led the Boston Braves to a world's championship. When reporters asked Walter Hapgood, who promoted the tour, how he'd managed to find such places as Dothan and Thomasville, Georgia, and Andalusia and Eufaula, Alabama, Hapgood replied insouciantly that he had never realized so many people "were begging for a chance to see the great Rogers Hornsby."[5]

Although the affable, hedonistic Babe Ruth had become the nation's baseball idol, for many people—including Rogers Hornsby himself—the intense, volatile, self-denying Ty Cobb was still the greatest player who ever trod the diamond. Hornsby had gained his first look at Cobb in the fall of 1921 in the California State League, where the antics of the "Georgia Peach" had resulted in his ejection from several games. But Hornsby had never seen Cobb at his worst until the Cardinals met Cobb's Detroit Tigers at Augusta, Georgia, their 1923 training site.

In the sixth inning, Cobb tried to steal second base and was tagged out by rookie shortstop Howard Freigau. In a fury, he cursed and threw dirt at umpire Cy Pfirman, who was touring with the Cardinals. Pfirman ordered him out of the game. When Cobb refused to leave, umpire in chief Harry "Steamboat" Johnson, employed by Detroit, drew his pocket watch, waited a minute, and, as Cobb stood his ground, declared the game forfeited to St. Louis. As people surged onto the field, the president of the Augusta baseball club and various civic leaders pleaded with fellow Augustan Cobb to leave, then with Johnson to let him stay, and finally with Branch Rickey to agree to resume play with Cobb on the field. Rickey absolutely refused, whereupon some 5,000 customers scrambled to the ticket windows to get their money back.

A short time later, Cobb stormed into the umpires' dressing room and told Johnson he was fired, only to relent before the teams entrained for Chattanooga. Johnson and Pfirman worked the game there the next day, as well as subsequent games at Birmingham and elsewhere in Alabama and Tennessee, with Cobb behaving himself comparatively well.

The Cardinals' annual spring matchup with the Browns consisted of only two games, both won by the American Leaguers. Conspicuously missing was George Sisler, who wouldn't play at all in 1923 because a stubborn sinus infection had damaged his vision and necessitated off-season surgery. Jacques Fournier was also gone, traded to Brooklyn and thus deprived of his profitable off-season income as Hornsby's coagent at Missouri State Life. "Sunny Jim" Bottomley, so called because he seemed always in good spirits, had come up from Syracuse late the previous season and taken over first base, the first important product of Rickey's farm system.

Hornsby was batting close to .405 on May 8, when, at Philadelphia, he caught his spikes trying to make a throw from behind second base and tore something in his left knee. The next day he walked with a cane and watched from the grandstand, absent from a regular-season game for the first time since 1920. He was back in the starting lineup ten days later at Brooklyn, but the knee was badly swollen and he couldn't run, cover his position adequately, or stride properly at bat. On May 26, at Pittsburgh, he limped to first after grounding a single through the infield, whereupon Rickey put in a pinch runner and sent Hornsby home to be examined by Robert F. Hyland, M.D., the Cardinals' team physician.

Hyland kept Hornsby's knee in a plaster cast for nearly two weeks, then removed it and gave him the okay to start working out. He returned to action on June 14 with a homer in a 3–2 victory over Boston at Sportsman's Park, after which the Cardinals resided in fifth place, four games above .500. The very next night, Hornsby left for Fort Worth, again called home by news that his mother seemed near death. Five days later, with Mary Rogers Hornsby out of danger for the time being, he rejoined his teammates and went hitless in a loss to New York.

His injury, his mother's crisis, his stressful love affair, and troubles with both his wife and his lover's ex-husband combined to make June 1923 one of the worst periods in Hornsby's life. Sarah Hornsby returned to St. Louis from California and filed for divorce; almost at the same time, John Hine's attorney subpoenaed Hornsby as a witness in Hine's suit in domestic relations court to overturn Jeannette Pennington's divorce decree.

Inasmuch as Hine's marriage was obviously finished, his action was probably an effort to lay the basis for a damage suit against Hornsby, on grounds of alienation of affections. According to an East St. Louis baker who testified in the hearing on Hine's motion, Hine had bragged, "I'll make a bunch of money out of a big ballplayer."[6]

Hine's lawyers decided not to call Hornsby to testify, but they did take his deposition, given on the evening of June 23 at the *St. Louis Times* building, following a loss to Chicago (the Cardinals' fifth defeat in a row). Hornsby went over the history of his relationship with Jeannette Pennington, trying to make it innocent looking and even claiming that his March 7 letter—which he said carried the salutation "Dear Miss Pennington"—hadn't been a love letter at all, in fact had been no more than a reply to a baseball fan! Asked about telephone conversations between Jeannette Pennington and Sarah Hornsby, he snapped, "I don't want you to ask anything about my wife. Don't ask a lot of foolish questions."[7]

While Judge Hogan delayed rendering a decision on Hine's motion, Hornsby became again a free man. He didn't contest Sarah Hornsby's divorce petition, neither appearing in person nor entering a formal denial. The hearing in circuit court before Judge Hogan, on June 12, lasted only fifteen minutes, most of which were taken up with testimony from two character witnesses for Sarah Hornsby. The decree stipulated that besides custody of Rogers Jr., she would receive a $25,000 lump-sum settlement.

That evening, at the new Chase Hotel, she met with reporters and handed out a typewritten statement denying that Rogers Hornsby was guilty of "any wrongdoing in the Hine matter." That disclaimer, which people who'd been following the story would have found hard to swallow, was no doubt a condition of Hornsby's agreement not to contest the divorce. Stopping from time to time to sob, she explained that because they'd usually lived in furnished apartments, their assets consisted of little more than cash and war bonds. Besides the $25,000 settlement, which she termed "more than generous," Hornsby had "made provision for the support and education of our boy."[8] Within a few days Sarah and Rogers Hornsby Jr. were again bound for Los Angeles.

"The Cardinals are an entirely different team when Hornsby is out of the game," remarked John McGraw on June 20, after his Giants had taken two of three at Sportsman's Park and built their lead over Pittsburgh to six games.[9] Yet even with Hornsby in the lineup, the 1923 Cardinals were a mediocre outfit. Jim Bottomley batted .371 in his first full season and justified the Fournier trade (even though Fournier also had a big year at Brooklyn), and Johnny Stuart, a rookie right-hander out of Ohio State University, pitched and won both games of a doubleheader at Boston—something that hadn't been done in the majors since the early years of the century.[10] But with the Cardinals clearly out of the running as early as July, it was generally an unmemorable season.

For Hornsby, the season was one he would mostly want to forget. Besides marital and extramarital muddles, he also fell into a bitter quarrel with the Cardinals management. It was all reminiscent of 1918, only much worse this time.

Late in August, at the Polo Grounds in New York, Hornsby reached third base and yelled for the batter to drive him in. With the count three balls and a strike, Rickey gave the "take" sign from the dugout. In plain sight, Hornsby threw up his hands in a gesture of frustration and disgust. He didn't score, and the Cardinals lost the game and dropped deeper into fifth place, seventeen and one-half games behind the league-leading Giants. Afterward, in the visitors' dressing room, Rickey sharply reminded Hornsby who was manager; the player replied with a barrage of what Rickey later described as "vile and unspeakable" language. Enraged, Rickey charged and swung at Hornsby, who simply pushed him away. Other players grabbed Rickey and held him until he regained his composure.

When the team returned to St. Louis a few days later, rumors again started to circulate that Hornsby would be traded. Rickey denied that any hard feelings remained; Breadon called the Rickey-Hornsby fracas "a closed incident." "It all came about in the heat of battle," said the Cardinals president. "Hornsby is not for sale or trade." The affair upset the veteran St. Louis sports scribe John B. Sheridan, who scolded "warring Christian" Rickey for losing his self-control and asked, "What is the advantage of a college education, if our leading college men are to settle things as angry wolves settle them?"[11]

Publicly, Hornsby said nothing, and on September 8, playing first base for an ailing Bottomley, he registered four hits in nine at bats as the Cardinals swept a doubleheader at Sportsman's Park and crippled Cincinnati's pennant chances. Pennant-bound for the third year in a row, the Giants took what proved to be an insurmountable lead over the Reds.

Shortly thereafter, Hornsby developed a severe skin rash on his chest and shoulders (conceivably a reaction to months of emotional stress) and, swathed in bandages and ointment under his clothing, sat in the grandstand during a series with Philadelphia. As the days passed, Hornsby still didn't make himself available, despite team physician Hyland's report that there was no reason he shouldn't play. When the rash was gone, Hornsby complained of recurrent pain in the knee he had injured four months earlier; the Cardinals management now became convinced that their number-one player was "dogging it."

Meanwhile Eddie Ainsmith went on a drunken spree, incurred the unforgiving wrath of Rickey and Breadon, and found himself sold to Brooklyn for the waiver price. Ainsmith announced that he wouldn't leave St. Louis until the Cardinals paid him $4,000—what they owed him in lump sum after he agreed to a regimen of compulsory frugality, whereby he received $200 per month during the regular season and the balance of his contract at the end. For several days he sat in the stands with his pal Hornsby, until he finally left for Brooklyn. As Hornsby saw things, "Eddie behaved all right; the grudge they got against him is that he's my friend. You oughta know that runnin' around with me, he wouldn't drink much; I never took a drink in my life."[12]

As a generally unpleasant season neared its end, the word around town was that—in Rickey's words—"a certain trouble-maker . . . who is associated with Hornsby in business and who has taken his baseball career in hand, seemingly" was giving the ballplayer bad advice—to wit, that he should force the Cardinals to trade him to an organization with greater appreciation of his talents. As many people in St. Louis were aware, Rickey was talking about Bob Newman of Missouri State Life. Queried by newsmen, Newman indignantly replied that he was far more interested in seeing a pennant winner in St. Louis than in Hornsby's problems. "I am not his adviser," said Newman. "I have no counsel to give him."[13]

On September 27 Breadon announced that Hornsby was fined $500 and suspended for the remaining five games of the season. "Hornsby was able to play yesterday [against Brooklyn]," said Breadon, "and he should have played." When the newspeople found Hornsby, he related that he went to the Cardinals' clubhouse and told Rickey his knee was still bothering him, but that he was willing to play in two upcoming exhibition games. He then went upstairs to the grandstand, where Breadon spotted him, called him over, and told him he was fined and suspended. "He simply persisted in forcing discipline," explained Rickey. "It was part of the plan. . . . But Hornsby will not be gratified by being traded."[14]

Hornsby did play those September 28 and 29 exhibition dates against nearby semipro outfits. In view of his suspension and the fact that he was the principal gate attraction, he thought he was doing the club a big favor. Most big-league clubs made extra money playing in-season exhibition engagements, but Hornsby's contract also allotted him a percentage of receipts from such games. What Hornsby *didn't* make from those two games, when added to his $500 fine and season-ending five-game suspension, amounted to an approximate personal loss of $3,000.

The Hornsby-less Cardinals ended the season on Sunday, September 30, splitting a doubleheader with Chicago that left them in fifth place with a 79–74 record—the same position in the standings as the Sisler-less Browns. Cardinals home attendance fell by more than 200,000; the organization ended up about $14,000 in the red.

Appearing in only 107 games, Hornsby slumped to .384 but still qualified for his fourth batting title. He hit seventeen home runs (twenty-four behind the league leader) and figured in none of the other major offensive categories except slugging percentage (.627).

Rickey and Breadon were convinced that John McGraw had again been "working on" Hornsby. Fearing that he might become the target of some kind of litigation undertaken by the Cardinals, Hornsby retained Frank J. Quinn, one of Jeannette Pennington's lawyers, to represent his interests. As Quinn phrased it in legalese years later (in a suit to recover the fee Hornsby hadn't paid him), the Cardinals officials believed "that said Hornsby had been incited to acts of insubordination by one John McGraw, of the New York Giants, for the purpose of causing such friction as would compel the said Cardinals to release said Hornsby from his contract with them, and thereby make him free to play ball with McGraw on the Giants."[15]

At season's end, Hornsby was unhappy about things in general. He said he didn't want to play for Branch Rickey again, but he'd never been a troublemaker and had always given his best. But he'd rather play in St. Louis than anywhere, "because the people . . . have been wonderful to me. . . . I mean that as honestly and sincerely as anything I have ever said in my life." If, though, his club wanted to trade him, "a baseball player has no hand in his affairs. . . . I will simply await developments."[16]

Breadon, whose word was determining in Cardinals operations, held his own press conference. Whether Hornsby wanted to play for Rickey or not, Breadon told local reporters (making sure they wrote down his emphasis), "The Cardinals POSITIVELY will not trade him. . . . If he declines to play with St. Louis next year, he will not play ANY place in organized baseball."[17]

Hornsby, having been in Organized Baseball nine years, knew how things worked. However antagonistic his relations with his employers might be, he would play for them in 1924—or he wouldn't play. The off-season found him still as much at odds with himself and most things in his life as when the season started. He was divorced; Jeannette was divorced; they were in love; but they couldn't do the right thing as long as a decision on her ex-husband's suit was pending. That autumn, Hornsby aptly fitted the characterization penned some years earlier by the Chicago sportswriter Hugh Fullerton: "Ball players are peculiar beings. . . . They are spoiled by overmuch praise if they make good, [and] they have about twenty-two hours a day to think about themselves and their troubles, to nurse grievances, and to develop peculiar turns of mind."[18]

Rogers Hornsby had plenty of time to think about himself and his grievances, and to develop peculiar turns of mind. Rickey and Breadon had time to think, too. Both Rickey, a straitlaced Methodist who doted on his large family, and Breadon, happily married with two daughters himself, no doubt viewed Hornsby's extramarital carryings-on with utmost distaste—but not so much that their baseball judgment was affected. Hornsby may have become a "bad actor," but if they unloaded him, they would have to have comparable worth in return.

Whether or not John McGraw actively cultivated Hornsby's discontents, the Giants leader wasn't the only one scenting the possibility of a deal for Hornsby. Rickey acknowledged that during the last series of the season, Bill Killefer, now the Chicago Cubs' manager, had inquired about the chances of acquiring the kid brother of his old Texas League batterymate. "Well, Bill," as Rickey reported his reply, "I would not give you Hornsby for every Chicago player in uniform in the park today."[19]

At the end of October, though, Rickey and Breadon met in Chicago for two hours with Killefer and William H. Veeck Sr., Cubs president. Since the purchase of the franchise by chewing-gum tycoon William K. Wrigley Jr. a few years earlier, the Cubs had become richer than ever— at least as rich as the Giants. Veeck told reporters afterward that the Cardinals wanted cash and several players, but not what the Cubs offered.

The day after the Cardinals leaders got back to St. Louis, Breadon went into conference at a downtown hotel with Dick Kinsella, ace scout for the Giants. Kinsella, according to Joseph Holland of the *Post-Dispatch,* arrived with a list of tradable players that included everybody but Frank Frisch and six others. A few days later, in New York, club secretary Jim Tierney cut the number of protected players to three; McGraw would trade anybody but Frisch, outfielder Ross Youngs, and shortstop Travis Jackson. The bidding for Hornsby, wrote Holland, "has developed into an open contest."[20]

When the Cardinals' brass met personally with McGraw, in New York just before he departed for Europe with wife and friends, Rickey still insisted that any deal must bring Frank Frisch to St. Louis. A .348 batter with 111 runs driven in and a majors-leading 223 hits in 1923, Frisch, at twenty-five, was faster and more sure-handed than Hornsby, and equally adept at either second or third base. As Giants captain, he was one of McGraw's favorites and, some New Yorkers speculated, McGraw's intended successor. Without Frisch, the Cardinals wouldn't deal; for Frisch, the Giants wouldn't deal.

"We told McGraw how we stood on the Hornsby [-Frisch] matter," Breadon said back in St. Louis, "and it was dropped immediately." Thoroughly frustrated after six years of intermittent dickering with Rickey, McGraw was in an ill temper when queried by reporters: "So far as I am concerned, the proposed deal for Hornsby is off for all time. . . . I wouldn't trade Frisch for Hornsby or any player in baseball." In a better mood when he alighted from the liner *Leviathan* in New York harbor six weeks later, McGraw was still adamant. Back in 1920, he said, the Giants had offered $300,000 in cash for Hornsby. "The Cardinals should have taken me then. I am not prepared to repeat it now."[21]

At last, that appeared to be that. Speaking to the Peoria, Illinois, Optimist Club, Rickey left no doubt about it: "Hornsby is not for sale, has never been, and never will be for sale." The *Post-Dispatch*'s John E. Wray showed some sympathy for Hornsby; after all, ballplayers were subject to a form of "peonage." Overall, though, Wray had to acknowledge that Hornsby's situation in St. Louis was favorable. Besides his handsome baseball salary, in past years his name had gained him big commissions on insurance sales. Hornsby had decided to give up that sideline, but now, Wray reported, he was using his name to market Christmas trees.[22]

That, it turned out, was a harebrained scheme whereby Hornsby bought up a great number of trees and flooded the local market—a strategy that only prompted established tree sellers to cut their prices, undersell him, and wipe out his entire investment. Poorer by an unknown amount from his Christmas-tree debacle, by $25,000 from his divorce settlement, and by steady losses on racing bets, Hornsby needed money—as he usually would for the rest of his life.

Late in the afternoon of February 21, 1924, Breadon and Rickey summoned sportswriters from the four St. Louis daily newspapers to disclose that Hornsby and his manager had talked at length the previous evening and again earlier that afternoon. They'd arrived at what—in uncharacteristically inarticulate fashion—Rickey termed "a settlement or whatever you call it." Rickey then showed the newspeople Hornsby's handwritten statement, attesting that "there is no longer any misunderstanding between us. I want to have the best year in baseball I have ever had and I want the Cardinal club to have the best year it has ever had."[23]

Rickey didn't convince anybody when he insisted that no discussion had taken place about the money Hornsby lost in fine, salary, and exhibition receipts the previous September. According to the common presumption, the Cardinals agreed to restitution, Hornsby to behave and play his best.

Five weeks earlier, Tony Foley, an old acquaintance of both Hornsby and Jeannette Pennington, was one of seventy-four people indicted by a federal grand jury investigating election fraud in St. Louis County. For not enforcing the laws, Boss Fred Essen and a number of county officials were charged with taking bribes from also-indicted gambling operators and liquor traffickers, including Foley.

If Hornsby and Jeannette Pennington commiserated over Foley's troubles, at least they were finally free to marry. Late the previous October, Judge Hogan had decided to deny John Hine's petition to set aside her divorce decree, which also undercut Hine's likely plans for an alienation-of-affections suit against Hornsby.

With his differences with the Cardinals evidently patched up and departure for spring training imminent, Hornsby was in a hurry to get married. At the same time, he feared bad publicity, given the local press's plentiful attention to his personal life over the past year. Frank Quinn came to his aid, "arranging . . . a lawful marriage under circumstances beyond the penetration of the forces of publicity."[24] On the afternoon of February 28, 1924, Hornsby and Jeannette Pennington went surreptitiously to the home of the city license clerk and purchased a marriage license. About five o'clock, Hornsby called the civil courts building to ask if Judge Hall were free; informed Hall was awaiting a jury's verdict, Hornsby, his intended, and Quinn went to the judge's courtroom, where, in the presence of the court reporter and several people also awaiting the verdict, Hornsby and Jeannette Pennington were married.

The next day, following a one-night honeymoon at Hornsby's rooms at the Jefferson Hotel, he departed for Bradenton, Florida, to begin his ninth full major-league season. If baseball always came first with Hornsby, he was still no more immune to the effects of personal turmoil than anybody else. In nearly every respect, the last year and a half had been a tough time. All he could do was persevere and try to prevail— and that's exactly what he did. The 1924 season would see him reach a level of batting excellence that, more than seventy years later, people would still talk about in awed tones.

6

· · ·

.424—and

Cardinals

Manager

Hornsby's remarriage was intended to be a secret, but it didn't remain one for long. Because the city license clerk conveniently "forgot" to report issuing the marriage license, no notice appeared in the regular birth and marriage listings in the local newspapers. At Bradenton, Hornsby refused to discuss the subject, but soon all the St. Louis papers managed to get the story and the ballplayer had to "fess up," in the slang of the time. In the end, all the secrecy proved of little consequence except for gossips in St. Louis. Baseball writers (as opposed to reporters on the regular news beats) cared about little besides baseball: What would the player do and what were the ballclub's chances in the upcoming season?

By 1924 the rest of the United States had discovered Florida, where a frenzied real-estate boom was under way. Energetic promotional efforts by local chambers of commerce also lured nine of the sixteen major-league teams—six from the National League—to the Sunshine State. Like much of the rest of the U.S. coastline, Tampa Bay proved easy for rum runners; when Branch Rickey reached Bradenton, he discovered that, as happened a year earlier, some of the early Cardinals arrivals had been patronizing local bootleggers. Rickey filed charges against one S. Desiderio for selling whiskey to his players and sent a rookie pitcher packing.

At Bradenton, Rickey and Hornsby posed smilingly for photographers and again seemed on good terms. In general, the weeks passed pleasantly, with Hornsby and the other regulars rounding into shape against nearby major- and minor-league teams and Rickey carrying on in his usual bustling and ebullient manner. Following chalk talks before morning practice sessions, he worked closely with Bottomley and other products of his farm-system enterprise, such as infielder Lester Bell and outfielders Taylor Douthit, Ray Blades, and Charles "Chick" Hafey.

When the team arrived in St. Louis, Jeannette Pennington Hornsby met her new husband in their chauffeured Lincoln sedan, and they were driven to a new home whose purchase Frank Quinn had arranged while Hornsby was at Bradenton. Bought for a reported $15,000, it was a twelve-room house with circular drive and stables, located on two wooded acres off Midland Boulevard, a mile or so beyond the western boundary of the city itself. It was an imposing place, but one that required servants and lots of upkeep and, despite the acquisition of an Irish setter, made Jeannette Hornsby lonely during the long stretches when her husband was away on road trips. They wouldn't live there long.

Only two games were scheduled in the annual preseason encounter with the Browns. The standing-room crowds at Sportsman's Park on Saturday and Sunday appeared to have forgotten all about Hornsby's well-known personal and professional foibles; mostly they wanted to check out George Sisler, who'd missed the entire previous season. With a triple and two singles in the first game, the Browns first baseman raised hopes for another year for himself and his team like 1922—maybe even better. (Browns partisans were in for a disappointment: Sisler would barely bat .300; the Browns, losing four more than they won, would finish a poor fourth.)

On April 15, opening day at Sportsman's Park, Commissioner Kenesaw Mountain Landis threw out the first ball and stayed to see Hornsby single and double off Chicago's Vic Aldridge, as the Cardinals scored three runs in the bottom of the ninth inning to win 6–5. It was the beginning of the most remarkable season at bat Hornsby would ever have, even if it wasn't the start of anything memorable for the ballclub.

With their team in seventh place by early June and again a noncontender, Rickey and Breadon sought to replace fading experience with promising youth. Doc Lavan drew his release three weeks into the season, and chronic holdout Milton Stock went to Brooklyn, as did "Spittin' Bill" Doak, winner of 144 games for St. Louis since 1914. By season's end, the Cardinals' roster consisted largely of players brought up through Rickey's farm system, which now included, besides Syracuse, Houston (Texas League) and Fort Smith (Western Association).

"Hustled on everything I hit" was the way Hornsby described that 1924 season.[1] He appeared in 143 of his team's 154 games (missing three in May with a jammed thumb and eight more in August with a sore back) and compiled the highest batting average at the major-league level since Willie Keeler's .432 in 1897 with the Baltimore National Leaguers.[2] In surpassing Napoleon Lajoie's 1901 American League mark by two points, Hornsby hit with remarkable consistency. He batted a high of .480 against Boston's pitchers, a low of .387 against Chicago's staff. His average at Sportsman's Park was .468; on opposing fields, .369. In the month of August, the hottest in St. Louis and the most wearing for ballplayers everywhere, he soared to .509. For the whole season, he failed to hit safely in only twenty-four games, with Boston's Johnny Cooney holding him hitless three times.

Hornsby ended at .424—227 hits in 536 at bats. National League president John Heydler, who watched him make thirteen hits in fourteen times at bat in an August series versus the Giants at Sportsman's Park, pronounced Hornsby "the greatest batsman of all time."[3] Such hyperbole might be expected from the league's president, but in fact what Hornsby did that year commanded everybody's attention—even

in the American League, where Babe Ruth won his only batting title (at
.378) and slammed forty-six home runs.

Hornsby himself hit twenty-five homers, second in the National
League to Jacques Fournier's twenty-seven. He also batted in ninety-five
runs, led his league in runs scored (121) and bases on balls (eighty-
nine), and reached base more than half the time. Yet while base hits
rained like money from the Texan's bat, the Cardinals finished in sixth
place with a 65–89 record.

Branch Rickey's standing as a manager wasn't helped by the fact that
in August—in his absence and under Burt Shotton's direction—the
Cardinals finally vacated the league cellar. Meanwhile St. Louis castoffs
Fournier, Doak, and Stock aided Brooklyn to a strong second-place
showing behind New York, which won its fourth National League
championship in succession (before losing the World Series for the second year in a row, this time to Washington). Hinting that Hornsby
might succeed Rickey, John E. Wray described the twenty-eight-year-
old ballplayer as "a man of few words but mighty deeds. He may lack
knowledge of the theory and mathematics of baseball so dear to the
heart of Branch; but he can tell the player what to do . . . and show
him how it's done." As such talk gathered over the winter, Hornsby's
only comment was that "every player hopes some day he'll have a club
to manage. But right now I wouldn't want such a job. I want to be just
a player until I feel that my best playing days are over."[4]

Meanwhile a controversy flared over naming the league's Most Valuable Player, a thankless task delegated to a committee chosen by the
Baseball Writers Association of America (BBWAA).[5] Besides a com-
memorative medallion, the player so named would receive 1,000 silver
dollars. With one writer from each of the eight National League cities
ranking players on a 1–10 scale, Brooklyn's Arthur "Dazzy" Vance,
who pitched twenty-eight victories and struck out 262 batters, received
seventy-four votes to Hornsby's sixty-two.

The St. Louis BBWAA members were initially puzzled by the vote,
then outraged when they learned that Jack Ryder of Cincinnati left
Hornsby off his ballot altogether. They formally protested such "bias or

prejudice" to league president Heydler, and Sam Breadon angrily called Fred Lieb of New York, chairman of the BBWAA selection committee. In turn, Lieb contacted Ryder and asked why he hadn't voted for Hornsby at all. "This contest supposedly is for a player who is most valuable to his team," explained Ryder. "I will concede Hornsby is a most valuable player to himself, but not to his team. On that basis I couldn't give him a solitary vote."[6]

"If Hornsby is not the most valuable player in the National League," declared Branch Rickey, "I must see things cross-eyed." Said John McGraw, "Hornsby is a far more valuable player than Vance." Hornsby himself was the epitome of gracious sportsmanship. "More power to Vance," he told the press. "He's a great pitcher. I certainly have no complaint to make."[7]

As a professional athlete, Hornsby was far more interested in pay raises than awards. Having completed a three-year contract that paid him $18,500 per year, he wanted another three-year deal—for a lot more money. With Rickey left out of their talks, Breadon and Hornsby came to an understanding quickly and amiably. For 1925–27, Hornsby would receive a total of $100,000. Babe Ruth, in the middle of a five-year pact paying $52,000 a year, was still way above everybody else. Yet Hornsby's $33,333 annual salary was not only the handsomest in his league but comparable to what player-managers Ty Cobb and Tris Speaker earned in the other league.

By now lots of baseball people—club officials, managers, fellow players, longtime fans, sportswriters, and of course John Heydler—shared the opinion of John P. Sheridan, who'd watched and reported baseball for forty years and seen every outstanding player in that period. Nobody wrote more perceptively than Sheridan about the post-1920 hitting boom and particularly Hornsby's batting prowess.

Hornsby, declared Sheridan in 1924, "probably is the greatest hitter of all time."[8] Pitching and fielding were better now, Sheridan thought; moreover, unlike batters before 1901, Hornsby had always played under the foul-strike rule, which counted the first two foul balls as strikes.[9] Moreover, Hornsby, unlike Ruth, was mainly a straightaway, line-drive batter; most of his long hits went from left-center around to right-center.

Sheridan observed that Hornsby used a thin-handled bat with a big knob, held it at the end, and stood as far back and away from the plate as he could and still remain inside the batter's box. He used his bat like a golf driver, its weight and thus its "driving power" concentrated in the end, and attacked the ball not as most men did—by stepping toward the *pitcher*—but by stepping toward the *plate* at right angles to the pitcher. Never bothered by anything over the outside of the plate, Hornsby was a superior curveball hitter, one who could "chase a curve to first base and hit it over the right field fence."[10]

Sheridan granted that some great batters—Ty Cobb and Napoleon Lajoie, for example—moved around in the batter's box, adjusting according to pitcher and circumstances. Hornsby, on the other hand, used what John McGraw had once called "the cigar sign pose": nearly erect, bat well away from the body, feet always in the same position. Hornsby himself advised (as quoted in *Athletic Journal*) that "a batter should never at any time change his style of batting to meet just one certain condition. He should perfect his style, and stick to it in all details."[11]

Hornsby rarely pulled the ball down the left-field line, and he once said that he never actually tried to hit a homer. "I just tried to meet the ball and didn't try to get fancy. . . . The pitcher was my target. I would have liked to hit him each time." His rules for good hitting were simple: (1) Don't swing at pitches outside the strike zone (vertically defined in Hornsby's day as knees to shoulders). (2) Hit the ball where it's pitched instead of trying to pull it. (3) Never guess: "A batter who tries to guess what the pitcher is going to throw is never a good hitter." (4) Be confident: "Never get the idea that you can't hit a certain pitcher." In sum, don't think a lot, because "you do or you don't."[12]

"You must believe in yourself," he avowed at the peak of his career. "I know I can hit the baseball." Asked many years later whether he'd preferred to bat against left-handers or right-handers, he replied with a degree of irritation: "I didn't care if the pitcher threw with his foot as long as the ball came in the strike zone." How did he feel about the pitchers he faced? "The only emotion or thought I ever had for a pitcher was to feel sorry for him. Maybe that's why I could hit."[13]

Often, with Hornsby at bat, pitchers must have felt sorry for themselves. Whenever Grover Cleveland Alexander—by Hornsby's estimation, the greatest of all pitchers—was asked about tough hitters, he always named Hornsby first. In 1926 he observed that Hornsby "has as much control of the bat, holding it at the end, as the old-time batter did when he choked the bat." Moreover, Alexander reminisced shortly before his death in 1950, "it was impossible to get him to swing at anything but strikes." He would take a pitch barely outside, then holler, "Come on, Alex, stop wastin' time and get that damn ball over the plate."[14]

In the spring of 1924, in a game with the Cardinals' Syracuse farm club at Jacksonville, Florida, Hornsby walked four times in four at bats, never once swinging at the ball. Afterward, when it was pointed out to him that the local fans paid to see him hit, he repeated what had already become his maxim: "The best way to become a bad hitter is to hit at bad balls."[15]

Clyde Sukeforth, a rookie catcher with Cincinnati in 1927, remembered that when Hornsby took pregame batting practice, "everything on the field stopped. Everybody turned to watch him swing. And that included the old-timers, the tough old pros. . . . when he had a bat in his hand, he had nothing but admirers."[16]

However much they admired him as a hitter, few contemporaries had much to say about Hornsby's other ballplaying qualities. He never stole more than seventeen bases in a season—which he did four times (1916, 1917, 1919, 1922)—and people rarely talked about his baserunning. Basestealing declined after 1920 with the arrival of "big-inning" baseball, but George Toporcer also remembered Hornsby as "slow getting away from the right side of the plate, due mainly to his vigorous follow-through swing, and therefore infield hits were a rarity with him."[17]

Yet Al Lopez, who came up with Brooklyn in the late 1920s and was behind the plate in nearly 2,000 major-league games, recalled

Hornsby's beating out more than his share of infield rollers. In Lopez's view, "he was one of the speediest men we ever had in baseball." Harold "Pie" Traynor, Pittsburgh's stellar third baseman in the 1920s and 1930s, once insisted that Hornsby would have beaten Mickey Mantle to first base from the right-hand batter's box. And during the 1922 season—according to the recollection of a sporting-goods sales-man at the scene—Hornsby's old high-school teammate Bo McMillin, then playing professional football, came out to Sportsman's Park, visited awhile, donned baseball shoes, challenged Hornsby to a foot race, and lost a 100-yard dash by a good margin.[18]

As for Hornsby afield, contemporary and later estimates have been mixed. He didn't settle at second base until 1920; even after that he played a number of games at first, third, and the outfield. His .958 fielding average for his career isn't impressive, especially compared with such premier second basemen as Eddie Collins (1906–30) at .970, Charlie Gehringer (1925–42) at .976, Bill Mazeroski (1956–72) at .983, or Joe Morgan (1963–84) at .981. Over the years Hornsby gained a particular reputation for having trouble with pop flies. Branch Rickey said flatly that "he did not like the fly ball in back of him," and Travis Jackson, the New York Giants' fine shortstop, recalled the time he was resting in the Polo Grounds clubhouse during the first game of a doubleheader, when John McGraw came bounding up the clubhouse steps exulting, "It finally happened! Hornsby got hit on the head by a pop fly!"[19]

That reputation resulted partly from the fact that with a runner on first base, Hornsby liked to position himself well in on the infield dirt and "cheat" toward second, in anticipation of a ground ball that could be turned into a double play. As a consequence, sometimes pop-ups that should have been caught fell between Hornsby and his right fielder.

Everybody agreed that Hornsby's forte as an infielder was in turning the double play. He made himself into an absolute master at getting to and across the base, taking the throw from the shortstop or third base-man with only the instep of his left foot in contact with the bag, and delivering the ball to the first baseman with an almost unerringly accurate flip across his chest. (Occasionally, some insisted, he didn't even bother to look to first when he got rid of the ball.)

Hornsby demanded perfect execution from his left-side infielders. "You throw that goddamn ball right at my chest," he instructed El-wood "Woody" English, Chicago's young shortstop, when Hornsby joined the Cubs in 1929. "Not above, not below."[20] Decades after he stopped playing, Hornsby couldn't understand why present-day second basemen straddled the bag, pivoted incorrectly on the double play, and put themselves in the way of base runners intent on preventing an in-time throw to first.

Yet while he could discourse learnedly on fielding, as well as base-running and sliding, Hornsby knew that his greatness was strictly a matter of what he did with a bat. "You know," he said about a year before he died, "I'd much rather talk about hitting. I think I'm on safer ground there."[21]

Hornsby also had pronounced views on ballplayers' personal habits. "Well, the most important thing in my schedule is sleep," he told an interviewer in 1925. Typically retiring at 10:00 or 11:00 P.M., he tried to get twelve hours of rest. Rising early wasn't advisable, because then a player would eat breakfast, have another meal at midday, and reach the ballpark "ready for a nap." In fact, a player was just starting his work-day at 3:00 P.M. (the usual starting time), and "you have to be wide awake to hit the ball and you can't be wide awake if you get up early in the morning."[22]

Spurning tobacco and liquor, Hornsby took up chewing gum with determination, and he went for food in a big way. He ate whatever and as much as he wanted, repeatedly attesting to the strength-building effects of "them juicy steaks."[23] Whatever meal he was eating, he usu-ally drank whole milk with it, and he enjoyed almost any kind of dessert. His special fondness was ice cream, in which he regularly in-dulged himself after games, after meals, or as a snack before bedtime. As a young man expending lots of calories on the ballfield, Hornsby kept his weight at 175–185 pounds. But as he grew older, played less, and followed the same eating habits, the pounds started to add up.

One of his most frequently mentioned traits was an obsessive concern for baseball's finest pair of eyes. "It is . . . bad business to do much reading," he said in that same 1925 interview. Hitters shouldn't read as they sat on swaying streetcars and trains; it was even worse for them to read in Pullman berths "until they fall asleep with a bright electric light shining in their eyes. . . . their eyes can't be in shape for batting when they abuse them that way."[24] Except for an occasional glance at baseball standings and averages, Hornsby himself read almost nothing.

Motion pictures were to be shunned as well. Once, during spring training about 1920, he agreed to accompany Branch Rickey to a movie. "That's all, Mr. Rickey," he said afterward. "I'm not going to ruin my batting eyes watching them movies. These are my eyes, not yours. I need them." (Many years later Hornsby admitted that he'd enjoyed the Wild West "shoot-'em-ups" of William S. Hart, "but only in the winter—never when I was with the ball club.")[25]

Other efforts on Rickey's part to broaden the Texan's interests were equally unavailing. At Bradenton in the spring of 1924, Rickey talked him into playing nine holes of golf. Hornsby, who'd never been on a golf course in his life, scored thirty-nine to Rickey's forty-eight—and never played again. A year later, during spring training at Stockton, California, Rickey persuaded him to attend a dance being given in the Cardinals' honor by the local chamber of commerce. Hornsby showed up, shuffled through one set, and went back to the hotel and to bed.

Although he made lots of friendly acquaintances and a number of genuine friends over the years, he impressed many people as being distant and preoccupied, if not downright unfriendly. "As a player," George Toporcer recalled, "Rog kept distinctly aloof from his teammates. . . . He usually insisted on rooming by himself. . . . Hard to approach, difficult to understand, he seemed to have nothing but contempt for the usual likes and dislikes of the average player." After Ferdie Schupp came to the Cardinals from the Giants in 1919, a New York writer asked him what kind of guy Hornsby was. "I don't know," replied Schupp. "You never see him except on the ball field, and he never talks to anybody. After a [home] game he comes into the club house, takes his shower, dresses, and walks out without a word, and nobody knows where he goes."[26] On road trips, when he wasn't at the local ballpark, Hornsby could usually be found sitting in the hotel lobby. He didn't read; he just sat and watched people come and go or talked—rarely about anything besides baseball—with reporters, players, and even passersby. Over the years he came to be regarded as the champion lobby sitter in baseball history.

In March 1925 Hornsby sat in unfamiliar lobby surroundings at the Hotel Stockton, the principal hostelry in Stockton, California. That rapidly growing San Joaquin Valley city of about 30,000 had become the Cardinals' new spring-training site, probably in the expectation that such an inland base might make for a liquor-free preseason. At $132 per person round-trip from St. Louis, the franchise could afford to have only thirty-three men in camp.

Although several players still paid the stiff fare for their wives, Jeannette Hornsby, expecting a child in about three months, remained in St. Louis. By then the Hornsbys had unloaded the mini-estate they bought a year earlier, had purchased an apartment house at 5308 Maple Avenue north of Forest Park, and occupied one of the building's four residences themselves.

As Hornsby's second marriage matured and took on new complexities, his first wife embarked upon a new life for herself and their son. In February 1925—some twenty months following her divorce—Sarah Martin Hornsby married Roy M. Finley of Denison, Texas. President of the Denison Railroaders when Hornsby played there and still Grayson County prosecuting attorney, Finley had known Sarah Martin for years before she married the ballplayer. "I wish a great store of happiness for them both," said Hornsby. "I'm glad to know she's happy."[27]

At Stockton, manager Rickey named Hornsby team captain, which made official his position as first among peers. At Rickey's request, he worked with rookie shortstop Tommy Thevenow and managed the regulars in exhibition games with the San Francisco and Sacramento clubs, while Rickey toured towns in the area with a second squad.

Worried about rumors that Breadon wanted to get rid of him, Rickey also asked Hornsby to speak in his behalf with the club president.

Accompanied by his wife, Breadon arrived at Stockton on March 18 and soon sought his star player's views on Rickey's managerial abilities. Hornsby replied that, as far as he was concerned, Rickey was the smartest man in baseball. All right, said Breadon, but how would Hornsby like to manage the ballclub? Still not twenty-nine and just at his peak as a player, Hornsby demurred. When he encountered Rachel Breadon, he asked if she would say something to her husband in Rickey's favor. That she did, and Breadon decided to keep Rickey in the dugout for the time being.

But a few days later, when the Cardinals moved into San Francisco for an exhibition series, Breadon summoned Hornsby to his hotel room and again offered him the manager's job. "I told Breadon," as Hornsby described the encounter decades later, "that if the Good Lord himself were to come down to California and manage this club, he couldn't do any better. It was a lousy team."[28] Again Breadon let the matter drop— for the time being.

After a 2,000-mile Pullman journey that took them home by way of San Antonio and Dallas for games with local Texas League outfits, the Cardinals split a two-game city series with the Browns. Then they left for Cincinnati to begin Hornsby's tenth full season as a big-leaguer. Whatever misgivings about the team's prospects he'd expressed to Breadon at Stockton, with the press he was upbeat. "It's the best Cardinal club I have played with since I came into the major leagues," he said before the opener at Redland Field.[29]

An overflow of 31,888 Cincinnatians was on hand to see their favorites debut under Jack Hendricks, who, following another stretch in the upper minors, had been hired to manage the Reds. It was a successful beginning for Hornsby's old foe, as Texan Pete Donohue shut out St. Louis on six hits.

Nine days later the Cardinals opened at home in impressive fashion, scoring eleven times in the first inning against Donohue and successors and beating Cincinnati 12–2 before about 14,000 people. The next day

Adolfo Luque's pitch hit Hornsby in the head and put the Cardinals captain out of action for four games. He singled twice when he returned on April 28, against Pittsburgh, but the team suffered its fifth straight defeat.

The Cardinals didn't win again until the streak reached seven; as they'd often done in recent seasons, they left home looking up at the rest of the league. Whether the team won or lost never seemed to affect Hornsby's batting fortunes; on May 16, at Brooklyn, he cracked his ninth home run and fourth in four games in a 6–4 loss—to which his own first-inning error contributed.

Thirteen days later, on Friday the twenty-ninth, the Cardinals lost a tough game at Pittsburgh. Facing a Memorial Day doubleheader with the hard-hitting Pirates on Saturday, they were in last place with only thirteen victories in thirty-six games. Still looking for ways to strengthen the ballclub, Rickey had recently pulled off what would prove one of his shrewdest deals, obtaining Bob O'Farrell, a first-rate catcher, from the Chicago Cubs for shortstop Howard Freigau and journeyman catcher Miguel "Mike" Gonzalez.

But in St. Louis, Sam Breadon was exasperated, especially after he checked on pregame sales for Sunday's game at Sportsman's Park and found that almost no tickets had been sold. "I couldn't stand it any longer and I suppose the fans felt the same way," Breadon later said.[30] He caught a train to Pittsburgh, arrived by nightfall of the twenty-ninth, and called Hornsby in, again to offer him Rickey's job. Again Hornsby demurred.

Next morning in the Schenley Hotel dining room, Hornsby was eating alone but unusually early, because the doubleheader was scheduled for separate morning and afternoon games. As he finished his eggs, bacon, and milk, traveling secretary Clarence Lloyd notified him that Breadon wanted to see him again, immediately. On his way out, he was intercepted by Rickey, who'd been sitting at a nearby table with Burt Shotton. While he knew he was being fired as manager, Rickey said, he wanted Hornsby to urge Breadon to give the job to Shotton.

Breadon wouldn't hear of Shotton, spoke contemptuously of Rickey's refusal to manage on Sunday, and still again insisted that Hornsby ought to manage his ballclub. "At least think it over, Rog," urged Breadon. A little later, Hornsby reported what had happened to Rickey, who went into a considerable snit. "If I can't manage, I don't want to hold any stock," he announced.[31]

Sensing the greatest financial opportunity of his life, Hornsby then told Breadon that he would take the job and continue under his player's contract at the same salary—if Breadon would help him buy Rickey's 1,167 shares, which amounted to 12.5 percent of total franchise stock. Breadon agreed, Rickey concurred in a taxi taking Breadon to the train station, and Hornsby walked into the visitors' dressing room as a twenty-nine-year-old manager and soon-to-be major stockholder in a big-league baseball franchise.

Putting it about as gently as he could, Breadon told the press: "We have been disappointed over the showing of the team, and we felt that Rickey was trying to do too much. . . . Everything is friendly between Rickey and Hornsby, and Rickey and I remain on the best of terms." Hornsby said of Rickey, "He's a mighty fine fellow. . . . We are mighty good friends, and I hope the combination of Rickey as vice president and Hornsby as manager of the Cardinals will be a winning one."[32]

More than anything else, Rickey suffered a blow to his pride. Long afterward he said that it wasn't giving up the field manager's job that hurt, but "the unnecessarily dramatic and clumsy way it was done." As for his own record, "I don't think I overmanaged. . . . It might be true . . . that I talked over the heads of the fellows at times. My fault as a manager, as I diagnose it, was due to my apparent zeal."[33] Rickey was out of the dugout and would never return, but he could console himself with his $25,000-per-year salary as vice president and, as his farm system began producing a superabundance of young talent, the small fortune he would accumulate from keeping 10 percent on all players' sales.

The *St. Louis Post-Dispatch*'s J. Roy Stockton subsequently attributed Rickey's managerial shortcomings to his "lawyer's instinct." He thought too much—juggling his players, going over losses in dressing rooms, "always citing past plays." Given his superior education, vocabulary, and intense manner, Rickey tended to intimidate his players, who resigned themselves to mediocrity.[34]

Hornsby threw out Rickey's chalkboard, held one fifteen-minute meeting to review the opposition at the beginning of each series, and generally let his men show what they could do—on the presumption that if they'd made it to the major leagues, they ought to know how to play the game. "Managing a ball club is mainly using common sense," he told an interviewer a year or so later. "There's no black art about it. It's hard work, getting players who can do a thing well and then letting them do it. . . . The less you meddle with players the better. . . . A baseball club is a machine. When you start the motor . . . let it run."[35]

On Hornsby's first day as Cardinals manager, May 30, 1925, his ballclub dropped two more games at Pittsburgh. After losing 4–1 in the morning, the Cardinals were overwhelmed 15–5 in the afternoon, despite Hornsby's two home runs into the right-field stands.

Twelve thousand curious St. Louis fans bought tickets on Sunday to see the Cardinals in their home debut under player-manager Hornsby. After Mayor Victor J. Miller escorted Hornsby to home plate for ritualistic gifts of floral pieces, rookie Flint Rhem, a folksy right-hander from South Carolina who'd briefly attended Clemson College before Rickey signed him, pitched a 5–2 victory over Cincinnati. Local baseball writer Herman Wecke noted "a dash that had been missing for some time" in the Cardinals' demeanor.[36]

On June 7, while Hornsby pushed his batting average to .401, his ballclub beat Brooklyn and climbed out of last place. Four days later, Breadon announced that Hornsby had purchased a "substantial block" of stock.[37] Giving Rickey $5,000 in cash, Hornsby borrowed the rest of what he needed from a local bank, with Breadon endorsing his note. He paid Rickey $42.85 per share for 1,167 shares—a total of $49,920.25. Breadon retained an option to buy Hornsby's stock at 6 percent interest, but a more visible factor in the arrangement was that

Hornsby's stock purchase entitled him to a seat on the Cardinals' board of directors.

While all that high finance was going on, Hornsby became a father for the second time. On June 2, 1925, William Pennington Hornsby was born at St. John's Hospital. Named for his father's deceased older brother and for his mother's family, "Billy" Hornsby inherited his mother's oval face and dark eyes, hair, and complexion.

Rogers Hornsby performed no miracles with the 1925 Cardinals, but under his leadership the ballclub righted itself and finished respectably. At the end they'd climbed to fourth place, with a record of 77–76. Hornsby's various personnel moves—such as bringing up Tommy Thevenow from Syracuse, abandoning Rickey's outfield platoon and installing Chick Hafey and Ray Blades as everyday players, and putting left-hander Bill Sherdel, previously used mostly in relief, into the starting rotation—all worked out well.

Flint Rhem recalled that Hornsby laid down three hard-and-fast rules (two for pitchers, one for hitters): (1) With a count of two strikes and no balls, Hornsby's pitcher had to knock down the batter with the next pitch. (2) If a batter hit a two-strikes-no-balls pitch, Hornsby's pitcher was fined fifty dollars. (3) If Hornsby's batter took a third strike with a runner on second or third base, it cost him fifty dollars. "If it's close enough to call," Hornsby preached, "it's sure as hell close enough to hit."[38]

Intensely competitive by nature, Hornsby as manager also took on a new combativeness. At Sportsman's Park on June 16, his club was trailing Philadelphia 4–0 in the sixth inning, when Phillies pitcher Jimmy Ring called time and asked plate umpire Cy Pfirman if he could leave the field to change his sweat-soaked undershirt. When Pfirman refused, catcher Jimmy Wilson turned on the umpire and said enough to get himself thrown out of the game. Walter "Butch" Henline replaced Wilson and took up the argument; Pfirman also chased him. At that point manager Art Fletcher ran to home plate and began waving his arms and yelling. Tired of the stalling and wrangling, Hornsby joined the pair at the plate; when Fletcher directed his tirade at him, Hornsby landed a left hook on his counterpart's jutting chin and sent him sprawling backward. Pfirman ordered Hornsby out of the game, but Ring (who took advantage of the commotion to change his shirt anyway) proceeded to yield three runs that inning and four the next, as the Cardinals completed a five-game sweep.

When league president Heydler received Pfirman's report on the St. Louis fracas, he fined Hornsby $100 and Fletcher $50, and let it go at that. So "The Rajah," as sportswriters had started calling him, remained in the lineup as the Cardinals, playing their best baseball in years, displaced the Browns as the city's favorite team.

The following August 4, when Jim Sweeney called him out on strikes in his first two times at bat, Hornsby cursed the umpire, drew another ejection, and that night received notification from Heydler that he was suspended for three days. Two weeks after that, in Boston, Hornsby stormed at Ernie Quigley until his players pulled him away and prevented another banishment.

Although Hornsby missed eleven games in July after he pulled something in his rib area on a swinging strike, he stayed atop the league in batting average and home runs. During the third week in September, the Cardinals took an unshakable hold on fourth place by sweeping three games from Brooklyn at Ebbets Field. Then they went over to the Polo Grounds and, with Hornsby hitting three doubles and two singles, won a doubleheader from the Giants. That killed John McGraw's hopes for a fifth-straight pennant and put Pittsburgh in the World Series for the first time in sixteen years.

On Sunday, September 27, in a doubleheader split with Boston at Sportsman's Park, Hornsby hit his thirty-eighth and thirty-ninth homers, as well as a triple, double, and single, and pushed his batting average to .403. During batting practice the next day, he fouled a ball off his big toe and split a toenail. From the clubhouse he summoned writers for both St. Louis and Boston papers to show them the bloody toe, because, he said, "some of those in the East may say that I'm stallin' because I want to save a .400 batting percentage."[39]

With a lead over teammate Jim Bottomley of nearly forty points,

Hornsby's sixth consecutive batting title was secure, whether he played or not. He sat out the three remaining games on the schedule, as well as exhibitions before disappointed customers at Detroit, Cleveland, and Sandusky, Ohio.

Three players—Bottomley, Pittsburgh's Hazen "Kiki" Cuyler, and Brooklyn's Zack Wheat—surpassed Hornsby in base hits, but over 138 games and 502 times at the plate, he managed a .403 average. Along with that went thirty-nine homers, 143 runs batted in, and 381 total bases—all league-leading marks.

Late in October the Hornsbys traveled to Fort Worth to introduce their four-month-old son to his grandmother Hornsby, who was now almost constantly bedridden. It was a somber visit, particularly inasmuch as the previous summer, forty-year-old Emory Hornsby had died in Fort Worth following an appendectomy, leaving a wife and daughter. Of the seven Hornsbys who'd once lived together on the farm at Winters, only four remained. Everett, the oldest, had married, retired from baseball, and taken a job with an oil company at Tulsa; Margaret had married, divorced, remarried, and now had two children.

At twenty-nine, Rogers Hornsby had married, fathered a child, divorced, married again, and fathered another child. Life went on, though maybe somewhat more complexly and perplexedly for Mary Rogers Hornsby and her offspring than for most people. But if the Hornsbys wouldn't have fit the mold of the ideal American family, at least their youngest member was whoppingly successful in his chosen profession. Ahead, moreover, was a season that would put him on top of the baseball world.

7

· · ·

The

Summit

S hortly after the conclusion of the 1925 season, Sam Breadon and Phil Ball ended years of squabbling over how much rent the Cardinals would pay the Browns if Ball enlarged Sportsman's Park, and Ball awarded contracts for the work. Completed by the following March at a cost of $600,000, the new edition featured a double-deck grandstand extending down both foul lines and a new bleachers in straightaway center field. Ball also had a roof put on the right-field bleachers, which now became a "pavilion." (Four years later the pavilion would be screened.) With a seating capacity of 32,000, the rebuilt ballpark also lengthened the foul-line distances from 340 to 355 feet in left, and from 315 to 320 in right.

In December 1925, the vote for the league's Most Valuable Player finally went Hornsby's way. With Tom Swope replacing Jack Ryder as Cincinnati's Baseball Writers Association representative, the panel gave Hornsby seventy-three of a possible eighty votes. That was one thing that made the 1925–26 off-season possibly the most pleasant of

Hornsby's career. Although Rickey stayed busy with evaluations of Cardinals-controlled minor-leaguers and planned additional farm-system tieups, his name was rarely mentioned. Hornsby enjoyed a free hand to hire the coaches he wanted and get rid of those he didn't. Burt Shotton was assigned to manage Syracuse, and, when Joe Sugden left to join Art Fletcher at Philadelphia, Bill Killefer, just fired after a last-place finish at Chicago, was hired to assist Hornsby.[1]

Over the winter the major-league joint rules committee made a concession to the struggling pitchers but also gave something more to the hitters. To help hurlers get a drier grip on the ball, the home team would have to place a resin bag at the mound before the start of each game. Batters, in turn, would gain a few extra points on their averages as a consequence of the liberalization of the sacrifice-fly rule; henceforth a time at bat wouldn't be charged if a fly ball advanced a runner to second or third base, as well as home plate.

About the only lamentable news for the Hornsbys that winter concerned the accumulating legal troubles of their friend Tony Foley. Having beaten the election-fraud charge on which he was indicted two years earlier, Foley was hit by another indictment for participating in an interstate theft ring that pirated 31,000 gallons of whiskey impounded in U.S. government warehouses, then sold the illegal liquor across the Midwest for more than $1.2 million. Late in December, a federal jury in Indianapolis convicted Foley and twenty-three others, including a Missouri state senator, a former federal circuit court clerk, and a former U.S. customs collector. Foley received a fifteen-month prison sentence; others got up to two years.

Neither Breadon nor anybody else publicly questioned whether Hornsby and his wife ought to have such friends as the Foleys. When, with hammers and drills pounding outside, Hornsby and Breadon met local baseball writers at Sportsman's Park, one scribe asked Breadon whether he was satisfied with Hornsby as manager. "Well, are you, Sam?" laughed Hornsby. Breadon beamed and said, "Well, I'll tell the world I'm satisfied."[2]

Hornsby's standing as a major stockholder became official early in

February, when he succeeded Hiram W. Mason (who'd recently re-signed as franchise secretary-treasurer) on the Cardinals' seven-person board of directors. Young Bill DeWitt, originally Rickey's office boy with the Browns and his personal secretary since 1917, became the new club treasurer, with Clarence Lloyd moving up from traveling secretary to franchise secretary.

Yielding to their manager's insistence that Texas was the best place in the world for spring training, Breadon and Rickey arranged for the Cardinals' return to the San Antonio area. Flashing newly capped front teeth and a couple of gold fillings, Hornsby left St. Louis with pitchers, catchers, coaches, and scouts on Saturday evening, February 20, bound for Hot Wells. Twenty-six hours later they pulled into the San Antonio train station, having traveled through Texas with window shades drawn to conceal their card playing, which was prohibited on the Sabbath under state law. Although it was nighttime when they arrived, various local dignitaries and a brass band were on hand to greet them, and automobiles conveyed them the five miles to the Terrell Hotel at Hot Wells.

They endured the spartan accommodations at Hot Wells only a week; when the rest of the players arrived, the Cardinals company moved into the elegant and historic Hotel Menger, in the heart of San Antonio near the Alamo chapel ruin, and shifted practices to Block's Stadium, home of the Texas League Bears. Abandoning Rickey's schedule of two-a-day practice sessions, with sandwiches served at the field, Hornsby held one daily workout—11:00 A.M. to 3:00 P.M.—which forced the players to follow his own two-meals-per-day eating routine.

During each batting practice, he stood behind the cage and advised hitters on what they might be doing wrong. He wanted no "second division ball players," he also told them, and there would be no "pets" on his team. If, to win, he had to use "some egg that I think is dumber than four humpty dumpties," then he would. He wouldn't need "snitches" to spy on his players, either, because "if somebody begins to slip," the manager would know it. "A ballplayer owes it to the club . . . to deliver the goods"; if he doesn't, "he's either gotta shake his habits or we'll shake him outta the league."[3]

Despite Hornsby's enthusiasm for Texas weather, it rained much of the time that March; early in April, in Dallas, the Cardinals even encountered light snow. Their manager was impatient to play every preseason game—and determined to win them all. Trailing by two runs when rain halted a game at Houston, Hornsby argued the umpires into resuming play. After the Cardinals rallied to win, Breadon asked why he'd been so anxious to complete the game. "The big thing is to get them into the habit of winning," Hornsby explained. "No game is unimportant. . . . the more of 'em you win, the better, regardless of the conditions."[4]

Besides getting his men in shape and into the winning habit, he found himself repeatedly called upon to attend banquets, luncheons, and other civic functions. Whereas previously Hornsby had been "of a retiring disposition," observed Bill McGoogan of the *Post-Dispatch,* now he had to socialize and at least pretend to enjoy it.[5]

He also spent a considerable amount of his off-field time with his wife and their new friends, the Frank L. Moores of Fort Thomas, Kentucky. Moore, a bookmaker who mostly took bets on horses running at the Latonia Track near Covington (but would cover the "action" almost anywhere in the country), had made Hornsby's acquaintance the previous summer, when the Cardinals were in Cincinnati. At San Antonio the Hornsbys picked up the Moores' hotel expenses, as they would again the following summer, when the Moores stayed several days at the Coronado Hotel during a Cardinals home stand.

As the Cardinals started north on their way out of Texas, they stopped in Austin to play the University of Texas Longhorns. Hornsby hurriedly arranged the game after learning that his mother, in the care of relatives at Austin for the past several months, had been hospitalized. When he visited her, as he recalled it, they talked some about the upcoming baseball season. His team would win the pennant and World Series, she believed, but she went on to say, "I don't think you will ever see me alive again." When he tried to cheer her up with assurances that they would see each other again next fall, she shook her head and said, "If I can live until the Cardinals win the pennant, I'll be happy."[6]

After beating the collegians and playing all but two of the rest of their games against minor-league competition, the Cardinals returned to St. Louis with a spring record of 22–1, their sole loss coming at the hands of the Chicago White Sox at Shreveport. Then, despite Hornsby's home run, they dropped the only game with the Browns permitted by weather. Nearly 23,000 braved cold and wet to get a look at the new version of Sportsman's Park.

Before the season opener at Sportsman's Park on April 13, Hornsby received the inevitable floral gratuities, plus a silver trophy donated by the Cleveland *Press,* which had held an off-season essay contest among its readers to choose the most popular American and National League players. (Babe Ruth, of course, was the choice for his league.) Then Jim Bottomley homered and singled, Hornsby doubled and singled twice, and Flint Rhem survived Pittsburgh's late-innings assault for a 7–6 victory. By the time the Cardinals won for the third time in the four-game series with the defending world's champions, St. Louis fans were already talking pennant.

Their team lost seven games in ten tries on the road. Even worse, on May 6, in a game with Cincinnati at Sportsman's Park, Hornsby collided at second base with Reds catcher Val Picinich and (as X rays eventually revealed) displaced two vertebrae. Although he was back in the lineup three days later, he struggled with his back from then on; that injury and a subsequent protracted bout with carbuncles on his neck, ears, and thighs would keep him in almost daily pain.

Saturday, May 22, was Rogers Hornsby Day—so designated by Mayor Miller, who urged St. Louisians to "show by their presence that they appreciate the splendid work that has been performed by this ballplayer."[7] Civic groups, Boy Scouts, and old St. Louis ballplayers paraded from Fair Grounds Park to Sportsman's Park, where James M. Gould, president of the St. Louis BBWAA chapter, presented the Most Valuable Player medallion and $1,000 in silver. Commissioner Landis, league president Heydler, and Sam Breadon were at home plate to con-

Reuben Hornsby, Rogers Hornsby's great-grandfather. (Austin History Center, Austin, Tex.)

Aaron Edward "Ed" Hornsby, seated right, with his four brothers, Travis County, Texas, ca. 1880. (Austin History Center, Austin, Tex.)

Rogers Hornsby, nineteen-year-old St. Louis Cardinals rookie. (*Sporting News* Photo Archive, St. Louis, Mo.)

Branch Rickey, ca. 1920. (National Baseball Library and Archive, Cooperstown, N.Y.)

Opposit
Hornsby in 1920, during hi
first batting-title season
(National Baseball Library an
Archive, Cooperstown, N.Y

Mary Jeannette Pennington Hine,
ca. 1922. (National Baseball
Library and Archive,
Cooperstown, N.Y.)

Coverage of Hornsby's marital
troubles in the *St. Louis Post-
Dispatch*, June 12, 1923.

Hornsby apparently scoring an inside-the-park, bases-loaded home run at the Polo Grounds, New York, 1927. Actually he missed the plate, collided with the umpire, and was tagged out by Chicago's Gabby Hartnett. (National Baseball Library and Archive, Cooperstown, N.Y.)

St. Louis Cardinals, 1926 National League and World Series champions. *Left to right, front row:* Billy Southworth, Tommy Thevenow, Vic Keen, Ernie Vick, Bob O'Farrell, Grover Cleveland Alexander. *Second row:* Jim Bottomley, Lester Bell, Jesse Haines, Otto Williams (coach), Rogers Hornsby (player-manager), Bill Killefer (coach), Ray Blades, Bill Sherdel, Taylor Douthit. *Standing:* Allen Sothoron, Jake Flowers, Herman Bell, Waddy Holm, Chick Hafey, Art Reinhart, Firmin Warwick, George Toporcer, Bill Hallahan, Edgar Clough, Flint Rhem. (National Baseball Library and Archive, Cooperstown, N.Y.)

Hornsby visiting with John McGraw before game one of the 1926 World Series, Yankee Stadium, New York. (National Baseball Library and Archive, Cooperstown, N.Y.)

Captain Hornsby, Boston Braves, and New York Giants captain and short-stop Travis Jackson, opening day 1928. Polo Grounds, New York. (Brad H. Hornsby)

Hornsby signing his player's contract with the Chicago Cubs, November 1929. Club president William H. Veeck to his right, owner William K. Wrigley Jr. to his left. (*Sporting News* Photo Archive, St. Louis, Mo.)

Left to right: Hornsby, Hack Wilson, Al Simmons, and Jimmie Foxx before game three of the 1929 World Series, Shibe Park, Philadelphia. (National Baseball Library and Archive, Cooperstown, N.Y.)

Joe McCarthy, *Chicago Cubs manager, 1929.* (National Baseball Library and Archive, Cooperstown, N.Y.)

Wagon transport from dockside to hotel, Catalina Island, February 26, 1929. *Left to right, standing in wagon:* Cliff Heathcote, traveling secretary Bob Lewis, Kiki Cuyler, Charlie Grimm, Woody English, Danny Taylor, unidentified. *Sitting:* Clarence Blair, Rogers Hornsby, Norman McMillan, John Schulte, Riggs Stephenson. *Behind wagon:* Hack Wilson. (Brad H. Hornsby)

Chicago Cubs, 1929 National League champions. *Left to right, front row:* Cliff Heathcote, Woody English, Mike Cvengros, Clyde Beck, Tommy Langtry (bat boy), Norman McMillan, Guy Bush, Johnny Moore, Riggs Stephenson. *Second row:* Jimmy Burke (coach), Grover Land (coach), Bob Lewis (traveling secretary), Bob Dorr (groundskeeper), John Seys (vice president), William H. Veeck (president), Margaret Donohue (secretary), William K. Wrigley Jr. (owner), Joe McCarthy (manager), Rogers Hornsby, Kiki Cuyler, Hack Wilson. *Back row:* John Schulte, Gabby Hartnett, Ken Penner, Sheriff Blake, Clarence Blair, Charlie Root, Zack Taylor, Andy Lotshaw (trainer), Hank Grampp, Mike Gonzalez, Hal Carlson, Chick Tolson, Pat Malone. *Missing:* Charlie Grimm. (National Baseball Library and Archive, Cooperstown, N.Y.)

gratulate Hornsby. The Phillies then obligingly lost 9–2, and for the first time in more than a month, the Cardinals' wins equaled their losses.

In mid-June, John McGraw made one of his worst trades when he sent Billy Southworth, a dependable outfielder who was batting .328 at the time, to St. Louis for Clarence "Heinie" Mueller, a local boy who'd put in four seasons of part-time duty. Southworth took over right field for the Cardinals, with Taylor Douthit as Hornsby's regular center fielder and Ray Blades and Chick Hafey sharing left. Hard-hitting Lester Bell found his place at third base; Tommy Thevenow ousted George Toporcer at shortstop; Jim Bottomley was the league's most productive first baseman; and Bob O'Farrell was both a steadying influence behind the plate and a timely hitter.

Hornsby's starting pitchers—Flint Rhem, lefties Bill Sherdel and Art Reinhart, off-season acquisition Vic Keen, and the veteran Jesse Haines—were less than formidable. But on the morning of June 23, the Cardinals claimed Grover Cleveland Alexander on waivers from Chicago. More than anything else, Alexander's arrival would prove the difference in the fortunes of the 1926 Cardinals.

Coming to Hornsby's club for only $4,000, Alexander brought sixteen years of big-league experience and 317 career victories, despite having pitched for only one pennant winner. "Pete" (as many players called him) or "Alex" (as he was known to Hornsby and others) was thirty-nine years old, 6' 1", and still a sinewy 185 pounds. He combined a good fastball, an outstanding curve, a seemingly effortless delivery, masterful control, and an uncanny knowledge of batters' weaknesses. Yet so far in 1926, his record was only 3–3, and he'd yielded fifty-six hits in fifty-two innings.

Alexander was an epileptic (long before anticonvulsant medications), and he drank heavily—by some accounts, because he thought that helped control his condition. With Bill Killefer, late manager of the Cubs and now Hornsby's aide, he'd gotten along fine; but Joe McCarthy, who succeeded Killefer after winning a pennant at Louisville, wouldn't tolerate Alexander's drinking and generally undependable behavior, and suspended him and then put him on waivers. In turn, Alexander took the same attitude toward career minor-leaguer McCarthy that Hornsby had taken toward Jack Hendricks. Big-leaguers of that era usually showed little regard for managers who hadn't played in the big time themselves; outstanding big-leaguers, moreover, often became player-managers—as had Hornsby and, for the 1926 season, six others.

Over the telephone from Chicago, Alexander told Killefer, "I'm in condition and ready to pitch now." When he arrived in St. Louis, he assured reporters that his arm still had some good games left in it, and he was "tickled to be with the team and Hornsby and Killefer. All Rog has to do is nod his head and I'll jump through a hoop for him."[8]

That afternoon Hornsby hit a bases-loaded homer—his 2,000th major-league hit—to beat Pittsburgh 6–2 and keep the Cardinals even in wins-losses. Three days later, on Sunday, June 27, Alexander made his debut for St. Louis before 37,196 seated and standing customers, the biggest baseball crowd in the city's history. He threw a four-hitter at Joe McCarthy's Cubs and, on Southworth's homer, gained what must have been an exceptionally satisfying victory.

Two days after that, team physician Robert Hyland ordered Hornsby admitted to St. John's Hospital for the removal of a badly infected carbuncle on his thigh. Killefer was in charge of the team and Toporcer filled in at second base until July 9, when Hornsby disregarded Hyland's advice and put himself back in the lineup. By then the Cardinals had moved into contention, jockeying with Pittsburgh for second place and trailing Cincinnati by a few games. Weakened by infection and hampered by pain and stiffness in his back, Hornsby batted consistently but with little power. "He has no more in his swing than a girl would have," observed J. Roy Stockton.[9]

After another week's absence, Hornsby returned to action early in August at Brooklyn, where the Cardinals won six straight games to tighten up a pennant race that, for the first time in eight years, didn't include the New York Giants. Hornsby played the Brooklyn series with a bandage covering the boil on his left thigh, another bandage on a boil on his left ear, and a bandaged spike wound on his right hand. Yet he still felt well enough to climb the railing behind the Cardinals' third-base dugout in an effort to reach a particularly abusive Brooklynite. Before he could land any blows, several Cardinals pulled him back onto the field.

Two weeks later, by beating the Giants three straight in St. Louis, the Cardinals briefly occupied the league lead; from then on, first place changed hands almost daily. Five games with Pittsburgh at the end of August and the beginning of September (one a rain-interrupted tie) drew 113,113 into Sportsman's Park, with the Sunday tie attracting thousands who arrived by excursion trains from as far away as Indiana, Oklahoma, and Texas.

Alexander, usually starting but sometimes relieving, pitched superbly, beating the Cubs in Chicago and then, with two days' rest, stopping Cincinnati. But then Hornsby's error on a pop fly—he fell on the back of his head and was briefly knocked unconscious—led to four first-inning runs as the Reds edged back on top by percentage points.

After a Labor Day doubleheader split at Pittsburgh that put St. Louis one game up on Cincinnati and three and one-half on Pittsburgh, Hornsby traveled to Youngstown, Ohio, to see James "Bonesetter" Reese, in the hope of getting some relief for his aching back. Hornsby was only one of many ballplayers who visited Reese, an elderly, totally unschooled former Welsh coal miner whose skills at skeletal manipulation were so renowned that the Ohio legislature gave him special medical certification.

Bonesetter Reese's efforts made Hornsby feel better physically, but on the late-night train back to Pittsburgh, he worried about his mother, now again in critical condition in Texas, and also seethed over difficulties he was having with both Branch Rickey and Sam Breadon. Besides dropping by the clubhouse or leaning over the railing near the Cardinals' dugout to offer unsolicited advice to Hornsby's players, Rickey also arranged for a federal prohibition agent to snoop after Alexander and other tipplers on road trips. In a lengthy tirade during the recent home stand, Hornsby had warned Breadon that he wouldn't manage or play for the Cardinals in 1927 if Rickey were still around. Afterward he told local baseball writer Herman Wecke that he was fed up with "that Ohio Wesleyan bastard."[10]

And earlier that Labor Day, between games at Pittsburgh, Breadon had come into the dressing room to tell Hornsby that, contrary to what they supposedly had agreed upon earlier, he wanted the team to keep exhibition dates in Syracuse and Buffalo on its way from Pittsburgh to Boston. Hornsby replied that his players were tired, and that for the sake of a couple of thousand dollars in receipts from "those silly exhibition games," Breadon was taking the chance of getting men injured and throwing away half a million in World Series money. Breadon persisted, until finally Hornsby stormed, "All right, but I won't send the first team! Now get the hell out of my clubhouse!"[11]

While Killefer took a couple of spare pitchers and mostly substitutes to Boston by way of Syracuse and Buffalo, Hornsby and most of the regulars and pitchers traveled by way of New York. There they rested and took in a game at Yankee Stadium, in the well-founded expectation that Miller Huggins's powerful club would be their World Series opponent. Hornsby, in street clothes, posed with Babe Ruth sitting atop the home team's dugout.

After splitting four games with the Boston Braves, the Cardinals were tied with Cincinnati, two and one-half ahead of Pittsburgh. Hornsby acknowledged that his team's errors had given away two games in Boston, but "don't worry about us crackin'."[12] Nor did they. They scored sixty-two runs in sweeping a six-game series at Philadelphia to pull ahead of Cincinnati and eliminate Pittsburgh from the race. Splitting two games at Brooklyn while Jack Hendricks's Reds lost their fifth game in a row, the Cardinals then moved into the Polo Grounds to face the Giants, who were playing out the season in the strange surroundings of fifth place.

On Friday, September 24—with the ballplayers and much of the country still buzzing over Gene Tunney's wresting of the heavyweight championship from Jack Dempsey the night before—Billy Southworth homered to beat his former teammates, and Hornsby and his men found themselves three games ahead of Cincinnati with only two to play.

Losses to the Giants on Saturday and Sunday made the final margin two games over the Reds, five over Pittsburgh. For the first time since the American Association Browns in the 1880s—after thirty-five seasons in the National League and twenty-five in the American—the city of St. Louis finally had a pennant winner.

Loudspeakers positioned at strategic points in downtown St. Louis carried a telegraphed play-by-play account of the pennant-clinching game, and people went into the streets to celebrate when it ended. They saved most of their energy, though, for their favorites' return after two World Series games in New York, the first of which wouldn't be played until Saturday, October 2.

Meanwhile baseball writers and Hornsby himself attributed the Cardinals' success to Alexander (who won nine games, lost seven, and pitched two shutouts after coming to St. Louis), to Southworth, and finally to Hornsby's policy of simplification—of signals, pitching instructions, things in general. As Bob O'Farrell put it long afterward, "Hornsby was a great manager as far as I'm concerned. That year in St. Louis he was tops. He never bothered any of us. Just let you play your own game."[13]

J. Roy Stockton, fast becoming St. Louis's foremost baseball reporter, offered a contemporary appraisal: From being "a colorless ballplayer," Hornsby had emerged as "a dynamic leader, a chief for whom his warriors would go to any limit to win." True, he would rather sit in a hotel lobby alone than be entertained at a governor's mansion, and "he swears like a trooper, a Texas trooper." Yet his outstanding characteristics were "courage, honesty, bluntness and determination . . . and you learn about the bluntness first." Stockton quoted an unnamed New York writer who remarked that Hornsby "is one of the most delightful characters I have ever met. He is the squarest, bluntest, cussingest and most convincing man I ever met in baseball." Concluded Stockton, "He's stubborn and bull-headed, he uses very bad language and he has some peculiar aversions. He can't mention a college without a few decorative adjectives. . . . But you can't help liking Hornsby. . . . He's just an honest-to-goodness person without guile or subterfuge. People trust Hornsby."[14]

At bat, Hornsby contributed much less to his team's championship season than he might have had he been healthy. Missing twenty games, he made only 167 base hits, homered eleven times, drove home ninety-three runs, and ended with a .317 batting average (thirty-six points below the league leader). It was his least-productive year since 1919, when he was still batting the dead ball. In the course of the season, moreover, he lost fifteen pounds, so that going into the World Series, he weighed less than he had since 1915.

On September 27, which was a Monday, the Cardinals practiced at Yankee Stadium. When Hornsby returned to the Alamac Hotel late that afternoon, a telegram was waiting from his wife, who simply passed along the contents of a wire from his mother's relatives. That morning, at age sixty-two, Mary Dallas Rogers Hornsby had died in Austin, Texas, where she'd been under relatives' care for the past year. The wire read: "Stay with Rogers. He needs you. All is done here. The Folks."[15]

According to contemporary reports and what Hornsby later said, his mother had insisted that her youngest offspring remain in New York to get ready for the World Series. At any rate, as his players trooped into his hotel room to offer half-articulated condolences, that's what he decided to do, reasoning that there wasn't a great deal he could accomplish by rushing off to Texas. He wired Austin that he would be there as soon as the Series ended, then called his wife to tell her to join him in New York.

Making their fourth appearance in six years, the Yankees were strong favorites with the bookmakers when the World Series—unrivaled as an annual American sports spectacle—began on Saturday at three-year-old Yankee Stadium. Before 61,658, left-handers Bill Sherdel and Herb Pennock each allowed a first-inning run, then pitched scorelessly until the sixth, when young Lou Gehrig, just completing his first full season, singled home Ruth with the game winner.

On Sunday, a couple thousand more people paid to watch Alexander even the Series with what was possibly his finest outing so far as a

Cardinal. He struck out ten Yankees and allowed four singles; Southworth's three-run homer and a bases-empty drive by Thevenow powered the Cardinals to a 6–2 victory.

After the game, the Cardinals dressed quickly, jumped into waiting automobiles, and, with motorcycle police leading the way, raced to make their train at Penn Station. At 3:50 P.M. the next day, they pulled into the Washington Avenue station under the Eads Bridge, where a crush of people were gathered for what was intended as a full-blown, official pennant celebration.

The jammed scene quickly became a wild one as well. Mayor Miller and his police escort pushed and punched their way through the crowd to get to the Hornsbys and the rest of the Cardinals contingent, and managed to present a bouquet of roses to the couple before they were enveloped by admirers. Women mussed Hornsby's hair, men pounded his back, and Jeannette Hornsby's hat was knocked askew. Separated from her husband in the crowd and genuinely frightened, she began to cry. In the Hornsbys' waiting Lincoln, little Billy Hornsby, in the care of his nurse, also cried for his mother.

Finally the police cleared an opening to a line of closed automobiles, and the Hornsbys and the other Cardinals players and wives proceeded down Washington Avenue to tumultuous cheers from tens of thousands of people lining the streets. Miller and Sam Breadon rode in the lead car, John Heydler in the next, and players and wives in following vehicles. The Hornsbys' Lincoln brought up the rear, a fact that wasn't apparent to parade watchers for several blocks. When they were finally identified, people crowded in to press their faces against the car windows; shouting boys stood on the rear bumper and running boards.

With red on display everywhere—banners, bunting, sashes, men's neckties, women's dresses—the line of automobiles proceeded through the biggest public demonstration St. Louis had seen since the Armistice eight years earlier. It took an hour to travel the thirteen blocks to Twelfth Street and over to Market Square, where, after speeches and more cheers, the celebration broke up and the Cardinals scattered to their homes. (Meanwhile the Yankees, arriving at Union Station a few minutes before the Cardinals got in, reached the Buckingham Hotel almost unnoticed.)

The Series resumed on Tuesday, October 5, before a record-breaking 37,708 at Sportsman's Park. A twenty-one-station midwestern radio hookup, anchored by the *Post-Dispatch*–owned KSD, carried a live play-by-play, with Graham McNamee at the microphone. On the field, Jesse Haines was nearly the whole show, pitching a five-hit shutout and making two hits, including a two-run homer.

But on Wednesday, before an even bigger St. Louis throng, Babe Ruth hit three home runs—the first time that had happened in Series play—as the Yankees piled up fourteen hits and ten runs and Hornsby followed twenty-game winner Rhem with four other pitchers. Thirty-five years later, the South Carolinian related that Hornsby had come to the mound in the first inning and instructed him not to throw Ruth anything fast, after which the Babe hit one of Rhem's slow ones onto the right-field pavilion roof. In the fourth, with Ruth again up, Hornsby came in with the same advice: pitch him slow; Ruth had just been lucky the time before. Rhem again followed his manager's instructions, only to watch the ball clear the pavilion roof and (so he later learned) break a Chevrolet dealer's show window across Grand Avenue. (That did it for Rhem; Ruth's third homer came off Herman Bell.)[16]

Thursday's game, the last to be played in St. Louis, drew the biggest crowd yet, nearly 40,000. Both Sherdel and Pennock again pitched splendidly, until, in the tenth inning, Tony Lazzeri, New York's rookie second baseman, lifted a sacrfice fly to score the go-ahead run. Pennock then set down the Cardinals without difficulty to put the Yankees ahead three games to two.

Back at Yankee Stadium before a disappointing turnout of less than 50,000, Alexander was again the master. Lester Bell's single and two-run homer keyed first- and seventh-inning rallies that gave Alexander ten runs, seven more than he needed in pitching his second complete-game win and pulling the Series even. Alexander scattered eight hits, struck out Ruth twice, and threw only twenty-nine called balls in his 104 pitches. Afterward he assured Hornsby that, if needed tomorrow,

"I can throw four or five of the damndest balls they ever saw. Maybe a couple of innings. But I won't warm up."[17]

The deciding game, played on Sunday afternoon, October 10, in an intermittent drizzle that held the attendance to 38,000, would become part of baseball fable and folklore—a golden moment in World Series history. Haines and Waite Hoyt both pitched well, until Yankees errors led to three unearned runs in the fourth inning, at which point Pennock relieved Hoyt. New York scored in the sixth to make it 3–2, then, in the bottom of the seventh, loaded the bases when Haines walked Gehrig with two out. In snapping off his curveball, Haines had raised and then burst a blister on the index finger of his right hand, and every pitch hurt. Hornsby came in from second, looked at the bloody finger, and, despite Haines's claim that he could keep going, signaled to the bull pen in the far left-field corner.

Rhem and Alexander were sitting in the bull pen; neither had been warming up. Alexander had celebrated in his usual fashion the previous night and, by Rhem's account, was dozing with a pint of whiskey in his pocket. Seeing Hornsby's signal, Alexander grinned, "staggered a little, handed me the pint, hitched up his britches and walked straight as he could to the mound." Hornsby walked out beyond the infield to meet Alexander and explain the situation: two out, bases loaded, Lazzeri up. "Do you feel all right?" Hornsby asked. "Sure, I feel fine," said Alexander. "Three on, eh. Well, there's no place to put Lazzeri, is there? I'll just have to give him nothin' but a lot of hell, won't I?"[18]

Alexander took off his red sweater, threw three or four warm-up pitches, and indicated that he was ready. In stepped Lazzeri (who, by a supreme irony, also suffered from epilepsy). O'Farrell squatted and faked giving a sign, but, as Alexander later explained, "he don't pay no attention to me and I don't pay no attention to him. . . . I just pitch whatever I happen to want to pitch and I know Bob will get 'em all."[19]

The first delivery was a curve that stayed too far inside—ball one. Another pitch caught the inside corner—strike one. Then another curveball, on which Lazzeri whipped his bat slightly too soon; the ball shot on a line toward the left-field corner and veered into the grandstand about ten feet foul. Alexander's next pitch was a fastball, low and outside; Lazzeri lunged for it but didn't come close. "How did I feel?" said Alexander afterward. "Go and ask Lazzeri how he felt. I felt fine. . . . The strain naturally was on Lazzeri."[20]

The score remained 3–2, Cardinals, but they still needed six more outs. Alexander retired the Yankees without incident in the eighth inning, but Pennock also held St. Louis scoreless, so that in the bottom of the ninth, Alexander found himself protecting a one-run lead and facing the top of the explosive New York batting order.

Earle Combs and then Mark Koenig were retired easily, each on groundouts. At that point, Alexander had retired twenty-four Yankees in succession, going back to the third inning of the previous day's game. Working with extreme care, he ran the count to 3–2 on Ruth, then walked him. With the slugging Bob Meusel and then Lou Gehrig coming up, the Babe might have been expected to stay put. But on the first pitch to Meusel, Ruth bolted for second base, trying, he later said, to get himself into scoring position. O'Farrell pegged perfectly to Hornsby, who had the ball waiting well ahead of the sliding Ruth.

On the long train ride back to St. Louis, Alexander imbibed freely and spoke glowingly of almost everybody, especially of his manager. "There's a great fellow if there ever was one," he told reporters. "Who couldn't pitch for Rog? . . . He makes this a great ball club. I've been in baseball a long time. But I was never treated as squarely as I have been treated by Rog and the St. Louis players and the St. Louis fans. But Rog is the man."[21]

Still experiencing back pain on almost every swing, Hornsby hadn't been much of a factor offensively. In twenty-eight times at bat, he batted only .250—six singles and a double. He did manage to drive in four runs, and he also played errorlessly throughout the Series, but his own subpar performance seemed to matter little in the aftermath of the greatest thing that could happen to any group of professional baseball players. Not at all inconsequential was the immediate cash payoff: $5,594.50 to each Cardinal—more than most of them were paid for the whole season. The Yankees had to content themselves with hefty losers' shares of $3,723 apiece.

Big things were again planned in St. Louis to honor the world's champions. Hornsby wired from New York that his players would participate in the city's celebrations but "[I] hope the fans will excuse me."[22] This time, with a reception committee waiting at Union Station (the main terminal), he slipped off at the Washington Avenue station. Together with Jeannette and Billy, he caught a later train for Dallas, with a connection to Austin.

On Tuesday night, October 12, 30,000 people gathered at Sportsman's Park to sit in darkness except for lights arranged around home plate, as ten Cardinals players (all that were still in town) received congratulations and various favors from Mayor Miller and other civic leaders. Inasmuch as another nine years would pass before Sportsman's Park had a loudspeaker system, not many could hear what was being said down on the field. The players stayed for an hour or so, tired of being lionized, and then left. Most of the crowd remained to frolic in the darkness of grandstand and bleachers; remarkably, nobody fell out of the upper deck.

The next day, in Texas, funeral services were held for Mary Rogers Hornsby at her sister's spacious house in Austin, where she had died. The pastor of Austin's First Southern Presbyterian Church preached the sermon, following which a letter from her ailing brother in Florida was read, hymns were sung, and prayers were offered. The big crowd—scores of relatives and family acquaintances—formed a motorized cortege that wound east over the nine-mile route to the cemetery at Hornsby's Bend, where the casket was reopened for those who hadn't attended the services in Austin.

The Associated Press account of the funeral was done in a vein of high-Victorian sentimentalism with southern touches, down to the ninety-year-old "Negro Mammy" who'd wet-nursed the baby Mary Dallas Rogers, and who now walked with a cane and relatives' support as she came for a last look at "Miss Mary Dallas." Onlookers marveled at "the naturalness of Mrs. Hornsby's appearance." Hornsby sat at the tent-covered gravesite with brother Everett and sister Margaret, and "tears streamed down his face and the hands which . . . swung the most feared bat in the National League trembled. His drawn cheeks clearly showed the ravages of his grief."[23]

Following the service, Hornsby greeted numerous aunts, uncles, and first, second, and third cousins, some of whom he hadn't seen since childhood. Then he walked around the cemetery, looking at the graves of the generations of Hornsbys, and finally returned to the automobile that would take him back to Austin. Jeannette and Billy weren't present, because on the way to the cemetery Ernest Jarmon, a cousin who was driving the Hornsbys, slammed on his brakes to avoid hitting the car ahead, threw Billy against the front windshield, and inflicted a wound that necessitated a flying trip back to Austin to have three stitches sewn in the toddler's forehead.

It was a sad (and unexpectedly hectic) anticlimax to what otherwise had been the greatest year in Rogers Hornsby's life. As he stood looking over the graves of his parents, brothers, and many other kin, he must have realized that, at the age of thirty, he'd already gained a kind of fame and fortune that could never be imagined by the vast majority of human beings. Although he couldn't have known it then, he'd already reached the summit of his career—the eminence of a life that would last another thirty-six years.

8

. . .

Touring the

National

League

I f joy reigned among the Cardinals' fandom, people close to the ballclub sensed that, as J. Roy Stockton put it, "the atmosphere around Breadon and Hornsby and the players [is] surcharged with friction and chill."[1] Although Breadon, Hornsby, and their wives posed together before the first World Series game at Yankee Stadium, Breadon remained indignant over being ordered out of the dressing room at Pittsburgh and then profiting little from those Buffalo and Syracuse exhibitions dates—a consequence of Hornsby's refusal to include himself or most of his regulars. A devotee of golf with a pronounced distaste for horseplaying, Breadon also couldn't reconcile his own and Hornsby's notions of appropriate off-field enjoyments.

For the Series games in St. Louis, the Cardinals owner allowed the players only two guest tickets apiece (presumably to spite his manager) and, after the seventh-game victory in New York, declined to come to the visitors' dressing room to congratulate his employees. On the long train ride back to St. Louis, Breadon summoned Bill Killefer to his compartment and asked whether he would be interested in managing the Cardinals next year, but Killefer remained loyal to the longtime friend who'd given him a job after his firing at Chicago. "I told [Breadon]," said Killefer two months later, "that I would not take the position under any circumstances or for any salary. I would not take Rogers Hornsby's job for any money."[2]

As for Hornsby, he was still unhappy over the run-in with Breadon in Pittsburgh and Rickey's meddling in on-field matters, as well as the $25,000 bonus Breadon had just paid Rickey—in accordance with a clause in Rickey's contract providing for such a bonus whenever the Cardinals won a pennant.

After burying his mother, Hornsby returned to St. Louis with his wife and young son, determined to change his circumstances. True, he owned the second-largest amount of stock in the Cardinals franchise and stood to realize a tidy dividend from a record home attendance of 681,535, and he was the second-highest-paid ballplayer in the majors, making more than $33,000 per year on a three-year contract that still had another year to run. But he hadn't received a salary increase in 1925 for taking over the manager's job, nor any kind of bonus for winning a world's championship sixteen months later. What he *had* received was quite a lot of front-office interference. If he had to put up with that, he wanted what he thought he'd earned—a three-year manager's contract paying $50,000 per season. And by J. Roy Stockton's report, Hornsby also sought to become the Cardinals' first vice president, superior to Rickey, "so that if anything happened to Breadon, Hornsby would be protected."[3]

Breadon and Hornsby went into conference on December 2, 1926, talked for an hour, and settled nothing, although Breadon announced that their meeting had been "very pleasant." Four days later, they met for two hours, talking entirely, Breadon reported, about the length of Hornsby's new contract. Yes, Hornsby wanted $150,000 over three years, but that was "more than the club's earning power for the past eight years justified." One year at $50,000 was "as far as I could reasonably see my way to sign." Said Hornsby, "I realize this is a business proposition and he has his side to consider. I must also think of my own."[4]

Not long before he died, Breadon looked back on his dealings with Hornsby and recalled, "I was so determined to get rid of Hornsby that I was afraid he might accept my one-year offer." At the annual gathering of major-league executives and managers in New York, starting December 12, 1926, Rickey conferred with John McGraw. If things didn't work out between Breadon and Hornsby, Rickey advised, then Hornsby would be on the market, and what would the Giants be willing to offer? McGraw, who'd had a bitter falling-out with Frank Frisch in St. Louis the previous August, said he would give up Frisch and a pitcher if St. Louis wanted to trade. "Then," Rickey recalled, "I asked him if he was aware of Hornsby's natural desire to take charge and manage." McGraw, always supremely self-confident, brushed that aside—he ran the Giants; it was Hornsby the player he wanted.[5]

So, in effect, the trade for Hornsby was already set when Breadon met with Hornsby for the last time on Monday, December 20, at Sportsman's Park. From his little office nearby, Rickey could hear angry, interrupted voices. Breadon, Hornsby later disclosed, again offered him a one-year, $50,000 contract, and also insisted that he must never again bet on horse races, go to tracks, or even associate with horse-racing people. His horseplaying was "nobody's damn business," shouted Hornsby, and Breadon could take his ballclub and (as Breadon delicately paraphrased it to Stockton later) "perform an utterly impossible act."[6]

After Hornsby stomped out of the office, Breadon called in Rickey, poured himself a drink of bootleg Scotch, tried to get Giants' owner Charles Stoneham on the telephone, received no answer, and left "visibly depressed." At his home he called Stoneham again, finally made contact with him through Giants' club secretary Jim Tierney, and asked whether Stoneham was still interested in a trade. Assured the Giants were, Breadon said, "Well, you've got Hornsby."[7] But, Breadon added, St. Louis had to have not only Frisch but a quality pitcher; Stoneham agreed to include right-hander Jimmy Ring (the same pitcher whose desire to change his shirt had precipitated the Hornsby-Fletcher rumpus in 1925). John McGraw, long hailed as baseball's Little Napoleon and supposedly the deciding influence in Giants affairs, didn't even know about the deal until Stoneham told him. But if the Hornsby trade signified the passing of power in the Giants organization from the renowned manager to the obese club owner, McGraw could at least exult in finally getting the player he'd sought for ten years.

By a totally unpredictable conjunction of events, Hornsby's trade was announced in time for the late editions of the afternoon newspapers, which also carried Commissioner Kenesaw Mountain Landis's disclosure of evidence in his possession that Ty Cobb and Tris Speaker, two of baseball's brightest and most venerated performers, had been implicated in a scheme to fix a Detroit-Cleveland game back in 1919. Landis subsequently cleared those two men and also dismissed recent allegations by Charles "Swede" Risberg and Charles "Chick" Gandil, two of the Chicago "Black Sox" banished from baseball, that in 1917 the Chicago team had bribed other Detroit players to throw games. Although the new scandals blew over quickly, the extensive off-season publicity given to two more highly questionable episodes in the sport's past strengthened Breadon's case against such an unregenerate gambler as Rogers Hornsby—at least in some quarters.

For several days following the announcement of Hornsby's trade, he and Breadon gave out interviews and issued written statements, each going over the particulars of their dealings and justifying himself. Inasmuch as Hornsby had gone through "a bad playing season" in 1926 and "might be finished as a player," Breadon couldn't go before more than 400 stockholders and defend a commitment of $150,000 for three years. "I expect to catch hell for the next few months," Breadon added, "but there is no ball player living, nor manager for that matter, who is going to run the club while I am president." Said Hornsby: "I gave the Cardinals all I had and I asked for a contract that I believed I was entitled to. Just tell the fans of St. Louis that I hate to leave." Thirty-five years later he termed the trade "the biggest disappointment I had in my life."[8]

No player-for-player deal until then surpassed Hornsby-Frisch for controversy. Although he'd never been a colorful, crowd-pleasing personality, Hornsby was, by general agreement, the foremost figure in St. Louis baseball history, and many local citizens took his departure as a devastating civic loss. For a while, Sam Breadon did catch hell.

Mark Steinberg, a member of the Cardinals' board of directors and Hornsby's stockbroker, called the trade "an insult to the fans of St. Louis" and resigned from the board; James M. Gould of the *Post-Dispatch* vowed never to cover another Cardinals game at Sportsman's Park (and didn't for nearly ten years); and officials of the local chamber of commerce asked Commissioner Landis to block the transaction, whereupon Breadon withdrew his membership in that organization.[9] At his downtown auto dealership, Breadon discovered crepe hanging above his office door; so many abusive calls were made to his home that he disconnected his telephone. At Broadway and Olive, a hoodlum jumped onto the running board of the Breadons' Pierce-Arrow and shouted insults until a traffic policeman chased him away. But Breadon, as stubborn (and stingy) as his Scots heritage was supposed to make him, rode out the storm. A week after the Hornsby trade, he named Bob O'Farrell, recently chosen the National League's Most Valuable Player for 1926, as his new manager. The loyal but luckless Bill Killefer joined the Browns as a coach.

On January 8, 1927, Hornsby arrived in New York to meet with John McGraw and sign a two-year contract for $36,500 per year, plus $500 for serving as team captain. Whereas he'd earlier lamented leaving St. Louis, now he implicitly denigrated not only the Cardinals' front-office management but the city itself. "Sure, I'm tickled to death," enthused Hornsby. "I'm glad to play ball in the greatest baseball town in the country for the greatest manager in the world." McGraw handled things "the way I like to do it—yes or no, without any hagglin' or moanin'—no small town stuff."[10]

Everything seemed in order—except that some things clearly weren't. From National League headquarters in New York, John Heydler had already announced that Hornsby couldn't play for the Giants while still owning stock in the Cardinals. On January 31, however, the Cardinals' board of directors held its annual meeting and elected Breadon president, Rickey vice president, Bill DeWitt treasurer, Clarence Lloyd secretary, William Walsingham as a board member to replace Mark Steinberg, and Rogers Hornsby to succeed himself on the board. A 10 percent dividend on 1926 profits was declared, which meant that Hornsby's stock earned him $2,916.

Asked about the anomaly of his being a ballplayer on one team while owning stock in another, Hornsby professed to be unconcerned. "I'm not worried about all this mess," he told St. Louis reporters. "It doesn't bother me a bit. Every time I meet a friend—I still have a few friends in St. Louis—I'm told to buck up and not let 'em get me down."[11] Actually, Hornsby and William Fahey, his attorney, knew they held the upper hand over Breadon, Heydler, and the entire National League. Unless Landis himself intervened, Hornsby would get something very close to his price—and Breadon or somebody else would have to pay it. Hornsby wanted $105 for each of his 1,167 shares, reasoning that in view of the Cardinals' success since he bought the stock—success for which he felt largely responsible—he was entitled to make a big profit.

Early in February, when Hornsby, Fahey, Breadon, and the largely forgotten Branch Rickey attended the annual Baseball Writers Association dinner in New York, all concerned denied discussions with either Landis or Giants officials about Hornsby's stock. But Hornsby did meet privately with Landis and, according to reports that leaked out, received a stern lecture on the need to curb his gambling habits. It was the first in a series of such admonitions, each of which would have the same negligible effect.

So Hornsby readied for spring training 1927 as both a big-time baseball stockholder and a big-time, handsomely paid ballplayer. With Jeannette and Billy, he left St. Louis bound for Sarasota, Florida, where, for the third spring in succession, McGraw's Giants would be based. Hornsby reported that his weight, which had fallen dramatically in the last half of the previous season, was now back to a normal 175 pounds.

In fact he gained about twenty-five pounds over the winter, so that he arrived at Sarasota weighing at least 185 to 190.

Both little Billy and Jeannette (still pretty but now plumper than when she'd first gained Hornsby's attention) enjoyed what, in those days, must have seemed truly a tropical paradise. When, following a couple of weeks of conditioning, the Giants were ready to start traveling to various exhibition sites, Hornsby's wife and son returned to St. Louis. From then on, while the rest of the players ate in groups, Hornsby sat alone in hotel dining rooms.

McGraw—late getting to Florida following his annual sabbatical at Havana's racetracks and casinos and then, once arrived, busy trying to straighten out his failed Sarasota real-estate schemes—left the early work to captain Hornsby. "Rog," remembered Frank Graham of the New York *Evening Sun,* "being a very literal person, took the captaincy very literally."[12]

Among the Giants regulars, Hornsby clashed particularly with third baseman Fred Lindstrom, who, at the age of twenty-one, was already a four-year major-leaguer. When Hornsby, from second base, called down Lindstrom on a particular play in practice, the brash young Chicagoan replied that "the old man [McGraw] always told me differently." Hornsby shouted that, in McGraw's absence, he was in charge, to which Lindstrom shot back, "You and your ideas. Once you lay aside your bat, you're a detriment to any club."[13]

Meanwhile the stock situation festered; Giants president Stoneham said flatly that Hornsby had to sell his St. Louis holdings, because "there must be no cry of syndicate ball." Yet Hornsby still went about his spring-training routine seemingly unruffled, and on March 8, 1927, he appeared in his first official game as a New York Giant, hitting two doubles and a single in a 13–1 pounding of the Browns. As Richards Vidmer of the *New York Times* described him, he performed "full of fire and fury . . . eager and enthusiastic, carefree but not careless."[14]

As usual, Hornsby was prepared to speak out on almost any baseball subject. At Venice, Florida, local civic dignitaries arranged a dinner to commemorate McGraw's twenty-fifth season as Giants manager. Hornsby and thirty or so other baseball people were on hand; afterward he walked in the hotel gardens with the *Sun's* Frank Graham. Strictly not for publication, asked Graham, what did Hornsby think about the Giants' prospects? "Before I tell you," replied Hornsby, "I want to say this. I don't talk 'not for publication.' Anything I say you can put in the paper, and if anybody don't like it, he can lump it." Over the winter, New York had acquired Edd Roush in a trade with Cincinnati, but the two-time batting titlist and far-ranging center fielder despised McGraw and still hadn't signed a contract. "Now I'll tell you what I think of the outfield," said Hornsby. "I think it stinks. They got to get Roush in here to keep those clowns from knockin' their heads together."[15]

The next day, while Hornsby managed and played against the Cardinals' Frank Frisch (for the first time since the trade) and the Philadelphia Athletics' Ty Cobb (for what proved to be the last time), John McGraw hurried to Chattanooga, Tennessee, where he signed Roush to a three-year contract—at what sportswriters calculated to be $23,000–$25,000 per year.

In announcing Roush's signing, McGraw took the occasion to blast league president Heydler for interfering with Hornsby's property rights and making up league rules as he went along. Yet Heydler remained determined, informing the National League's board of directors that, failing all else, "Hornsby will be stopped by me from playing on or after April 12 [opening day]." While Heydler privately described Hornsby's position as "most unjustifiable and unfair," he was also impatient with Sam Breadon, who, as he said in a circular to the other National League club presidents, could buy up all of Hornsby's stock anytime he wanted.[16]

On April 6 Heydler finally contacted Hornsby personally. Speaking by telephone from the Richmond Hotel at Augusta, Georgia, the ballplayer was generally uncooperative, repeatedly referring Heydler to Fahey, his attorney in St. Louis. He did suggest that he might be willing to exchange his stock for a majority interest in the Houston Texas

League franchise, which the Cardinals controlled. When Heydler called Fahey in St. Louis, the attorney's response was "Let Landis decide it." Heydler, jealous of his prerogatives as National League president, proposed that the whole thing might be resolved at a meeting of National League club representatives that he intended to convene on April 8 at the William Penn Hotel in Pittsburgh. He wanted Fahey and Hornsby to attend as well.[17]

On the morning of the eighth, Leo J. Bondy, the Giants' attorney and Stoneham's official representative, went to Hornsby's room at the William Penn and found the ballplayer, who'd arrived from Washington the previous night, lying on his bed, propped up on an elbow, and obviously resentful at having missed his usual sleep. When Bondy started to talk about what Hornsby ought to do, the response was "Why don't you mind your own business?"[18]

In accordance with official league practice, Hornsby and Fahey weren't allowed to be physically present but sat in another room and kept in telephone contact as Heydler and the club executives debated the issue for eight hours. "The theory of the meeting," as Heydler later put it, "was, first, that good sportsmanship and fair dealing must prevail ahead of either the interest of the player or club; second, that the interests of the National League should prevail ahead of any individual."[19]

Heydler finally persuaded Breadon to agree to a price of $100,000 for Hornsby's holdings, which came out to a little more than $95 per share. That wouldn't do, said Hornsby, speaking through Bondy (who shuttled between rooms) and by telephone through Fahey; he had to get $105 per share, or it was no deal. By a seven-to-one vote, with Bondy the lone dissenter, the group endorsed Heydler's offer and adjourned at 7:00 P.M.

While Fahey returned to St. Louis, Heydler, Bondy, and Hornsby all took the same train to New York. Arriving late the next morning, they went directly to the Giants' offices in the Hart Building (at Sixth Avenue and Forty-second Street) and into conference with Stoneham and McGraw. Bondy emerged to tell waiting reporters that Hornsby had

131

agreed to sell for $100,000, plus another $12,000 to cover his legal costs. Of the total of $112,000, Breadon would pay $86,000, with the other seven clubs contributing $2,000 each and the Giants picking up the extra $12,000.

"All's settled and that's another worry off my mind," said a smiling Hornsby as he headed up to the Polo Grounds for that afternoon's preseason game with Washington. Reported Heydler to Landis, "It was a high price to pay for a principle." "What looked like a mole-hill proposition at the start," Heydler wrote J. G. Taylor Spink, publisher of the *Sporting News,* "grew into a mountain, and I feel we were lucky to escape an unpleasant ending."[20]

What with getting more than twice as much for his stock as he paid for it, as well as tidy profits from the sale of the Maple Avenue apartment building and another at 6647 Kingsbury Boulevard he and Jeannette had purchased the previous year, Hornsby appeared to be in the chips. But he still owed the bank about $22,000 plus interest on what he'd borrowed to purchase Cardinals stock in 1925, and he was being sued by Frank Quinn, his wife's former attorney, for $5,250 in unpaid fees, dating back to 1923.

Quinn's suit turned out to be more of a long-running nuisance than anything else, but another civil action proved a far more serious matter. Brought by Hornsby's erstwhile bookmaker friend Frank L. Moore and coming in the midst of the stock-ownership controversy, it became both a public embarrassment and a threat to whatever financial stability Rogers and Jeannette Hornsby may have been trying to achieve.

In mid-January 1927 Moore, accompanied by his Kentucky attorney, arrived in St. Louis and retained seventy-three-year-old Thomas Rowe to represent him under Missouri law. The three met vainly with William Fahey and then, on the twenty-fourth, filed suit in St. Louis City circuit court for $92,000, the sum Moore said Hornsby owed him in gambling and other debts.

During January and February 1926, Moore alleged, he'd bet $70,000 in Hornsby's behalf—in amounts ranging from $400 to $4,300—on races at the Latonia track in northern Kentucky and at tracks in various other states. Hornsby had also hit Moore for a variety of loans: $7,500, which became the down payment on the Kingsbury Boulevard apartment building; $4,000 for Hornsby to invest in a dog track at Jacksonville, Florida; $4,930, which went to pay off a New York City bookmaker; and various sums in ninety- and sixty-day notes Hornsby signed during 1925 and 1926, involving loans to both Hornsby and his wife.

"I don't owe Moore a dime," insisted Hornsby. "I did borrow $7,500 from him to help pay for my apartment [building] here, but every cent of that debt has been paid." That much Moore and his attorney eventually agreed to; by late February they'd amended their petition on that and other claims, so that they now claimed Hornsby owned Moore $70,075. Fahey described Moore as a "hero-worshipper" who sought Hornsby's friendship by including him in bets Hornsby knew nothing about; in fact, declared Fahey, Hornsby "never made a sizable bet on a horse race until he met Moore."[21] People familiar with Hornsby's gambling habits well before his association with Moore simply found that impossible to believe.

With Hornsby about to leave for spring training, the proceedings couldn't go forward without his being present to defend himself. Judge McElhinney ordered the suit carried over to the fall term of his court, and the Hornsbys were off to Sarasota.

So with two lawsuits pending in St. Louis, the victorious manager in the most-recent World Series wore a New York Giants' uniform for his twelfth major-league opening day. The Giants began robustly at Philadelphia, battering the perennially "Phutile" Phillies 15–7 before a capacity crowd of about 22,000 in intimate, shabby Baker Bowl. Batting fourth, Hornsby doubled and hit a two-run homer over the scoreboard in right-center field—where marks on the short, high wall made by hard-hit balls in previous seasons remained unpainted.

The Giants had to start the season without Travis Jackson, disabled by an emergency appendectomy shortly before the season opened; Eddie "Doc" Farrell, a University of Pennsylvania dental school graduate, took over at shortstop. A few days into the season, Hornsby shared a dining-room table in the Copley Square Hotel in Boston with Farrell and the *Times*'s Vidmer. When Vidmer inquired how the team looked, Hornsby seemed oblivious to Farrell's presence: "This team can't win with Farrell at shortstop. He can't make the double play."[22]

Of course Hornsby was the acknowledged best at that particular play, and Wilson Sporting Goods had recently paid him a fee to market a Rogers Hornsby Glove. Advertised as "ready broke," expensively priced (at nine dollars), and specially designed for middle infielders, it featured a "Hornsby tunnel loop web" between thumb and index finger and a three-finger design, with the third and fourth fingers combined to deepen the glove pocket. (Within a few months the Spalding company, capitalizing on the presumed rivalry between Hornsby and Frank Frisch, would bring out a rival glove designed to Frisch's specifications).[23]

On May 10, 1927, in New York, Frisch's and Hornsby's ballclubs met for the first time in regular-season play, Frisch going hitless and Hornsby doubling, homering, and batting in five runs as the Giants walloped St. Louis 10–1. McGraw, who the previous season had complained that he couldn't rely on Frisch as his captain, relied heavily on Hornsby; later that month, with McGraw already suffering from the chronic sinusitis that made his summers miserable, Hornsby was in charge of the team when it returned to Boston.

There Hornsby benched Farrell (even though the little shortstop was batting close to .400), installed a barely recovered Jackson at shortstop, and thereby constituted a unique infield, all of whose members— Hornsby, Jackson, Bill Terry, and Fred Lindstrom—would eventually be named to baseball's Hall of Fame. Though handicapped by mediocre catching and pitching, the 1927 New York Giants were still the most talented group of men with whom Hornsby had played thus far.

After a good start, the high-powered Giants went into a slump and, week after week, barely won more than they lost. In June, McGraw (no doubt with Hornsby's counsel) sought to bolster his pitching in a six-player swap that sent Farrell to Boston and brought right-hander Larry Benton, hitherto the Braves's ace, to New York.

On their first trip into St. Louis, the Giants split four games before big crowds, Frisch making six hits and Hornsby a like number, including a two-run homer. Before the first game, Mayor Victor Miller presented a wristwatch to Hornsby "from the fans of St. Louis," and the next day the Giants captain was the luncheon guest of the Exchange Club at the Chase Hotel.[24]

On Saturday, June 18, Charles A. Lindbergh landed his *Spirit of St. Louis* monoplane at Lambert Field, from which, thirty-five days earlier, he'd departed for New York to undertake his epochal nonstop flight to Paris. With more than 33,000 on hand at Sportsman's Park, Lindbergh led players and dignitaries to the flagpole in center field for the hoisting of the 1926 championship pennant. Then, as Sam Breadon stood by uncomfortably, Commissioner Landis awarded the World Series rings; Breadon's former manager, in his gray visitors' uniform, received the first one.

McGraw started something of a controversy when he was quoted in St. Louis as saying, "it has been agreed Hornsby will become the active manager of the team next year." The story quickly went out over the wire services; in New York, Charles Stoneham hastened to reassure everybody that McGraw wasn't about to step down, that he could manage the Giants as long as he liked. McGraw himself hurriedly qualified what he'd said; he only meant that if he ever did quit, he would like Hornsby to be his successor. Whereupon Hornsby added that he was satisfied to be "just a player in the ranks."[25] Still, suspicions persisted that Hornsby was the heir apparent to baseball's choicest managerial post.

On July 19 the Polo Grounds was the scene of a John McGraw Silver Jubilee, marking a quarter century in which his teams had won ten pennants and three World Series. Mayor Jimmie Walker, Commissioner Landis, league president Heydler, six club presidents, a number of former Giants players, and assorted celebrities were on hand for protracted pregame ceremonies, then for an 8–5 loss to the Chicago Cubs. That put the Giants' record at 47–43—fourth place in the standings behind Chicago, St. Louis, and Pittsburgh—and prompted boos from the

25,000 or so customers, many of them directed at Hornsby. At that point Hornsby, batting in the .330s, trailed Pittsburgh's Paul Waner by fifty or sixty points and Frisch by a good margin as well. Although he drove in runners and pounded out home runs with regularity, the horseshoe-shaped Polo Grounds, with its uniquely short distances down the foul lines but vast terrain from right-center around to left-center, cut down on his power output at home.

With McGraw again in upper-respiratory misery, Hornsby took the team west, won four of seven games from St. Louis and Chicago, and moved to within seven games of the first-place Cubs. Returning to New York after an 8–3 road trip, the Giants then won ten straight and seventeen of twenty at the Polo Grounds, with McGraw remaining at his Pelham, New York, home much of the time. When, with Hornsby in charge, they left on their final western swing, New York was bunched with Pittsburgh, Chicago, and St. Louis—four teams separated by only three games.

Assuming the full prerogatives of manager, Hornsby drove the Giants toward a pennant. Besides enforcing a midnight curfew, he banned smoking, card playing, and even reading in the visitors' dressing quarters. The Giants grumbled, but they kept on winning. After splitting a four-game series at Chicago and taking seven of twelve games (played over seven days) in the dense St. Louis and Cincinnati heat, Hornsby, twelve pounds lighter than when he left New York, had his team established in second place, although they still trailed red-hot Pittsburgh by four and one-half games.

On Thursday, September 22, before a capacity crowd of some 37,000 at Forbes Field, the Pirates and Giants split a doubleheader; Pittsburgh won the first game 5–2, while Hornsby's two-run homer (his twenty-sixth) accounted for all the runs Fred Fitzsimmons needed in the nightcap. The Pirates scored their first run that afternoon when a line drive (recorded as a base hit) ricocheted off Larry Benton's and then Travis Jackson's gloves. That evening, as Hornsby prepared to go down to dinner at the Schenley Hotel, club secretary Jim Tierney came by his room to complain that the Giants might have won both games if Jackson hadn't played out of position and let in that run in the opener. Hornsby exploded: Tierney didn't know a goddamn thing about baseball; all he was expected to do was "take care of the cabs and the hotel rooms and the tickets and we'll take care of playing ball."[26]

That night McGraw and Stoneham arrived from New York; when Tierney reported his encounter with Hornsby, the Giants owner was furious. Stoneham, who owned racehorses and gambled quite a lot himself, had never liked the idea of Hornsby's welching on his gambling debts, and now Hornsby had bawled out a club official who also happened to be Stoneham's close friend. Hornsby might be the best ballplayer in the National League, but he was still, in Stoneham's view, no more than a ballplayer. As of that night, Hornsby's future with the New York Giants was in doubt.

Yet everything seemed all right the next afternoon, when McGraw sat with Stoneham behind the visitors' dugout and roundly praised Hornsby. Asked if he would resume direction of the team, McGraw replied, "I don't think so. No one possibly could run the club any better than it is being run right now."[27] After victories on Friday and Saturday, the Giants left town only one and one-half games out of first place.

McGraw returned to the dugout at Brooklyn on the twenty-fifth. A seven-inning tie there and a dreary 9–2 defeat at Philadelphia (only the fiftieth time the Phillies had won all season) shoved the Giants three and one-half games back and into third place, with only five to play. They won the two remaining games at Baker Bowl, while Pittsburgh and St. Louis took a game apiece at Chicago and Cincinnati, respectively.

On the twenty-ninth, as a tornado devastated St. Louis's west side, killing about 100 people and narrowly missing Sportsman's Park, the Cardinals lost in Cincinnati; Pittsburgh and New York were idle. The Reds also beat Pittsburgh the next day, but at Brooklyn's Ebbets Field, Dazzy Vance outlasted three Giants pitchers, and that evening New York stood three games out of first place with only two games remaining. Pittsburgh's victory over Cincinnati on Saturday, together with St. Louis's rain-out, clinched the Pirates' second pennant in three years.

After the meaningless season-closing games on Sunday, the standings were: Pittsburgh (94–60), St. Louis (92–61), New York (92–62).

Hornsby could hardly be accused of doing anything short of his utmost for McGraw, Stoneham, and everyone else connected with the New York Giants. He played in all 155 games (which included one tie), hit twenty-six home runs and drove in 125 runs (third in the league in both categories), led the league with 133 runs, and batted .361, second to Paul Waner, Pittsburgh's spray-hitting second-year outfielder. In addition, he managed the Giants in roughly half their games, and he was in charge nearly all the time during the 45–12 surge that brought them within two games of a pennant.

Frank Frisch captained the Cardinals, batted .337, and led both majors with forty-eight stolen bases. Frisch also topped second basemen in both leagues in assists, double plays, and fielding percentage. Although he didn't make St. Louis fans forget Hornsby, he played a dashing style of baseball that won over nearly all of them. Moreover, they turned out in record numbers—763,715 for the season. Said Sam Breadon shortly before he died, "I never will forget Frankie Frisch for saving my life."[28]

While Pittsburgh, a good ballclub, fell in four games to the Yankees powerhouse, Hornsby settled his bill at the small residential hotel near the Polo Grounds where he'd lived half of the past season, and headed back to St. Louis and his nominal home. Since the early part of the year, the Hornsbys' residence had been the Forest Park Hotel, where Jeannette and Billy lived full-time and Hornsby stayed when the Giants were in town. From there the Hornsbys entrained for Texas to visit relatives in the Fort Worth and Austin areas.

Rogers Hornsby and John McGraw genuinely and greatly admired each other. "They were like two peas from one pod," said Giants outfielder Heinie Mueller. "They went together all the time, went to the races together, and we all thought Rog would be manager some day."[29] Under different circumstances, Hornsby and McGraw might have experienced a close and productive relationship for the next few years, until McGraw decided to retire and leave the ballclub in Hornsby's hands.

That outcome had been generally predicted, almost from the time Hornsby joined the Giants.

But if he really wanted to remain a New York Giant, Hornsby did himself no good by saying publicly in Philadelphia (and subsequently in St. Louis, Fort Worth, and elsewhere) that "there would have to be a new ownership of the Giants before I would consent to being manager. There are too many people attempting to dictate the club's policy. I had a taste of that in St. Louis, with Breadon and Rickey each having a finger in the pie. As manager I would want complete authority in the playing end."[30] For Charles Stoneham, already unhappy with his prickly and high-priced ballplayer, that may have decided the issue.

What undoubtedly sealed it, though, was Hornsby's conduct in the matter of *Moore* vs. *Hornsby,* the litigious history of which resumed in December 1927. In New York, Joe Vila, the veteran baseball reporter for the *Evening Sun,* predicted that Hornsby wouldn't "hide behind [Missouri's] anti-gambling laws. . . . Men who don't make good [their] gambling debts here, especially at the race track, soon lose caste."[31] But that was exactly the strategy Hornsby and attorney William Fahey decided upon.

By the time the case came to trial—now in St. Louis County circuit court, with Judge McElhinney still presiding—Frank L. Moore had again reduced his claims against Hornsby, which now totaled $45,075. The trial on his suit opened in Clayton, Missouri, on December 19. In constituting the all-male jury, both Fahey and Thomas Rowe, Moore's Missouri attorney, asked pointedly whether Hornsby's trade to New York eleven months earlier would influence their judgment—a voir dire that may have been unique in legal annals.

On December 19, as Hornsby, incessantly chewing gum, sat at a table with his wife and Fahey, Frank Moore took the stand. He testified that when he was introduced to Hornsby in 1925 at the Cincinnati baseball park, "the first thing Hornsby asked me after the usual 'pleased to meet you' was, 'have you any tips on the horses?' " Moore provided a few tips; Hornsby gave him ten dollars to bet for each race Moore mentioned. After that, Hornsby started calling his Fort Thomas, Kentucky, home from New York, Philadelphia, and other cities to get tips on that day's action and have Moore make bets. For a period of more than a year, "I was supplying Hornsby with tips on the races and placing bets for him." When Rowe asked why Moore hadn't been willing to make an out-of-court settlement, the Kentuckian declared, "I won't let Hornsby get out of this. It's not the money, but the principle."[32]

Hornsby and Fahey contested Moore's claims on the general grounds that inasmuch as the debts Moore insisted he was due were all gambling debts, then Hornsby, a citizen of Missouri—where any gambling was illegal—couldn't be held liable. They also entered demurrers to two counts in Moore's petition, both having to do with money loaned to Jeannette Hornsby to bet (and lose) for her husband. Ruling that Hornsby couldn't be held liable for his wife's debts, McElhinney reduced the remaining value of Moore's suit to $36,320.

After that, Hornsby himself—"clean cut of limb and bronze of face," in a navy blue suit with well-matched accessories, vigorously working over his wad of gum—gave his testimony, which proved to be the only other in the trial. He'd been told, he said, that Moore was the best racing handicapper in the country, and he acknowledged that in 1925 and 1926 he bet almost daily on Moore's advisories—often $1,000 at a time, sometimes $1,500, once $2,400. But, he insisted, he paid for all his losses. When Rowe, on cross-examination, asked whether Hornsby was a professional gambler, he quickly said no. Then was he an amateur gambler? "I'll leave that for you to decide, Mr. Rowe," he answered. "Rogers," exclaimed Jeannette Hornsby when he stepped down, "you were wonderful!"[33]

On December 21 McElhinney instructed the jury that while Hornsby's gambling debts were inadmissible under Missouri law, they could still rule that he owed money to Moore for gambling loans or whatever purpose. Early that afternoon, the jurors reported back their 10–2 verdict (only a three-fourths majority being needed in civil cases), opting for McElhinney's first instruction and finding Hornsby liableless. Both Hornsbys were absent from the courtroom because Jeannette had become ill, but Moore bitterly told reporters, "I'm through with this case and with St. Louis."[34]

Twenty days later, early in the evening of January 10, 1928, Hornsby telephoned J. Roy Stockton in a futile effort to obtain John McGraw's address in Havana, Cuba, for which destination (Hornsby learned after calling New York) McGraw had just departed. Hornsby was trying to help Kirby Samuels, just fired from his job as Cardinals trainer, and he figured McGraw might be able to find something for Samuels.

Three hours later Hornsby again called Stockton. "Remember I wanted to get Kirby a job with the Giants?" Hornsby said. "Well, I'm out of a job now. Not exactly out of a job. But I've been traded to the Boston Braves." He then read a telegram just received from Boston president Emil Fuchs.[35]

For the second time in thirteen months, Hornsby was the subject of front-page news, but this time the story wasn't just sensational; it seemed incomprehensible. In what was announced as a straight player exchange, Hornsby went to the Boston Braves for Jimmie Welsh, a run-of-the-mill outfielder, and James "Shanty" Hogan, a promising but chronically overweight young catcher. Jim Tierney made the deal public at 9:45 P.M. (New York time) in the form of a typewritten statement, signed by Charles Stoneham and John McGraw, copies of which were handed out to the local press at the Giants' offices in the Hart Building. Undertaken "after due deliberation" between club president and manager and involving no cash, the deal was made with "the best interests of the New York Giants" in mind. As reporters shouted questions, Tierney replied that the statement would have to speak for itself.[36]

The *New York Daily Mirror* (rarely the most reliable source) claimed that at the end of the season, eight Giants, including stalwarts Lindstrom, Terry, Jackson, and Roush, had told Stoneham they wouldn't play again if Hornsby continued to do any managing. So Stoneham "decided that the players . . . were far greater assets to the Giants than Hornsby." Nobody ever confirmed that story, but when he was asked about possible friction with various Giants players, Hornsby spoke freely and harshly of Fred Lindstrom: "He's just a cry-baby. He always has something wrong with him in a tight series, especially if he's near the .300 mark in batting." If a tough pitcher started warming up, "Lindstrom started to sob. He'll always cry, whether I'm on the club or not."[37]

When reporters caught up with John McGraw at Savannah, Georgia, the Giants manager would only say, "There is nothing to add to the original announcement. The trade has been made and there's all there is to it." Back in New York, Stoneham talked vaguely about possible conflicts in authority; in St. Louis, Hornsby seemed genuinely nonplussed. No, there was never any friction between himself and McGraw; no, he never tried to undermine McGraw, "a great manager, the best I ever knew"; no, there couldn't be any "horse-race betting angle to this."[38]

Yet in fact the "betting angle"—what Stoneham perceived as Hornsby's welching on honest bets—did much to speed his departure. Tierney acknowledged as much a few days later; eventually even Hornsby came to realize that offenses against "that drunken bum," as he referred to Stoneham, decided his fate with the New York Giants.[39]

How determined Stoneham had been to rid himself of Hornsby became evident in subsequent weeks, when McGraw in Havana and other National League club officials confirmed that before the deal with Boston, Hornsby had been unsuccessfully shopped around: to Brooklyn for fastballer Dazzy Vance; to Chicago for outfielder Hazen "Kiki" Cuyler (recently obtained from Pittsburgh); and to Cincinnati, where Jack Hendricks, still carrying a grudge from his stint as the Cardinals manager, vetoed an exchange for second baseman Hughie Critz and catcher Eugene "Bubbles" Hargrave. Only after those three clubs had turned down the Giants was Boston brought into the picture.

That publicity may have chagrined Hornsby, but his comment was typical: "It don't matter to me whether I'm with the Braves or any other club." As for the Giants' prospects without him, "How the hell should I know anything about the Giants? I'm with Boston now." But he added that he wouldn't believe McGraw had approved the trade "until he tells me with his own lips."[40]

That never happened. In fact the trade was wholly Stoneham's idea, and McGraw—owing money to Stoneham and now struggling to square things with investors in his Florida land fiasco—could do nothing but acquiesce. The Little Napoleon was no longer Napoleonic, at least not when it came to crossing Charles Stoneham.

While rumors circulated that Commissioner Landis might investigate the circumstances of the trade, Emil Fuchs announced that Landis knew all about it beforehand and gave his approval. Therefore, said Fuchs, "it would not be good sportsmanship or fairness to reflect further on Mr. Hornsby's integrity, fidelity, loyalty and honor."[41]

"Judge" Fuchs (so called because he'd once been a minor magistrate in New York City) was fifty years old, portly, dark complexioned, and, by all accounts, an exceptionally likable man. What he lacked in baseball savvy and financial resources, he tried to make up for with optimism and enthusiasm. As president of the Boston National Leaguers, he needed plenty of both, because the Boston franchise had fallen on sad times since the "Miracle Braves" won everything back in 1914. Since 1921, except for a fifth-place showing in 1925, the Braves had finished either last or next to last every year. Although they occupied the newest ballpark in the league (opened in 1915), the Braves couldn't play home games on Sundays under Massachusetts law and usually trailed everybody in attendance. But with the addition of Hornsby, bubbled Fuchs, the Braves would be "the greatest since 1914."[42] They might even be able to pay their bills.

Although Frank Moore's suit was out of the way, Hornsby's legal complications persisted. Frank Quinn's suit for unpaid legal fees was still pending (as it would be for the next eight years), and yet another civil action, brought by John H. Barto, M.D., the previous summer, alleged that Hornsby owed him $387 dating back to January–March 1925. During that period, as the Hornsbys' itemized account showed, Barto visited the Maple Avenue apartment almost daily to treat Jeannette Hornsby, then pregnant.[43] Although Barto obtained a judgment in justice of the peace court early in March 1928, William Fahey managed to secure a reversal in city circuit court on a technicality. Otherwise, as Hornsby said good-bye to his wife and little boy and left for St. Petersburg, Florida, to start spring training with his third team in three years, his personal affairs seemed to be in better order than for some time.

Both the Braves and the Yankees trained at St. Petersburg, the Yankees at Crescent Lake Park at Thirteenth Avenue and Fifth Street, on the north side of the little city, the Braves at Coffee Pot Park, located at the head of the bayou of the same name that ran into Tampa Bay.[44] Hornsby arrived on February 21 and was met by Fuchs and Jack Slattery, the Braves' new manager. Until Fuchs hired him the previous fall, the fifty-two-year-old Slattery, a onetime second-string big-league catcher, had been coaching the Boston College baseball team.

Hornsby and Slattery shared a room at the Vinoy Park Hotel on the bay and, to all outward appearances, got along fine. Fuchs met with his prize acquisition and offered him a three-year contract to supersede his two-year pact at New York. Hornsby would receive $40,600 per year (including $600 annually for serving as team captain), an arrangement that sustained Hornsby's status as the second-best-paid player in the majors. It was also about four times as much as Fuchs paid Slattery. Hornsby said he looked forward to batting at Braves Field, where the late-afternoon shadows from the single-deck grandstand bothered him less than the shadows at the double-deck Polo Grounds. Moreover, bleachers in front of the left-field fence (originally installed for the Boston College–Holy Cross College football game the previous fall) shortened the 403-foot home-run distance by more than eighty feet.

Carrying an aggregate .361 major-league batting average, Hornsby began a season that turned out to be no more than an interlude in his career as both player and manager. The Boston Braves were a deplorable outfit that had won only fifty-one times in 1927 and finished dead last. Early on, Hornsby may actually have entertained some notion that his presence—as well as that of Lester Bell, obtained late in March from St. Louis at Hornsby's urging—might make the Braves at least respectable. But while Hornsby would play up to form, so, unfortunately, would most of the rest of the team.

Hornsby didn't hit well in the games in Florida and on the trip north, and started the season in a slump. At the Polo Grounds, where the Braves opened with the Giants, he posed with rookie Andy Cohen, his replacement, and John McGraw, who appeared in a uniform for the first time in nearly seven years. While Hornsby managed only an infield single, Cohen drove in three runs on a double and two singles, scored twice, and made a nice stop and throw on Hornsby's hard-hit grounder to clinch the Giants' 5–2 victory. The heavily Jewish crowd of 30,000 cheered Cohen's every move; after the final out, he was hoisted on admirers' shoulders and carried around the field.

For the next couple of weeks, Cohen continued to bat torridly and field deftly, and wags in New York were asking "Who's Hornsby?" Sick with flu for a couple of days, Hornsby suggested that "it ain't fair to the kid. As soon as I get goin', I'll lose him."[45]

A month into the season, Cohen was hitting about .270 and Hornsby was leading the league at .410, but the Braves lost nineteen of their first thirty games and remained out of last place only because the Phillies proved even more inept. On the evening of May 23, Fuchs announced that Slattery had resigned and that, "after much persuasion," he'd obtained "the consent of Rogers Hornsby to accept the management of the Braves."[46]

Again some people were ready to suspect Hornsby of undermining his field boss and maneuvering himself toward the manager's job. Walter "Doc" Gautreau, a five-foot-four Boston native and Holy Cross graduate and a part-time second baseman for the Braves since 1925, later described how Hornsby sat by himself and made critical remarks when Slattery held pregame strategy sessions and then, during games, sneered at "that dumb collegiate coach out there."[47]

Gautreau also remembered an occasion when, with the Braves losing badly at Chicago going into the top of the ninth inning, Hornsby, assuming he wouldn't come to bat, "was already in the dressing room before we had been retired." By Gautreau's account, Hornsby cared for

nothing but his batting average. In a game with Pittsburgh, Eddie Farrell didn't tag up at first base on Hornsby's long fly to right field, and,
according to Gautreau, "he bawled the life out of . . . Farrell. . . .
We were seven runs behind at the time. Hornsby was looking for a
sacrifice fly."[48]

Gautreau was among four players released within a week after
Hornsby succeeded Slattery. The question of whether Gautreau and at
least two others were let go because they were Roman Catholics would
arise indirectly the following January, as a consequence of hearings
conducted by the Boston city finance commission on allegations that
William G. Lynch, a city councilman, sought payoffs for himself and
other councilmen in exchange for approving a local ordinance authoriz-
ing Sunday baseball. In the course of the hearings, Lynch's lawyer
asked Emil Fuchs whether, the previous summer, Fuchs hadn't complained to Lynch that both Hornsby and Bruce Whitmore, who sat on
the Braves' board of directors, were members of the Ku Klux Klan, and
that the absence of Catholic players was hurting attendance at Braves
Field. Although Fuchs denied saying anything of the kind, the suggestion that Hornsby might be a Klan member—when combined with
similar suspicions Jim Tierney had encouraged in 1927—raised dis-
turbing implications about Hornsby both personally and professionally.

It's quite possible, though unprovable, that several years earlier,
when the post–World War I Klan movement was at the peak of its
membership and influence, Hornsby may have joined the secret organization in Fort Worth (a Klan stronghold) or possibly St. Louis. Local
Klan units assiduously sought to recruit prominent figures in politics,
business, the ministry, as well as sports—provided they met the basic
requirements of being native-born, white, and at least nominally Protes-
tant. Fred Lieb, who reported on baseball for fifty years for various New
York newspapers, claimed that both Hornsby and fellow Texan Tris
Speaker told him "they were members of the Ku Klux Klan."[49]

How does one square such suspicions with Hornsby's obvious fondness for John McGraw, a practicing Catholic, or his friendship with
Mark Steinberg, his Jewish stockbroker and ardent champion in

St. Louis? One thing seems fairly certain: if Hornsby actually belonged to the Klan, his membership, like that of hundreds of thousands of other Americans who joined the secret fraternal order, was never more than semiactive. By 1927–28, moreover, most people who'd ever been Klan members had dropped out; that seems a safe assumption as well where Hornsby is concerned.

In any case, it's doubtful that Hornsby really wanted Jack Slattery's job, however scornful he may have been of the "dumb collegiate coach." As when he took over at St. Louis from Branch Rickey, Hornsby received no boost in pay for managing the Braves. Trying to win games with a pitching staff that yielded close to 900 runs would have been a trial for anybody. "If our pitchers could deliver," he complained shortly after succeeding Slattery, "we would hold our own with the best. . . . there the trouble lies."[50]

On May 27 George Sisler cleared waivers in the American League and joined the Braves in exchange for the $7,500 waiver price, paid to Washington. Sisler could still swing the bat, as he proved by hitting .340 in 118 games over the remainder of the season. Yet neither the addition of Sisler nor Hornsby's efforts to fire up his team by getting himself thrown out of a game and suspended for three days did much good.

It turned out that the left-field bleachers helped the Braves' opponents more than the home team. Most of Hornsby's home runs at Braves Field cleared the fence in right center; of forty-eight homers landing in the new bleachers during the Braves' first fifteen home games, two-thirds resounded off visitors' bats. Fuchs first ordered the erection of a screen in front of the bleachers, then, in July, decided to dismantle them altogether. For the rest of the 1928 season (and until 1930, when the fence itself was moved in) the distance down the left-field line remained a respectable 353 feet.

Despite a bad stone bruise on his right heel incurred in July and then a pulled leg muscle suffered in August, Hornsby stayed in the lineup nearly every day. His seventeenth and eighteenth homers at Cincinnati on August 18 pushed his batting average to .377, several points better than Paul Waner's.

In September the Braves struggled through nine doubleheaders in sixteen days and lost thirteen of their last fifteen games, ending with a 50–103 record (39–83 under Hornsby). Their late-season woes coincided with a hot streak for their manager that clinched his seventh batting championship. In 140 games Hornsby averaged .387, seventeen points better than Paul Waner, and banged twenty-one homers and drove in ninety-four runs. Opposing pitchers often worked around him, so that he drew 107 walks, more than anybody in the majors besides Babe Ruth.

As bad as the Braves were, they weren't bad enough to land in last place, because Philadelphia finished at 43–109. Meanwhile the Cardinals, under Bill McKechnie's low-keyed direction, won for the second time in three years, beating out New York by two games and Chicago by four.

About six weeks before the season closed, Hornsby signed a new three-year contract to manage the Braves. Although Fuchs made the re-signing into quite a show, hardly anyone expected that the spring of 1929 would find Hornsby still with Boston. The Braves' financial circumstances were expected to improve if Massachusetts voters approved a Sunday baseball referendum on November 8 (as in fact they did), but in the present season, said a *Sporting News* observer, the Braves had "lost almost everything but the players' shirts."[51]

In fact, Hornsby was actively working to get himself traded to the Chicago Cubs. The Braves couldn't really afford his salary, he told Fuchs, so it would be the smart thing to trade him while he still had some good years left. The new contract Hornsby signed in August was actually a matter of ensuring that he would receive the same $40,000 salary wherever he played during the coming three seasons.

Early in September, when the National League presidents met in New York to discuss World Series arrangements, Chicago president William H. Veeck found Fuchs receptive to a deal for Hornsby. Veeck then traveled to Boston, where the Cubs were in town for a three-game set at Braves Field. During pregame practice, as Veeck and manager Joe McCarthy chatted beside the visitors' dugout, Hornsby walked over, shook hands, and said he hoped the Cubs could arrange a trade for him.

At the World Series (which the Yankees again swept), Hornsby sat in the Yankee Stadium press box and told reporters he expected to be traded; twenty feet away Fuchs was denying that such a deal was in the offing. According to one Chicago writer, Hornsby offered to bet $20,000 that with his bat in the lineup, the Cubs would win a pennant.

The widely anticipated deal was finally announced on November 7, 1928. The Cubs acquired Hornsby for $200,000—the most cash involved in any player transaction up to that time—plus five nondescript players. Backed by William K. Wrigley Jr.'s enormous fortune and further enriched by record National League attendance totals for the past two seasons, the Chicago franchise had become the league's richest. Wrigley, it was generally agreed, had just bought a pennant for the Cubs.

Describing Joe McCarthy as "the slickest manager I ever encountered," Hornsby said nobody need worry about whether he would get along with his new field boss. "My troubles at St. Louis and New York were personal matters," he added. "If people take a dislike to you or you to them, it's something that can't be avoided. Nothing of that kind will occur at Chicago because it's not that kind of organization."[52]

A week later, Hornsby arrived in Chicago, beamed with Wrigley and Veeck as he signed his contract at the Wrigley Building, then donned a Cubs uniform and posed some more. His contract called for $40,000 for each of the next three seasons, but inasmuch as first baseman Charlie Grimm would continue as Cubs captain, Hornsby actually took a $600-per-year pay cut.

Then it was back to St. Louis to spend the off-season at the fourth residence Rogers and Jeannette Hornsby had shared in the past four years. After various apartments and hotel suites and a handsome suburban residence, they became farm folks. Since his childhood, Hornsby had resided on a farm for only about five months, but like many other

Americans of his day, he nurtured both a sentimental attachment to rural living and a notion that somehow owning a farm spelled long-term security. The previous summer he'd paid $18,600 for a place at Robertson, Missouri, a rural community located a couple of miles north of Lambert Field and some fifteen miles from Sportsman's Park. Once owned by a horse breeder named Barney Schreiber, the farm consisted of ninety-three mostly uncleared acres, a fourteen-room house, and pens, paddocks, stables, and various other outbuildings.

That December, the *Sporting News* carried a feature piece on the Hornsbys on the farm, with Rogers, Jeannette, and Billy pictured in various outdoor settings. Wearing an old leather jacket and battered hat, Hornsby climbed down from his tractor to explain that he was out every morning by eight o'clock to tend his chickens, pigs, and cows and calves. The farm's animal population also included hunting dogs, geese, turkeys, and even a couple of pheasants. Hornsby intended to make the farm pay by marketing milk-fed broilers and bluegrass turf, which he touted as ideal for baseball fields and golf courses. Late the previous summer, he'd hired "a couple of darkies" to come up from Texas and cultivate his bluegrass. Concluded the *Sporting News*'s visitor, "He's contented, busy and was never in any better physical condition."[53]

After two and one-half years filled with controversy on the ballfield and in club and league officials' offices and the courts, it appeared that Hornsby might have arrived at some kind of professional and personal stability. The thriving Chicago Cubs, the latest stop on his tour of the National League, might even prove to be the last he would have to make.

I n the late 1920s the Chicago Cubs and professional baseball as a
whole benefited from the most prosperous peacetime conditions in
the nation's history. As stock prices soared to previously unimagined
levels, both business spokesmen and professional economists postulated
that the United States had entered upon a new era of plenty—that
American productive and distributive capabilities rendered obsolete the
historic cycle of boom followed by bust. With the major exception of
the struggling agricultural economy (of which Rogers Hornsby's farm
was now a part), the country appeared to be riding a permanent wave of
prosperity.

With a population nearing three million, Chicago was more than
ever the "city of the big shoulders" acclaimed by the poet Carl
Sandburg. The legend of the "roaring twenties" was largely the legend
of Chicago, with its unrelenting civic boosterism, stunning commercial
architecture, throbbing nightlife, and, most of all, its big-time criminals.
Although organized crime flourished in New York, Philadelphia,

St. Louis, and most other major American cities, the bloody struggle among Chicago's gangs to control the traffic in bootleg liquor gave that city a particular renown for systematic violence. Chicago's gang wars reached a climax in February 1929, when Al Capone's assassins first killed rival criminal chief Dion O'Banion in his flower shop, then, a week later, trapped and gunned down seven henchmen of George "Bugs" Moran, O'Banion's successor, in a North Clark Street garage.

For the next two weeks, as Chicago's newspapers detailed the circumstances of O'Banion's murder and the St. Valentine's Day Massacre, groups of Chicago Cubs made the 2,000-mile, two-and-a-half-day train trip to Los Angeles to begin spring training. At Long Beach they boarded a ferry for a twenty-seven-mile voyage south to Santa Catalina Island, the club's training site for the past seven springs.

Since 1919, Santa Catalina had been the sole property of William K. Wrigley Jr., who bought the island from the Banning family for $3 million. About twenty miles long and eight miles across at its widest, Santa Catalina (usually called simply Catalina) contained a silver mine, rock quarry, and tile factory. At the little town of Avalon, where ferries docked, Wrigley built a first-class hotel named the St. Catherine's, as well as a golf course, bird sanctuary, and baseball field. Most of the island was covered by semitropical forest; Hollywood film crews regularly came over from the mainland to shoot "jungle movies."

Reaching the ferry landing at Avalon on the morning of February 26, Hornsby and the rest of the Cubs regulars—following what had become a local custom—piled into a wagon drawn by two aged horses for the ride to the St. Catherine's. After lunch the new arrivals suited up, walked the short distance to the ballfield, and joined the pitchers, catchers, and rookies who'd already been working out for a week.

Hornsby shared accommodations at the St. Catherine's with shortstop Woody English, who would remain his roommate away from Chicago for the coming two seasons. English was pleased to discover that for a clean-living young man such as himself, Hornsby was the perfect roommate—neat and orderly, habituated to regular hours, mindful of his own business, and little interested in others'. While Hornsby worked with English on his batting and loved to talk baseball, he neither inquired about bachelor English's private life nor talked about his own; English couldn't recall a single mention of Hornsby's wife or son.[1]

Hornsby and William Wrigley quickly took to each other. When Wrigley arrived at Catalina, Hornsby spent one whole practice session explaining baseball's finer points to the Cubs' owner. Wrigley delighted in Hornsby's knowledge of the game, remarking afterward, "I heard more baseball today than I have heard in my whole life."[2]

Meanwhile Joe McCarthy—from whom, by implication, Wrigley hadn't heard much baseball—readied his men for the 1929 pennant race, which most prognosticators had already conceded to them. The addition of Hornsby made McCarthy's team, contenders since he'd arrived in 1926, into a true powerhouse. "The Cubs had the best group of individual players of any team I ever played on," remarked Hornsby many years later.[3]

The Chicagoans featured a heavy-hitting outfield of Kiki Cuyler, Lewis "Hack" Wilson, and Riggs Stephenson; proficient infielders in first baseman Charlie Grimm and shortstop English; and four solid pitchers in Charlie Root, Guy Bush, Perce "Pat" Malone, and John "Sheriff" Blake—all right-handers. It would have been an even more formidable aggregation if Charles "Gabby" Hartnett, the National League's foremost catcher, hadn't developed a bad throwing arm that spring and missed virtually the entire season.

The club's principal power hitter was Hack Wilson, National League home-run leader for the past three years and a popular figure with teammates and Chicago fans. Drafted by the Cubs from the American Association after a stint with John McGraw's Giants, Wilson was oddly configured: 5′ 6″ tall and 195 pounds, with a massive torso, short arms, small hands, and tiny feet. Like Hornsby, Wilson drove most of his homers into the arc from left-center to right-center field; unlike Hornsby, Wilson liked to drink—frequently and a lot.

As in past springs, the Cubs worked out twice a day on Catalina, played a few intrasquad matches, and then took the ferry to Los Angeles for games with the local Pacific Coast League Angels. Wrigley also owned the excellent Los Angeles ballpark and the Biltmore Hotel, where the Cubs lodged. Although the hotel boasted one of the city's better restaurants, Hornsby discovered a lunch wagon up the street where he could get steaks to his liking. About nine each evening, he would usually vacate his lobby chair to go out again, this time for a pint of ice cream before bedtime.

After series on the Coast with Los Angeles, San Francisco, and the Detroit Tigers, the Cubs traveled east with the Detroit team through Tucson, El Paso, and Beaumont, concluding the preseason schedule at Kansas City against the American Association Blues. They reached Chicago with an exhibition record of 23–5–1.

The Chicago National League ballpark, where an overflow crowd watched the Cubs lose the season opener to Pittsburgh, was situated at North Clark and Waveland Streets on Chicago's North Side. Originally built for Charles Weeghman's Federal League entry, it became the Cubs' home in 1916 after Weeghman bought the local National League franchise and moved his new club into the steel-and-concrete facility, which then seated about 15,000. Two years later Weeghman sold out to William Wrigley, who began a program of expansion and improvement that climaxed in 1926 with the addition of a grandstand upper deck, bringing the seating capacity of Wrigley Field (as it was now called) to nearly 38,000. One bleacher section extended from the foul line across right field; another, in left-center, terminated well short of the foul line. The ballpark's dimensions when Hornsby joined the Cubs were 348 feet down the line in left, 447 to the flagpole behind a metal fence in dead center, and 318 down the right-field line.[4]

Hornsby's bases-loaded home run beat Pittsburgh the next day. It was an auspicious beginning for what proved to be his last big season as a player, as well as a big year in Chicago baseball history. Along the way, some 1.25 million people paid to get into Wrigley Field; for the third season in a row, the Cubs set a new National League attendance record, with an exceptionally high proportion of their patronage consisting of women. Over the past four years, many women had become fans by listening to radio broadcasts of Cubs games—permission for which the franchise freely granted to as many local stations as wished to carry games. Women also responded enthusiastically to the Cubs Ladies Day promotions, which admitted them to Wrigley Field without charge, with or without male escorts.

Tuesday, August 6, 1929, came close to being a Ladies Day riot. Nearly 29,000 women and 11,000 or more men overpowered the ticket sellers and turnstile keepers, overran the playing field, stood in the aisles, and sat atop the outfield fences to watch the Cubs end a five-game winning streak by losing to Brooklyn, despite Hornsby's twenty-third home run.

That was Chicago's only loss over a fifteen-game stretch. Although the first half of the schedule featured a close battle with Pittsburgh, New York, and defending-champion St. Louis, the Cubs' hot streak in August and ten straight wins at the beginning of September enabled them to pull away from the rest of the league. After a Labor Day sweep of the Cardinals, Chicago's lead reached twelve and one-half games; two weeks later the Cubs clinched the pennant when Pittsburgh lost at Boston. At the end, Chicago led the Pirates by nine and one-half games, New York by five more, St. Louis by twenty. The Cubs batted .303 as a team, hammered 140 home runs, led the majors with 982 runs, and tied for the majors' best fielding average.

Hornsby played in every inning of the Cubs' 154 decisions, plus two ties. Although he made 229 hits and batted .380, he still trailed Phila-delphia's Francis "Lefty" O'Doul and Brooklyn's Floyd "Babe" Herman. His thirty-nine home runs tied him for third in the league with Wilson, behind New York's Mel Ott and Philadelphia's Chuck Klein. He scored 156 runs, a new "modern" (twentieth-century) record for the National League, and led all second basemen in assists and double plays while committing only twenty-three errors.

The season exacted its toll on the thirty-three-year-old Hornsby. The stone bruise suffered the previous season developed into a calcified condition in his right heel, and he played in increasing pain. "There wasn't any use in telling the world about my foot," he said afterward. "The ball club needed me and it was up to me to get around the best I could." Besides, "What good would it have been to tell 'em about my heel? They'd have just said that Hornsby was offering his heel as an alibi for slowing up." Only manager McCarthy and trainer Andy Lotshaw knew of his problem—later described as a "heel spur." Lotshaw taped both ankles with the idea that Hornsby wouldn't favor his sore foot, but "believe me," said Hornsby, "at night I didn't feel like doing any visiting. . . . All I wanted to do after a ball game was to get to my room and lay the body down."[5]

In dethroning the New York Yankees in the American League, Connie Mack's Philadelphia Athletics won 104 games, batted .296 as a team, and scored 901 times. Besides a powerful everyday lineup built around sluggers Jimmie Foxx and Al Simmons, the Athletics boasted outstanding pitching, especially from Bob "Lefty" Grove (twenty-nine wins) and George Earnshaw (twenty-four).

On form the Cubs matched up about evenly with Philadelphia, but almost nothing about the 1929 World Series went according to form. Connie Mack astonished everybody by picking fourteen-year veteran Howard Ehmke, who'd pitched in only eleven games all year and in none since midseason, to start the opening game at Wrigley Field. A crowd of nearly 50,000 (including more than 10,000 occupying temporary bleachers built on platforms behind the outfield fences) watched in dismay as Ehmke used an assortment of motions and speeds to strike out thirteen Cubs—a new Series record. Root pitched almost equally well until Foxx homered in the seventh inning. It ended 3–1, Philadelphia.

The next day's game was far less suspenseful. Foxx homered with two on base, and Simmons unloaded with one aboard. The Athletics knocked out Malone and totaled twelve hits and nine runs, while the Cubs managed only three runs off Earnshaw and Grove, who combined for another thirteen strikeouts.

Hornsby was Ehmke's strikeout victim twice, and in game two Earnshaw and Grove fanned him once apiece. That night, on the train to Philadelphia, he seemed mystified by his ineptness at the plate. "I struck out on pitched balls that in the season I would kill nine times in ten," he said. "When I missed them I actually thought they must have gone through my bat."[6]

Against Earnshaw in game three, at Philadelphia on October 11, Hornsby went down swinging his first two times up, then singled in the sixth inning to drive home Guy Bush for Chicago's first run. The Cubs put over two more runs that inning—enough for Bush, who scattered nine hits and yielded a single run. It was the National League's first Series victory since Hornsby's Cardinals won the seventh game in 1926.

Like that one, game four of the 1929 World Series would go down as one of the most memorable ever played, but for wildly different reasons. Until the home half of the seventh inning, Charlie Root pitched scorelessly, allowing only three hits. Meanwhile the Cubs piled up eight runs on three Philadelphia pitchers, Hornsby contributing significantly with a single and triple. Then occurred what the Chicago writer Edward Burns described as "the greatest debacle, the most terrific flop, in the history of the world series."[7]

By the time Pat Malone, the fourth pitcher of the inning, finally got the third out, the Athletics had pushed over ten runs. The critical events in the rally were Wilson's two misplays on fly balls, on one of which George "Mule" Haas circled the bases behind a runner while Wilson chased the ball to deepest center field. Wilson touched neither ball and ended up charged with only one error for the whole game—on a fly he'd dropped two innings earlier. Lefty Grove came on to pitch the eighth and ninth innings and struck out four of the six batters he faced, so that the final score was Philadelphia 10, Chicago 8. Along with many other witnesses, Burns had trouble believing what had happened: "We've looked at our scorebook glassy eyed for an hour now, thinking there must be some mistake, but 10 she is, folks."[8]

Pennsylvania's persistent Sabbatarianism kept the teams idle on Sunday. While Hornsby sat in the lobby of the Benjamin Franklin and calmly predicted victory tomorrow, Wilson acknowledged, "I'm a big chump . . . and nobody is going to tell me different."[9]

Following Saturday's bizarre encounter, Monday's was something of an anticlimax. Ahead 2–0 in the bottom of the ninth inning, Malone retired the first batter, then yielded a double to Max Bishop. Haas followed with a home run over the right-field fence, and after catcher Gordon "Mickey" Cochrane grounded out to Hornsby, Simmons doubled, Foxx drew an intentional walk, and Edmund "Bing" Miller ended the Series with a drive to right-center between Wilson and Cuyler, scoring Simmons.

One of the more talented ballclubs of the period, the Cubs nonetheless played poorly in almost every respect. Besides striking out fifty times and managing only seven extra-base hits and seventeen runs, they committed seven errors. With eight singles, Wilson led both teams in batting average, but what people would always remember was his disastrous outfield play in game four. Hornsby's second and—as it happened—last World Series was a dreary experience all around. After going hitless in four times at bat in the last game, he ended with only five hits in twenty-one official plate appearances, and his eight strike-outs led everybody. Although he made no excuses, his hurting right heel undoubtedly hampered both his stride and swing at bat and his mobility afield.

The Cubs' losers' shares came to about $3,500 each. A number of them would end up needing the money more than they'd anticipated, because by the end of October the bottom had fallen out of the dazzling securities market. Hornsby was one of tens of thousands of Americans—including a lot of other baseball people—caught in the Great Crash of 1929.

Back in 1926, on the advice of stockbroker Mark Steinberg, his St. Louis friend and admirer, Hornsby had bought 1,000 shares in Radio Corporation of America, obtaining most of it on margin at fifty-two dollars per share. Within two years RCA had soared to 276 1/2, but Steinberg predicted the stock would continue to rise, so Hornsby held on to his 1,000 shares. He still held them when the Crash came, and although most of his losses were on paper, he came away from the experience soured on both Steinberg and stocks. "I lost a lot more money in Wall Street than I ever did on the race track," he said a few years later. "Those sanctimonious cusses with side whiskers can take your money faster than the bookmakers, and leave you less for it."[10]

Then there was Hornsby's farm, which became another losing proposition. His plans for making profits from the sale of bluegrass turf, chickens, and an occasional pig or heifer never materialized. By the middle of 1930, with general economic conditions steadily worsening, the farm had become a thorough liability, and Hornsby was complaining that he would sell the place if he could find somebody willing to pay him what he'd put into it.

Late in November 1929, he entered St. John's Hospital in St. Louis, where Robert Hyland shaved off the calcified area of his heel, removing about a dozen bone particles in all. Two days later he traveled to Chicago to show the heel to Cubs president Veeck and fill out forms for the insurance coverage the ballclub maintained on its players. Hyland predicted that the heel would be sound by spring; if it still hurt, Hornsby assured reporters, he would just tape it up again and play.

One heartening note in a generally cheerless off-season was Hornsby's selection for the second time as his league's Most Valuable Player. The Baseball Writers Association's committee gave him sixty of eighty possible votes—six more than Lefty O'Doul, who led the league with a .398 batting average and helped the Phillies climb to fifth place.

Despite being, by common agreement, the goat of the Series, Hack Wilson spent an enjoyable off-season. After signing a contract for $22,300 for 1930, he turned back a $20,000 damage suit brought by a Chicago milkman who claimed to have suffered permanent injuries when Wilson climbed into the Wrigley Field grandstand and punched him in 1928. But on orders from Commissioner Landis, Wilson had to cancel plans for a boxing match at the new Chicago Stadium with Art Shires, the White Sox's colorful young first baseman, for which both contestants were to have been paid $15,000.

The Cubs were again pennant favorites when they gathered at Catalina, especially after Gabby Hartnett tried out his throwing arm and decided he was his old self. That spring, it later came out, William Wrigley let Joe McCarthy know that his job depended on winning it all in 1930. When McCarthy offered to resign then and there, Wrigley quickly assured him that he had no intention of changing managers—at least not for the present.

If McCarthy's prospects were unsure, Hornsby's became downright discouraging. He limped noticeably and couldn't run at full speed; at the end of March, in Los Angeles, he gave up trying to play, had his heel x-rayed by an orthopedic specialist, and was told that new spur growth had shown up. In no mood for local boosterism, Hornsby cut short a local radio interviewer who asked whether he didn't think California was the greatest place in the world for spring training. "No," grunted Hornsby, "Texas is better."[11]

He left the team at Los Angeles and traveled to Chicago for more examinations and X rays by a specialist recommended by club officials. Advised this time that his heel ailment had been "grossly exaggerated," he rejoined the team at Kansas City, limped badly after running from first to second, and told McCarthy to put somebody else in.[12]

Hornsby was at second base on April 15, when the Cubs opened the season at St. Louis, singling twice in a 9–8 victory. But he met the ball with little power, still limped when he ran and couldn't slide at all, and had trouble getting in front of grounders and reaching second base in time to turn double plays. In and out of the lineup and periodically reexamined and x-rayed, he was batting only .227 on May 7; he didn't hit his first home run until the season was a month old.

Hornsby's heel was only part of the Cubs' troubles. Lester Bell, purchased from Boston at Hornsby's urging to fill a weak spot at third base, developed a bad shoulder and couldn't get the ball across the diamond, and Charlie Grimm missed the early part of the season with a cracked rib.

Matters were about to turn considerably worse. Early in the morning of May 28, right-hander Hal Carlson, a thirty-eight-year-old veteran of both the National League and the World War and the Cubs' principal reliever, died suddenly from a hemorrhaging stomach ulcer. That afternoon's game at Wrigley Field was played as scheduled, Kiki Cuyler homering in a victory over Cincinnati that made the Cubs' record

20–19—good for fourth place. After a day off, St. Louis was on hand for a morning-afternoon Decoration Day doubleheader.

In the lineup for the past week, Hornsby had pushed his average close to .300 and seemed to be working his way back to form. Then, in the third inning of the morning game with the Cardinals, he doubled in Woody English and tried to advance to third base on Wilson's fly to right field. As the throw came in, he started to slide, changed his mind, and managed to twist his left ankle in such a way that it snapped.

After having his ankle set at a nearby hospital, Hornsby reappeared at Wrigley Field for the afternoon game, walking on crutches, his lower leg encased in plaster. Although the Cubs won both games to move into third place, gloom prevailed among the customers at Wrigley Field and fans listening by radio, among Cubs officialdom, and in the Chicago dugout, where even teammates who found Hornsby distant, brusque, and generally unlikable still understood that their chances for another World Series share had dimmed.

The next day, a Saturday, Hal Carlson was buried at nearby Rockford, his hometown. At Wrigley Field, Hornsby poled himself to home plate to receive a bronze medal from James A. Crusinberry, president of the Baseball Writers Association, and a bag containing $1,000 in gold from league president Heydler—both emblematic of being 1929's Most Valuable Player. After that he returned to his farm to heal.

Ironically, the National League's most prolific season offensively since the 1890s happened when its premier hitter for the past decade was out of action for nearly the entire schedule. By consensus, the 1930 ball was livelier than ever. As extra-base hits and runs piled up and batters who'd never connected with power cleared the fences regularly, Bill Klem, a National League umpire since 1905, was among many veteran observers upset over the ball's rabbity behavior. "I'm telling you," said Klem as early as May, "they will have to get it out of there. It is making the game ridiculous." John McGraw (who rarely agreed with Klem otherwise) also thought that "the game has become a case of burlesque slugging, with most of the players trying to knock home runs and many of the pitchers becoming discouraged."[13]

The absence of Hornsby's bat no doubt hurt the Cubs, but how much is questionable. Wilson, Hartnett, Cuyler, and nearly everybody else hammered the ball for what would later be termed "career numbers." After ten wins in succession and twenty-four in thirty-one games, Chicago moved into first place; by late August, Hornsby's teammates held a five-game lead over McGraw's Giants, with Brooklyn and St. Louis in close pursuit.

In the meantime, stories surfaced that Hornsby, at odds not only with manager McCarthy but with various teammates, was about to be traded, and that his gambling proclivities had again come to Commissioner Landis's attention. As to the first matter, Hornsby was uncomprehending. "I can't understand why they call me a troublemaker," he said in July. "I'm not worried. I'm just puzzled."[14] As to the second, he remained publicly silent, as did Landis.

Sixty-one years later, the son of Leslie O'Connor, Landis's secretary and chief assistant, would discover in his father's papers a statement dated July 17, 1930, written under the Chicago National League Ball Club letterhead, addressed to Landis at his Chicago office on North Michigan Avenue, and signed by Hornsby. Its one paragraph read:

I wish to inform you that I do not in the future intend to have anything to do with gamblers, bookmakers, horse races or bets, etc. I also wish you to know that I do not play cards or shoot craps; and intend taking no part in any of these enterprises.[15]

It was an interestingly phrased document, in the first part of which Hornsby lied about what he intended to keep on doing, while in the second part he pledged not to do what he'd never been interested in doing.

Hornsby pinch-hit a few times beginning on August 18, started in three games early in September, told McCarthy his legs were killing him, and returned to pinch-hitting duties. The Cubs continued to play good baseball but couldn't stem the onrushing Cardinals, who gained the lead in mid-September. Meanwhile Wrigley talked as if the pennant was already lost, attributing his ballclub's "failure" to such misfortunes as Carlson's death, Bell's and Hornsby's disabilities, and recent injuries to Charlie Root and Riggs Stephenson.

Yet as late as September 21, after Hartnett's thirty-fourth home run gave Pat Malone his nineteenth victory, the Cubs were only two games behind front-running St. Louis. Two days later, with his team still trailing by only two and one-half games, Wrigley summoned press representatives to his Lake Shore Drive mansion to say he'd made up his mind. "We simply decided to make a change," he said. Given all the rumors in circulation, it seemed better to make the announcement now than later that, for 1931, Rogers Hornsby would manage the Cubs. "Since the day I entered baseball as an owner," he added, "I have had my heart set on winning a world series."[16]

Wrigley's unhappiness with McCarthy went back to last year's Series, wrote Irving Vaughan, because, for one thing, McCarthy insisted on pitching inside to the Athletics hitters, whereas Hornsby argued that they ought to be worked outside. Going against his own "always-for-publication" rule, Hornsby had privately confided as much to Vaughan on the train east following Philadelphia's two-game sweep at Wrigley Field. According to local reports, Wrigley also was unhappy with the excessive celebrating of Wilson and others after they clinched the pennant; McCarthy, Wrigley believed, simply lost control of his players.

The presumption was that at the end of a current series in Boston, McCarthy would accompany the Cubs home, manage the season's remaining four games, and continue as nominal manager until the end of 1930, thereby fulfilling his twelve-month contract and drawing the balance of his $35,000 salary. Understandably umbraged, McCarthy would have none of it. He got off the train at Buffalo to see his wife, stayed over two days, and arrived in Chicago on September 27 to announce his resignation. While McCarthy's admirers at the Chicago Board of Trade hosted him at a luncheon, Hornsby had to take over the ballclub by default. The Cubs won the four remaining games of the season from Cincinnati, but St. Louis clinched the pennant at Pittsburgh. At season's end, St. Louis led Chicago by two games.

In the press flurry that followed McCarthy's dismissal and Hornsby's appointment as Cubs manager, Rud Rennie of the *New York Herald-Tribune* offered perhaps the sagest analysis. The problem, said Rennie, was what to do with Hornsby, a $200,000 investment, if he couldn't play again—as it appeared he might not. "So Hornsby stays and McCarthy goes," wrote Rennie. "Having killed the plain goose that layed the golden eggs, Mr. Wrigley will try a golden goose."[17]

The postseason city series—played each year when neither Chicago team was in the World Series—drew fine crowds at both Wrigley Field and the White Sox's Comiskey Park on the South Side. In fact the total attendance of 163,000 for six games was close to what the Cardinals and Athletics drew in that year's World Series (which Philadelphia again won, four games to two). The city series went to the Cubs, with Hornsby leaving the dugout only to occupy the third-base coach's box. The winning players' shares came out to $1,300 each after McCarthy, popular with nearly all the Cubs, was voted a full share.

Although a general economic downturn was under way by mid-1930, what came to be known as the Great Depression worked a delayed reaction on Organized Baseball. Overall major-league attendance for 1930 reached 10.5 million—a figure that wouldn't be equaled for another sixteen years. For that same period, neither the Cubs nor anybody else would equal that season's 1,463,624 paid admissions at Wrigley Field.

Booming bats in both major leagues accompanied 1930's record attendance. Despite the presence in the American League of sluggers such as Ruth, Gehrig, Foxx, and Simmons, the National's offensive output was even more spectacular. The league as a whole averaged .303; six teams recorded .300-plus averages, topped by New York's .319. A twentieth-century record was set for total runs (7,025), as well as all-time records for home runs (892) and slugging average (.448). Bill Terry of the Giants led the majors with a .401 batting average; Hack Wilson, besides batting .356, clubbed fifty-six homers and drove in 190 runs—league and majors marks, respectively, that would remain unmatched sixty-five years later. The Cubs hit a record 171 homers, while the Philadelphia Phillies scored 944 runs, hit 126 homers, batted .315 as a club, and still managed to win only fifty-two times.

Hornsby's contribution to the 1930 batting barrage was negligible: a .308 average in only 142 plate appearances, with two home runs and seventeen runs batted in. People who'd followed his career could only conjecture about what kind of statistics he might have piled up that season if he'd managed to stay healthy.

Late in October, Joe McCarthy signed a handsome contract to manage the New York Yankees. When Cubs coach Jimmie Burke followed McCarthy to New York, Hornsby added Charley O'Leary, onetime Detroit infielder. Ray Schalk, former White Sox catcher and manager, stayed on to work with the Cubs' batterymen.

At the end of the year Hornsby returned to Chicago for the formality of signing a two-year player-manager contract for the same $40,000 annual salary he'd received since 1928. He'd been tramping over his farm with a shotgun and his dogs, he reported, and his legs felt fine. Asked if he thought the Cubs would hustle for him as they had for McCarthy, he answered with customary candor: "Why shouldn't they? They're still playing for a living, aren't they? I don't care whether they like me personally, just so long as they play for me." He went on to say, "McCarthy and I parted friends," and "I didn't undermine him and he knew I didn't."[18] Others—notably Gabby Hartnett and team captain Charlie Grimm—weren't so sure of that. Both had been close to McCarthy; neither looked forward to playing for Hornsby. Grimm's situation became especially uncomfortable when Hornsby tried throughout December, without success, to arrange a deal with St. Louis for Jim Bottomley.

One Cub, though, wasn't worried about Hornsby or much of anything else that winter. Hack Wilson took a vaudeville turn at a Chicago theater, then went home to bask in the adulation of the home folks in Martinsburg, West Virginia—especially his pals at the Elks Club bar. Recently named his league's Most Valuable Player, Wilson told everybody that he wanted a big raise over what he'd received in 1930, and that he got after meeting with Veeck in Pittsburgh. At $33,000, Wilson became the second-best-paid player in the National League.

Yet changes were afoot that would contribute to making 1931 a bitter, disheartening year for Wilson. Agreeing that the offense-defense balance needed to be redressed, American and National League presidents and owners voted to do away with the sacrifice-fly rule altogether, as well as instruct the Spalding Company (exclusive suppliers for more than fifty years) to modify the baseball itself. But whereas American Leaguers were satisfied with higher stitching, so that pitchers could snap off curveballs more effectively, president Heydler and his owners ordered a ball with both raised stitching and a thicker cover, which would have a deadening effect.

Hornsby downplayed the significance of the new ball as he left St. Louis for Los Angeles by automobile, going by way of Fort Worth and Austin to visit relatives. He wanted to reach Catalina Island at least five days ahead of the rookies and batterymen to test his ankle and heel. Nearing his thirty-fifth birthday and now weighing 200 pounds, he'd thickened around the middle and jawline, acquired a few gray hairs, and begun to look less like a superbly conditioned athlete than an ordinary citizen of early middle age.

At Catalina, the Cubs players soon discovered that under Hornsby things would be different. As he'd done with the Cardinals, Hornsby instituted one four-hour, lunchless practice per day; he also drew up a weight chart, kept track of everybody's poundage, and enforced a midnight curfew. Ed Burns marveled that "lads who haven't been in a hotel lobby in the early evening in the memory of man" now idled around the St. Catherine's. As always, Hornsby himself was part of the lobby scene, where, as described by a Los Angeles writer, "he sits for hours staring out of a chair . . . like a farmer boy on his first big trip to a big city."[19]

If Wrigley thought McCarthy had been too easygoing, then Hornsby meant to have discipline. Horseplay during practice prompted scoldings; misplays, harsh criticism. "He expected you to be as good as he was," remembered Woody English. Once the Cubs left Avalon and moved into Los Angeles, their manager laid down strict clubhouse rules. "We weren't allowed to smoke [or] eat," recalled Grimm, nor was any kind of reading material—even newspapers—permitted in the dressing area. As English put it, "Everybody was afraid to open his mouth in the clubhouse."[20]

For Hornsby, it wasn't only a matter of keeping his players' minds on baseball; it also had to do with professional appearances. As he put it a few years later, "How does it look to the fans to see a guy walking down the runway to the dugout sucking on a cigarette? That's bush-league stuff. . . . When I put on my uniform, I put it on to go to work and not to sit around and smoke and kid about last night. That uniform belongs to the public and when you're wearing it you belong to the public."[21]

Hornsby played in most of the exhibition games that spring, but he usually sat out the last several innings; it was obvious that his feet and legs were bothering him. Amid rumors of friction between Hornsby and various players, the Cubs reached Chicago with a 22–14–1 exhibition record.

They opened the season before a Wrigley Field overflow by beating Pittsburgh 6–2, behind Charlie Root. At bat, Hornsby started in high gear, winning the season's second game with a home run, hitting a three-run shot two days later, and then, at Pittsburgh's Forbes Field on April 24, homering three times in succession and driving in eight runs to defeat the Pirates almost single-handedly. It seemed that whatever had been done to the ball made little difference where Hornsby was concerned.

Afield, though, his movements were "distressingly slow and shaky," reported Burns.[22] In fact, the whole Chicago infield was worrisome. Grimm was still a timely hitter, but he no longer covered much ground to his right; Hornsby covered even less to his own left. Lester Bell remained an all-around disappointment, so Hornsby shifted English to third base and stationed rookie Bill Jurges at shortstop.

Late in May, Hornsby rankled Gabby Hartnett when he persuaded Veeck to trade substitute catcher Earl Grace to Pittsburgh for Ralston

"Rollie" Hemsley. Although Hemsley was batting only .171 and, in three years with the Pirates, had earned a reputation mainly as a carouser, when Hornsby put him behind the plate more than half the time, he lived up to his new manager's expectations by batting .309 and bringing needed speed to the slow-footed lineup.

Hack Wilson started the season in a slump and never got over it. As the season progressed, he complained to everybody willing to listen about the dead baseball, as well as the elimination of the sacrifice fly (which had saved him eighteen outs in 1930). In truth, given the fact that Wilson rarely pulled his hits, the deader 1931 ball meant that drives he lifted over fences the previous season now fell harmlessly into outfielders' hands. By mid-June, Wilson was playing only part-time, alternating in left field with Riggs Stephenson (until Stephenson broke his leg) and in center with Danny Taylor and rookie Vince Barton.

After playing in forty-four of the first forty-eight games, Hornsby himself went into a slump and sat down in favor of Clarence "Foots" Blair. From then on he put himself in the lineup only about half the time, using Blair and Jurges at second base and trying a few games at third. Juggling his daily lineup and getting steady pitching from Root, Bush, Malone, and Bob Smith (purchased from Boston in the off-season), Hornsby kept the Cubs in contention with St. Louis, New York, and Brooklyn.

As Hack Wilson struggled, so he drank. The addition of Hemsley gave Wilson another speakeasy companion to go with Malone, and in Boston late in June the trio ran afoul of Hornsby. Wilson and Malone missed curfew; Hemsley made it back to his room before midnight, though roundly drunk. Wilson and Hemsley drew a one-day suspension; Malone, given a reprieve, labored to victory three days later in ninety-five-degree heat at Philadelphia, with Hornsby hitting his thirteenth and fourteenth homers and enjoying Malone's discomfort.

Asked about rumors that Hornsby was on the way out, Wrigley assured reporters, "Hornsby will be around after most of the others have gone. Make that as strong as you can." Hornsby's recent disciplinary problems were "just a hangover from last season." Under McCarthy, some of the players "got into habits that can't be broken over night." When he was interviewed by the *New York World-Telegram*'s Joe Williams, Hornsby sounded as hard-nosed as ever. "Sure, I know there are a lot of people that dislike me," he said. "But then there are a lot of people I don't care for. I don't go around trying to make enemies, but somehow I seem to make them. . . . I don't worry about not being popular. I have a notion that popularity won't do you much good if your team ain't up there."[23]

After winning three of four games from the Giants at the Polo Grounds in mid-July, the Cubs were in third place, barely behind John McGraw's club and five behind league-leading St. Louis. The next day, at Brooklyn, Hornsby was ejected by umpire Harry McGrew in the first inning of a game Malone eventually lost 3–2. The Cubs never came that close to the top again, as the Cardinals, now managed by Charles "Gabby" Street and assembled almost wholly from Branch Rickey's growing farm system, steadily built their lead. By early September, with his team fifteen games out of first place and six and one-half behind second-place New York, Hornsby conceded the race and began using several new players. The most talked-about newcomer was second baseman Billy Herman, purchased from Louisville for $50,000 and generally presumed to be Hornsby's successor.

Meanwhile Wilson—who a year earlier had been on top of the baseball world—suffered humiliation, suspension, and finally rejection at the hands of his superiors. Late in August, when he again missed curfew in New York, Hornsby told him to catch a train for Chicago, because he was suspended for ten days. But after he apologized to Hornsby and then, at the manager's insistence, made amends in front of the whole team, he won still another chance.

In Cincinnati the next week, when injuries and Barton's absence for his father's funeral left the Cubs with only three outfielders, Hornsby put pitcher Arthur "Bud" Teachout in left field and kept Wilson in the bull pen warming up relief pitchers.[24] That evening, as the players boarded the train after their fourth straight loss to the last-place Reds, Wilson got into a quarrel in the vestibule between Pullman cars with two Chicago sportswriters: Harold Johnson of the *Evening American* and Wayne Otto of the *Herald and Examiner.* Malone happened through, joined the dispute, and, with Wilson's encouragement, ended up punching both writers because, he said later, they'd been "on me" in their columns.[25]

When the ballclub reached Chicago, Hornsby immediately reported what had happened to club president William Veeck, who agreed to fine Malone $500 and suspend Wilson without pay for the remainder of the schedule. Said Hornsby, "Hack knows he's through as a Cub, so it would hardly be fair either to himself or the team to play him."[26] Altogether, Wilson lost about $6,500 in fines and suspension money, climaxing a totally frustrating season in which he appeared in 112 games and batted .261, with only twelve homers and sixty-one runs batted in.

At Comiskey Park on Wednesday, September 9, the Cubs defeated the White Sox in a game that drew 35,000 and raised $44,489 for the Governor's Unemployment Fund, one of many such charitable ventures in the early Depression period. Wilson, accorded only an upper-deck right-field seat for the game, complained about that, about how much money he'd lost, and, most of all, about Hornsby's playing a pitcher in left field in that game in Cincinnati.[27]

On September 13 Hornsby belted a bases-loaded home run in the eleventh inning to defeat Boston for a doubleheader sweep. Although it was the Cubs' eighth win in a row since coming home, many in the still-plentiful Wrigley Field crowds gave out with boos whenever Hornsby came to bat. With thirteen victories in its last fifteen games, his club secured third place with an 84–70 record, four and one-half games behind New York and a distant seventeen from repeat-winner St. Louis.

By most ballplayers' standards, Hornsby put in a solid season. Taking part in an even 100 games, he batted .331, hit sixteen home runs, and drove in ninety runs. Again, though, he struggled afield, making twenty-two errors, turning double plays with difficulty, and having trouble getting to anything hit to his left side.

Hornsby was a nonparticipant during the postseason city series, which the White Sox won in seven games. While that was happening on Chicago's South and North Sides, Al Capone stood trial in U.S. district court for income-tax fraud; on October 18 he was convicted on five counts and, a week later, sentenced to eleven years in federal prison.

It was perhaps symbolic that the ascendancy and undoing in Chicago of both Al Capone and Hack Wilson virtually coincided. Almost at the same time that Capone entered prison, Wilson received word that he was traded to St. Louis for the durable spitballer Burleigh Grimes (who since 1917 had defeated the Cubs in twenty-five of thirty decisions). Reached by telephone at Martinsburg, West Virginia, Wilson shouted, "That's great. I'm sure glad to get away from Chicago!" Hornsby, he went on, "took the bat right out of my hands [by ordering him not to swing at 2–0 and 3–1 pitches]. I had to . . . take a lot of sweet strikes I might have hammered out of the lot. The fans don't realize what I was up against when I played under the Hornsby system."[28]

For the Hornsbys, the off-season months were full of new legal troubles. They had to settle out of court with Ruth Wismer, a St. Louis woman struck by their chauffeured automobile the previous spring, and then again with Effie M. Blume, their "family nurse," who claimed to have lost her sight in one eye as the result of an injury sustained late in May when the Hornsby automobile, carrying Blume and Jeannette and Billy Hornsby from St. Louis to Chicago, went off the road near Atlanta, Illinois.

Then, in June 1931 the U.S. Bureau of Internal Revenue (BIR) charged that the Hornsbys had filed incorrectly and underpaid on their 1927 tax return. Claiming Fort Worth rather than St. Louis as their place of residence, they tried to take advantage of Texas's community-property law, which permitted a husband to list half of his annual income in his wife's name. Ruling that the Hornsbys must file as Missouri residents, the BIR doubled the $36,603 that Hornsby listed as his 1927 income, added $1,000 he hadn't reported ($300 in fees for ghostwritten newspaper columns and $700 in second-place money from World Series receipts), and denied a deduction of $5,835 in legal costs connected with the sale of his Cardinals stock.

All told, it came out to $8,782 in unpaid federal taxes and penalties. William Fahey, still Hornsby's attorney, formally contested the ruling before the Board of Tax Appeals in Washington, to no avail. Moreover, when the Missouri state auditor looked into the Hornsbys' 1927 state return, they ended up having to pay an undisclosed additional amount into the treasury at Jefferson City.

Although the 1931 Cubs again led the majors in home attendance, they drew half a million fewer fans than in 1930. Meanwhile the Cardinals barely topped 600,000 for the regular season with a team that easily repeated as pennant winners and finally downed the mighty Athletics in the World Series. Overall major-league attendance fell by some three million, and only nineteen minor leagues finished the season, seven fewer than in 1930.

That December, at their annual meetings in Chicago, Commissioner Landis, the league presidents, and the sixteen club presidents officially agreed to reduce the June–September roster limit from twenty-five to twenty-three and, unofficially, to institute general salary rollbacks. One of the biggest losers in the austerity drive was Hack Wilson, first offered only $7,500 for 1932 by Branch Rickey, then sold to Brooklyn, where he finally settled for $16,500, half his previous year's salary.

Based upon an industry that, like soft drinks and tobacco, proved Depression-proof, William Wrigley's chewing-gum fortune remained secure, and his Chicago Cubs were better positioned to cope with the hard times of the 1930s than most other franchises. Wrigley had always spent freely to build winners, but so far his money had produced only one pennant, and his personal dream of a World Series champion had gone unrealized.

It never would be, because on January 26, 1932, at the age of seventy, Wrigley died of a stroke at his winter home outside Phoenix, Arizona. He left an estate worth about $21 million, not including Santa Catalina Island, the Los Angeles and Phoenix Biltmore Hotels, Wrigley Field, the Los Angeles Angels and their ballpark (also called Wrigley

Field), and other properties in Chicago and Pasadena, California. At the memorial service in Chicago preceding Wrigley's burial at Pasadena, Hornsby told reporters, "I have lost the best boss I ever had. . . . Mr. Wrigley was the prince of them all."[29]

Ownership of the Chicago franchise passed to thirty-seven-year-old Philip K. Wrigley, whose interests mostly ran to golf and mechanical tinkering. "I don't know much about baseball," confessed the younger Wrigley upon inheriting the ballclub, "and I don't care much for it, either."[30] President William K. Veeck now gained a virtually free hand to run the franchise.

Waiting for Hornsby and the first group of Cubs when they reached Catalina Island was Grover Cleveland Alexander, down and out and reduced to touring with bearded House of David baseball teams during the summer. At age forty-five, Alexander may have hoped for a chance at a comeback, but all he did that spring was pitch batting practice in exchange for room and board at the St. Catherine's and $100 in wages.

Hornsby worked out daily with his players and, to please the paying customers (usually no more than a few hundred at a time that spring), played the early innings in games with Pacific Coast League teams, Pittsburgh (based at Paso Robles), and the New York Giants, who trained at Los Angeles. But his feet swelled and his legs hurt, and Billy Herman was at second base most of the time. As the Cubs started east, it was evident to Chicago writers that Hornsby intended to play as little as possible in the season ahead. Meanwhile Jurges and English divided time at shortstop, and young Stanley Hack, purchased from Sacramento the previous fall, showed so well at third that Lester Bell drew his release.

With English nursing a split finger on his throwing hand and Riggs Stephenson still limping from last year's broken leg, Hornsby put together an opening-day lineup that included veterans Grimm, Hartnett, and Cuyler but also such unfamiliar names as Herman, Jurges, Hack, Barton, and Johnny Moore (an outfielder who'd appeared in only eighty games in three seasons). After splitting six games on the road, Chicago debuted at home in perfect weather before far less than the usual

173

capacity-plus assemblage. With the flag at half-mast in memory of William Wrigley, Hornsby's men were held to five hits by Cincinnati's Charles "Red" Lucas, and lost 7–2.

Four days later Cuyler broke his foot rounding first base and was put out of action for seven weeks. When Stephenson was finally able to move into left field, Hornsby optioned Barton to the International League and shuffled Moore, Danny Taylor (soon sold to Brooklyn), and Lance Richbourg in center and right.

Philip K. Wrigley saw his first game at Wrigley Field on May 8—a 12–5 victory that ended a four-game sweep of Brooklyn. Throughout that series, the Robins' Hack Wilson dodged lemons tossed from the grandstand; in the second game he revived painful memories of the 1929 World Series when he stumbled and let two drives go over his head. Within another two years, Wilson would drink himself out of the majors, but in 1932 he made a considerable comeback with Brooklyn, batting close to .300, slamming twenty-three home runs, and driving in 123 runs.

Especially after losing Kiki Cuyler, Hornsby may have wished that he still had Wilson's bat to put into the lineup. Although the Cubs won twenty-five of their first thirty-five games and maintained a small lead over the surprising Boston Braves, Hornsby wasn't happy with his personnel. Asked by a New York writer about the Cubs' prospects, he answered with characteristic tactlessness: "How the hell can I win a pennant with this lousy outfield?" When Veeck read that in Chicago, he telephoned to ask Hornsby to tone it down, stop being so openly critical of his own team. Replied the manager, "Why not? It is a lousy outfield"—and hung up.[31]

Desperate for some punch, Hornsby kept Hartnett in the lineup despite his preference for Rollie Hemsley's defensive and base-running skills and, at the end of May, put himself in right field for back-to-back doubleheaders with Pittsburgh and St. Louis. Although he homered in the second game of the Memorial Day split with St. Louis, he didn't do much else at bat and covered little territory during a week's outfield duty.

On June 1 Hornsby was held hitless in the Cubs' first encounter with the Cardinals' Jerome Herman Dean, an Arkansas sharecropper's son whose madcap minor-league antics had already gained him the nickname "Dizzy." The rookie right-hander—long, lean, and blazingly fast—beat Pat Malone 1–0 in a rain-terminated seven-inning game. Two days later, after two balls bounced by Hornsby for triples in an eleven-inning defeat at Pittsburgh, he took himself out of the lineup. "Hornsby's experiment on himself as a chaser of flies . . . hasn't been a howling success," commented the *Tribune*'s Irving Vaughan.[32]

That same June 3, across the state in Philadelphia, the Yankees' Lou Gehrig became the first twentieth-century player to hit four home runs in one game—a feat that was eclipsed on the next day's sports pages by John McGraw's resignation after thirty years as Giants manager, in favor of first baseman Bill Terry. Hornsby must have wondered whether, had things worked out differently back in 1927, he himself might not have succeeded McGraw—maybe two or three seasons ago.

The Cubs' offense picked up somewhat with Cuyler's return on June 14, but pitching was the main reason Hornsby's club stayed in the pennant race. Although Burleigh Grimes and Bob Smith, both in their late thirties, were about washed up, Malone, Guy Bush, and Charlie Root could usually be relied upon. The new mainstay of the staff, though, was Lon Warneke, a skinny young right-hander brought up from Reading late the previous season. A couple of years younger than fellow Arkansan Dizzy Dean, close to the same size and almost as fast, Warneke was on his way to twenty-two wins.

With the Giants struggling toward a sixth-place finish under Terry and the injury-plagued Cardinals destined for seventh, it became a three-team race between Chicago, Pittsburgh, and Boston. In July, though, Bill Jurges lost two weeks of the season and almost his life when, early on the morning of the seventh, a young divorcee who danced and modeled under the name Violet Valli came to Jurges's room at the Hotel Carlos on Sheffield Avenue and drew a .25 caliber revolver. Jurges tried to get the pistol away from her; as they struggled, it discharged three times. One bullet bounced off Jurges's ribs and exited near his right shoulder; another grazed the little finger of his left hand; still another broke the woman's wrist. In her room at the same hotel, Valli left a couple of empty gin bottles and a note that read: "To me, life without Billy isn't worth living, but why should I leave this earth alone? I'm going to take Billy with me."[33]

Tearful, blaming gin and Kiki Cuyler (who'd advised Jurges to break up with her), Valli went quietly with the police. When Jurges refused to file charges, the police went ahead and booked her for attempted murder. Out on bail a week later, she sat in a Wrigley Field field box on the first-base side and stared at the patched-up Jurges, who occupied the owner's box behind the Cubs' third-base dugout.[34]

That day Hornsby put himself in at third base for the slumping Stanley Hack and stayed for six games in a row, during which he failed to reach grounders that went for nominal base hits, fielded bunts with difficulty, committed four officially scored errors, and heard frequent boos from the Chicago fans. After a 13–3 rout by New York on July 18, he sat himself down for good. Four days later Jurges was able to return to shortstop; English took over full-time duties at third.

On July 26, with their record 49–42, the Cubs left for Boston to start an eastern tour, trailing Pittsburgh by four and one-half games and leading Boston by two. Both players and the complement of Chicago writers noticed that club president Veeck had decided to come along, and that Hornsby, who always enjoyed the privilege of a private compartment, sat in the players' Pullman. At the Somerset Hotel, they also noticed, Veeck and Hornsby ate at separate tables.

After winning three of four games and dumping the overachieving Braves nine and one-half games back, the Cubs moved on to Brooklyn. At Ebbets Field on July 30, Hack Wilson's bases-loaded homer beat his old buddy Pat Malone and dropped Chicago another game behind Pittsburgh. After two days of rain, the teams resumed play on Tuesday, August 2. Warneke gave up three runs in the eighth inning, with Wilson and Danny Taylor providing Brooklyn's key hits; Frank Demaree— an outfielder brought up from Sacramento two weeks earlier with a stipulation that the Cubs would pay $50,000 to the Pacific Coast League franchise if he made good—popped out to end the game.

That night, on the train to Philadelphia, Veeck fumed in his private compartment. Besides the fact that former Cubs Wilson and Taylor had mostly accounted for the two losses at Brooklyn, Veeck was angry because Hornsby hadn't put himself in as a pinch hitter for Demaree in the ninth inning. A week earlier, in Pittsburgh, Hornsby also had failed to hold a clubhouse meeting to talk over the Pirates' batters; when Veeck asked him about that, the reply was, "If you don't like the way I'm handling the Cubs, pay me off." To which Veeck had shot back, "Not just now, but remember that crack."[35]

On the train to Philadelphia, Veeck became convinced that the time had come. He called Hornsby to his compartment, where the two men disputed all the way into the Broad Street station over what Veeck considered managing mistakes and Hornsby deemed front-office interference in on-field matters. "I've had enough of second-guessers," snapped Hornsby. At the Benjamin Franklin Hotel, they disappeared into Veeck's room, then came out to meet reporters. "Rog is leaving the club," announced Veeck. "We have asked waivers on Hornsby as a player and they have been given. Hornsby is a free agent."[36] The affable, popular Charlie Grimm—who'd known as early as July 21 that he would be taking over the team—was the new Chicago manager.

Asked about specifics, Veeck turned to Hornsby: "There has been no quarrel, has there Rog?" Chuckling, Hornsby said, "I guess we won't call it a quarrel. Only big differences of opinion about the ball club and the way it should be handled."[37] Then and in several later statements, both Veeck and Hornsby repeated that official line and denied Hornsby's gambling was an issue.

Yet in fact, for the past three years Hornsby had been borrowing money from team members to cover his racing bets and losses, and his firing, wrote Irving Vaughan, created "a mild panic" among the players.[38] Within a few hours after Veeck and Hornsby met the press, the club president and ex-manager were meeting with Hornsby's creditors. Some of his debts—$250 borrowed from Malone, $200 from Bob

Smith, and $745 from English—he'd already repaid. But he still owed English $1,115, Charley O'Leary $2,000, and the First National Bank of Chicago $2,000 on a note Guy Bush had signed for him just before the start of the present road trip. (As far back as 1929, moreover, Bush had signed Hornsby's $5,000 note with the same bank, although that debt was clear by 1932.) After getting all the numbers down, Veeck worked out a schedule whereby Hornsby would pay back everybody in five installments, beginning on August 18, with the money to be deducted from the nearly $17,000 the ballclub still owed him on the balance of his contract.

The next day, in Chicago, Philip Wrigley said that while he knew nothing of Veeck's intentions until after Hornsby's dismissal, "anything Veeck does is all right with me. I don't know much about baseball. It's Veeck's job to see the Cubs win a pennant." Meanwhile Hornsby sat in the hotel lobby in Philadelphia, chatting with reporters and occasional well-wishers. "Hell, I've been fired before," he noted with implicit if not technical accuracy. "The Cubs have my best wishes. I hope Charley leads 'em to a pennant. I'll begin to think about my future after that [December 31] contract date comes around."[39]

When Hornsby arrived in St. Louis the following afternoon, he went directly to Sportsman's Park, where he watched a Browns-Athletics game in the company of Robert Hyland, with Browns owner Phil Ball in the adjoining box. The game over, Hornsby signed autographs at the exit gate and finally started home to his farm at Robertson. John E. Wray, among others, suspected that Hornsby might be in line for the job of Browns manager, but the next morning Ball announced the rehiring for 1933 of Bill Killefer, his manager for the past three years.

Questions about gambling—not only Hornsby's but others' on the Chicago ballclub—persisted in the aftermath of his firing. The *Chicago Daily News* reported a horse-race betting pool among Cubs players, one of whom, it was alleged, had been involved with Hornsby in running up a $38,000 debt to bookmakers. On August 11—the morning after the Cubs moved into first place by defeating the Pirates in ten innings—Commissioner Landis arrived in Pittsburgh, talked with various players at their hotel, watched the Cubs win again that afternoon, and returned to Chicago without a public word to anybody.

Veeck termed the *Daily News* stories "a cheap, cowardly attack," while in St. Louis, Hornsby remarked that players on every team gambled, and if they were to be punished for that, "it would disrupt the entire league."[40]

Two days after his appearance in Pittsburgh, Landis turned up in St. Louis, where he met at the Park Plaza Hotel with Hornsby, English, Bush, O'Leary, and Pat Malone. Hornsby acknowledged borrowing money from various Cubs, said he told Veeck all about it on the train from New York to Philadelphia, and produced a copy of the statement he signed for Veeck, setting up a repayment schedule. But he went on to insist that he used the money to cover mortgage payments on his farm, the Bureau of Internal Revenue's extra tax assessments, and "bills and so forth."[41] The others present readily seconded Hornsby's explanation for his borrowings.

Hornsby also denied ever going to the track in the company of a Cubs player. When Landis asked if he'd "run bets" through Cubs trainer Andy Lotshaw, he answered, "Hell no," he'd always handled his own bets. "If I wanted to get on a horse, I did"—always before and never during games, never through ballpark ushers or anybody else.[42]

After Hornsby spoke, Bush, highly agitated, denied being part of any betting pool, and he was particularly upset when Landis asked about rumors that he and Hornsby were seen at a North Side bookmaker's place with (as Landis phrased it) "two ladies known as blondes." "I don't give a damn what anybody says," protested Bush, "the gambling stories printed in Chicago are lousy."[43]

Whatever misgivings Landis may have harbored about Hornsby's denials or what others said in his or their own defense, the commissioner apparently deemed it unwise to go any farther with the inquiry. Landis simply released a thirty-six-page transcript of his meeting with Hornsby and the other four men. "There will be no formal decision," he told reporters. "The transcript speaks for itself."[44]

Privately, Landis considered Hornsby to be unregenerate and incorrigible. "That fellow never will learn," he commented to J. G. Taylor Spink of the *Sporting News*. "His betting has got him in one scrape after another, cost him a fortune and several jobs, and still he hasn't enough sense to stop it." Editorially, Spink was almost as censorious: Hornsby was paying the price "for having an outside interest that he refused to give up, even when years ago it appeared certain that it was proving a grave obstacle in his path to enduring baseball fame and fortune." Hornsby would be remembered "as the man who couldn't give up the horses."[45]

The Cubs' record when Hornsby was fired was 53–46; they trailed Pittsburgh by five games. With onetime Yankee Mark Koenig, purchased from the Pacific Coast League, established at shortstop and solidifying their infield, the Cubs won twenty of their first twenty-five games under Grimm, while Pittsburgh went into a tailspin. By the end of August, Chicago enjoyed a commanding lead of six and one-half games, and on September 20 Grimm's team clinched the pennant by winning the opener of a doubleheader at Forbes Field. Cuyler hit a bases-loaded triple, Bush won his nineteenth game, and Billy Herman became only the tenth player to make 200 base hits in his rookie season.

Before the next day's game, the Cubs met to decide how they would divide their World Series money. They voted for twenty-two full shares and gave Koenig—whose steady work afield and strong hitting many considered the key to their pennant drive—only half a share. Hornsby was voted nothing, whereupon he appealed in writing to Landis, taking credit for the development of Herman, Warneke, and Jurges, claiming that the Cubs were just peaking when he was fired, and noting that he was on the active roster as a player for nearly two-thirds of the season. "I don't know what the rules on the subject say—I did not read them," wrote Hornsby. "But I do feel that I deserve a share more than some of those who will receive full portions."[46]

Landis waited two weeks before turning down Hornsby's appeal. Citing a provision in league bylaws, the commissioner noted that for a player who hadn't been on a team's roster as of September 1 to receive a Series share, he must be voted one unanimously. "He can overrule the vote of the players any time," growled Hornsby. Besides, several Cubs would have voted to give him a share "if they hadn't been ordered what to do"—presumably by Veeck.[47]

Although the *Sporting News* believed that many people "thought the freeze-out [of Hornsby] bordered on persecution," the New York Yankees, who provided the World Series opposition, concerned themselves not at all with Hornsby's plight.[48] It was the half-share voted their old teammate Koenig that gave the Yankees their battle cry. As Joe McCarthy watched in satisfaction and found it necessary to do little else, his team proceeded to demolish the "cheap-skate" Cubs in four games, reaching Grimm's pitchers for thirty-seven runs and slamming a record eight homers, including Babe Ruth's fabled "called shot" off Charlie Root in game three.

Contacted at his farm, Hornsby said he wasn't even listening to radio broadcasts of the Series games, and he didn't care who won or lost. Deprived of Series money (which came out to $4,244.60 per full loser's share), he also lamented the $20,000 he'd lost on his farm. "Sometimes I wish I had my money back," he said. "But if I hadn't put it in real estate, I'd have put it somewhere else where it would've shrunk even more."[49]

It was another low point in Hornsby's life, but he wasn't about to change his ways. By the end of the year, the Cubs would have paid him off, minus deductions for his debts. After that, he was going to need a job.

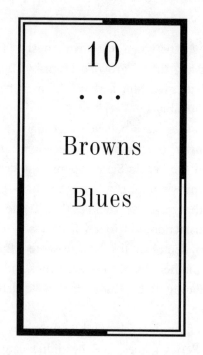

10

· · ·

Browns

Blues

In the past, Rogers Hornsby had felt bitterly and spoken harshly about Branch Rickey, but now he found himself having to turn to Rickey for help. Christian gentleman that he was, Rickey came to Hornsby's rescue, convincing Sam Breadon that—strictly as a player— Hornsby could help the Cardinals in 1933. As John E. Wray of the *St. Louis Post-Dispatch* put it, the Cardinals thus "relieved what promised to be an embarrassing, even mortifying position for the one-time King of Swat."[1]

On October 24, 1932, Hornsby met with Breadon and Rickey in the Cardinals' Sportsman's Park offices and signed a one-year contract for $15,000. The contract specifically omitted the standard reserve clause, so that Hornsby would become a free agent after one season. Breadon also exacted a pledge that Hornsby had no designs whatsoever on manager Gabby Street's job.

People who knew Sam Breadon had no trouble believing him when he said, "I'm not taking this step for sentimental reasons." If Hornsby could still handle second base, Frank Frisch would move over to third. Rickey, asked if Hornsby's off-field conduct had been discussed beforehand, would say only, "Yes, a great deal."[2]

Honestly grateful, Hornsby ate about as much crow as people who knew him could have expected. "I feel like I'm coming back home," he said, "and I want everyone to know how much I appreciate the chance offered me. . . . I may have had some misunderstandings with officials of the club in the past, but in the six years I have been away I've had a chance to do a lot of thinking and studying. . . . You can take it from me that there are no two finer men to work for in baseball [than Breadon and Rickey]. I'll give Street everything I've got and I understand I'm not considered as manager now or at any future time."[3]

A couple of weeks later, Rickey took Hornsby with him when he addressed the annual membership drive of the St. Louis Young Men's Christian Association. Hornsby announced that he was joining the Y, and indeed he did. Over the winter he worked out five days a week at the downtown YMCA, pulling weights and oars, throwing around a medicine ball, and running ten circuits on the indoor track in an effort to lose pounds and strengthen his legs.

Dick Farrington, a local sportswriter, caught him during a workout, "unconcerned and smiling." Recently, Hornsby acknowledged, he'd driven to the St. Louis county seat at Clayton to witness the auction of his farm. He didn't receive anything like what he put into the place, but said, "No, I ain't going into any of my troubles. What do the fans care about that?" The important thing was the next baseball season: "Watch me next year." If he made a big comeback, "wouldn't that make a better story?"[4]

After moving his wife and son into a rented house in the city, Hornsby prepared for a kind of short-term employment he wouldn't have considered in better times. A professional sports promoter named Ray Doan, who handled everything from donkey baseball games to touring House of David teams, hired Hornsby as an instructor at his new All-Star Baseball School, which would open at Hot Springs, Arkansas, during the last two weeks in February. Besides Doan and

Hornsby, the school staff included George Sisler (recently unemployed following a season managing in the Texas League), Grover Cleveland Alexander (waiting to catch on with one of the House of David squads), Les Mann (now an official with the national YMCA), and Cardinals scout Jack Ryan.

Sixty-five baseball hopefuls in their teens and early twenties, from thirty states, converged on Hot Springs and suited out for "classes" at Whittington Park, the municipal baseball field. Some arrived in their own or family automobiles; most hitchhiked along the highways or sneaked aboard railroad freight cars. They all paid sixty dollars in tuition and an additional fifteen to twenty dollars for room and board—a princely outlay in the depths of the Great Depression.

Hot Springs had once flourished as a major health spa, attracting, among other well-paying clients, ballplayers seeking to boil out winter indulgences in the local mineral baths. But the town had struggled since 1919, when the state government shut down Oaklawn Track and the routlette wheels, blackjack tables, and slot machines in the hotels. Doan's baseball school brought in some needed outside money, even if the boys had little to spend once they arrived.

Hornsby mostly coached and demonstrated batting during the morning and afternoon sessions at Whittington Park. At most, he made $200 for his two weeks' services, but he showed that he could work effectively and agreeably with youngsters, and actually seemed to be enjoying himself most of the time.

As the Cardinals began spring practice at Bradenton, Florida, Gabby Street acknowledged that over the winter he'd received "hundreds" of letters from fans about Hornsby, and that most had argued it was a mistake to sign him. But, said Street, Hornsby was "a determined, courageous fellow," and "I know he'll give me everything he has said and be loyal."[5]

Hornsby arrived at Bradenton by automobile, driving from Hot Springs in the company of young John Flaherty, to whom he'd taken a liking at the school. Flaherty hung around for a week or so, shagging flies and catching a little batting practice. Asked what impressed him most at Hot Springs, he laughed and said it was watching Hornsby hit.

Bradenton had improved its hotel and baseball facilities since the mid-1920s, but it was still quite a comedown from the lush surroundings on Catalina Island. Hornsby's salaried income represented even more of a comedown—less than 40 percent of his pay with the Cubs. And again he was just another player, theoretically subordinate even to captain Frank Frisch.

At Bradenton, it quickly became evident that Hornsby wouldn't be able to give the Cardinals nearly as much as they hoped for. Although he raised oohs and aahs with batting-practice drives into the moss-covered live oaks that ringed the unfenced outfield, and appeared in several exhibition games, he suffered from feet blisters, leg cramps, and especially a strained right Achilles tendon, apparently the legacy of years of favoring his sore heel. While the Cardinals played their way north and west across the southern states, Hornsby traveled ahead to St. Louis to see Robert Hyland, who examined the troublesome tendon and wouldn't predict when he might be ready to play.

Hornsby finally got into the lineup for the Cardinals' ninth game of the season, versus Pittsburgh at Sportsman's Park. Frank Frisch, still bitter over taking a big pay cut, was also unhappy about having to handle shortstop, not third base, as planned, because over the winter Charley Gelbert, the Cardinals' regular at that position since 1929, had nearly blown a leg off in a hunting accident. If Hornsby cheated to his right from his second-base position, then Frisch cheated to his left from shortstop; with John "Pepper" Martin, nominally an outfielder, occupying third, the St. Louis infield was decidedly porous.

Two days later Hornsby rode the bench as Dizzy Dean and other Cardinals yelled taunts and obscenities at Chicago's Guy Bush, until Bush left the game trailing by four runs. A St. Louis newspaper quoted Hornsby as accusing Charlie Grimm and Gabby Hartnett of undermining him in 1932. "Jolly Cholly" was less than jolly when he read the piece, threatening to go to the Cardinals' clubhouse and "drag Hornsby out and give him a good trimming." William Veeck advised Grimm that he wouldn't prove anything by getting into a row with "a washed-up ballplayer." Said Hornsby, "As far as anybody beating me up—well, I'll be in there playing for the Cards when we go to Chicago. . . . they'll have to take back that one about me being all washed up."[6]

On Sunday, April 30, the Cardinals moved into Wrigley Field for a doubleheader, and all the talk about bad blood between Hornsby, Grimm, and others on the two teams helped draw a rainy-day crowd of 22,000. Although they saw no fisticuffs, the Chicago fans jeered the Cardinals and particularly Hornsby through the long, wet afternoon. Unruffled, Hornsby singled and doubled in the first game, which Chicago won 7–3, then lined a two-run homer into the left-field bleachers off Pat Malone to provide the difference in St. Louis's 5–3 victory in the nightcap.

Hornsby went on to play seven more games in a row, but Street and Rickey agreed that something had to be done about the infield. Rickey negotiated a deal with Cincinnati whereby St. Louis gave up Paul Derringer, a promising right-hander, and two other players in exchange for Leo Durocher, a loud-mouthed, weak-hitting, but slick-fielding short-stop. In effect, Durocher displaced Hornsby, because, with Frisch back at second base, Street used Hornsby mostly as a pinch hitter.

In that role, he became the best in the majors. In one stretch of games in June, he made five consecutive pinch hits, including his second homer of the year in a losing effort at Philadelphia that left the Cardinals' record at 35–25. At that point they trailed Bill Terry's New York Giants by a game and a half, but by the middle of July they'd slumped to fourth.

Amid increasing talk in St. Louis and elsewhere that Street's days were numbered, J. Roy Stockton of the *Post-Dispatch* inquired whether Hornsby would like to succeed him. "I'll dig ditches before I'll take that job," declared Hornsby. "I've never undermined anybody in my life but if I'd take the Cardinal job again, I'd be branded for life."[7]

Hornsby wasn't about to close the door on anything else. On June 4, at Sportsman's Park, Phil Ball watched his listless, last-place Browns lose a doubleheader to Chicago. At one point Ball remarked to White

Sox owner Louis Comiskey, who shared his box, "I wish I had a fellow like Hornsby running this team. He'd make those fellows click their heels." "But you wouldn't get along with him," suggested Comiskey. "The hell I wouldn't," said Ball.[8] On July 19 Bill Killefer, Ball's manager since 1930, announced his resignation. Coach Allen Sothoron took over for the time being, but Hornsby's name quickly popped up as Ball's likely choice to succeed Killefer.

Meanwhile Hornsby pinch-hit and occasionally substituted for Frisch in late innings. He played second base the entire game on July 22—a loss to Boston at Sportsman's Park that dropped the Cardinals to fifth. As it happened, his one base hit in that game—a run-scoring double in the first inning off right-hander Leo Mangum—would be his last in National League competition. After forty-six games, including twenty-four pinch-hitting appearances, he was batting .325, with two home runs and twenty-one runs batted in.

Two days later, Hornsby watched as James "Tex" Carleton defeated the Braves in the first game of a doubleheader. During the break between games (the second of which was finally rained out), the Cardinals' front office issued a press release announcing Gabby Street's firing. Frisch became player-manager, under a new contract that presumably restored most or all of what had been slashed from his 1932 salary. Branch Rickey had already quietly asked waivers on Hornsby, at the same time that he arranged talks between Hornsby and Phil Ball, starting perhaps as early as the day Killefer resigned.

In a telegram to Ball, American League president William Harridge warned that Hornsby was "undesirable on certain counts," but the Browns owner remained undeterred. "Mr. Harridge means well," said Ball, "but I think he's allowed prejudiced opinion to influence him." Whether he hired Hornsby or not was "strictly a club matter."[9]

On Wednesday morning, July 26, Hornsby and Ball met again at Ball's downtown office in the Security Building. They were interrupted by a call from Rickey, who reported just hearing from National League president Heydler that Hornsby had cleared waivers. That meant the Browns, at the bottom of the American League, had first claim on player Hornsby. Ball produced a contract for three years (including the balance of 1933), which specified an annual salary of $15,000 for Hornsby's services as player and manager of the St. Louis Browns.

Philip deCatesby Ball was roundly admired by his peers, who also sympathized with his predicament. Gruff, honest, and generous, he was a little-schooled, self-made multimillionaire who built his fortune first in manufacturing and supplying ice, then in marketing refrigeration systems. After getting into baseball in the Federal League enterprise, he purchased the Browns early in 1916 and amalgamated them with his defunct Terriers. Although the Browns came within one game of a pennant in 1922 and contended in a few other seasons, usually they finished in the bottom half of the league and cost Ball a lot of money. Since 1916 the franchise had reported a dividend only five times; John E. Wray put Ball's losses since 1927 at $500,000.

Potentially the Browns were a valuable property. Ball owned Sportsman's Park (on which he'd spent $600,000 for improvements in 1925–26) and, with the purchase of the Milwaukee (American Association) and San Antonio (Texas League) franchises, had begun to build a farm system. But the whole enterprise depended ultimately on how many people paid to watch the Browns at home, and precious few had done so in recent years. Even in 1930, as overall major-league attendance reached new highs, turnouts for the sixth-place Browns were so poor that, as one observer put it, "there always is a funereal atmosphere about Sportsman's Park while a battle is in progress."[10] It was ironic that, largely because of Rogers Hornsby, St. Louis had changed from a predominantly Browns town to one predominantly Cardinals.

Ball once described his team as his hobby and "a source of relaxation. I think every business man who can afford the hobby should own a [baseball] club." But he wanted a winner, and in Hornsby, who was much like him in personality and temperament, he thought he finally had the right man. "The Browns need the driving force that Hornsby possesses," he told the press. "They'll work for him, or else. Rog has no use for the indolent, soft type of player. He demands action and usually gets it." But when he suggested to Hornsby, "This can be a great ballclub, Rog," his new manager would have none of it. "It's a lousy ballclub," said Hornsby.[11]

That it was, although the Browns numbered a few quality players. Sammy West and Carl Reynolds, both Texans obtained in a trade with Washington the previous December, and young Bruce Campbell made up a solid outfield; Oscar Melillo played a capable second base; and Irving "Bump" Hadley and George Blaeholder were pitching stalwarts. But with the possible exception of first baseman Irving "Jack" Burns, the rest of the roster consisted of players who were at best marginal big-leaguers. With a 37–54 record, the 1933 Browns trailed the rest of the league in both standings and attendance.

Hornsby acknowledged not knowing much about the American League, but "baseball is baseball in any man's league," he said as he left for Chicago to join the ballclub. On Friday morning, July 28, he introduced himself individually to his players at breakfast, then convened them in a conference room for a general get-acquainted session. "I'm going to like this job," he beamed. "We're starting from the bottom. . . . We can't move anywhere but up."[12] Idle that afternoon, the Browns won their first game under Hornsby on Saturday, when Hadley and Sammy Gray combined to limit the White Sox to two runs while St. Louis pushed across three.

The Browns won six of their first eleven games under Hornsby, including back-to-back victories over Cleveland in their first home dates since his arrival. For a while things seemed to be looking up; Hornsby, reported one local observer, "has the chins of the boys in the air, they are tagging all the bases and not taking short cuts to the clubhouse." Will Harridge, in St. Louis to honor New York's Lou Gehrig for surpassing the previous consecutive-games-played record of 1,307, now predicted better days for the Browns. With Hornsby on hand, "the St. Louis situation is more encouraging . . . than for many years."[13]

Hornsby quickly improved his catching by claiming Rollie Hemsley on waivers from Cincinnati, where Hemsley's drunken sprees had exasperated manager Owen "Donie" Bush, as they also had Jewel Ens at

Pittsburgh and, after Hornsby left the Cubs, Charlie Grimm as well. "Oh, yes, I know Rollie is supposed to be a playboy," said Hornsby indulgently. "He's a scrappy player, wants to win, and that's the kind of man I want."[14]

Yet hopes for a respectable showing in August and September proved illusory; after Hornsby took charge, the Browns won only nineteen of fifty-two games. They finished nine games behind seventh-place Boston; first place—occupied by Washington for the third (and last) time in the history of baseball in the national capital—was forty-five games distant. Although the Browns made the second-fewest errors in the league, they also yielded the second-most and scored the second-fewest runs.

Playing out the season with that "lousy club" did bring Hornsby one highly satisfying moment, on August 17 at Sportsman's Park against New York. All afternoon, the Yankees had razzed Hornsby, calling him, among other things, a washed-up National Leaguer. In the bottom of the ninth inning, the Browns trailed by two runs and were down to their last out but had two men on base. Hornsby put himself in as a pinch hitter, and when Yankees ace Vernon "Lefty" Gomez threw one within reach, he lifted it onto the pavilion roof in right-center.

As the downcast Yankees headed for their dugout exit, Hornsby trotted around the bases in a state of rare animation. "Yeah," he yelled, "this is the great National League hitter, the great Mr. Hornsby—still good enough to beat you sons-a-bitches!" (Before the next day's game, the garrulous Gomez happened by the Browns' dugout. "Hell," he kidded Hornsby, "I thought you were the on-deck batter, you were standing so far away from the plate.")[15]

Only a few thousand people were present that Saturday afternoon for Hornsby's heroics, even though the attraction was the reigning world champions: Ruth, Gehrig, and company. For the season, the Browns managed to attract slightly more than 79,000 paying customers, which, except for the abbreviated 1918 season, was the smallest attendance for any big-league franchise since the 1890s.[16] At the same time, total majors' attendance improved by nearly 30 percent over 1932 (when the sixteen clubs drew only 3.5 million); the minor leagues, bolstered by wholesale conversion to nighttime baseball and the adoption of post-season championship playoffs, had survived the worst of the Great De-pression—though reduced in number by 40 percent.

Whatever hopes Hornsby may have entertained of building a winner with Ball's money faded when Ball died in St. John's Hospital in St. Louis on October 22, his sixty-ninth birthday. The cause of death was septicemia, supposedly a result of Ball's drinking contaminated water at his vacation home in Michigan. He was survived by his wife, son, daughter, and son-in-law.[17]

For the second time in two years, Hornsby found himself deprived of the support of an owner he genuinely liked, and with whom he ex-pected to have a durable and profitable relationship. L. Carle McEvoy, Browns vice president and business manager, later said of Ball's death: "That was the club's worst break. We had a lot of thought for the future, players that could help Hornsby, but with Ball's death there no longer was a wealthy man . . . who cheerfully could take the club's losses while we tried to build up again from the bottom."[18] Ball left an estate worth nearly $2.5 million, not including Sportsman's Park; but he also left heirs whose main object was to dispose of the Browns as soon as a buyer surfaced. Moreover, his will made no provision for the Browns, so that, the following summer, it was necessary for McEvoy and Louis B. Von Weise, executor of the estate and now Browns presi-dent, to secure a probate court award for $328,992 to keep the fran-chise going.

Off-season 1933–34 was a time for retrenchment and searching for needed cash. The Milwaukee franchise was sold to a local group, leav-ing San Antonio as the Browns' sole farm club. Hornsby was at his Sportsman's Park office by 9:00 A.M. every weekday to send out letters (composed by club secretary Willis Johnson) to prospective dealers in baseball flesh. Through a succession of transactions starting that winter, Hornsby obtained funds that kept the Browns afloat, at the same time that he gave up most of the quality material he'd inherited from Bill Killefer.

Hornsby's first major deal typified how he would have to operate for the next three years. Carl Reynolds went to Boston in exchange for outfielder Smead Jolley, pitcher Ivy Andrews, and about $40,000. Hornsby then sent Jolley, shortstop Jim Levey, and pitcher Wally Hebert to Hollywood of the Pacific Coast League for shortstop Alan Strange. So the Browns came out with $40,000, a pitcher, and a rookie shortstop.

As he had the previous winter, Hornsby worked out daily at the downtown YMCA, but now he also submitted to the ministrations of "Dr." Leo J. August, a masseur who ran a St. Louis "health institute." Besides using massage and heat treatments in an effort to stretch Hornsby's Achilles tendon, August put him on a diet that involved foregoing breakfast except for a glass of milk and another of orange juice, then eating nothing until evening. Hornsby's goal (which he would never attain) was to get down to 186 pounds. "I'm more than satisfied with my own condition," he said. "Of course, I'm not tryin' to fool anybody. I know I ain't as fast as I used to be or as fast as I ought to be."[19]

Weighing about 200 pounds, Hornsby drove 400 miles from St. Louis to Hot Springs to work again in Ray Doan's baseball school. More than 100 youths showed up that February, to be instructed by "chief of staff" Hornsby as well as by George Sisler, Les Mann, Grover Cleveland Alexander, Burleigh Grimes, Lon Warneke, Dizzy Dean and his younger brother Paul (a Cardinals rookie), and others on hand at various times. Hot Springs, after its long travail without legalized gambling, was about to undergo something of a renaissance because, on March 1, 1934, Oaklawn Track reopened.

When Hornsby departed for the Browns' training site, his jammed automobile included Charley O'Leary and Grover Hartley, his new coaches; Jack Ryan, who'd left the Cardinals to scout for Hornsby; and two hopefuls from the baseball school. Covering 700 miles in seventeen hours, they arrived at West Palm Beach, Florida, and occupied rooms at the El Verano Hotel.

Overcoming real-estate crashes and destructive hurricanes and not wholly thwarted even by the Great Depression, West Palm Beach and the whole southern half of Florida had developed remarkably over the past fifteen years. With the end of national prohibition late in 1933, "sin," as many Americans still understood it, could again thrive at West Palm Beach, hand in hand with horse racing.

Aloys "Ollie" Bejma, the son of Polish immigrants from South Bend, Indiana, came up from San Antonio that spring and made the roster as an infielder. He remembered Hornsby's taking a liking to him, so much so that he invited the rookie along when he visited a local bookmaker's joint; after making a substantial bet for himself, he gave Bejma ten dollars to get down on a horse.[20]

At practice that spring, Hornsby helped Bejma and various others with their hitting, convinced that he could make big-league hitters of sub-.300 minor-leaguers. He also became convinced that Leo August's diet wasn't helping him lose weight; in fact it was diminishing his energy. By late March he'd returned to hearty breakfasts: pork chops, liver, bacon, eggs, juice, and milk. From then on, he would show no interest at all in following a diet.

Among the newcomers at West Palm Beach, two were especially impressive. Twenty-one-year-old Harlond Clift, a rare Washington State product, came up from San Antonio as a third baseman and pounded the ball all spring. Louis Newsom, a husky, boastful South Carolinian who'd received a trial two years earlier with Hornsby's Cubs, posted thirty victories in the Pacific Coast League in 1933 and became the Browns' property in the annual minor-league draft. Nicknamed "Buck" (later familiarly known as "Bobo"), Newsom was at the start of what would prove a long and extraordinarily peripatetic major-league career.

Back in St. Louis, meanwhile, the Cardinals' Sam Breadon and Browns president Louis Von Weise agreed on at least two matters: major-league baseball wasn't ready for the nighttime play that had become standard throughout the minor leagues; and, given current economic conditions, radio broadcasts of games inhibited live attendance. Despite experience to the contrary on the part of the Chicago Cubs, the

Cardinals and Browns joined most other teams in banning broadcasts of home games for the coming season.

None of that concerned Rogers Hornsby. After winning two, losing two, and tying one in the annual foul-weather series against the Cardinals, his ballclub traveled to Cleveland to open the season. Hornsby started the game at third base, then gave way to Clift in a 5–2 loss, which Newsom absorbed. Twelve years later much media attention would be given to the infield shifts employed against the Boston Red Sox's Ted Williams—first by Cleveland player-manager Lou Boudreau, then in the 1946 World Series by Cardinals manager Eddie Dyer. In fact, in that 1934 opener and whenever the Browns met Cleveland, Hornsby ordered his infielders to shift one position when the Indians' Hal Trosky or Earl Averill, both left-handed pull hitters, came to the plate.

Hornsby now wore a number on the back of his uniform, as had been the general practice since 1929 in the American League and 1933 in the National League. Queried about why he wore "11," Hornsby explained that his son Billy told him it was his lucky number. "I don't believe in it myself," disclaimed Hornsby, "but just to make him feel good I told him I would."[21] (Once school was out, Billy Hornsby appeared regularly as the Browns' batboy, proudly wearing his father's number at Sportsman's Park and accompanying the team on a midsummer road trip.)

The 1934 St. Louis Browns played good baseball over the first third of the season, reaching a peak on June 8 when their 24–20 mark put them briefly in third place. An Associated Press writer hailed Hornsby as the season's "miracle man" for taking "a bunch of fellows named Joe" and turning them into contenders, but Hornsby knew it wouldn't last. "We're hittin' over our heads," he said in mid-June. A month later, with his team in sixth place, he sputtered that instead of pitchers he had "throwers" who habitually got behind in the count and then had to put a fastball over the plate, usually with bad consequences.[22]

Things weren't going well in the Hornsbys' household, either. Their marriage had been under plenty of strain, what with Hornsby's annual job changes and the financial woes that climaxed with the loss of the farm. Hornsby continued to bet—and lose—on horse races, even though he became more cautious about his personal associates.[23] For her part, Jeannette Hornsby drank and put on weight. The glamour and big money of the 1920s were gone; now she was an early-middle-aged mother whose looks were fading, married to a man who worked for an impoverished franchise and managed a bad team. Life with the renowned "Rajah" held little excitement anymore. On July 27, 1934, she filed for divorce in St. Louis County circuit court, and although her husband shortly talked her into withdrawing the suit, their marriage remained troubled.

While Frank Frisch's Cardinals, sparked by the Dean brothers' mound brilliance, surged to their fifth pennant in nine years, the Browns floundered through the second half of the season. With much of the continent in the grip of a protracted drought that had already transformed the Great Plains into the "Dust Bowl," most afternoons at Sportsman's Park were staggeringly hot. Losing most of the time in that heat, Hornsby and his players were often out of sorts with each other. His pitchers resented having to worry about a fifty-dollar fine if they threw a strike on an 0–2 count; on one occasion Buck Newsom made that particular mistake and actually yelled at the umpire to call a ball! Newsom hadn't liked Hornsby at Catalina Island and still didn't, especially after Hornsby made him endure a twenty-hit, thirteen-run hammering at Detroit on August 9. That was one of Newsom's twenty losses for the season, including a game at Sportsman's Park on September 18 in which he held Boston to one unearned run and no hits for nine innings, only to lose the game in the tenth.

Rollie Hemsley tried Hornsby's patience again late in August when he got drunk and fought with a sailor inside a Philadelphia bar, then fought outside with a policeman who wouldn't let him drive his rented car. Awakened at 5:00 A.M., Hornsby went to magistrate's court, secured Hemsley's release, and then sent him back to St. Louis under suspension. "I'm more afraid of Hornsby than I am of the Magistrate," said the catcher.[24] Reinstated on September 1, Hemsley suffered a knee injury that ended his season for good.

Meanwhile the Browns won ten times in twelve outings, and Hornsby was talking about finishing fourth and gaining a share of the World Series money. They proceeded to lose fourteen of their next twenty games, including a September 9 doubleheader defeat by New York before some 15,000 people, the Browns' biggest home crowd in years. Most of those in attendance were drawn by a last chance to see Babe Ruth, who'd said he would retire at the end of the season.[25] After he pulled a muscle on the base paths in the first game, the Babe didn't play for the rest of the four-game series.

The Yankees finished the season in second place, seven games behind Detroit. The Browns, by losing a doubleheader to the champion Tigers, ended up sixth with a 67–85 record, two games behind Philadelphia and a game ahead of Washington (which experienced one of the most disastrous turnarounds in major-league annals). Hornsby appeared in only twenty-four games, playing a few times at third and once in right field, but performing mostly as a pinch hitter. He made seven hits, one of which was his 300th major-league home run.

After picking up $200 by lending his name to a ghostwritten daily column on the World Series (which the Cardinals won in seven games), Hornsby again settled into trade discussions. The Browns' home attendance had increased by only a few thousand; the franchise needed ready cash as much as ever. Even more, it needed a buyer. American League president Harridge publicly disapproved of a franchise's being controlled by an estate, but at $400,000, which was what Ball's heirs were said to be asking, nobody seemed interested. Hornsby, wrote John E. Wray, "feels like he is standing on a globule of mercury."[26]

Cleveland paid the Browns about $20,000 and gave up a utility infielder and a run-of-the-mill pitcher for Bruce Campbell, and Washington got Bump Hadley for cash and catcher Luke Sewell, who was then sold to Chicago. Supposedly Hornsby cleared about $30,000, but the ballclub again suffered a net loss in talent.

For the third February in a row, Hornsby ran Doan's baseball school at Hot Springs, again working with Alexander and the Deans, and also using the National League's George Barr to instruct aspiring umpires.[27] The school had acquired enough of a reputation that the 1935 enrollees included several actual professionals who'd played the previous year in lower minor leagues.

Hornsby drove into West Palm Beach on February 26. Announcing that he felt fine, he now attributed his feet and leg problems over the past two years to those off-season workouts on the hard floor of the St. Louis YMCA. But as he also acknowledged, "I'm my age—no more, no less."[28]

After losses to Brooklyn at Orlando, Florida, and Columbus, Georgia, the Browns headed for St. Louis with a 12–5 exhibition record. They dropped three of four games to the Cardinals at Sportsman's Park, where, in line with what other majors clubs were doing, the Browns had installed an electrically amplified loudspeaker system. People in every corner of the ballpark now heard the announcement of batters, pitching changes, and a variety of other information.

Newsom's luck hadn't changed; in the season opener—before some 3,500 at Sportsman's Park—he battled Cleveland's Mel Harder for fourteen innings before losing 2–1. Hornsby played the entire game at first base, handled thirteen chances errorlessly, and singled in the Browns' run. He also put in nine innings in each of the next two games, at Chicago, but then pulled up lame and gave way to Jack Burns, who'd been abed with tonsilitis.

The previous winter, when Hornsby had complained to Von Weise and McEvoy that he had too many "humpty-dumpties" and "banjo-hitters," they hadn't understood his own distinctive terminology. But as the 1935 Browns started out by losing their first ten games and twelve of their first fourteen, they understood all too well their manager's meaning. Yeah, remarked Hornsby sarcastically, the team was in a slump, "and I must say, one of the most successful slumps I've ever encountered."[29] Except for Newsom, Hornsby's pitchers were awful. Over the first fifteen games, he used forty pitchers—an extraordinary circumstance at a time when starters were usually expected to go the distance. His players were also woefully slow; it wasn't until May 30 that Ollie Bejma achieved the team's first stolen base of the year. Home attendance was the worst so far; early in May, when the Detroit Tigers left St. Louis after two games and two rain-outs, they'd amassed a total of $250 in visitors' receipts.

So the departure of marketable Browns continued. On May 21 Newsom went to Washington for $40,000 in straight cash, and George Blaeholder, one of the higher-paid Browns, was traded to Philadelphia for pitcher Merritt "Sugar" Cain and outfielder Ed Coleman. A few days later, while his team was in Boston, the "dimpled dictator of the Browns" (as sportswriter Dick Farrington called Hornsby) traded Oscar Melillo to the Red Sox for outfielder Julius "Moose" Solters and $35,000 of owner Tom Yawkey's seemingly inexhaustible wealth.[30]

Solters immediately made the trade look good by hitting a triple and two doubles, which, along with Bejma's homer over Fenway Park's high left-field wall, gave St. Louis a 6–5 victory. For the rest of the season, Solters would be the club's principal offensive threat, ending with a .330 batting average, eighteen homers, and 104 runs batted in.

Detroit's Mickey Cochrane, manager of the reigning American League champions and thus his league's field boss for the third-annual All-Star Game on July 8, chose Hornsby as one of his two coaches. Rollie Hemsley, named to replace the injured Bill Dickey of the Yankees, caught the whole game, which drew nearly 70,000 people into Cleveland's huge Municipal Stadium. The American Leaguers won 4–1, their third victory in the three years of the game's existence.

At the All-Star break the Browns were working on an eight-game losing streak; another loss when the schedule resumed made their record 19–50. Disgusted by his team's performance, Hornsby told Frank Graham in New York, "I'm running a ball club, not a popularity contest. . . . The way I look at it, too many managers baby their ball players. What for? They're grown men, aren't they? And they're supposed to play ball the best they can all the time. That's what they're up here for, ain't it?" Meanwhile Von Weise tried to allay suspicions that

Hornsby might not return for 1936: "Why, Hornsby is my boy. I have implicit confidence in him and I think he feels the same toward me."[31]

The Browns became a hard-to-beat ballclub in the second half of the season, mainly because of Solters's bat and the subsequent addition of veteran shortstop Lyn Lary (secured from Washington for Alan Strange) and second baseman Tom Carey (brought up from the International League to replace the disabled Bejma). By August 26, having won three of five games from New York to wound the Yankees' pennant chances, they'd improved their record to 43–72 and threatened to seize seventh place from Connie Mack's once-mighty Athletics.

Hemsley behaved himself, caught 139 games, batted .290, and generally played the best baseball of his nineteen-year career, but Hornsby's club included other "bad actors." One was Dick Coffman, a right-hander in his ninth big-league season, who thus far in 1935 had given up more than six earned runs per nine innings, won only five of sixteen decisions, and endured steady criticism from his manager. On the evening of September 2, as the Browns prepared to leave St. Louis for the East, Coffman downed several drinks at a bar near Union Station and weaved aboard the train. Hornsby was sitting in his compartment with coaches O'Leary and Hartley when he saw Coffman in the aisle outside the door. "I couldn't hear what he was saying," Hornsby later told Frank Graham in New York, "but I knew he was popping off." A few minutes later, Hornsby went to the dining car, ordered dinner, and then decided "there wasn't any use taking [Coffman] around the circuit."[32]

He returned to his compartment, called Coffman in, and told him to get off the train at Edwardsville, Illinois, and report to McEvoy back in St. Louis. Coffman, a considerably bigger man, followed Hornsby out into the aisle and cursed him, "so," Hornsby later said, "I belted him and knocked him into Willis Johnson's lap." Hornsby started back to the dining car, but when Coffman got up and rushed at him, they clinched and wrestled until parted by players and coaches.[33]

Put off the train, Coffman returned to St. Louis cut and bruised, complaining of a sore back, and telling everybody who would listen,

"As a manager, Hornsby is a wash-out. He's got good men on the club, but he doesn't know how to handle them—always nagging, always nagging. No wonder the team is in last place."[34] Given a ten-day suspension after McEvoy and Hornsby talked by telephone, Coffman went home to Veto, Alabama, and didn't come back.

A week later, at Philadelphia, the Browns contributed to the Athletics' thirteen-game losing streak and finally vacated the league cellar. A season-closing doubleheader loss at Cleveland gave them an overall 65–87 record, but after mid-July they won forty-three and lost only twenty-three—and probably saved Hornsby's job. Except for the repeat-champion Tigers, they set the hottest pace in the league.

Two weeks before the season ended, Hornsby met with Von Weise in New York, where the Browns president now maintained his business office, and was rewarded with a new three-year contract at $18,000 per year, plus 25 percent of franchise profits—if there ever were any. Hornsby would continue to be a rostered player, even though in 1935 he appeared in only ten games and made just five base hits.

While Detroit won the World Series from Charlie Grimm's Cubs in six games, Rogers, Jeannette, and Billy Hornsby embarked on what was undoubtedly the greatest adventure and probably the best time they ever enjoyed as a family. The Hornsbys joined an expedition of American All-Stars, bound for Mexico for ballplaying and vacationing. The group included the Athletics' Jimmie Foxx and Washington's Earl Whitehill, their wives, and nine other American Leaguers who made the trip spouseless. Organized and led by Earle Mack, Connie Mack's son and coach, the expedition departed St. Louis on October 2, on the Missouri Pacific's *Sunshine Limited.* A week later they reached Mexico City, after stopping at various places in Texas to raise expense money in games against local semipro clubs.

They were in Mexico eighteen days, during which they played sixteen games. Using a converted soccer stadium, they won seven of ten games in Mexico City from the strong Aztecas club, which bolstered itself with a couple of Texas League pitchers as well as Philadelphia Phillies infielder Jose "Chile" Gomez, a Mexican citizen. After defeating

Santa Rosa and La Liga (the latter a club of picked amateur players), they exhibited their talents on excursions into the states of Hidalgo, Puebla, and Veracruz. Besides attending several jai alai matches, they became acquainted with Mexican cuisine and generally enjoyed themselves.

Whitehill, Chicago's Ted Lyons and Vern Kennedy, and the Browns' Jack Knott did the pitching; Foxx caught and played third base; and Hornsby played second base in all sixteen games. The sports daily *La Aficion* reported that Hornsby's "style of batting, standing so far back in the box, was a matter of astonishment to the fans."[35]

The highlight of the Mexican sojourn was a three-game series in Mexico City, October 25–27, between the All-Stars and the Pittsburgh Crawfords, fresh from defeating the New York Cubans to claim the Negro National League pennant.[36] Managed by first baseman Oscar Charleston, already a legend in the Negro leagues, and featuring such standouts as catcher Josh Gibson, third baseman William "Judy" Johnson, and center fielder James "Cool Papa" Bell, the Crawfords were arguably the best team black professional baseball ever produced. Although their series with the white All-Stars in Mexico City received little publicity in North America, it was one of the outstanding black-white matchups in the era of segregated professionalism.

The first game, played before 10,000 aficionados, was an eleven-inning, 6–6 tie that ended in controversy. The All-Stars built a 4–2 lead against Crawfords ace Leroy Matlock, but in the top of the ninth Clarence "Spoony" Palm pinch-hit a two-run homer and Pittsburgh ended up scoring four times off Whitehill. Foxx then tied the game in the bottom of the ninth, homering with Henry "Heinie" Manush aboard off reliever Roosevelt Davis.

Two innings later the All-Stars loaded the bases with one out, whereupon Foxx hit a smash to Judy Johnson, who knocked the ball down and threw home to force Eric McNair. The All-Stars protested that in making the play, Johnson touched third base, which would negate the force play and necessitate Josh Gibson's tagging McNair, which he hadn't done. Consequently, the white players argued, the winning run had scored. Finally the two umpires ruled McNair forced; when play resumed with the bases still loaded, Hornsby grounded to shortstop Chester Williams, who stepped on second to force Foxx and retire the side. At that point the umpires judged it too dark to continue.

The other two games with the Crawfords were far less dramatic. Behind Knott and Lyons, the All-Stars won by scores of 11–7 and 7–2, with Hornsby singling, homering, and driving home three runs facing Harry Kincannon and Ernest Carter on the twenty-sixth, then doing the same against Bert Hunter the next day. Some of his plays at second base, enthused *La Afición,* "would doubtless have even taxed the ability of a younger Hornsby ten years ago."[37]

When they left Mexico City, Mack paid each of the All-Stars $700 plus expenses, and they made an additional $125 apiece from a stop-over game at Nuevo Laredo. In San Antonio, at the end of what he termed "a baseball missionary tour," Hornsby described Mexico as having "the grandest scenery I've ever seen . . . and the climate is ideal." Although the ballparks were too small and lacked grass, baseball had great potential in Mexico. All that was needed was "some major league players to take them in hand and teach them the fundamentals and fine points of the game."[38]

In St. Louis, Hornsby's off-season business included putting waivers on Dick Coffman. The troublesome pitcher ended up with the New York Giants, where he would win twenty-three games over the next two seasons and realize two losers' shares in back-to-back World Series against the Yankees. But major trades weren't to be had that winter—at least not by the Browns (who in truth possessed little that other clubs wanted).

"For criminy's sake," huffed Hornsby, "you'd think all these managers had outfields of nothing but Ty Cobbs and infields of nothing but world beaters, the way they talk when you want to make a trade." He guessed he'd have to wait until spring, when managers realized what "humpty-dumpty players" they really had. More broadly, he complained about what he saw as a shortage of young talent throughout Organized Baseball, which he attributed to too many youthful distractions. "Why, kids these days are more interested in riding around in an automobile and going to dances than they are in playing baseball."[39]

Hornsby at least got rid of one personal annoyance when, at the end of January 1936, Frank J. Quinn finally dropped his nine-year-old suit against Hornsby for $5,250 in unpaid legal fees. Presumably Quinn decided that, after all those years, he wouldn't be able to establish whether he'd performed services for the Hornsbys under retainer or strictly as a matter of personal friendship. He may also have come to doubt whether Hornsby still had enough money to pay a judgment—even if he did win his suit. So he gave up, "with prejudice."[40]

Early in February the Baseball Writers Association of America held the first of three polls to elect the initial class of inductees for the National Baseball Hall of Fame, which was to open at Cooperstown, New York, in 1939 in commemoration of the game's mythical centennial. One hundred seventy of 226 votes (75 percent) were necessary for election; Ty Cobb received all but four votes, seven more than Babe Ruth. With 105 votes, Hornsby placed ninth, and inasmuch as men still listed as active players were excluded from subsequent ballots, his election to the Hall of Fame would have to wait until 1942.

No doubt reflecting the general improvement of economic conditions, Ray Doan's 1936 baseball school drew a record 361 young ballplayers, with Hornsby, Sisler, Tris Speaker, and ten other past or present big-leaguers handling instructional duties. When somebody asked Hornsby how he felt about his situation in St. Louis, he said he was "having more fun" managing the Browns than he'd had with the Cardinals. Yet a remark to J. Roy Stockton earlier that winter carried a more convincing ring: "You know me. I don't get no kick out of a humpty-dumpty club."[41]

At West Palm Beach, Hornsby announced that he was glad to be rid of "dead wood and trouble-makers," looked over the thirty-seven ballplayers on hand, and predicted the Browns would "lead the second division." He preached self-confidence to Ed Coleman, working on him, according to Dick Farrington, "like a first rate psychologist."

Hornsby was "far from a back-slapper," but he was effective "in his gruff, straightforward way."[42]

The Browns often looked good in preseason play, beating other big-league clubs twelve of seventeen games and compiling an overall 21–6–1 record. After splitting a pair with the Cardinals in St. Louis, they opened the season with the veteran National Leaguer Jim Bottomley, claimed on waivers from Cincinnati, at first base and Roy "Beau" Bell, a Texas A & M graduate purchased from Galveston of the Texas League, in left field in place of the hobbled Solters.

Bell and Coleman homered in the season opener at Chicago, but Ivy Andrews blew a lead and the White Sox won 7–6. The next day Jack Knott did the same thing, with young Monty Stratton getting the win for Chicago. At most, 1,500 people showed up on April 17 for the Browns' chilly home opener, which they lost to Cleveland, 13–10 in ten innings. After losing three more games, they finally won one at Detroit, then lost the remaining eleven games of that road trip and another two when they returned home.

Desperate for pitching, Hornsby traded Jack Burns to Detroit (which was equally desperate for a first-base replacement for the injured Hank Greenberg), in exchange for left-hander Elon Hogsett plus $17,500. Hogsett became one of Hornsby's starters, but he was battered regularly and did little to improve the mound staff. Even less help was right-hander Les Tietje, swapped by Chicago for Merritt Cain. Besides an intense dislike for his new manager, Tietje also developed an arthritic condition that made him useless the last half of the season.

Although he praised his players' hustle, Hornsby admitted that "the pitching was worse than I thought."[43] It didn't help his disposition—or that of the Browns' dwindling fandom—when former Brown Buck Newsom struck out eleven in handing Hornsby's club its twenty-third loss in twenty-seven games.

That was on May 15. Six days later, at Detroit, Hornsby hit a pinch single in the ninth inning to score Hemsley with the winning run. That victory completed a three-game sweep of the world's champions and improved the Browns' record to 11–30. Although they were still buried in last place, at least the $15,000 in visitors' receipts they took out of Detroit would pay the bills for a while.

"I ain't so young as I used to be," said the forty-year-old manager after his second—and last—appearance of the season on June 9, when he played in place of the lame-backed Bottomley at New York and drew a walk to force in the winning run. Citing the 186 runs recently scored in one day, he complained that major-league baseball was "verging on bush league stuff. . . . There isn't any chance for scientific baseball."[44]

Determined to make his players keep their minds on business during that road trip, Hornsby prohibited card playing not only in dressing rooms but on trains and at hotels. While the other Browns griped but at least stayed sober, Rollie Hemsley, put out of action by a split finger, boarded the train from Boston in a painless condition and proceeded to amuse himself by dropping lighted matches into teammates' Pullman berths. Hailed before Hornsby and McEvoy back in St. Louis, Hemsley drew a week's suspension and a fine that, by Les Tietje's recollection, amounted to $1,500. "I'm surprised Rollie didn't kill Hornsby," Tietje said.[45]

Hemsley, though, never lost his admiration for Hornsby, or Hornsby his fondness for the ne'er-do-well Ohioan. Earlier in the season, when Sid Keener had asked about Hornsby's reputation for toughness, the catcher replied, "Hornsby tough? He's made me what I am."[46] Again he was the only Brown named to that year's American League All-Star team.

With a 23–47 record at the All-Star break, the Browns still had last place all to themselves. Their home attendance, like that for most other teams, was running well ahead of 1935, even though, for the third straight summer, most of the United States suffered from drought and reeled under ghastly heat.[47]

Louis Von Weise came into St. Louis in mid-August and watched his first home game of the year. As local reporters listened incredulously, he maintained that the franchise was sound because Ball had built a reserve fund in the 1920s, and "at no time have we sold a player because we needed cash." As for Hornsby, with two more years to go on his contract, "we are satisfied with his leadership."[48]

All that was strictly for public consumption; in fact Von Weise and McEvoy were far from satisfied. During the Browns' recent stopover in New York, Von Weise had talked with several St. Louis players and heard a chorus of complaints about the manager. On the trip east, he was told, four players (never named but probably Solters, Lary, Andrews, and reserve outfielder Ray Pepper) stood outside the door of Hornsby's Pullman compartment and yelled for him to come out. Presumably afraid, Hornsby refused to open the door. (The story didn't appear in print until the following October; when it did, Hornsby denied the whole thing. If some people were outside his door, he said, "they must have been whisperin' or I would have had enough curiosity to go out and see how tough they were. . . . Maybe they was back in the buffet car, guzzlin' a bottle of beer.")[49]

In St. Louis, Von Weise talked with Hornsby about that night on the train and how and when the Browns' fortunes might improve. If Von Weise didn't like the way he was running the team, offered Hornsby, "then you can pay me and I'll be on my way."[50] Therein, of course, lay the difficulty: if Hornsby were fired, the financially strapped franchise would still owe him $36,000 on the remaining two years of his contract.

With McEvoy's connivance, Von Weise undertook to force Hornsby out. For the remainder of the season, McEvoy (like William Veeck four years earlier) refused to reserve a Pullman compartment for Hornsby, who had to be content with a lower berth. Hornsby also found that he was being billed for complimentary tickets left for acquaintances at the Sportsman's Park pass gate. The Browns club officials went so far as to hire private detectives to gather evidence on Hornsby's betting habits, which the franchise's attorney then presented to Commissioner Landis in Chicago, in the hope that Landis might do something about Hornsby's contract. Landis's response was that the Browns had known all about Hornsby before they hired him; he was their problem, not the commissioner's. So, because the ballclub couldn't afford to fire him and he couldn't afford to quit, Hornsby stayed on.

On August 23, at Cleveland's League Park, the Browns helped make baseball history when they faced seventeen-year-old Bobby Feller, who'd just completed his junior year at Van Meter (Iowa) High School. In his first big-league start, with a crowd of about 8,500 on hand, the youth went the distance and gained a 4–1 victory. What made the game historic was that Feller threw his fastball past fifteen Browns, thereby coming within one strikeout of Rube Waddell's American League record (set in 1908) and within two of Dizzy Dean's total in 1933. Two weeks later, at League Park, Feller again subdued the Browns, pitching his second complete game and striking out ten. It was the beginning of one of baseball's most spectacular mound careers.

Feller wasn't working against a weak Browns batting order; that season they batted .279 as a team and scored more than 800 runs. Solters batted in 134; Harlond Clift topped .300 and hit twenty homers; and Beau Bell, who credited Hornsby with teaching him how to hit to all fields, emerged as one of the league's most dangerous batters, averaging .344 and driving home 123 teammates. It was the Browns' "throwers," whose collective 6.24 earned run average was the highest in the majors, that kept the team submerged.

Another September collapse pushed Philadelphia's losses to an even 100 games and again prevented Hornsby's club from finishing last. After being rained out of the second game of a doubleheader at Chicago, the Browns ended the season at 57–95, a staggering sixteen games behind sixth-place Boston. With consummate hypocrisy, Von Weise said in New York, "we are not holding Hornsby responsible for the Browns' failure to do better."[51]

That fall, Phil Ball's heirs finally unburdened themselves of the St. Louis Browns. Branch Rickey served as agent for the estate in arranging the Browns' sale to forty-two-year-old Donald L. Barnes, a six-year resident of St. Louis who controlled a string of loan companies from New York State to Missouri. Another key figure in bringing about the deal was William O. DeWitt, Rickey's longtime assistant, who persuaded Barnes to take the plunge—and to give DeWitt a share in the ownership as general manager.[52]

On November 7 Barnes and DeWitt completed their negotiations with William O. Cady, Phil Ball's son-in-law, who managed the family's business. Barnes paid $325,000 for the franchise, which included an 80 percent interest in the Texas League San Antonio Missions. Sportsman's Park remained the property of the family-controlled Dodier Realty Company, so that henceforth both St. Louis teams would be renters—the Browns at $30,000 a year, the Cardinals at $35,000. For his services, Rickey came away with a $25,000 commission.

Barnes warmly described Hornsby as a definite asset to the franchise. "They can rant and tear Hornsby to pieces," he went on, "but I'm sold on him. . . . In spite of his admitted lack of tact, here and there, he knows how to run a ball team." The people who'd been in charge of the Browns hadn't given Hornsby "the right kind of disciplinary support," but things would be different now. For his part, Hornsby dared anybody to say he'd neglected his job. He wanted to stay on, but "I am what I am and I ain't one to pretend. . . . If they want me as I am, I'll be pleased to go ahead with the job, but nobody's going to dictate to me about how I'm going to enjoy myself."[53]

One might have read potential trouble into Hornsby's pronouncement, but everything was bright and cozy when he met with Barnes and DeWitt at Barnes's Chesterfield, Missouri, country place shortly before Thanksgiving. Hornsby thanked Barnes for the flowers he'd sent Jeannette Hornsby during a recent hospital stay, and then agreed to a new two-year contract for a total of $18,333 per year. Hornsby would receive nothing from whatever profits that might materialize, because, said Barnes, "he didn't think he was entitled to any profits that the new owners of the Browns might make through their efforts."[54] At the same time, Barnes inserted an intricately worded clause whereby he could avoid paying off Hornsby's contract—if the manager's services were terminated.

The new owners began ambitiously but in some frustration. Barnes and DeWitt were interested in night baseball, and by now so were Sam

Breadon and Branch Rickey. Both St. Louis clubs received authorization from their leagues to play up to seven home dates at night, but Barnes and Breadon deadlocked on how much each would pay toward the installation of a lighting system. So for 1937 the Cincinnati Reds, who'd inaugurated night ball in the majors two years earlier, would continue to be the only team in either league playing part of its home schedule under lights.

DeWitt quickly undertook to develop a farm system for the Browns, as his mentor Rickey did for the Cardinals starting in the early 1920s, and as other major-league franchises, most notably the Yankees, had been doing in the Depression years. Although the Browns couldn't afford to buy controlling interests, within six months DeWitt had signed working agreements with a dozen minor-league clubs.

Assured he would continue to have a free hand in player dispositions, Hornsby sold Ray Pepper's contract to Buffalo and exercised waiver claims on outfielder Ethan Allen, who carried a .300 batting average after eleven National League seasons. The Browns manager then got rid of Solters, Lary, and Andrews—"real playboys," as he termed them; "problem players," in John E. Wray's words.[55] All three were traded to Cleveland in an even-up swap for outfielder Joe Vosmik, pitcher Oral Hildebrand, and infielder Bill Knickerbocker. The key man in the trade for the Browns was Vosmik, who'd enjoyed several strong seasons for the Indians and, although he slumped in 1936, was only twenty-six. The addition of the Cleveland native to a batting order that would include Allen, Sammy West, Harlond Clift, Beau Bell, Jim Bottomley, and occasionally Hornsby was expected to make the St. Louis offense more potent than ever.

Hornsby also persuaded Barnes and DeWitt to move spring training to San Antonio, his favorite preseason haunt, and to give his fifty-two-year-old brother Everett a job scouting the Oklahoma-Arkansas-Missouri area.

Following his annual two-week instructional stint for Ray Doan, Hornsby, accompanied by Charley O'Leary and Grover Hartley, caught the Missouri Pacific at Benton, Arkansas, for San Antonio. At city-owned Tech Field, Maurice O. Shevlin, sports editor of the *St. Louis Globe-Democrat,* found "serenity and a feeling that the Browns are going somewhere this season." Barnes and DeWitt arrived and told the assembled players that Hornsby enjoyed absolute front-office support; Clift and Bell settled their salary demands for about $7,000 apiece; and Hornsby expressed delight that, with new owners and money in the club's treasury, "I don't have to peddle my stars to meet expenses."[56]

An extraordinary number of Browns brought their wives and children to spring training and installed them (at the players' expense) at the Hotel Menger, where the Browns stayed. That situation didn't please Hornsby a bit. "Women are never no help around the ball club," he growled. "Wives don't do no good." On the ballfield, he had no time for anything but baseball. When a newsreel cameraman asked him to stay past two o'clock the next day so that Texas Governor James V. Allred could be filmed with Hornsby and his players, the native Texan snapped, "If the Governor's out there at two o'clock, we'll be there, but not much later." But couldn't the Browns use some free publicity? "Publicity never won a pennant," said Hornsby. "Have the Governor there on time."[57]

John E. Wray noted that although city officials had recently shut down establishments known for their high-stakes card games, plenty of slot machines, bingo sessions, and barely disguised bookmaking joints were available; moreover, enforcement of Texas's postprohibition laws—which legalized beer but not liquor by the drink—was "about as active as a chicken with the pip." Few cities surpassed San Antonio in cuisine. At a chamber of commerce dinner at the Casa Rio restaurant, Wray and most of the rest of the Browns' contingent found the *muy picante* feast daunting, but not the St. Louis manager. "Gimme some more of that stuff," he said delightedly. "What's the matter with you guys, can't you take it?"[58]

Availing himself of salt baths and rubdowns after practices, Hornsby attested that his feet and legs felt fine. His new bosses had made it plain that he should play as much as possible to promote exhibition-game receipts, as well as attendance in the early part of the season. So, still using the three-finger glove the Wilson sporting goods firm had marketed in his name for the past ten years, he appeared in nearly every preseason game. Getting to those games involved much arduous travel by bus—accompanied by breakdowns, flat tires, and other delays—to Harlingen, Laredo, and other places along the Rio Grande.

At Lockhart, scene of Hornsby's now-famous "farming out," the Browns played an intrasquad game so that their manager could visit with his uncle H. T. Rainey and family. (The game was sponsored by the local American Legion post, which was named for Hornsby's cousin, killed in France in the last war.) At Austin, where the Browns played the University of Texas, Hornsby and Bell were honored in a ceremony at home plate. "After it was over," recounted Wray, "they gave him a book—something he seldom reads—and a four-quart hat, which he'll never wear."[59]

After he singled and doubled and turned three double plays in a ten-inning victory over the Chicago Cubs at Fort Worth, Hornsby pronounced himself ready to play a lot: "This ain't braggin'; it's just giving you the lowdown on what I think of myself as the Browns' second baseman."[60]

Following a two-game sweep of the Cardinals in the annual spring series, the Browns drew their biggest opening-day crowd since pre-Depression days—about 7,500. If that turnout betokened better times economically in the St. Louis area, it also indicated higher expectations for the Browns under their new ownership. Especially for fans who loved slugfests, it was a happy occasion, with the locals battering Chicago 15–10 and Hornsby singling twice and lining a pitch from Vern Kennedy into the center-field bleachers, 430 feet away. After three more games—another at home and two at Cleveland—Hornsby sat down in favor of Tom Carey, and from then on, regardless of front-office wishes, he was willing to play only when it wasn't cold and the ground was dry.

Following a promising start at home and in the western cities, the Browns went east, lost thirteen of fifteen games (including a no-hitter to Chicago's Bill Dietrich), and settled into last place. As expected, the everyday lineup registered plenty of base hits; early in June, the team average was .290, with Bell among the league's best at .377. But Hornsby's pitchers, whose average age was thirty, were as ineffective as ever. "I've got a lot of softball pitchers," he protested. "They can't put anything on the ball and what's worse, they can't get their pitches near the plate."[61] Barnes was along on that first eastern trip—ostensibly to acquaint himself with the ins and outs of his club's operations—but people familiar with Hornsby's managerial career might have taken that as an ominous sign.

By mid-June the Browns had drawn some 73,000 to Sportsman's Park, but they'd managed to win only a third of their forty-five games. On their second trip into New York, a local writer quoted Hornsby as saying that, aside from Clift, nobody on his team hit with power—that he couldn't win with "banjo-hitters." When fans in Boston greeted the Browns with chants of "banjo-hitters," Hornsby repudiated the interview to both Barnes (who was again traveling with the ballclub) and his team. Later, back in St. Louis, he denied that he would "put the slug" on any of his players. Asked about rumors that Bottomley was about to succeed Hornsby, Barnes sounded eminently supportive: "There are a few snipers here in St. Louis who welcome every chance to take a shot at Hornsby. But he has been one-hundred per cent with us and we are backing him the same way."[62]

In the meantime Hornsby had to deal with Rollie Hemsley's regular fall from grace. In Cleveland, Hemsley boarded the train well under the influence and busied himself with a knitting kit he'd picked up somewhere. Unamused, Hornsby received Barnes's approval for a ten-day suspension. Hemsley was back behind the plate on July 14, when Boston's Buck Newsom overcame Clift's seventeenth home run and won his fifth straight game since coming to the Red Sox from Washington six weeks earlier.

A couple of hours before the next day's game, feeling good and having little to do, Newsom strolled around Sportsman's Park and happened upon Hornsby talking on a pay telephone and getting what was obviously some hot betting information. What Newsom heard was one

end of a conversation with a jockey named Martin, who rode at Fairmount Park near Collinsville, Illinois. As Hornsby himself remembered
it twenty-five years later, he and Martin had both invested in a horse
named Quince King, who was up in years but still known as an excellent "mudder." When Martin reported that the Fairmount track was
deep in mud, Hornsby went across the street to a Grand Boulevard
bookmaking joint. As Les Tietje remembered his betting practices, "He
wouldn't bet a two-dollar bet, it was always $100, $100, $100 across
the board."[63]

On this particular occasion, Hornsby went a lot deeper: "I had
$1,000 across the board for myself and $100 across for Martin [on
Quince King]. . . . At the first [quarter-mile] call he was 10 lengths in
front and he won in a romp." At $44–1 to win, $22–1 to place, and
$8–1 to show, Hornsby collected about $35,000 from his distraught
bookmaker—his biggest winnings ever.[64] (Newsom, who followed
Hornsby from the ballpark to the bookmaker, hurriedly got down on
Hornsby's horse and made a nice killing of his own.)

That grand score proved Hornsby's undoing in his relations with
Donald Barnes. The previous fall, Barnes had talked him into borrowing money to invest in Barnes's loan enterprises. On the morning of
July 16, when Hornsby walked into Barnes's Sportsman's Park office
with a cashier's check for $4,000 to pay the balance on the loan, the
Browns president refused to accept it on the grounds that it had been
gained through gambling. When Hornsby protested that he "won it fair
and square," Barnes pointed out that it came from a bookmaker. "Hell,"
exploded Hornsby, "I never promised anybody I wouldn't play
horses. . . . The money is as good as the money you take from people
in the loan-shark business. It's better than taking interest from widows
and orphans."[65]

That about did it. Four days later, Hornsby pinch-hit for Tom Carey
in the tenth inning of the first game of a doubleheader with the Yankees at Sportsman's Park. With the bases full, he tapped a pitch from
rookie Frank Makossky into a force play at home plate, after which
Ethan Allen flied to right fielder Tommy Henrich, who threw home to

213

double up Bill Knickerbocker, trying to score from third, and give New York a 5–4 win. After another loss in the nightcap, the Browns' record tumbled to 25–52.

Late the next morning, July 21, Hornsby showed up at Sportsman's Park as usual, took note of local press people on hand, and encountered Bill DeWitt, who steered him into Barnes's office. A few minutes later, Barnes came out to read a typewritten statement in the form of a notification to Hornsby that his contract was "hereby canceled and terminated as of this date," and that coaches O'Leary and Hartley and scout Everett Hornsby were dismissed as well. Jim Bottomley, added Barnes, would be the new Browns manager. Pressed about Hornsby's firing, Barnes would only add, "Well, just say he was released for cause. Draw your own conclusions." Tommy Heath, a Browns utility first baseman-outfielder, remembered that "quite a lot of happiness spread around the clubhouse when we heard the news."[66]

In a written statement, Hornsby protested, "My betting at no time interfered with my handling of the club," then admitted that "while my contract did not forbid betting on horse races, both Mr. Barnes and Mr. DeWitt have objected to my doing so." Had he been fired for gambling? "Aw, they always bring that up," said Hornsby. "That's the theme song, so let 'em sing it if they want to."[67]

Again Hornsby refused to acknowledge that his betting habits could always serve as a reason to fire him—if and when an owner felt so inclined. It soon came out that, like Von Weise and McEvoy, Barnes had hired "spotters" to report on Hornsby's movements on the road and in St. Louis. The Browns' president also talked personally to various people, including Milton "Alabam' " Delmas, clubhouse boy for the Browns, who denied ever placing bets for Hornsby. Delmas went on to say, though, that he frequently made bets for visiting players. "The first thing I know," said Delmas, "I became the betting runner for almost every team that came here."[68]

Hornsby conferred with John M. Lashly, his current attorney, who advised him that, given the provisions in the contract he'd signed the previous November, he ought to settle for whatever Barnes was willing to give him. On July 23 Barnes agreed to pay his ex-manager $7,500 (roughly the balance of his salary for 1937)—and Hornsby took it. Said Lashly, "There is no doubt that betting was at the bottom of [Hornsby's] dismissal." Added Barnes unctuously, "We have the kindliest of feeling toward Rogers and wish him every success in his future activities."[69]

"So a gallant old figure stands waiting for the lightning to strike again," commented Dick Farrington. "Where he will go he doesn't know. . . . It marks a tragic finale to a man who has meant so much to the game."[70] Farrington's epitaph—if that's what it was intended to be—would prove wonderfully premature.

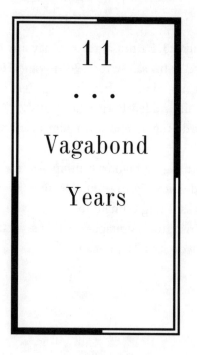

11

· · ·

Vagabond

Years

H ornsby's big winnings on Quince King at Collinsville and the $7,500 buyout by the Browns provided a temporary financial cushion, but he had little to show for a salaried baseball income that, over twenty-three years, approached $500,000.[1] Given past bad investments, persistent profligacy with the horses, and the affluent lifestyle the Hornsbys took for granted, he had to have a job—some kind of baseball job. Again he turned to Branch Rickey, but this time Rickey had to tell him, what with Dizzy Dean out of commission and the Cardinals floundering, "I've got troubles of my own." There was just no way he could help.[2]

Hornsby never officially retired as a player; his name had appeared on the active roster of every team he managed. In 1937, in fact, he was at second base in seventeen of the seventy-seven games the Browns played up to his firing. He wielded his bat with effect, too, hitting .321 in fifty-six trips to the plate, with a home run and eleven runs batted in. Forty years later, some American League ballclub would doubtless have taken him on as a designated hitter; but in an era when all nine players had to field a position as well as swing a bat, nobody wanted a wide-girthed, sore-legged, forty-one-year-old, regardless of what glories he'd known in younger days.

So Hornsby had played his last big-league baseball. At the end, only Ty Cobb (at .367) surpassed his .358 lifetime batting average, and he was ahead of all National Leaguers in home runs (297), runs batted in (1,549), and extra-base hits (1,765).[3] In the National League's records, he trailed only Honus Wagner in runs scored and base hits. Besides the highest season's batting average for either league since 1897, he also held the National League record for most bases-loaded home runs (12) and the "modern" league record for consecutive games with safe hits (33). On several occasions during his last spring training with the Browns, Hornsby had mentioned that he would like to reach 3,000 base hits (although as yet that figure hadn't acquired the magical connotation it would have for later generations of ballplayers, fans, and Hall of Fame electors). Had he remained the St. Louis Browns' player-manager for another season or so, he might have made it; as it was, he ended up seventy hits short.

If nobody in the majors wanted Hornsby that summer of 1937, others elsewhere did—at least on a short-term basis. The *Denver Post*'s annual semipro baseball tournament had acquired considerable national stature in the 1930s, because many ballplayers who would have been full-time professionals if not for the Depression-driven contraction of the minor leagues now picked up money performing for hundreds of business-sponsored teams across the county. Once Hornsby became available, the Bay Refiners, based in Denver, sought to strengthen their chances in the sixteen-team *Post* tournament by hiring him for $500 per game. It was a considerable comedown, but Hornsby could use the money and, for the moment, had no better prospects.

Grover Cleveland Alexander, in considerably worse circumstances, managed the Springfield, Illinois, Empires; an oil-company outfit from Pampa, Texas, featured third baseman Sammy Baugh, better known as a football All-American at Texas Christian University. A group of Negro leaguers who'd just won the Dominican Republic championship for dictator Rafael Trujillo, led by Satchel Paige and featuring such notables as Josh Gibson and Cool Papa Bell, entered the *Post* tournament as the Ciudad Trujillo team.

Paige, Gibson, Bell, and company—some of the best ballplayers in the world—swept through the tournament and claimed the $14,000 prize money. Hornsby, experiencing his first nighttime baseball, earned the $1,500 the Bay Refiners paid him, homering in a 25–0 massacre of a team from Worland, Wyoming, then singling and doubling twice in a ten-inning victory over Alexander's club. In the semifinal game, Bob Griffith of Ciudad Trujillo struck him out three times, as the black stars pounded the Bay Refiners 12–0. After that, Hornsby did what most Americans in 1937 would have considered a daring thing—he took a commercial airliner from Denver back to St. Louis.[4]

While Jim Bottomley managed the Browns to a 21–56 record for the balance of 1937 and then received his notice after the ballclub's worst season in twenty-six years, Hornsby sought some kind of long-term employment.[5] Nothing turned up at the National Association convention in Milwaukee early in December or at the annual major-league gathering in Chicago a week later. Informed that Commissioner Landis wanted to see him (presumably about the circumstances of his dismissal by the Browns), Hornsby dutifully went to Landis's Chicago office suite, where he was met by Leslie O'Connor, the commissioner's secretary. The judge, said O'Connor, had instructed him to take Hornsby's statement. Nothing doing, Hornsby told O'Connor; he'd talk to Landis or nobody. "The Judge didn't send back no word to me," as Hornsby later told it, "so after a few minutes I left his office, and from that day on I never talked to him."[6]

"Why are they always pickin' on me?" Hornsby asked his longtime confidant Sid Keener, now sports editor of the St. Louis *Star-Times.* "I get tips on the horses," he pointed out, "and yet club owners pass out tips on stocks listed on Wall Street." "My gambling," he continued, "has never interfered with my playing on the ball field or in managing a ball club. . . . I've won many games with a base hit in the pinch on days when I lost a chunk of money with a bookmaker."[7]

Perhaps so, but for the present the only thing Hornsby had going was Ray Doan's baseball school at Hot Springs, where he again tried to teach enthusiastic youngsters how to play the game—and again took his percentage of the school's receipts. When it was over, he picked up a few dollars in Chicago as guest speaker before the annual convention of the American Society of Bakery Engineers. Young players weren't as strong as they used to be, he told his unlikely audience, because they "smoke, drink and carouse much more than they used to."[8]

From Chicago he drove to Daytona Beach, Florida, where owner Mike Kelley of the Minneapolis Millers, of the Class AA American Association, hired him as a spring-training batting coach, although Hornsby also hoped to hire on as manager Donie Bush's adjutant for the full season. Dick Hackenberry, then covering the Millers for a Minneapolis newspaper, remembered Hornsby's arriving in a rumpled suit, with the heels of his socks worn through. Over the next couple of weeks, Hackenberry drove him several times to a local bookie joint. Hornsby's presence made Bush thoroughly uncomfortable; at one point the Millers' manager told Hackenberry, "I don't need this guy. If he stays another day, it's between me and him who Mike wants to run this club. I'm fed up with him here."[9]

Hornsby, generally conceded to be the greatest right-hand hitter of all time, made little impression on a tall, spindly, left-hand-batting nineteen-year-old named Ted Williams, who, by many later estimates, became baseball's greatest hitter—period. A half century later, Williams remembered nothing Hornsby had told him, except the commonplace wisdom to get the pitch he could hit best, not the pitcher's best. About to start a 1938 season in which he pummeled American Association pitchers for a .366 average, forty-three home runs, and 142 runs batted in, Williams neither needed nor wanted Hornsby's coaching.

Finally something came through for Hornsby—a job as player-coach with the Baltimore Orioles of the International League at $5,000 for the coming season. Baltimore business manager John Ogden, who'd pitched against Hornsby in the National League, held no illusions about

Hornsby's intentions. "Rog will be with us until a better job presents itself," he said.[10]

Since the doldrums of 1933, when only fourteen leagues completed the season, the minors had undergone a renaissance; thirty-seven circuits would complete their schedules in 1938, and that year Jersey City set a new International League attendance record, drawing 337,000 despite finishing seventh. Part of the reason for the minors' comeback was the shift to night baseball, in Baltimore and nearly everywhere else. For the rest of his life, most of the baseball Hornsby saw would be played under the lights.

Although he held active-player status, Hornsby found himself with little to do if he didn't want to interfere with catcher-manager Clyde "Bucky" Crouse. He appeared in sixteen games—mostly as a pinch hitter—and hit safely only twice. Most International Leaguers viewed Hornsby with indifference, if they even knew him. After he struck out Hornsby with the bases loaded, Montreal's Dick Porter was asked if he realized who that was. "Sure," said Porter. "He's Baltimore's third base coach."[11]

Early in June, Hornsby decided he'd had enough of Baltimore and signed to manage the remainder of the 1938 season for the Southern Association's Chattanooga Lookouts—now classified by the National Association as being one and one-half rungs below the majors at Class 1A—for the same salary he'd been receiving with the Orioles.[12]

In joining Chattanooga, Hornsby had to accommodate to the whatever-sells-tickets ethic of his new boss, the zany, flamboyant Joe Engel. A forty-five-year-old former big-league pitcher, Engel headed a syndicate that had purchased the Chattanooga franchise from Washington owner Clark Griffith. Operating independently, Engel attracted crowds by such productions as a "wild elephant hunt," which featured local black youths wearing loincloths, carrying spears, dancing to tom-toms, and herding six canvas-bedecked "elephants" into a circle, where six "hunters" shot them with blank pellets. After that extravaganza, a costumed ostrich laid an egg on second base; Engel then led a costumed duck to the spot to deposit an egg twice as large.

Clearly, Hornsby's days with such a man would be limited. On June 27 he arrived in Chattanooga and signed a contract with Engel, who candidly acknowledged that he wanted Hornsby for his box-office appeal. Hornsby went along with Engel to a certain extent, such as accompanying the Lookouts' president to the city jail to be photographed presenting a birthday cake to inmate Virginia Winston in her cell, as well as accepting a "gift" at home plate of a swaybacked mule that supposedly signified Hornsby's "old gray mare" status. Yet Hornsby hadn't lost any of his renowned bluntness. Named honorary mayor by the Chattanooga city council in still another home-plate ceremony, Hornsby told the crowd (and his assembled players), "I'm in favor of floating a bond issue to buy a couple of pitchers."[13]

Neither the bond issue nor much help otherwise was forthcoming, although Pat Malone, just released by Baltimore, joined his old Chicago boss and pitched effectively for the rest of the season. At the end of the schedule, Chattanooga was in sixth place with a 66–85 record. Hornsby twice put himself on display in pinch-hitting roles, homering at Lookout Field before 5,000 on one of Engel's numerous promotional nights, then singling in the season finale at Atlanta.

From Chattanooga, Hornsby returned to Baltimore, where John Ogden hired him to replace Bucky Crouse as Orioles manager for 1939. Some estimated his salary at $10,000, which was probably at least $2,000 more than it really was. Kiki Cuyler, Hornsby's onetime teammate, succeeded him as Chattanooga manager.[14]

A few weeks later, Hornsby wrangled a press pass for the first two Yankees-Cubs World Series games at Wrigley Field in Chicago, but when Landis heard about that, he immediately ordered the pass withdrawn. "Maybe the Judge thought I was trying to chisel my way in," remarked Hornsby, "but he's wrong. . . . I don't know if Landis was trying to block me because I bet on horse races."[15] After the second game (of a Yankees sweep), he returned to St. Louis.

That December the *Sporting News* published Hornsby's reflections on his experiences in baseball, as set down by Dick Farrington. He didn't want "to sound like a squawk," he said, "because everybody knows I can take it. Besides, I don't like a cry-baby." Yet in fact he squawked at some length, especially over accusations that he couldn't get along with anybody, that he'd undermined various managers, and that his betting got in the way of his baseball. Although critics depicted him "as a hard guy, a bull-dozer and a self-centered mug," he'd actually saved Branch Rickey's managing job in the spring of 1925, and when he agreed to manage teams had often done so reluctantly. As for his troubles with club executives, "if some of the fellows who think they know it all, would keep their noses out of the managerial end, which they know nothing about, baseball would be a lots better off." On his horseplaying: "Never—get that—never has my wagering in any way interfered with my affairs on the diamond. . . . The races have cost me a lot of money, it is true, but it's my dough and as a free-born American citizen, I can do what I want with it. . . . It's the only real fun I get—betting on the horses."[16]

That winter the *Sporting News* also carried weekly advertisements for the Rogers Hornsby Baseball College, which would be held at Hot Springs from February 15 to March 3. Ray Doan and Hornsby had parted ways, Doan inaugurating a new baseball school at Jackson, Mississippi, and Hornsby taking over Hot Springs as his exclusive operation. Soon the two camps were issuing rival claims about size, cost, duration, and quality of instruction. Ray Doan's Original All-Star Baseball School, founded on "six years of successful operation," charged only forty dollars for six weeks, claimed to have enrolled 250, and featured Babe Ruth, Dizzy Dean, Gabby Street, and Burleigh Grimes. Although Hornsby's full tuition was fifty dollars, he also advertised a special four-week course for thirty-five dollars, plus instruction by himself and, among others, Lon Warneke, Earle Mack, and former National and Federal Leaguer Benny Meyer. An added attraction at Hornsby's camp was the presence of seventeen members of his Baltimore team, who in effect did their spring training at Hot Springs. While his school (which enrolled about 100) wasn't "a haven for autograph-seekers," his people, said Hornsby, knew how to teach fundamentals and get along with boys.[17]

Once the baseball-school war ended, Hornsby could gather his forces in Baltimore to start the International League season. Going against the trend throughout the minors toward major-league tie-ups, Baltimore continued to operate as an independent franchise under John Ogden's front-office direction and the ownership of the Dunn family. Again Baltimore would find it hard to compete with the league's farm clubs, especially the Newark Bears and Rochester Red Wings, owned outright by the New York Yankees and St. Louis Cardinals, respectively.

For 1939 Hornsby decided to stay on the sidelines altogether and do the best he could with weak pitching and a shaky infield. After playing at around the .500 mark over the first third of the season, the Orioles slumped to sixth place and remained there, finishing ahead of Toronto and Montreal (also both independents). It was perhaps the least-interesting season of baseball Hornsby had ever been part of.

Hornsby's future at Baltimore was in doubt as early as August, when Ogden announced that he was leaving the Orioles at the end of the year to become the Philadelphia Phillies' business manager. Informed by the Dunn family that he wouldn't be needed next season, Hornsby talked with club officials at Syracuse and also at Montreal, where Branch Rickey put in a word for him with Royals president Hector Racine. But the Syracuse job went to somebody else, and Racine, whose franchise had recently come under the control of the Brooklyn Dodgers, had to comply with the preference of Dodgers' front-office boss Larry MacPhail for Clyde Sukeforth. At the annual National Association and major-league meetings late in 1939, Hornsby's job search was equally unproductive, so as he traveled to Hot Springs to reopen his baseball school, he lacked employment prospects in Organized Baseball for the first time since he was eighteen years old.

After the school ended, Hornsby covered expenses for rent and food, gave his instructors what they were due, pocketed the $500 or so that was left, and effectively joined the approximately nine million Americans still jobless after a decade of the Great Depression and seven years of the New Deal's multifaceted recovery efforts. Then, early in June, he received a telephone call from John Holland, president of the Oklahoma

City Indians of the Class IA Texas League, asking him to succeed manager–first baseman Jim Keesey. Hornsby didn't have to think it over; he packed quickly, said good-bye to his wife and son, and drove into Oklahoma City early Sunday morning, June 9. A couple of hours later he met with Holland and business manager Jimmy Humphries, and signed a contract specifying $1,000 per month for what remained of the season.

That afternoon 3,000 fans came out to see Hornsby and cheer the Indians as they swept a doubleheader from Dallas and vacated last place. Given a standing ovation as he left the field, Hornsby then had to push his way through massed admirers to get into the clubhouse.

Although Holland and Humphries received players on assignment from major-league clubs, Oklahoma City, like Baltimore and Chattanooga, was still trying to compete as an independent. Hornsby's mainstays were second baseman Don Kolloway and outfielder Thurman Tucker (who both belonged to the Chicago White Sox); shortstop Millard "Dixie" Howell (former University of Alabama football All-American); catcher George Dickey (younger brother of the Yankees' Bill); and pitchers Dewey Adkins (subsequently purchased by Cleveland) and Orval Grove (on option from the White Sox).

Sparked mostly by those men, Hornsby's Indians spurted to sixth place and, after a brief slump, put on another spurt to move up to fourth. Hornsby, wrote the *Sporting News* Oklahoma City correspondent, "prowls the coaching box like a caged bear. . . . Skillful handling of moundsmen and inspirational leadership to the hitters are the Rajah's strong points."[18]

In July, at Fort Worth, he managed the North team to an eleven-inning, 7–6 victory in the league's annual All-Star Game. Eddie Dyer—once Hornsby's teammate on the Cardinals and now managing first-place Houston—had charge of the South All-Stars. Tulsa's Dizzy Dean, who was trying to throw enough sore-armed junk to get back to the majors, pitched an inning for the North team.

On the last day of the regular season, with a playoff berth locked up, Hornsby came up as a pinch hitter at Tulsa, hit the ball against the center-field fence, and essayed no farther than first base—in his only appearance as a player in two years. By losing that game, his team finished at 82–78, a solid fourth place.

Although guiding Oklahoma City from last place into the playoffs added considerable luster to his managerial reputation, Hornsby said frankly that he didn't like the playoff system because it cheapened the pennant race (which Houston had won by sixteen games). Yet whatever his objections to the first-through-fourth tournament that had become standard postseason fare across the minors, Hornsby wouldn't have been unhappy upsetting the odds. The Indians didn't accommodate him, falling to Houston in the opening round three games to one (in a best three-of-five series).

With a few thousand dollars in his possession that he didn't have back in the spring and with hopes of finding something better, Hornsby put off Holland and Humphries about his plans for next year. After he again came up empty-handed at the winter meetings, he finally signed for another season at Oklahoma City. The contract—which the Indians officials personally brought to St. Louis for his approval and signature—was a month-by-month agreement specifying $1,000 per month. At the end of each month, in other words, Hornsby would be free to leave. He joined the Indians at Atlanta, Texas, their spring-training site, eleven days late—only after his baseball school closed.

Inasmuch as most teams lost money during the 1940 Houston run-away, Texas League owners and presidents agreed to prune the per-team roster limit from eighteen to seventeen men and the aggregate salary limit from $5,200 to $4,750 per month. Oklahoma City went even further, abandoning train travel—despite the league's great distances—and relying on rickety buses to get the Indians to their away-from-home schedule commitments.

Nothing much worked for Hornsby, Holland, and Humphries. Houston, loaded with young Cardinals-system talent, again left everybody behind and discouraged attendance around the league. After an exhausting road trip that left Oklahoma City tied for fourth place but, at 32–37, far out of the running, Hornsby had seen enough. On June 23, at the local hotel where he'd been living, he called Humphries to report that he was leaving for St. Louis. "I'm sorry it didn't work out," he said when he got home. "But I wasn't doing Oklahoma City much good, and they're having a little trouble at the gate. I didn't expect them to pay me that kind of dough when they're not taking it in. Holland and Humphries are good fellows and I didn't want to work a hardship on them."[19]

All of that sounded quite magnanimous, but Hornsby wouldn't have given up a $1,000-per-month job if something better hadn't been in the offing. In fact, the ownership of the Fort Worth Texas League franchise had already contacted him about assuming dual authority as business and field manager of the local Cats. On November 18 Hornsby arrived in Fort Worth to sign a one-year contract with the franchise's new owners—president Stanley A. Thompson, an oilman, and vice president Tom J. Brown, a Coca-Cola executive—who each had put up $13,000 to cover the Cats' existing deficit. The reason he was willing to take the job, said Hornsby, was that all authority would be "in one man's hands. That eliminates indecision, buck passing and alibi-ing. I'll be able to second-guess myself from now on," he joked.[20] Hornsby's salary would be $9,000, plus a percentage of whatever profits might be generated.

Although none of his immediate family still resided in Fort Worth, other relatives as well as a large number of acquaintances lived in the area, so that, even for such a confirmed nonsentimentalist as Hornsby, taking the job with the Cats was like coming home. While sixteen-year-old Billy remained in Missouri as a student and star athlete at Mexico Military Academy, Hornsby and his wife rented a house in Fort Worth. Early in December he left for the National Association meeting at Jacksonville, Florida, where, reported the *Sporting News,* he was "one of the busiest men at the convention."[21]

Two days after the Jacksonville meeting ended, swarms of carrier-launched Japanese aircraft crippled the U.S. fleet at Pearl Harbor in the Hawaiian Islands, triggering U.S. entry into the wars raging in Asia since 1937 and Europe since 1939. Hornsby noted that most of the players on Fort Worth's reserve list held 3-A (dependent-deferred) draft status, but "if Uncle Sam wants some of our players, he's more than welcome to them. I'd be proud to know they're serving their country in this fight against the most despicable tyrants who ever tried to conquer the world."[22] That was about as close as he ever came to a political statement—at least for public consumption.

On the evening of January 19, 1942, Hornsby received several calls and telegrams from writers in the East and Middle West, all reporting that they'd heard the results from the Baseball Writers Association's annual Hall of Fame poll—Hornsby had made it. In his first year of eligibility (under rules adopted in 1939 whereby one's active major-league playing career must have ended at least five years earlier), he received 182 of 233 votes. Nobody else came near the required three-fourths majority.

Officially notified by a local BBWAA member the next morning while he was getting a shave and haircut, Hornsby said he would meet reporters later at the ballpark. "Mighty nice honor," he said as he sat behind his desk in his LaGrave Field office, "and I certainly appreciate the honor. But baseball in 1942 is the thing with me now and . . . my thoughts are on a successful season for the Cats." They would have to excuse him, because he had to try to sell season boxes to local businesses. At the end of the day, having received not "a single turn-down," he went to a nearby café and celebrated both that success and his Hall of Fame election with a double serving of vanilla ice cream.[23]

Asked how she felt, Jeannette Hornsby described herself as "thrilled," and she went on to say that it had been "a thrill to me to see how Rog is tackling his new job here. He's as enthusiastic as a boy fresh out of school embarking on a career." Whenever something about him appeared in the local papers (as happened almost daily), she sent a clipping to Billy in Missouri.[24]

Again the Hornsbys' affairs seemed on the upswing. In Dallas, at the annual Texas League meeting, the club presidents adopted a resolution honoring his Hall of Fame admission; in Fort Worth, some 300 Junior Chamber of Commerce members feted him at a Welcome Home luncheon at the Hotel Blackstone; and Thompson and Brown readily approved his holding that spring's baseball school at LaGrave Field. Zeke Handler, the Cats' year-round publicity agent as well as ballpark announcer during the season, thought Hornsby was generally satisfied with his situation in Fort Worth, and remembered that he took particular delight in lunching at Carshon's Café, a local kosher restaurant. As Hornsby liked to say, "Can't beat Jew soup."[25]

The Texas League was one of thirty-two minor circuits completing that first wartime season. Although a considerable number of players had been called to military service before Pearl Harbor, the initial exemption of married men and those under twenty-one still left sufficient manpower to stock rosters throughout Organized Baseball. As a rule, farm clubs, usually consisting of younger, unmarried players, ran into trouble earlier than did independents, which tended to employ older men with families.

Fort Worth's opening-day pitcher, for example, was thirty-seven-year-old Earl Caldwell, who'd worked for Hornsby on the St. Louis Browns. The Cats got off to a good start, Caldwell surviving Oklahoma City's ten hits and hanging on for a 9–7 victory. Listed on the roster, the forty-six-year-old Hornsby appeared as a player only once—on May 3, 1942, in the second game of a doubleheader at Houston. He put himself at second base and, in what were to be his last times at bat in Organized Baseball, lined out and struck out twice before singling in the two runs that won it for his Cats.

It was a generally good year for Hornsby and the Fort Worth franchise. He received strong mound work from Caldwell and minor-league veterans Ed "Beartracks" Greer, Claude Horton, and Hank Oana (a Hawaiian-born outfielder whom Hornsby installed in his pitching rotation). Besides making some key infield additions, Hornsby again enjoyed stellar center-field and leadoff play from speedy Thurman Tucker (returned to the Texas League by the White Sox), and Fort Worth also featured the league's home-run and runs-batted-in leader in first baseman Mervyn Connors. The Cats drew their largest crowds in a decade and more than doubled their previous year's attendance of 46,000.

A nine-game winning streak late in the season hoisted the Cats into third place, where they finished with an 84–68 record—behind Shreveport (an independent) and pennant winner Beaumont (a Detroit farm). When a crowd estimated at 4,000 came to LaGrave Field on September 4 for Rogers Hornsby Night, Hornsby seemed less uncomfortable than he usually was on such occasions. Besides gift certificates from local civic boosters, he received a hand-tooled belt from his players. Wrote Zeke Handler (who also happened to be one of the *Sporting News*'s Texas League correspondents), "Frankly, how does the Rajah stay in the minors?"[26]

As field manager, business manager, and profit sharer, Hornsby stood to benefit all around from a good showing by his ballclub in the Texas League playoffs; but the red-hot Shreveport Sports eliminated Fort Worth, four games to three. (The Sports—thirteen of whose members had been with the team the previous year—then beat pennant winner Beaumont for the right to play Nashville in the annual Texas League–Southern Association Dixie Series, which Nashville won in six games.) Despite the Cats' playoff failure, the Fort Worth owners were generally happy, as was Hornsby, who took a few hundred dollars out of franchise profits. Early in October, he signed a contract for another season as front-office and field boss of the Cats.

Yet a general air of uncertainty hung over the Texas League that autumn. Selective service call-ups increased; problems created by gas rationing and railroad-transportation priorities seemed unmanageable; and Houston, San Antonio, and Tulsa—the league's remaining farm-club members after Detroit dropped Beaumont at season's end—were pessimistic about fielding teams for the coming season. Whatever prospects the Texas League may have had for 1943 went down the drain when Shreveport owner Bonneau Peters sold his entire roster to St. Paul of the American Association and announced that he was shutting down operations. Late in February, league president J. Alvin Gardner conducted a telephone poll and disclosed that a majority of the seven remaining franchises had agreed to suspend play "for the duration"—in the common phrase of the war years.

Only independents Fort Worth and Oklahoma City wanted to carry on. Hornsby, whose livelihood was directly involved, tried to convince his colleagues that with sports of all kinds (and of any caliber of performance) booming under the full-employment wartime economy, they should stay in business. "You fellows are afraid to take a chance," he protested. "You think more of a dollar than you do of baseball." "No one offered a refutation," wrote an Oklahoma City newsman; another, from Tulsa, thought that "two or three more determined, daring fighters like Rogers Hornsby . . . could have swayed the league into starting."[27]

Draft call-ups and war-imposed restrictions on civilian travel made it impossible for Hornsby to run his annual baseball school. For 1943 he continued to draw a salary (albeit in reduced form) to look after the affairs of the Fort Worth franchise in its wartime dormancy. Per the owners' instructions, he sold everybody on the Cats' reserve list to Milwaukee of the American Association.

By the end of 1943, Hornsby was just about broke. "If" had become pretty much the story of his professional life: if, for example, he hadn't alienated Sam Breadon and then Charles Stoneham; if William Wrigley or Phil Ball hadn't died; if John Ogden hadn't decided to leave Baltimore; and if (most grandiosely) World War II hadn't happened at all. At least he no longer bore the expense of educating and otherwise maintaining his son Bill (as the youth now preferred to be called). Early in 1943 the top athlete at Mexico Military Academy decided to pass up the remainder of his senior year and enlist in the Marine Corps.

If he had to, Hornsby was willing to take a baseball job in another country, namely the Federal Republic of Mexico. Jorge Pasquel, who with his brothers had built a fortune in liquor distributorships and other enterprises, dreamed of promoting *La Liga Mexicana* into an authentic rival to *Las Ligas Grandes* to the north. In January, Hornsby flew from Dallas to Mexico City to discuss a job as player-manager of the Vera Cruz Blues in Pasquel's six-team circuit. Although Pasquel offered him as much as a five-year contract, Hornsby decided on one year. "Mr. Pasquel is a very enthusiastic baseball man," he told reporters in Mexico

City, "and we could make a winning combination." Back home, he was more candid: "It's baseball, ain't it? I don't know any other business and I don't want to. There's no place left for me in the game here. United States baseball has forgotten me."[28]

That's the way it looked to plenty of people, who were as puzzled as Zeke Handler why nobody in the big leagues—or anywhere else in his own country, it seemed—wanted Hornsby's services. A widely shared view in baseball circles held that once the Browns fired him, Kenesaw Mountain Landis put out the word that Hornsby wasn't to be employed again in the major leagues. Though never documented, the notion that Hornsby had been blacklisted was at least plausible.

So Hornsby signed for $1,500 per month to manage in Pasquel's Mexican League—for however long his employment lasted. Though consisting mostly of Mexican- and Cuban-born players, the league also featured such Negro-league standouts as pitchers Chet Brewer, Theolic Smith, and Ferris McDuffie; infielder Ray Dandridge; and catcher Quincey Trouppe—all of whom had cast their lot with Pasquel for $400–$500 per month (the league maximum). Scheduling games only on Thursdays, Saturdays, and Sundays, Pasquel's circuit operated with teams in Monterrey, Torreón, Tampico, Puebla, and Mexico City, where both the Mexico City Reds and Hornsby's Vera Cruz Blues (named for Pasquel's home city but also based in the capital) played their home games.

Hornsby's team included Dandridge, as well as former Philadelphia Phillies' and Washington Senators' infielder Chile Gomez (who'd played against Hornsby in the 1935 Mexican games), former Syracuse infielder Antonio "Chico" Rodriquez, and catcher Salvador Hernandez, who'd spent the past two seasons with the Chicago Cubs. Inasmuch as only those four players spoke English, Hornsby recalled, "I had to give my team pep 'talks' by waving my arms and making all kinds of odd gestures."[29]

On opening day, some 20,000 people showed up at the Mexico City ballpark, pushed down the right-field fence, crowded around the infield, pelted police and opposing players with fruit, and, when the game was over, threw dirt on wealthy women patrons as they left the grounds. Although most of his players were used to such disorderly scenes, for Hornsby it was a strange environment in which to try to play baseball. He stuck it out through eight games over three weeks, riding buses hundreds of miles at a stretch, sleeping in shabby hotels, and eating food that was usually to his liking but often didn't agree with the non-Mexicans on the team. At the end of the month, the Blues came home and won the first of a three-game set with Puebla.

On Saturday, March 31, his club trailed 14–13 in the bottom of the ninth inning, when, with the bases full, Hornsby put himself in as a pinch hitter. As he recounted it a few weeks later, "I got hold of one. The air is pretty thin down there and the ball carries. It went out of the park for four runs and we won again, 17–14. The peons carried me off the field and threw fruit at the other team."[30]

The next morning Pasquel called Hornsby into his ballpark office. "Mr. Hornsby," said Pasquel, "that was a nice hit yesterday, but it would have been better if we hadn't won the game." Although Hornsby knew that Pasquel owned a piece of all six teams in the league, he was astonished to learn that the Mexican mogul actually wanted his Blues to lose, so they could draw a bigger Sunday crowd for what would have been the deciding game of the series. "Now," Pasquel complained, "we have already won the series." Shaking his head in disbelief, Hornsby suggested that maybe it would be better for everybody concerned if he and Pasquel parted company. "I finally decided that I'd rather be a lamp-post in America than a general down there," Hornsby said when he got back to St. Louis, "so I quit." Yet he remained enthusiastic about the future of baseball in Mexico, which "can be made into a baseball paradise."[31]

Shortly after his return, radio station WTMV, across the river in East St. Louis, hired him to do a fifteen-minute baseball report and commentary, airing six nights a week. The station paid him $150 per month through the baseball season—$900 in all. Awkward and stiff early on, Hornsby eventually learned to read his copy clearly and ad lib effectively. Having lived most of his life in midwestern and eastern U.S.

cities, he no longer spoke with a pronounced Texas accent; now he sounded much like a typical lower Middle Westerner.

That winter, the Hornsbys' twenty-year marriage effectively came to an end. Although neither filed for divorce, they lived apart from then on. Jeannette continued to reside in St. Louis; in the absence of a formal separation agreement, Rogers sent her a monthly check.

Early in 1945 he moved to Chicago, rented an apartment at 1260 North Dearborn, and went to work year-round as director of a citywide youth baseball program called Diamond Schools for Boys sponsored by the *Chicago Daily News* and the city recreation commission. The program offered free clinics for boys between the ages of ten and sixteen, with instruction to take place on the recreation commission's seventy baseball diamonds. Assisted by Tom Sheehan, a former big-league pitcher, Hornsby would visit all the diamonds, do some teaching himself, and oversee several dozen neighborhood instructors.

In August, Hornsby, Sheehan, Jack Ryan, and University of Illinois baseball coach Wally Roettger traveled by station wagon to Galesburg, Peoria, Springfield, Decatur, Danville, and Champaign for baseball clinics, radio and newspaper interviews, and luncheons with local civic groups. Hornsby also sold (for twenty-five cents apiece) five instructional booklets he'd put together in the late 1930s on batting and pitching. "I liked every minute of it," he said at the end of the 600-mile trip. "The boys are attentive and punctual. They're interested." In turn, "We give 'em a chance to play and don't bore 'em with talk. They find out we sincerely seek to help them."[32]

By the end of that summer of 1945, the war had ended and professional baseball was entering a period of unprecedented and previously unimagined popularity and profits. If in fact Commissioner Landis had blacklisted Hornsby, the judge was no longer around to interfere with his professional life; in November 1944, after nearly a quarter century as baseball czar, Landis died at age seventy-eight. Albert B. "Happy" Chandler, the new commissioner, found too much else to worry about—such as players' salary and pension demands, impending racial integration, and Jorge Pasquel's designs on major-league rosters—to concern himself with Rogers Hornsby's past imbroglios.

As yet nobody in either the majors or the minors had called Hornsby about a job, but for now he wasn't doing badly. Reestablished in a city where he knew a lot of people, he could count on a steady twelve-months income of about $6,000—some of which he actually saved. Half the year he was out on baseball fields working with kids, something he clearly enjoyed.

He also wasn't long without female companionship. Sometime in 1945 he met a divorcée named Bernadette Ann Harris. Little would ever be known of her life before she met Hornsby, except that she was born in Rose Creek, Minnesota, in 1898, that she was a former nurse who married a Milwaukee physician named Robert Harris, and that they were divorced in 1940. Hornsby later said that she became his "personal good friend and secretary."[33] Bernadette Harris obviously was (or became) more than friend and secretary; when, in 1948, Hornsby bought a six-unit apartment building at 1249 West Thorndale Avenue, they moved in together on the first floor.

Early in 1946, after more than two years with the Marine Corps in the South Pacific, Bill Hornsby received his discharge and came to see his father in Chicago. Now nineteen and a muscular six-foot-one and 194 pounds, he aimed for a career in professional baseball, even though, he told reporters, he knew he couldn't hit "like Dad." About to "go home to St. Louis" to see his mother, he intended to rejoin Hornsby later and help out in the Daily News baseball school.[34]

In the meantime, Hornsby finally gained major-league reemployment, albeit only briefly. Manager Jimmy Dykes of the Chicago White Sox contacted him about coming out to Pasadena, California, and working with his hitters for a week in spring training; shortly thereafter Charlie Grimm put aside his dislike for Hornsby long enough to invite him to do the same thing for the Cubs on Catalina Island.

Bill Hornsby accompanied his father as far as Pasadena, where Rogers Hornsby Jr. was working for an engineering firm. A graduate of Denison (Texas) High School, at age sixteen, Hornsby's older son had always been more interested in fly-fishing and electricity than competitive sports; as a teenager he built his own crystal radio sets.[35] After studying electrical engineering at Texas A & M College, he married, worked in Pasadena, then, in 1942, enlisted in the Army Air Corps. Following training stints in Texas, he joined a bomber group in Britain and flew fifty missions as a navigator.

That March in Pasadena, after many years, Hornsby renewed his acquaintance with his son by his first marriage, and also met Wanda Grace Hornsby and little Ann, his two-year-old granddaughter. It was the first and only meeting for the Hornsby half brothers; within another year and a half, Rogers Jr. would have rejoined the air force and lost contact with Rogers and Bill Hornsby.

In April, while Hornsby again got the *Daily News*'s clinics under way, a Boston Red Sox scout looked over Bill Hornsby and signed him to a minor-league contract with Lynn, Massachusetts, of the Class B New England League. Bill found the company too fast at that level; by July he was with the Red Sox farm at Oneonta, New York, in the Canadian-American League, one classification lower. There he proved himself a capable infielder who hit with occasional power, but he had trouble with anything besides a straight fastball. For 1947 he was elevated to Lynn, but he would never be more than a journeyman minor-leaguer.

Meanwhile his father put in another year as administrator and pedagogue for the *Daily News*. At South Bend, Indiana, after he finished speaking at a service clubs luncheon, the master of ceremonies presented a certificate of appreciation for his work in youth baseball. Hornsby looked at it, scowled, and handed it back. "This isn't for me," he said crossly. "My name is *Rogers* Hornsby. This is made out to *Roger* Hornsby." Jack Ryan jumped up to grab the microphone and smooth things over. "Now, Rog," Ryan laughed, "take it easy, old boy. They didn't take a basehit away from you. They just dropped a letter from your name."[36]

Hornsby might be excused for showing irritation when people still got his name wrong, because, for all his renown, a full-time post in Organized Baseball hadn't materialized. Sam Breadon, for one, wouldn't hear of reemploying Hornsby. That October, in Breadon's hotel suite in Boston (where the Cardinals opened the World Series versus the Red Sox), the venerable sports journalist Grantland Rice asked Breadon why he didn't hire Hornsby to work with young players in the Cardinals' farm system. Hornsby knew more about hitting and how to teach it than anybody, Breadon granted that, but "I couldn't look those fathers and mothers in the eye and say we'd look after their boys' welfare, their health and their morals, if Hornsby was going to be one of their teachers."[37]

Another temporary instructorship did come along for Hornsby early in 1947, when William H. Veeck Jr., the brash young showman who headed a syndicate that had acquired the Cleveland franchise, invited him to come to Tucson, Arizona, and work in the midwinter sunshine with players from the Indians' organization. Hornsby again brought along his ballplaying son, who donned an old Cleveland uniform and practiced with several minor-league prospects under the scrutiny of Tris Speaker, Bill McKechnie, and Al Lopez—all full-time coaches for player-manager Lou Boudreau. Hornsby's particular assignment was to try to help catcher Jim Hegan and outfielder Pat Seerey, who'd both been with the team for several years. Tall and lanky, Hegan hit for neither power nor average; Seerey, stocky and perpetually overweight, had slammed twenty-six homers in 1946 but batted only .225. For the past three seasons he'd led the American League in strikeouts.

By now, Hornsby himself—fifty years old and almost completely gray—tipped the scales at about 225 pounds. But when he picked up a bat, he could still scorch line drives to all parts of the ballpark, which in itself may have worked a discouraging effect on his subjects. At any rate, neither Hegan nor Seerey profited from their sessions at Tucson. By midsummer Hegan's hitting had improved, but only after he abandoned Hornsby's advice to stand virtually upright and away from the plate. Battling an awful slump as well as his waistline, Seerey went back to his old crouching stance; yet, he moaned, "it's still no hits. . . . Aw, hell, I'm still striking out. Right now I don't know what the hell [Hornsby] tried to tell me. I musta forgot it."[38]

At Tucson, as the *Cleveland News*'s Ed McAuley remembered him, Hornsby was "tireless, patient and hard-working." He stood for hours behind the batting cage, making suggestions, giving encouragement, being, McAuley thought, "more constantly interested in baseball than anyone else I've met"—except possibly Joe McCarthy. At night Hornsby sat in the lobby of the Santa Rita Hotel, waiting for his pupils to join him and talk baseball. "Some of them did, but not enough for the Rajah," wrote McAuley. "Mac, I can't understand it," he recalled Hornsby's saying. "I've been around a long time and I have something to contribute. Yet very few of the youngsters are interested enough to talk with me."[39]

Like other managers in the past, Lou Boudreau found Hornsby's presence discomforting. Whereas Tris Speaker readily deferred to the twenty-nine-year-old Boudreau, Hornsby put in his two cents' worth about everything. It soon became apparent, McAuley felt, that "Hornsby was the 'outsider' of the brain trust—that the sooner he left camp, the better Boudreau would like it."[40] Finally Bill Veeck called with orders that Hornsby was to visit Cleveland's Oklahoma City farm club at Jacksonville, Florida. Hornsby lingered in Tucson and, when Veeck arrived a few days later, made an unsuccessful effort to talk the Indians' president into letting him stay on.

After spending a week at Jacksonville looking over Oklahoma City's personnel, Hornsby returned to Chicago to start the *Daily News* schools, no doubt disappointed that he hadn't turned up something long-term with the Indians. The following fall he decided to supplement his annual salary by reestablishing his Hot Springs baseball school, which he'd last operated in 1942. Proclaiming "Rogers Hornsby Reopening His Great Baseball School" over a photo of a jowly Hornsby, advertisements stipulated charges of $100 plus room and board for six weeks from mid-February to the end of March. Hornsby also succeeded in getting his school certified with the Veterans Administration for GI Bill educational benefits.[41]

In January 1948, with what must have been mixed feelings, he traveled to St. Louis for a dinner at the Hotel Jefferson in honor of Sam

Breadon, who'd sold the Cardinals the previous November. When his turn at the microphone came, Hornsby made a few nice remarks, after which Breadon beamed as he posed with Hornsby, Gabby Street, Frank Frisch, Billy Southworth, and Eddie Dyer—five of the six managers of his nine Cardinals pennant winners.[42]

Breadon's death in May 1949 from cancer followed Babe Ruth's the previous August (also from cancer) and Hack Wilson's in November (from drink). All three men affected Hornsby's life in important ways: Breadon, by putting the Cardinals on their feet financially so they could build upon Hornsby's talents as player and manager; Ruth, by popularizing power-oriented baseball and establishing a standard for judging not only Hornsby's batting prowess but his salaries; and Wilson, by doing much to make possible Hornsby's second World Series, then helping him lose it, and finally, in 1931, performing so badly on and off the field that Hornsby couldn't win with the most-talented ballclub he ever managed.

In 1948 Hornsby conducted both his baseball school at Hot Springs and the *Daily News* clinics in the summer months in Chicago. Of the 132 young players at Hot Springs the next year, sixty-four signed professional contracts, including fourteen taken en masse by the independent Centralia, Illinois, franchise of the Class D Mississippi–Ohio Valley League. Meanwhile, in Chicago, Hornsby was credited with overseeing a program that, over four summers, had taught baseball to some 100,000 boys.

Hornsby's association with the *Chicago Daily News* baseball program ended in 1949, when WENR-TV made him what he termed "a very attractive offer" to do play-by-play for the Chicago Cubs' home games.[43] As yet, in that nascent period in television sports, such qualities as grammar, diction, and hyperbolic embellishment seemed less important than having an authoritative voice in the broadcast booth; if nothing else, Hornsby's voice would be authoritative. So he gained the opportunity to work closely with the Cubs franchise (which, ironically, dismissed Charlie Grimm and hired Frank Frisch during that same season); he also reinforced his presence both within baseball circles and

Hornsby and Hack Wilson, supposedly making up following Wilson's suspension, 1931. (Rev. Jerome C. Romanowski, Laurel Springs, N.J.)

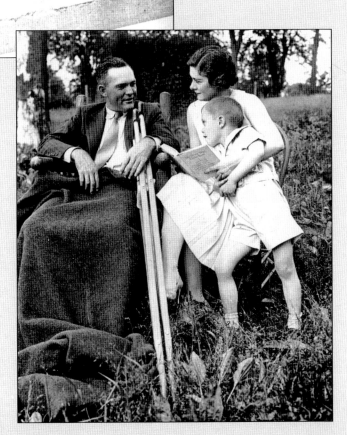

Disabled with a broken ankle, Hornsby rests at his Robertson, Missouri, farm with wife Jeannette and five-year-old son Billy, June 1930. (National Baseball Library and Archive, Cooperstown, N.Y.)

Ray Doan's first baseball school, Hot Springs, Arkansas, late winter 1933. *Front row, left to right:* Doan and instructors Rogers Hornsby, Les Mann, Grover Cleveland Alexander, Jack Ryan, and George Sisler. Bob Scheffing from Decatur, Illinois, future major-league catcher and manager, is in the fourth row, fourth from right. (*Sporting News* Photo Archive, St. Louis, Mo.)

Hornsby shaking hands with Phil Ball, St. Louis Browns
owner, after signing to manage the Browns, July 26, 1933.
Standing: Browns vice president L. C. McEvoy.
(*Sporting News* Photo Archive, St. Louis, Mo.)

Second Lieutenant
Rogers Hornsby Jr.,
U.S. Army Air Forces,
ca. 1944. (*Sporting
News* Photo Archive,
St. Louis, Mo.)

t. Louis Browns at the start of the 1935 season: *Left to right, first row:* Ivy Andrews,
)scar Melillo, Charlie O'Leary (coach), Rogers Hornsby (manager), Grover Hartley
:oach), Heinie Mueller, Rollie Hemsley, Frank Grube. *Second row:* Buck Newsom, Ray
'epper, Bob Weiland, Jack Burns, Johnny Burnett, Harlond Clift, Jack Knott, Dick
:offman, Bill Strickland. *Top row:* Sammy West, Debs Garms, Jim Walkup, George
3laeholder, Beau Bell, Ollie Bejma, Tommy Heath, Alan Strange. (Rev. Jerome C.
Romanowski, Laurel Springs, N.J.)

Rogers and Bill Hornsby,
Tucson, Arizona,
February 1947.
(*Sporting News* Photo
Archive, St. Louis, Mo.)

At a banquet in St. Louis,
January 1948, honoring
St. Louis Cardinals owner
Sam Breadon. *Left to right:*
Hornsby, Eddie Dyer,
Breadon, Billy South-
worth, Gabby Street.
(*Sporting News* Photo
Archive, St. Louis, Mo.)

Hornsby with Guy Airey,
Beaumont Roughnecks
president, Stuart Stadium,
Beaumont, Texas, 1950.
(*Sporting News* Photo
Archive, St. Louis, Mo.)

Hornsby visiting with former Beaumont Roughnecks *(left to right)* Gil McDougald, Ernie Nevel, Bob Marquis, and Clint Courtney t New York Yankees spring training, Phoenix, Arizona, 1952. (*Sporting News* Photo Archive, St. Louis, Mo.)

Hornsby signs to manage the St. Louis Browns in Bill Veeck's New York hotel suite, October 8, 1952. (*Sporting News* Photo Archive, St. Louis, Mo.)

Hornsby with Mrs. Grover Cleveland Alexander and Ronald Reagan, Browns spring training, Burbank, California, 1952. (*Sporting News* Photo Archive, St. Louis, Mo.)

The play that prompted Hornsby's firing by Browns president Bill Veeck. Yankee Stadium, June 7, 1952: As Hornsby watches from the third-base coaching box, a fan interferes with Gil McDougald's effort to catch a foul ball. (*Sporting News* Photo Archive, St. Louis, Mo.)

Left to right: Powel Crosley, Hornsby, and Gabe Paul, opening day, Crosley Field, Cincinnati, 1953. (National Baseball Library and Archive, Cooperstown, N.Y.)

Hornsby testifying in Chicago on September 8, 1953, at the coroner's inquest into the death of Bernadette Ann Harris. To his right is Cook County coroner Walter McCarron. (*Sporting News* Photo Archive, St. Louis, Mo.)

Hornsby instructing boys in the Chicago Recreation Department's baseball program, ca. 1955. (National Baseball Library and Archive, Cooperstown, N.Y.)

Hornsby with Marjorie Hornsby, to his right, and stepdaughter Mary Beth Porter, to his left, Chicago, February 1957. (*Sporting News* Photo Archive, St. Louis, Mo.)

Hornsby as batting coach of the New York Mets, spring 1962. (*Sporting News* Photo Archive, St. Louis, Mo.)

with a new generation of fans. By the end of the year, feelers for managing jobs had started to come in.

About midnight on December 23, 1949, Hornsby received a call from a wire-service reporter, who told him that a couple of hours earlier, his son Rogers Jr. had been killed in a plane crash. By dawn he knew the particulars: A B-50 bomber (a B-29 modified for in-flight refueling) had left Chatham Air Force Base at Savannah, Georgia, on a routine training mission. Five minutes after lifting off to the northeast, the huge aircraft lost power and plunged into a swamp on the South Carolina side of the Savannah River—within sight of U.S. Highway 17 but virtually inaccessible. As described the next day, the crash site was "a crater of marshy ooze," with nothing visible but "bits of metal and dirty water."[44] All eleven crew members (all married men) were killed, including First Lieutenant Hornsby, the navigator. It took several days for searchers, working in shoulder-deep mud, to recover the bodies.

Barely twenty-nine years old, Rogers Hornsby Jr. left a wife, a five-year-old daughter, and a two-year-old son (whom his grandfather had never seen). When Hornsby called his son's mother to share her grief, she told him that under no circumstances was he to attend the funeral services. So, in deference to her wishes, he ordered a huge floral spray "from Rogers and Bill" sent to Denison, where services were held before burial in the military cemetery at San Antonio. When Sarah Finley saw the spray, recalled her granddaughter, "she threw a fit."[45]

If the year ended in sadness, hurt feelings, and no doubt considerable regret on the part of both Hornsby and his onetime wife, at least his professional prospects had brightened. He'd spent the past twelve years as something of a baseball vagabond, always hopeful of returning to the big leagues but with little more than hope to go on. Now, at last, he was about to get his chance to make it back.

12

· · ·

Making

It

Back

On January 26, 1950, Martin G. "Chick" Autry, a former American League catcher who'd managed the Beaumont Exporters of the Class AA Texas League for the past two seasons, died of a heart attack in Savannah, Georgia, at age forty-six. Those sensitive to human irony might have noted that Autry died within a few miles of the spot where Rogers Hornsby Jr. was killed a month earlier, and that Autry's death finally created an opening for the return to Organized Baseball of Rogers Hornsby Sr.

Actually, George Weiss, architect of the New York Yankees' farm system and now their general manager, and Casey Stengel, coming off the first of what would be five straight world's championships as Yankees field manager, had been thinking about Hornsby for some time. With Chick Autry's death, they decided to bring him into the New York organization as manager of the Yankees' Beaumont farm club.[1]

Early in February, Hornsby arrived in Dallas and, in the presence of Guy Airey, president of the Beaumont franchise, and league president

J. Alvin Gardner, signed a one-year contract at what Airey called "the second highest salary ever paid a Texas League manager."[2] Although Airey would be Hornsby's nominal boss, the New York organization picked up the bulk of his salary. Airey never disclosed the actual sum, but it was around $18,000—by far the most anybody had paid Hornsby since he left the St. Louis Browns.

Hornsby's salary was still well below what Dick Burnett, a hugely rich Texas oilman, had recently agreed to pay Charlie Grimm to manage Burnett's independently operated Dallas Eagles. "Jolly Cholly," dismissed as Chicago Cubs field boss the previous June (but kept on in the front office), received the fattest minor-league manager's contract in history—$30,000 for one season. So eighteen years after Grimm took over the Cubs from Hornsby, the crisscrossings of their careers within the little universe of professional baseball again made them adversaries.

Like most other minor leagues, the Texas League was coming off four unprecedentedly prosperous seasons. Since 1938 (when Shreveport replaced Galveston), the league's membership had remained unchanged: Beaumont, Houston, San Antonio, Dallas, Fort Worth, Tulsa, Oklahoma City, and Shreveport. Aggregate league attendance for 1949 exceeded 2.7 million, which surpassed not only the counterpart Southern Association but the Class AAA American Association as well. For 1950, Texas League club owners agreed to raise the roster limit from nineteen to twenty and the monthly salary limit from $8,500 to $10,000. Overall it was a very strong minor league—"better than ever," Hornsby later described it.[3]

Finally installing lights when the Texas League resumed play in 1946, the Beaumont franchise shared in baseball's postwar attendance surge. Although the Exporters were on the bottom at the end of every postwar season except 1946 (when they finished fifth), in 1948 they drew a record 152,000 customers, about 50,000 more than the city's population.

The Yankees operated the majors' third-biggest farm system and controlled a wealth of ballplayers; so far, though, the best prospects had ended up elsewhere, usually on Yankees-owned franchises such as Kansas City, Quincy, Illinois, and Binghamton, New York—as opposed to those under working agreements, such as Beaumont. Understandably feeling shortchanged by the New York organization, Airey and Beaumont's loyal baseball following hoped Hornsby's hiring signaled better treatment by George Weiss and associates.

Hornsby still hadn't given up his Hot Springs baseball school, but early in March he put Benny Meyer in charge and left by automobile for Cuero, Texas, the Beaumont team's spring-training site. A town of about 5,000 some sixty miles east of San Antonio, Cuero offered cheap hotel rates and a semipro baseball diamond—circumstances befitting the Texas League's doormat. Bill Hornsby, twenty-four years old and now a free agent, arrived with his father and worked out with twenty-five or so other hopefuls. Keith Thomas, up from Quincy, remembered him as a slick fielder who "couldn't hit a lick."[4] Within a couple of weeks he left to play semipro ball for the coming summer.

The Roughnecks, as they were renamed in a local newspaper poll over the winter, were the youngest group of players Hornsby ever managed. Aside from Ford Garrison, a thirty-five-year-old outfielder who'd played for Hornsby at Fort Worth in 1942, and Ernie Nevel, a thirty-year-old pitcher, their ages ranged from twenty to twenty-five, even though a few (such as Thomas) were former GIs. They were also all white men. The Brooklyn Dodgers' Jackie Robinson, who'd broken Organized Baseball's color line at Montreal four years earlier, was the National League's reigning Most Valuable Player; in the coming season, eight other black players would appear on big-league rosters (albeit on only four clubs). Blacks also dotted the minor leagues from New England to California, but the Texas League, Southern Association, and other southern circuits still played all-white baseball.[5]

For his young charges, Hornsby was a revelation in more ways than one. He didn't shower with his players after workouts or games, changed quickly into his street clothes, and left the premises with scarcely a word to anyone. He rarely smiled and was characteristically brusque and sometimes cuttingly sarcastic, as when he remarked to Elvin Tappe, a young catcher, that his name fit him perfectly, because all he did was "tap" the ball.[6] Pitchers didn't like the fact that instead of coming to the mound to make pitching changes, Hornsby stood in the dugout and waved new men in. They also objected (privately) that he then made the relieved pitchers watch the rest of the game from the bench instead of letting them proceed to the showers.

Yet the hitters soon learned to listen to him. Bob Marquis, a lean, fleet-footed center fielder, recalled that while Hornsby was "always on my butt," he taught Marquis to quit trying to pull the ball, because he would never be a home-run hitter. When Hornsby undertook to show by example how it ought to be done, Tappe, catching batting practice, wondered aloud why he stood so far from the plate. Hornsby gestured toward the pitcher and growled, "Tell him to throw the damn ball." In Marquis's words, "Buddy, he hit line drives—bam! bam!"[7]

When a Dallas reporter visited Cuero, he found Beaumont's manager in his hotel room, attired in blue-striped pajamas, and already in bed, although it was still early evening. Hornsby immediately launched into a complaint. A few nights earlier, he'd accompanied George Scheppes, former Dallas owner, to the town of Alice to help work up interest in Scheppes's new Rio Grande Valley League (Class C). "And do you know what they play in Alice?" asked Hornsby, staring at the ceiling. "Softball. Softball—I never thought they'd do that in Texas, with all the room there is to play baseball." (A couple of months later, speaking at a Beaumont Rotary Club father-son banquet, he urged the youngsters to play lots of baseball but avoid "sissy" softball, apparently oblivious to the widespread sponsorship of recreation-league softball teams by Rotary and other service organizations.)[8]

Hornsby quickly saw that Gil McDougald, a gangly, twenty-two-year-old Californian, would likely be his second baseman and best hitter. While others gawked at McDougald's eccentric batting stance—feet wide apart, left foot pointed toward third base, bat drooped at a forty-five-degree angle—Hornsby watched him hit once and turned his attention to other things. When Yankees scout Atley Donald dropped in, Hornsby told him to make sure nobody in the organization tried to change McDougald's stance.

Like most of the other Beaumont players, McDougald respected Hornsby without really liking him. "Playing under Hornsby," he later commented, "was like being out on probation from reform school. . . . Believe me, Hornsby eats and sleeps baseball and then chews it up again." When another player asked to change roommates because he had nothing to talk about with his present one, the manager responded, "My boy, you're greatly mistaken. You two boys have everything in common to talk about—baseball."[9] Yet a genuine mutual fondness developed between Hornsby and at least one Roughneck rookie. Clint Courtney, from Coushatta, Louisiana, was a short, stocky, bespectacled catcher whose ferociously competitive disposition compensated for what he lacked in natural ability. Courtney was exactly Hornsby's kind of ballplayer, while Hornsby's tough, no-nonsense managing style exactly suited the young man who came to be known as "Scrap Iron."

Knowing that Beaumont was probably his last chance to regain the big time, Hornsby told his men he wanted to win every exhibition game. They did win eighteen of nineteen (all with Texas League and lower-minors teams) and then came home to a city that hadn't been so baseball-hungry since prewar days, when, as a Detroit farm, the local franchise featured the likes of Hank Greenberg, Lynwood "Schoolboy" Rowe, Paul "Dizzy" Trout, and Dick Wakefield.

Although McDougald homered off San Antonio's Bob Turley for the winning margin in the Roughnecks' home opener, what happened in Dallas that night eclipsed everything else around the league. Dick Burnett staged the Dallas-Tulsa opener in the vast Cotton Bowl, where he arranged for Ty Cobb, Tris Speaker, Dizzy Dean, Mickey Cochrane, Travis Jackson, Frank Baker, Duffy Lewis, Charlie Gehringer, and Charlie Grimm (except Grimm, all Hall of Famers) to take the field in Dallas uniforms at the start of the game. After Dean threw one pitch, they gave way to the Eagles regulars, thus concluding a stunt that brought out a paying crowd of 53,578, the largest in minor-league history.

As most people expected, the Fort Worth Cats—managed by the colorful Bobby Bragan and loaded with talented youngsters from the

Brooklyn Dodgers organization—quickly pulled away from the rest of the league.[10] Early in June, with Hornsby's team in seventh place and drawing poorly, Guy Airey borrowed $25,000 from the league reserve fund and warned that unless attendance picked up, Beaumont might lose its franchise. Actually, Beaumont's attendance decline over the first quarter of the season was the smallest in the league, which showed an aggregate loss of nearly 111,000 from the same point the previous year.

The Texas League wasn't unique; after peaking in 1949 with fifty-nine leagues and forty-two million in paid attendance, the minors quickly entered a long-term process of decline and disbandment. Although hardly anyone understood what was happening, a number of factors affecting postwar demography and lifestyles—such as suburbanization, a growing variety of outside entertainment and recreation options, and, most of all, spreading ownership of in-home television sets—had permanently changed the minors' circumstances. Had some seer tried to explain all that to Rogers Hornsby, he would have found it irrelevant to the business at hand, which was to win ball games and let long-range problems take care of themselves.

Bill Curry, Airey's business manager, recalled that when the ballclub was at home, Hornsby phoned in every morning to ask if Curry or Airey needed him at the ballpark or elsewhere. He was readily available, because he'd sold his car and rented a little house within easy walking distance of Stuart Stadium, the baseball plant on the city's south side occupied by Beaumont's teams since 1929. Hornsby lived by himself except for one period that summer when Bernadette Harris flew down from Chicago. Occasionally he could be seen away from the ballpark, usually at local soda fountains eating ice cream.

When anybody brought up the subject of his gambling, he gave out mixed responses. Sometimes he claimed that he hadn't bet for a year because his handicapper (whom he would never identify) had died, and he couldn't make sense of a racing form anyway. At other times he said that now he bet only in the off-season. In fact, he continued to place bets on races in various parts of the country. In Jefferson County, Texas, the sheriff's department and police forces took an indulgent attitude toward gambling and prostitution—as long as neither became excessively overt. One tavern in Beaumont's central business district, for example, stood wide open in summertime; passersby could easily glimpse a racing chart on the rear wall, with a man busily chalking in entries and results.[11]

Meanwhile, in Fort Worth one night, Beaumont outfielder Keith Thomas watched the league-leading Cats going through infield practice and, within Hornsby's hearing distance, observed, "That's a helluva ballclub." "Thomas," snorted Hornsby, "why don't you look at your own ballclub? You've got a helluva ballclub right here."[12] He didn't speak to Thomas again for two months.

"Well, Thomas," Hornsby abruptly inquired in August, "what do you think about your ballclub now?" By then, the Roughnecks had won nine straight games and climbed to second place. "We don't have the best club in the league," Hornsby told the press, "but we have spirit and confidence." When Sid Keener, his old St. Louis newspaper friend, wrote to ask how he'd achieved such a turnaround in his team's fortunes, Hornsby replied with characteristic simplicity: "I tell my boys to go out and do the best they can every day, and to out-hustle the other club. There's nothing unusual in that system. You can't burden a ballplayer with too many signals, too much coaching."[13]

After June 7 Beaumont played .709 baseball. They gained first place on August 30 and held on, clinching the regular-season pennant with two games to play and finishing at 91–62—two and one-half games ahead of Bragan's Cats. Meanwhile Charlie Grimm's well-paid Dallas Eagles, made up mostly of retread major- and minor-leaguers and woefully lacking in pitching, could do no better than fifth place.[14]

Two acquisitions from tail-end Houston proved critical to the Roughnecks' late-season drive: shortstop Jack Cusick, bought for the league waiver price, and pitcher Clarence Beers, signed as a free agent. Beers, a St. Louis native whose father had taken him to see Hornsby at Sportsman's Park and then paid his way to the Hot Springs school in 1938, went to Hornsby's room at the Rice Hotel in Houston, where he was greeted by a pajamaed boyhood idol. "He offered me a $2,000 bonus and $500 a month," recalled Beers, "and I didn't ask any questions."[15] Cusick stabilized Hornsby's young infield; Beers won nine of twelve decisions after joining Beaumont.

By the time his Cuero originals and midseason pickups clinched the pennant with two games to play, the Hornsby-Beaumont story had attracted national press coverage and prompted speculation about Hornsby's prospects for next year. "Sure," he said, "I'd like to get back in the majors in 1951. The majors are the only place." Nobody had contacted him, "but I'd be in a receptive mood if they do."[16]

Despite Hornsby's graceless behavior on the night of September 5, when 6,259 Beaumont-area people turned out to see him given a new Cadillac, Guy Airey remained pleased by just about everything. Not only had Beaumont won its first pennant since 1942 and only its fourth since joining the Texas League in 1912, but more than 170,000 people had passed through the Stuart Stadium turnstiles, more than ever before (or ever after). Even after repaying his loan from the league reserve fund, Airey showed a tidy profit. Hornsby, Airey later said, was the most conscientious and considerate manager he'd worked with in twenty-seven years in baseball. "All Hornsby ever asked," said Airey, "was to be left alone to run his ball club. In turn, he leaves the business department up to the owner, and that made things lovely here in Beaumont."[17]

Sportswriters in the Texas League cities named McDougald Player of the Year after the youngster with the strange stance batted .336, hit thirteen home runs, and drove home 115 runs. Thomas batted in 111 runs, Marquis hit .296 and played a sparkling center field, and Ernie Nevel tied for the league lead in victories with twenty-one.

After they clinched the pennant, Hornsby told his players that he was satisfied with what they'd already accomplished; he didn't care if they won or lost in the playoffs. Beaumont fans expected something more than what followed: a four-game collapse at the hands of fourth-place San Antonio (which then went on to defeat Tulsa for the playoff championship and the Southern Association's Nashville Vols for the Dixie Series title). But as far as Hornsby was concerned, he'd made his point. He showed that he could take a group of mostly young players and win

247

in a tough league—that he still knew baseball and how to get the most out of his men.

Yet Hornsby remained as "deficient in the social relation"—in John B. Sheridan's phrase—as he'd ever been. When he returned to Chicago, Jack Brickhouse, covering Cubs games for WGN-TV, invited him into the Wrigley Field broadcast booth. After welcoming him back from doing a great job at Beaumont, Brickhouse mentioned Grayle Howlett, president of the Tulsa franchise. "Whatta guy!" bubbled Brickhouse. "He's been my friend for years, a real good pal, a right guy. Do you know him, Rog?" "Yeah, I know him," Hornsby replied. "I don't like him."[18]

A few weeks later Rogers and Bill Hornsby flew to Puerto Rico, where Hornsby was to manage the Yankees-subsidized Ponce club in the Commonwealth's six-team winter league. Of Ponce's five non–Puerto Rican players (the maximum permitted), three—Clint Courtney, Bob Marquis, and Ernie Nevel—had been with Hornsby the previous summer. (The other two non–Puerto Ricans were infielder Bill Skowron and pitcher Lew Burdette, also Yankees farmhands.)

Caguas, which eventually won the league title while Hornsby's Ponce club finished third, featured Manuel "Jim" Rivera, a Manhattan-born, left-handed outfielder of Puerto Rican ancestry, who'd played the previous season at Pensacola in the Class B Southeastern League. Rivera had started late in Organized Baseball, having served several years in the federal penitentiary at Atlanta after a wartime army court-martial found him guilty on a charge of attempted rape. Now twenty-eight, he made a strong impression on Hornsby with his combination of power, speed, and relentless hustle.

Early in December, Hornsby left his Ponce team and flew to St. Petersburg, Florida, for the annual minor-league convention. There, as baseball insiders had been predicting for the past couple of weeks, he met with Emil Sick, owner of the Pacific Coast League's Seattle franchise, and signed to manage Sick's Rainiers in 1951.[19] No salary figure was given out; most estimates placed it at around $20,000. Hornsby's first official act was to draft Jim Rivera.

In January, following Bill Skowron's departure for military service, Bill Hornsby filled in at third base for a few games, but again he found the competition too strong. Within a week he drew his release and was on his way back to the States in the company of his father, who took leave of the Ponce team for good.[20]

Along with Ty Cobb, Tris Speaker, Dizzy Dean, and eleven other Hall of Famers, Hornsby traveled to New York City for an open house and banquet commemorating the National League's seventy-fifth anniversary. The festivities took place in the Broadway Central Hotel, which had somehow survived since February 2, 1876, when, as the Grand Central Hotel, it hosted a gathering of baseball entrepreneurs who brought the National League into existence.

Hornsby's annual baseball school was still a source of needed income, so he went directly from New York to Hot Springs. As he'd done a year earlier, he stayed around only until the end of February, coaching and demonstrating batting to 100 or so enrollees (who still each paid $100 tuition), before turning things over to Benny Meyer and leaving for his new job.

Hornsby drove the Cadillac given him at Beaumont all the way to Palm Springs, California, where the Seattle Rainiers would do their preseason conditioning. At Phoenix he stopped to look over the Yankees spring-training operation; visit with McDougald, Courtney, Marquis, and Nevel from his Beaumont champions; and tell Casey Stengel and his coaches what he'd told scout Atley Donald at Cuero, Texas, a year earlier: Don't mess with McDougald's batting style. (They did anyway, having the rookie hold his bat upright; McDougald still hit .306 and won American League Rookie of the Year honors for 1951.)[21]

In 1950, along with many other minor leagues, the Pacific Coast League (PCL) had suffered a substantial attendance drop, so that for 1951 its schedule was reduced from 200 games to 168. Players would be paid for six and one-half weeks' less work, which imposed a particular hardship on PCL veterans and prompted a number of futile holdouts.

Seattle was the last independently operating franchise in the PCL, and the Rainiers also began and ended the 1951 season as the only all-white team in the league. That was partly because black prospects were usually signed directly by big-league organizations, then sent to farm clubs in the northern states and Canada. As a nonaffiliated franchise, Seattle would logically be the last in the PCL to have black players, although it's doubtful that either Emil Sick or Hornsby wanted a racially mixed roster. When asked about the Rainiers' all-white composition, Hornsby would only say, "We would be very happy to have a Negro player on our team if we could find one who would help us."[22]

Hornsby later affirmed that the PCL—Seattle, Portland, Sacramento, San Francisco, Oakland, Los Angeles, Hollywood, and San Diego—was the best minor league he'd ever seen. Apart from its longer playing season, it was unique in several other respects. The aggregate population of PCL cities exceeded those in the American Association or International League; the PCL's annual attendance (even with the 1950 falloff) was the highest in the minors; and salaries—not confined by an official league limit—reached $15,000–$17,000 for star players. The PCL also benefited from excellent rail and air service, first-class hotels, and a meal allowance that, at five dollars per day, was only slightly below what big-leaguers received. PCL enterpreneurs and fans had long nourished major-league aspirations and sought exemption from the annual major-league draft, but so far they'd had to content themselves with general recognition as the best of the minors.

On the night of March 27, at Los Angeles, a disappointing crowd of about 5,000 paid to see the season opener between the local Angels and Hornsby's Rainiers. Baseball commissioner Happy Chandler, serving out his term after being denied another by the major-league owners, threw out the first ball, and three hours later Hornsby claimed his first PCL victory. At the end of a 12–9 slugfest, the difference was two home runs by Joe Montalvo, Seattle's towering catcher, and another round-tripper by left fielder Jim Rivera.

A couple of weeks later, the 1951 Texas League season began with Bill Hornsby in the infield for Oklahoma City, where he'd found a roster spot with what was now an independently operating ballclub.[23]

Batting only .206 after sixty-nine games, he again received notice of his release. When his father heard the news, he commented that it never made any sense to waste time in the minor leagues, and that he was "glad Billy learned early that he wasn't a real player. . . . Imagine how I would have felt, seeing the Hornsby name down in the batting averages with the pitchers."[24]

Although Seattle remained officially independent and consisted mostly of former major-leaguers and veteran minor-leaguers, Emil Sick readily accepted particular players on assignment from the big leagues. As a consequence, of the twenty-six men with Hornsby at the start of the season, only thirteen remained by August. Along the way, Hornsby experienced trouble with several of his veteran players, despite the efforts of coach Benny Huffman to mediate between the abrasive manager and his men. When Hornsby persuaded Sick to release pitcher Dewey Soriano, Soriano told the local press, "I like Seattle as a baseball town, but I don't like Hornsby and I don't like the way I was handled." Later in the season, when left-hander Jim Davis thought he wasn't being used enough, he told Hornsby, "Wherever you go from here, I wish you all the luck in the world—all of it bad."[25]

"In a way, I liked pitching for him," recalled right-hander Harold "Skinny" Brown, who won sixteen games in both relief and starting roles after joining Seattle on option from the Chicago White Sox. "He liked to win and so did I. But there was no give and take." Brown found Hornsby unapproachable and sometimes downright disagreeable, as when he scolded Brown and Davis, who shared an apartment in the same complex where Hornsby lived, that they were neglecting their careers by going trout fishing on days off. Brown also thought Hornsby only managed game by game, giving little thought to longer-range matters such as pitching rotations and lineup shifts.[26]

Hornsby hadn't changed. He upbraided his players for pregame fraternizing with members of other teams, still waved pitchers out and in from the dugout, still made pitchers he removed stay around for the rest of the game. He still didn't shower with his players, remaining after a game only long enough to change from uniform to street clothes.

Brown remembered him haunting hotel lobbies, usually alone, just sitting and watching.[27]

Brown, out of the University of North Carolina, was representative of
a new generation of better-educated, more independent-minded ballplayers—a different species from what Hornsby had known (or at least
been willing to accept). "Players are now too well satisfied," Hornsby
lamented to a writer as he sat in the lobby of the Hollywood Plaza Hotel,
"and they also have too many things to look forward to—like golf and
owning their own automobile. Too often nowadays a boy doesn't even
have to work for what he gets." Hornsby went on to denounce the
current practice of offering hefty signing bonuses to unproven teenagers.
"A big pocketful of dough is handed [them] on a silver platter. In my
book that's all wrong," he argued, because a bonus reduced a youngster's
incentive. "If I owned a major league club, I wouldn't even pay a Ty
Cobb until he made good." Still, he didn't begrudge youngsters their
bonuses if owners were "saps enough to give it to them."[28]

Hornsby may have been as set in his ways and beliefs as ever, but he
did have a warm side, which some people in Seattle saw that year. A
young man named Dave Kosher, suffering from cerebral palsy, was
wheelchair-bound when Hornsby befriended him early in the season.
Under Hornsby's rough, persistent encouragement, Kosher made himself leave the wheelchair and start walking. He eventually became sufficiently mobile for Hornsby to make him assistant clubhouse attendant;
in return, he became Hornsby's permanent acolyte.

By winning twenty-four of thirty-one games from late June through
July and taking four of five from the second-place Hollywood Stars,
Seattle built a five-game lead. Pleased with Hornsby's managing job,
Sick offered him a three-year contract at the same salary, but Bill Veeck,
who headed up a group that had just purchased the St. Louis Browns,
was already in contact with Hornsby about managing the Browns in
1952. By August, Veeck was calling him every week to talk about
changes needed for "our club"; Hornsby had to keep telling the impetuous Browns president that he didn't know where he would be next
year.[29]

By beating Oakland 4–2 on September 5, behind former big-leaguer Charley Schanz, Hornsby's club clinched Seattle's first PCL championship in ten years. The Rainiers finished at 99–68, six games in front of Hollywood, and topped the PCL in attendance for the third year in a row, pulling 465,727 into Sick's Stadium.

PCL writers voted Rivera the league's Most Valuable Player. Appearing in 166 games, Rivera won the batting title with a .352 average, also led in runs scored, hit twenty home runs, and drove in 111 runs. Only Bob Boyd, Sacramento's black first baseman, stole more bases. Said Hornsby of Rivera, "I don't know where we would have finished without him."[30]

In the dressing room after the pennant clincher, for once Hornsby lingered to congratulate his players. "The Rajah just grinned," wrote Royal Brougham, a local journalist. "He shook hands with Charley Schanz and passed a few quiet remarks to several other Rainiers." Outfielder Walt Judnich, a seven-year major-leaguer at odds with Hornsby most of the season, shook his hand and affirmed that he was the best manager Judnich had played for. Gushed Brougham, "The goose hangs high for the old fence-buster in this, his 55th [*sic*] year of an exciting life."[31]

However much Hornsby disliked minor-league playoffs, he had to be pleased with the outcome of what the PCL called the Governor's Cup Series. After eliminating fourth-place Los Angeles in a two-of-three-game set, the Rainiers left no doubt about who was the league's best by taking three of five from Hollywood, with Rivera doubling twice in the 9–2 clincher at the Stars' Gilmore Field.

Hornsby had no intention of staying on at Seattle, especially after Sick refused to give him either a pennant-winning bonus or a chunk of the $67,500 the White Sox paid for Rivera's contract. By the time he left the West Coast, Hornsby was talking about a possible deal with Gene Autry, the wealthy star of numerous low-budget western movies, whereby Autry would buy the San Francisco Seals and install Hornsby as general and field manager. San Francisco, said Hornsby, was "a good city and a good franchise," and "Autry would be a great asset to the league and to baseball. He's a high type of individual." But so far, he explained, Autry hadn't been able to get together with San Francisco owner Paul Fagan. Hornsby had talks scheduled during the World Series with other ballclubs, and, he said, "That's why I'm frettin' now. I'm in the middle and on the spot."[32]

Nothing ever came of Autry's San Francisco project. On the morning of September 30, Hornsby flew to St. Louis to meet with Bill Veeck and watch the Browns' season closer against the White Sox. After squirming through a comedy basketball game between the Harlem Globetrotters and a team led by professional clown Max Patkin (played on a wooden surface put down behind third base), Hornsby watched Ned Garver stagger to a 9–5 victory that gave the boyish-looking Browns right-hander a heroic twenty-win season. The Browns won only thirty-two times otherwise, finished dead last, and, despite Veeck's outrageous promotional efforts (which included once using a midget to pinch-hit), totaled only 293,770 in home attendance.

Nine days later, in New York, where the Giants were losing the World Series to the Yankees, Hornsby and Veeck met again, at Veeck's Savoy Plaza Hotel suite, and the Browns president offered him a three-year contract at $36,000 per year. Earlier Hornsby had talked with president Fred M. Saigh of the Cardinals (who'd just fired Marty Marion) and received an offer from Saigh that exactly matched Veeck's. He chose to go with the Browns, Hornsby later said, "because they were down, and I believed there was a greater opportunity to get results." The Cardinals' fans were used to contenders, "and if the club didn't win the pennant right away under my direction, there'd be a lot of criticism of the manager."[33]

At the age of fifty-five, Rogers Hornsby finally made it back to the big time—hired by the same franchise that fourteen years earlier had fired him from his last job in the majors, and hired by the son of the man who'd fired him at Chicago in 1932. The original partnership of Hornsby and Veeck hadn't worked at all; longtime baseball observers shook their heads, wondering what possible future a Hornsby–Veeck Jr. partnership might have.

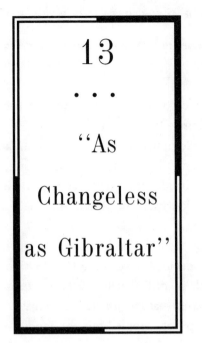

13

· · ·

"As

Changeless

as Gibraltar"

ornsby's new boss was perhaps the single most dynamic, atten-
tion-getting (and attention-loving) man in baseball. Thirty-seven
years old when he hired Hornsby, Bill Veeck was a native Chicagoan
and self-described "hustler" who grew up watching Hornsby perform at
Wrigley Field for the St. Louis Cardinals, New York Giants, Boston
Braves, and finally the Chicago Cubs—the franchise Veeck's father
served as president. When William H. Veeck Sr. died in the fall of
1933, his son dropped out of Kenyon College and went to work for
the Cubs in a variety of posts, from advertising and food service to
ticket sales and park maintenance. (In later years he liked to tell how in
1938 he helped sprig the ivy on the walls of the rebuilt Wrigley Field
bleachers.) By 1941 he was club treasurer and assistant secretary.

Before the next season, young Veeck and Charlie Grimm raised
enough money to purchase the Milwaukee Brewers of the American
Association. Introducing an array of promotional stunts that rivaled Joe
Engel's at Chattanooga, the Veeck-Grimm combination capitalized on

war-generated prosperity and scarce wartime entertainment options and, with three-straight pennant winners, broke all Milwaukee attendance records.

Veeck also hatched ambitions for acquiring a big-league franchise, namely the moribund Philadelphia Phillies. He made the mistake, though, of telling Commissioner Kenesaw Mountain Landis that if allowed to purchase the Phillies, he intended to sign several outstanding Negro-league stars. Landis, who never favored the integration of Organized Baseball, quickly took the Phillies off the market and eventually found another buyer.

By late 1944 the restless Veeck, closed out of the majors and bored at Milwaukee, had decided to join the U.S. Marine Corps. A leg injury suffered in an artillery drill developed into osteomyelitis and led to a succession of surgeries that eventually took most of his left leg and left him, as he liked to put it, crippled but not handicapped. After the 1945 season, Veeck sold the Brewers; in the summer of the next year he organized a group of investors that bought the Cleveland Indians.

Moving the Indians full-time into huge Municipal Stadium, Veeck lured fans by promoting Bob Feller's pitching dates, as well as hiring clowns and acrobats, staging fireworks spectacles and beauty pageants, and offering numerous contests and giveaways. He also signed Larry Doby, the American League's first black player, and thereby won over thousands of black fans from the Negro American League's Cleveland Buckeyes.

In 1948 it all came together for Veeck, player-manager Lou Boudreau, and the Indians, who drew 2.6 million people—more than any baseball franchise had ever attracted—and, after defeating the Boston Red Sox in a one-game pennant tiebreaker, bested the Boston Braves in the World Series. Satchel Paige, whose midseason signing was widely criticized as another Veeck stunt, pulled in big crowds, provided critical pitching help, and permanently won Veeck's heart.

Veeck sold his interest in the Indians following the 1949 season and, after a year and a half out of baseball, purchased control of the downtrodden St. Louis Browns. He resigned Paige (released by Cleveland after Veeck left), pulled out all his old promotional tricks, added a few new ones, and boosted attendance considerably in the last half of the 1951 season. Yet except for Paige and twenty-game-winner Ned Garver, the Browns remained a sorry lot.

Veeck had long admired Hornsby, first as a player, then as an exceptionally knowledgeable baseball man. His work at Tucson in 1947 with Jim Hegan and Pat Seerey especially impressed Veeck (despite the fact that it apparently did nothing to improve either player's hitting). Firing the mild-mannered Zack Taylor, Veeck went against the advice of various people (including even his mother) and brought in Hornsby to manage the Browns. Although Veeck later claimed that in hiring Hornsby he mistakenly "put publicity and promotion ahead of operations," he also honestly expected that "the Rajah" would reverse the Browns' misfortunes.[1]

"There will be no clowns," said Hornsby in New York on October 8, when he and Veeck held a press conference to announce his hiring. Fireworks shows after games were okay, but "I take my baseball seriously, and if my club is getting beat, I don't want anybody laughing at some clown." "One thing I'll tell you," he went on, "I'll spend a lot of time at the ball park. . . . That's all I got to do, baseball. It's my life and if workin' will do any good, Bill and I ought to do all right. You know he isn't going to sit still and have a lot of humpty-dumpties playin' ball for us." "I won't let any team I manage finish last," he declared. Why was he so certain the 1952 Browns wouldn't finish last again? "Me," he said without hesitation.[2]

Conspicuously missing from anything either Hornsby or Veeck said publicly were references to Hornsby's unhappy experience with Veeck's father, or his somewhat less unhappy encounter with Bill DeWitt, the Browns' second-in-command when Donald Barnes fired Hornsby in 1937, and now Veeck's vice president and general manager.

Hornsby would still live in Chicago, although he observed that he was only an hour and twelve minutes from St. Louis by air. And he'd continue his longtime practice of signaling pitching changes from the dugout instead of going to the mound. "When I want [a pitcher] out," he said, "I'll say so from the dugout and he'll get the hell out of there. . . . I believe half the time when a manager walks out to the mound he just wants to get into the television picture or be seen by the crowd." And yes, he'd still coach at third base, "because the manager belongs there whether winning or losing. He ought to be responsible for sending runners home."[3] No, he would no longer operate his early spring baseball school at Hot Springs.

Without anybody bringing up the subject, Hornsby brought it up himself: "Maybe you're wondering if I'd object to playing Negroes on my club. That's all wrong. If they're good players, they'd be welcome to play for me. . . . In Puerto Rico last winter, Negroes were on our roster and they did all right for me."[4] Hornsby was making reference to Saturnino "Nino" Escalera, a slightly built outfielder on his Ponce team. Although most of his auditors were thinking of Satchel Paige, the Browns' only black player, a more reminiscent Hornsby might have added that, going back to 1935 in Mexico, he'd periodically competed against, managed, and managed against black players.

Publicly, Hornsby went out of his way to tout the White Sox's Jim Rivera; privately, he all but demanded that Veeck acquire the outfielder. "He's the only player I've seen in a long time that I would pay into the park to see play," enthused Hornsby. "He loves to play ball, he can run and hit and throw and he gives you quite a show. Wait'll you see him." Five weeks later, Veeck negotiated a trade with Chicago that brought Rivera and three others to St. Louis for three dispensable Browns. Acceding to Veeck's wishes that he give up Puerto Rican winter ball, Rivera flew to St. Louis to sign his 1951 contract. "Whatever success I've had, or might have in the future," said Rivera, "I owe to Mr. Hornsby."[5]

While Hornsby named Bob Scheffing (a onetime Hot Springs pupil) and Bill Norman as his regular coaches and Marty Marion as player-coach, Ned Garver drove to St. Louis from the family farm at Ney, Ohio, and signed for $25,000—the biggest salary in the Browns' history. The Browns also obtained Clint Courtney in a trade with the Yankees and negotiated other deals that, by the following spring, left only Garver and five others from the team that had completed the 1951 season.

At the end of January, Hornsby said good-bye to Bernadette Harris, flew from Chicago to St. Louis, and with his coaches, pitchers, catchers, and rookies boarded a Missouri Pacific train for El Centro, California, where the Browns had scheduled preliminary workouts before the White Sox occupied the site for regular spring training. In the early going, Roy Sievers, the 1949 American League Rookie of the Year, aggravated a shoulder injury sustained the previous season. Although Sievers required surgery (and would miss all of 1952), Hornsby seemed little concerned over the loss of the Browns' principal right-handed power hitter. "If you can hit, you can hit any kind of pitching," he remarked. "This is still a man's game."[6]

As always, Hornsby scheduled one continuous workout session— 11:00 to 2:00—with no lunch break. Besides pitching up to a half hour each day during batting practice, occasionally he grabbed a bat, stepped to the plate, and rapped long drives to all parts of the outfield. Asked one day whether he might not be working the players too hard, he snapped, "Hey, they're men, aren't they? Hard work is good for 'em."[7] At the end of February, the full Browns squad gathered at Burbank, California, and worked out at Olive Memorial Stadium, a city-owned facility. By then, another trade, with Detroit, had added left-hander Gene Bearden (the American League Rookie of the Year with Cleveland's 1948 champions), as well as right-hander Bob Cain and first baseman Dick Kryhoski.

The Browns' workouts took place only a short distance from Universal Studios. By still another of many ironic twists in Hornsby's life, Universal happened to be filming *The Winning Team,* a highly sanitized version of the life of Grover Cleveland Alexander, who had died the previous December. When the pitcher's widow visited Olive Stadium in the company of Ronald Reagan, cast as Alexander in the movie, Hornsby neglected practice long enough to pose with them for photographers.

Outwardly, the weeks at Burbank were hardworking but harmonious. Ned Garver was quoted as saying that the ballclub had "a new spirit," not "the defeatist attitude anymore. . . . It's just like being with an entirely new group" (which it nearly was). After ten victories in fifteen games—against the White Sox, Cubs, Giants, Pirates, San Francisco, and Oakland—the Browns headed east and won two more from Cleveland at Tucson. "St. Louis looks like a brand new ballclub," commented Indians manager Al Lopez.[8]

Yet much of the team was already seething with resentment and anger toward Hornsby. Milton Richman, who spent much of that spring covering the Browns, remembered that in the bottom of the first inning of games at Burbank, the public-address man always announced: "Coaching at third base, Rogers Hornsby, the greatest right-handed hitter who ever lived." Various players liked to mimic that tribute when Hornsby was paged at the Los Angeles Biltmore: "Paging Rogers Hornsby, the greatest right-handed hitter and the most miserable manager who ever lived." One night on a railroad platform, Gene Bearden nodded toward Hornsby and said to Richman, "Look at him standing there by himself. It's no wonder. He doesn't have a friend in the world and he doesn't deserve one."[9]

It was the same thing that had surfaced at least as early as 1951 at Seattle: hard-nosed, demanding, and critical as he'd always been, Hornsby couldn't relate to a new generation of ballplayers who were better educated, more family oriented, and sometimes less professionally dedicated than the prewar generation. Hornsby could never understand that it might help if he got to know his players personally—and they got to know him as well.

Ned Garver remembered Hornsby's remaining "completely aloof. He wouldn't speak to you except to ridicule you." He didn't even eat with his coaches, and in the various cities where the Browns played that spring, he seemed to have no friends. As Garver remembered it, when the Browns stopped over in Houston for an exhibition game, Bill Hornsby, now working out of St. Louis for the Falstaff Brewing Company, dropped by the Rice Hotel lobby to visit his father. Sternly disapproving his son's occupation, Hornsby refused to speak to him. With

Hornsby, said Garver, what passed for conversation consisted of one-sentence pronouncements. He never reminisced about his long and picturesque career—never said a word about John McGraw, Hack Wilson, his World Series experiences, anything. "See," lamented Garver many years afterward, "he could have shared those things with us, but he wouldn't talk with us."[10]

Hornsby didn't help his standing with his players or Bill Veeck when he fined Satchel Paige $100 for arriving late for an exhibition game at Corpus Christi, Texas. When Paige explained that he'd had trouble getting a taxi at his black-operated rooming house, Hornsby shot back, "What do you expect me to do, lead you around by the hand?" Paige appealed to Veeck, who promised the pitcher he wouldn't deduct the fine from his paycheck. Commenting on the whole incident, Hornsby offered, "Paige don't do it on purpose. He just forgets what time it is."[11]

After games at Corpus Christi, San Antonio, Houston, and Beaumont (where no more than a couple of thousand people turned out for Hornsby's first appearance since his 1950 triumph), the Browns sat through rain-outs of two scheduled exhibitions with the Cardinals at Sportsman's Park and then headed for Detroit to open the season.[12] Whatever rumblings of discontent writers traveling with the club may have detected, Hornsby's team had shown well in preseason play, ending with a 19–10 record. As he put it later on, "I never saw a club with better team spirit or one in better physical condition than the squad that opened the 1952 season in the uniforms of the Browns."[13]

Even those uniforms were different when Hornsby's team took the field at Detroit's Briggs Stadium. In place of the busy brown-and-orange-trimmed flannels they'd worn for the past two decades, the 1952 edition of the Browns appeared in simpler motif: brown caps and stockings, no trim on gray shirts and pants, just scripted "St. Louis" across the shirtfront ("Browns" on the white home attire). If Hornsby hadn't personally demanded a change (as was generally assumed), at least the new uniforms typified his plain, no-nonsense style. As Queen Juliana of the Netherlands and 43,111 others watched at Briggs Stadium, Garver threw a three-hit shutout. Of the Browns' starting nine that day, only Garver and second baseman Bobby Young had appeared regularly in St. Louis's 1951 lineup.

For a while, it seemed that Hornsby might actually have wrought the transformation Veeck hoped for. After eight games, the Browns held first place with a 7–1 record, which included seven completed starts by Hornsby's pitchers. Of those route-going efforts, the most impressive was that of Bob Cain, who on the night of April 23, at Sportsman's Park, permitted Cleveland one hit and no runs over nine innings. Bob Feller gave up only one hit as well, but Feller lost his game in the bottom of the ninth on third baseman Al Rosen's error.

According to Cain, Hornsby never congratulated him on his splendid outing; when reporters sought a comment from the Browns manager, he replied simply, "What the hell, you saw it, didn't you? Why ask me about it?" More positively, Hornsby said that he wasn't surprised by his team's early showing, and he wasn't "conceding a thing until the other clubs prove we can't win it."[14]

Early season home attendance also delighted Veeck. The turnout of 27,910 for a doubleheader with Chicago on Sunday, April 20, was the biggest since 1944—when the local American Leaguers won the only pennant in their fifty-two-year history. Moreover, unlike previous big-league executives for whom Hornsby had worked, Veeck appeared totally unconcerned about his manager's gambling habits, past or present. As the Cubs' manager and in his earlier stint with the Browns, Hornsby had denied using club employees to "run bets" for him, but in 1952, according to various accounts, he regularly dispatched the Browns' clubhouse man across the street to place wagers with bookmaker Louis "Murph" Calcaterra.

On their first extended road trip, the Browns started to play up to most people's expectations. Garver was knocked out twice and began complaining about not knowing when he was scheduled to pitch. Hornsby, he said, ordered him to do off-days sprints before the first game of a doubleheader, then told him between games that he was to pitch the nightcap. The poor early showings of "Hornsby's pets"—the label Garver and others laid on Jim Rivera and Clint Courtney, as well as third baseman Leo Thomas and first baseman George Schmees (both drafted out of the Pacific Coast League on Hornsby's word)—added to the gathering discontent. "I've never seen a whole ballclub go into a batting slump at the same time like ours has," groaned Hornsby with obvious disregard for his own baseball experience. "I guess the boys are pressing too hard." As for Garver's succession of disappointing outings, "It's brutal the way Garver has been beaten this season. . . . Garver knows how to take it. He doesn't grumble or complain."[15]

Yet whatever palliatives Hornsby might deliver for public consumption, Garver and most of the rest of the Browns had already turned against him. His pitchers couldn't understand why Hornsby made them watch their opponents' batting practice, although the manager insisted that somebody might pick up something that would help the team. And why didn't Hornsby have the grace to come out and take the ball from a pitcher? Why must a big-leaguer have to wait, hand the ball to his successor, and then troop to the dugout? (To which Hornsby insisted he must return as soon as he changed his sweatshirt.)

After sweeping a Memorial Day doubleheader at home from Detroit before 13,000, with Paige saving the opener and getting credit for his fourth win in the nightcap, the Browns headed east in sixth place with a record of 20–24. For twenty-one home dates, they'd drawn 201,350, triple the attendance at that point in 1951.

At Philadelphia, Garver lost another tough one, 2–1, with the Browns scoring their first run for him in forty-two innings. While Garver's record fell to 2–6, Paige continued to excel in relief. At Washington, he pitched five and one-third scoreless innings, made three singles in three times at bat, and drove in the winning run in the top of the seventeenth to gain his fifth victory against a single defeat.

During their stays at Philadelphia and Washington, Hornsby gave Bobby Young permission to leave the ballclub and visit his wife and children at Baltimore. But when Hornsby, in a team meeting at Washington, singled out Young for being more interested in getting home than winning games, Young angrily retorted (as he told it later),

"Hornsby was never to mention anything about my family and if he did again I'd punch his face in."[16]

On Friday, June 6, the Browns moved into Yankee Stadium and beat the locals 9–3, third baseman Jim Dyck homering twice and Courtney once. The next day, after making only three hits off Allie Reynolds and losing 2–1, St. Louis remained tied with Philadelphia for sixth place with a 22–26 record.

On Sunday the teams met in a doubleheader. In the top of the fourth inning of the first game, Browns pitcher Tommy Byrne lifted a foul fly back of third base. With Hornsby watching nearby from the coaching box, Gil McDougald tried to make a catch at the field-box railing, only to have a spectator clutch at the ball and fumble it out of McDougald's reach. Umpire Joe Paparella immediately signaled Byrne out, judging that McDougald was interferred with in trying to make the play. Hornsby briefly discussed the play with Paparella, then resumed his position.

From St. Louis, where he was listening to a radio broadcast of the game, Veeck telephoned Yankee Stadium, reached traveling secretary Bill Durney, and instructed him to have Hornsby register an official protest with the umpires. Durney made his way to the Browns' dugout and passed along Veeck's order, whereupon an infuriated Hornsby stomped to home plate to explain to umpire in chief Art Passarella that he was sorry, he knew official protests weren't allowed on umpires' judgment calls, but that's what Veeck wanted, so he had to do it. It was too late for that anyway, replied Passarella; under the rules, the umpire in chief had to be notified of a protest before play resumed. Meanwhile the Yankee Stadium public-address announcer, evidently acting on prior word from Durney, intoned that the Browns were playing the game under protest. A few minutes later, after the umpires sent word upstairs to the contrary, the announcer corrected himself.

It was all pretty confusing, although it made no difference in the outcome, which was a 5–2 Yankees victory that was aided by five St. Louis errors. The winners of the last three World Series also won the nightcap on a shutout by right-hander Vic Raschi; Hornsby's club dropped into seventh place.

From New York, the Browns traveled by train to Boston and checked into the Hotel Kenmore. As soon as he got to his room, Hornsby called Veeck to say that he'd been embarrassed in New York before his players and the umpires, and that he wouldn't stand for such interference from a club owner or anybody else. Beyond that, he wanted Veeck to know that he listened too much to "yes men," notably Durney and Bill DeWitt. Essentially he told Veeck what he'd told Veeck's father twenty years earlier: stop meddling in on-field matters or pay me off.

Veeck flew into Boston the next morning and went directly to the Kenmore and into conference with Hornsby. All right, he would pay Hornsby off. Although Hornsby's contract called for three full years' salary, Veeck talked him into taking full pay for the remainder of the present season and all of 1953, but only half pay ($18,000) for 1954. Then Veeck summoned local and traveling newspeople to disclose that he'd dismissed Hornsby and named Marty Marion as the Browns' new manager. "I just made a mistake," said Veeck. "I thought Hornsby had mellowed, but he hadn't."[17] He went on to say that he'd decided on the change a week earlier; his quarrel with Hornsby over the protest in New York had no bearing on his decision. While the newspeople scribbled that down and reported it, few actually believed it.

Talking separately to the press, Hornsby said of the incident in New York, "I didn't protest [at first] because it was strictly a judgment call. . . . There's no use in arguing with umpires about a thing like that." Had he been fired? "You can say I was fired or quit," he replied. "I don't care. But nobody can send messenger boys down on the field to tell me what to do when I'm runnin' the team. When you work for a screwball, you get screwball questions and screwball answers." Wound up, Hornsby went on to say, "In my baseball code, we're all gettin' paid to do one thing—win! . . . I didn't put my arm around any of my players and kiss 'em if they won. . . . Every day, a ball player is the same with me, win or lose." When Veeck sent Durney to the Yankee

Stadium dugout to tell him what to do, he "decided that was too much." For now, he intended to fly to St. Louis, pick up his automobile (the Beaumont Cadillac), and drive home to Chicago.[18]

Early in the afternoon of June 10, when word of Hornsby's firing got around the Kenmore, somebody—a group of Browns players by one account, Durney by another, Veeck himself by still another—concocted the idea of having a trophy to honor Veeck made up at a local department store. A three-foot-high trophy was delivered to Durney at the hotel, and in the Browns' dressing room at Fenway Park that evening, with a battery of photographers on hand, Ned Garver presented it to Veeck. An inscription read: "To Bill Veeck. For the greatest play since the Emancipation Proclamation." Many oldtime baseball people gagged at that gesture (or self-gesture), including the New York writer Frank Graham, who'd known Hornsby since the 1920s. "Whom did [Veeck] think he was hiring?" Graham asked plaintively. "Little Lord Fauntleroy?"[19]

Yet most of the Browns who talked to the press sounded as if they actually were liberated from some form of involuntary servitude. "He didn't show me any respect as a twenty-game winner," protested Garver. "He never gave anybody a pat on the back or a smile or a word of encouragement." George Schmees (who, without Hornsby's recommendation, would still have been in the minors) hadn't liked being ordered to take first pitches. Besides being unhappy over the lack of praise for his one-hit victory, Bob Cain complained about being removed early in four other games and told by Hornsby that he was "only a night pitcher." Gene Bearden said, "They ought to declare a national holiday in St. Louis," and Bobby Young told everybody, "If I thought I could make as much money in some other profession, I would have given up baseball rather than continue playing for Hornsby."[20]

While the slump-ridden Jim Rivera, the foremost of Hornsby's alleged "pets," remained publicly silent, Clint Courtney refused to take part in the vilification of a man he admired. "Hornsby was like a father to me and helped me tremendously with my batting," pronounced the young catcher. "I still think he's a fine manager."[21]

As the newspeople continued to quiz him, Veeck expanded on various players' grievances: Hornsby played favorites; he couldn't get along with anybody; he was even cheap with his tips to clubhouse attendants around the league. "I saved Hornsby from getting whacked," the Browns president insisted. "Several of the players were ready to give it to him, physically, when I stepped in and removed Rog from the picture. . . . The men were tense, fired up against Hornsby for his methods in dealing with them."[22]

In a telephone interview from Boston with St. Louis sports broadcaster Harry Caray, Hornsby spoke honestly of himself: "I'm not too friendly a fellow. I told them about myself—that I wasn't a fellow who mixed freely with the players—that I wasn't a fellow runnin' around with a lollypop in my hand and kissin' them after they won a game or got a hit." Yet when passions cooled somewhat a couple of weeks later, he was remarkably generous to men who'd not been so to him. "I thought every player on the club gave his best at all times," he said. "I still think they're a fine bunch of fellows who gave me one-hundred percent of their ability, and I tried to give them the same thing out there as manager."[23]

One of the more incisive commentaries on Hornsby's latest trouble came from the St. Louis sportswriter J. Roy Stockton, who'd pretty much grown up in baseball with Hornsby. As Stockton saw things, Hornsby both carried a grudge from the past in the case of Bill DeWitt and, for the present, understood neither today's ballplayers nor today's baseball writers. Contemporary writers haunted the dugouts and clubhouses, less interested in the game on the field than inside information—the "quotable quote." Hornsby, observed Stockton, missed the old-time writers such as John Wray, Sid Keener, Jim Gould, and even Stockton himself—men with whom he could be comfortably honest. As for his players, "it never entered his mind that a friendly atmosphere, a warmth between players and manager, might be important." If the men wanted to win as much as he did, they would respect him. "But they didn't."[24]

Two days after Veeck fired Hornsby, the biweekly magazine *Look* published an article under Hornsby's name—complete with outdated pictures of him with various Browns players—entitled "It's Still Baseball, Ty Cobb!" The article was intended as an answer to a two-part piece published the previous March under Cobb's name in the weekly *Life*. Cobb had lambasted nearly everything about contemporary baseball: the game itself, which relied on power-hitting at the expense of speed, strategy, and finesse; today's ballplayers, who were overpaid, often poorly conditioned, and "a particularly fragile lot" when compared to the rugged men of Cobb's era; and executives who gave big bonuses to kid prospects, who often never became anything else.[25]

Although Hornsby often talked in much the same vein, Cobb's claim that Hornsby was weak on pop flies and his choice of Eddie Collins as second baseman on his all-time team left Hornsby thoroughly peeved. After deriding Cobb's *Life* articles in hotel lobbies across the country, he readily accepted *Look*'s invitation to publish a rebuttal. Ghostwritten by Tim Cohane, Hornsby's article admonished Cobb that "it's still baseball" and defended today's performers. If Cobb were playing in 1952, Hornsby noted, he simply wouldn't be allowed to run at will, wouldn't steal anywhere near as many bases, and, in general, would have to adjust to a different kind of game. When Hornsby listed his own all-time outfielders, he returned Cobb's slight by ignoring him in favor of Babe Ruth, Tris Speaker, and Joe Jackson. ("Relative to Hornsby," said Cobb in a telegram from his Atherton, California, home to an eastern acquaintance, "any person can express [any] opinion he desires whether in good spirit or not. I am sorry to see him lose his job.")[26]

While Hornsby's old nemesis Charlie Grimm returned to the majors, succeeding Tommy Holmes as manager of the struggling Boston Braves (and positioning himself for a far better situation when the Braves shifted to Milwaukee ten months later), Hornsby found himself again on the job market. Over the next two and a half years, it would cost Bill Veeck about $67,000 to pay off his contract, but Hornsby always needed to keep working somewhere in baseball.

On top of everything else, waiting for Hornsby when he arrived in St. Louis from Boston was a copy of a petititon his long-estranged wife had just filed in circuit court in St. Louis. Alleging that Hornsby possessed a "violent and ungovernable temper" and struck her on several occasions before abandoning her in 1945, Jeannette Hornsby asked the court to order him to pay a regular maintenance allowance.[27]

Meanwhile Hornsby's name came up with increasing frequency as a possible successor to Cincinnati manager Luke Sewell, who was talking about resigning. Hornsby saw the Reds in action on July 10, when he took part in Hall of Fame Night at Crosley Field (as the former Redland Field had been known since the mid-1930s, when Powel Crosley Jr., a multimillionaire manufacturer of radios and other appliances, bought the Reds). With Jimmie Foxx, Carl Hubbell, Paul Waner, Mickey Cochrane, and about a dozen other Hall of Famers, Hornsby watched the Reds defeat Boston to improve their record to 34–44.

Twelve days later Reds general manager Gabe Paul telephoned Hornsby and asked him to fly from Chicago to Indianapolis for a meeting. Over coffee in the airport terminal, Hornsby told Paul that he was definitely available if and when Sewell was out of the way. Then, on July 26, Paul flew to Chicago and met Hornsby at the Hilton Hotel, where they agreed on a contract that Hornsby would sign as soon as Sewell quit. A two-year arrangement, it would pay Hornsby something less than $10,000 for the remainder of the present season and $20,000 for 1953. Sewell accommodatingly resigned two days later, just before a doubleheader loss to Philadelphia that dropped the Reds into seventh place. As he left, Sewell denounced second-guessing local sportswriters who "brought the fans down on my head," adding that Cincinnati's was "the worst fan clientele in the country."[28]

The next morning Paul called in the press to announce Hornsby's hiring—as approved beforehand by Powel Crosley, vacationing in Canada. "I picked Hornsby because I wanted a hard-nosed baseball man," said Paul.[29] For the next week, Hornsby would be on the road, looking over Cincinnati-controlled minor-leaguers; until August 5, when he assumed active direction of the team, coach Earle Brucker (Sr.) would be in charge.

Several months later, Paul expanded on the circumstances of

Hornsby's hiring. "When a change was imminent," he said, "I thought of only one fellow—Hornsby." Besides Crosley, who'd always liked Hornsby, he talked with Branch Rickey and George Weiss, "both of whom gave Hornsby tremendous recommendations." Some of the Reds players thought that "a fellow with horns was coming in to take over," but that interested Paul less than what Hornsby thought of the players. If, in the past, Hornsby had experienced trouble with particular players, Paul was convinced that "it has been with fellows . . . who do not like Rog's antipathy toward anyone who takes it easy."[30]

Hornsby visited the Milwaukee and Kansas City American Association teams, to which the Reds had assigned particular players, and the Texas League Tulsa Oilers, a full-fledged Cincinnati farm club. Yet the minor-leaguer he liked the most belonged not to the Reds but to the Yankees. In Tulsa, Beaumont's Jim Greengrass, a blond, broad-shouldered outfielder, hit a towering home run over the center-field fence; what impressed Hornsby even more, he later told Greengrass, was his all-out hustle. "I even ran full speed to first when I got a base on balls," Greengrass recalled.[31] One way or another, Hornsby intended to have the Beaumont outfielder on his ballclub.

When the Reds' new manager returned to Cincinnati, sixty newspaper and radio people gathered for a welcoming luncheon at the Netherland Plaza Hotel. Hornsby talked for thirty-five minutes—no doubt a personal record. "I'm no diplomat," he conceded, but "neither am I a Simon Legree." He promised to have "an interesting ball club. A real fighter." Although the talk was well received, Lou Smith of the *Cincinnati Enquirer* remained skeptical about how successful Hornsby might be at a time when "such self-denial and singleness of purpose" as he'd always demanded were "foreign to the makeup of most present-day ballplayers."[32]

Defensively one of the best in the majors, the team Hornsby inherited from Sewell lacked batting punch and was decidedly pitching-poor. Ted Kluszewski, a hugely muscled first baseman, was the only consistent threat at the plate; the veteran lefty Ken Raffensberger was Cincinnati's one reliable starting pitcher. Since 1945 the Reds had finished no higher than sixth place and, despite the city's rich baseball tradition, usually ended near the bottom of the majors in home attendance.

On August 5 the Reds won their first game under Hornsby on the strength of Raffensberger's shutout pitching and Kluszewski's two-run triple. Besides Powel Crosley, who flew in from Canada for the game, 12,651 paying customers—the second-biggest crowd of the season— came out on a weeknight to inspect the Hornsby-edition Reds. At 42–61, Cincinnati trailed the sixth-place Cubs by a game and a half.

As he'd done the previous fall with the Browns, Hornsby quickly started exchanging players he didn't like for players he wanted. Veteran outfielder Wally Westlake was sold to Cleveland, and Ewell Blackwell, a great pitcher a few years earlier but no longer effective, went to the Yankees in a trade that brought Ernie Nevel and Bob Marquis from Kansas City and Jim Greengrass from Beaumont. As soon as Greengrass arrived early in September, Hornsby put him in left field in place of Joe Adcock, a tall, powerful Louisianian who hated the outfield but had no chance of supplanting Kluszewski at first base. For eighteen games, Greengrass batted .309, hit five homers (including a grand slam against Brooklyn), and drove in twenty-four runs.

At ten every morning when the Reds were at home, Greengrass met Hornsby for a session on how to play the unique embankment in front of Crosley Field's left-field wall. Although the rookie appreciated the extra help, the truth was that Hornsby, as Greengrass put it long afterward, just "loved to be in that ballpark." As he got to know his manager, Greengrass came to realize that baseball was too much Hornsby's whole life. He spent a lot of time in the dugout, just sitting alone and, thought Greengrass, probably reminiscing to himself about the old days.[33]

The Reds won twenty-seven and lost twenty-four games after Hornsby assumed control. They finished in sixth place, in front of the Boston Braves and a Pittsburgh team that won only forty-two times and received general recognition as one of the worst in major-league history. Although overall major-league attendance fell nearly 1.5 million,

Cincinnati's home crowds totaled 606,824, a slight improvement over 1951.[34]

Once the season was over, Hornsby and Paul cleared out Luke Sewell's three coaches, replacing them with Ford Garrison (another Beaumont alumnus) and fellow Texan Buster Mills. They then worked out two major off-season trades, the first of which turned out to be among the most successful in Reds history.

Following Brooklyn's failure to win the 1950 pennant, Branch Rickey had sold his interest in the Dodgers for approximately $1 million and joined Pittsburgh as vice president and general manager. Signing youngsters for lavish bonuses, trading with abandon, and hurriedly putting together a farm system, Rickey sought to do for the Pirates what he'd done for the Cardinals and Dodgers—only much quicker. So far, though, nothing had worked, and Rickey was on the outs with his best young player, power-hitting outfielder David "Gus" Bell. Rickey was willing to take a substitute outfielder and catcher from the Reds in exchange for the twenty-two-year-old Bell.

In the other trade—a four-way deal involving Cincinnati, Boston, Brooklyn, and Philadelphia—Joe Adcock ended up with the franchise that was about to shift to Milwaukee; Everett "Rocky" Bridges, a squat infielder known more for his peerless tobacco chewing than his ballplaying, joined the Reds. It was the most fortuituous event in Adcock's life, because, given custody of first base by Charlie Grimm, he became one of the National League's premier power hitters.

Interviewed at his Thorndale Avenue apartment building, Hornsby complained about Chicago's winters and about being generally bored. Not only were the racetracks closed, but "card-playing is silly. Most of the movies are lousy. Them television comedians stink. Basketball and hockey don't mean nothin'." He couldn't wait to leave for spring training.[35]

Part of that winter, Hornsby occupied himself working with J. Roy Stockton on a book that would combine his reminiscences about baseball past, ruminations on baseball present, and instructional tips for youngsters. In a period before tattling tomes by and about professional athletes came into vogue, *My Kind of Baseball*—published the following spring—was an unusually candid baseball book. Hornsby was particularly open regarding his experiences with "Bill Veeck and his office clerks." It ended on an upbeat note, with Hornsby looking forward to big things in Cincinnati. But, no, he never had permitted beer in the dressing room after games, and he still wouldn't. "Beer and baseball don't go together," he remarked. "I have to wait for my milk shakes, don't I?"[36]

For the seventh spring in succession, the Reds trained at Tampa, Florida, using a minor-league facility named Plant Field. Although he still held to his routine of one long practice and two meals per day, Hornsby also decided upon a softer approach than he'd used with the Browns. "Baseball is fun, not work," he announced to his assembled players. "Just hustle, play the best you can and we'll get along and have a lot of fun doing it." He divided his players, stationed them on two diamonds, and for three days had them do nothing but play the old kids' game of "work-up," with a player remaining at bat until he was put out, whereupon everybody in the field moved up a position. "I believe in letting ball players train the way I wanted to train when I was a player," said Hornsby. Lou Smith was surprised to find him "anything but the whip-crackin' skipper he was pictured to be."[37]

Lots of players' wives and small children were on hand at Tampa, and Hornsby didn't even seem to mind that. Besides, for several days Bernadette Harris—"an attractive brunette" (in Lou Smith's description), who introduced herself as "Mrs. Rogers Hornsby"—could also be seen at the ballpark and the Floridian Hotel.[38]

For 1953 the Cincinnati Reds would continue to play as one of the majors' dwindling number of all-white teams. The Puerto Rican outfielder Nino Escalera appeared in several spring-training games as the first black player to wear a Cincinnati uniform, but by the beginning of the season he was back in the minors.

Hornsby spent considerable time at Plant Field with Ted Kluszewski, trying to get the brawny first baseman to level his swing and thereby, Hornsby believed, increase his home-run output. Meanwhile, at Crosley

Field, a screen was being erected in front of the right-field bleachers to cut the distance for Kluszewski and Gus Bell from 366 to 342 feet.

For all the relaxed atmosphere Hornsby obviously tried hard to create, he began spring training on bad terms with infielder Grady Hatton, whom he scolded for not reporting for the first day's practice, even though Hatton was already in Tampa. Hornsby further antagonized the veteran Hatton by leaving him behind with the second squad for a final exhibition game at Tampa, while the first squad started home, playing a series with Washington on the way north. Inasmuch as Hatton was the Reds' player representative in dealings with management, animosity between the two native Texans didn't bode well.[39]

When the Reds returned to Cincinnati for two games with Detroit (which they split to end the exhibition season at 16–14), Bernadette Harris rejoined Hornsby. Having completed a deal for the sale of his apartment building in Chicago, Hornsby rented a house on the northwestern side of Cincinnati, at 3716 Homelawn Avenue in the municipality of Cheviot, where he introduced Harris to neighbors as his "housekeeper." A month later, in St. Louis, a circuit court judged ruled on Jeannette Hornsby's petition for separate maintenance, ordering Hornsby to begin payments of $400 per month.

The Reds opened the season on Monday, April 13, before a full house at Crosley Field. The opposition was the Milwaukee Braves, whose owners, just twenty-six days earlier, had finally secured authorization from the other National League clubs for the first major-league franchise relocation in fifty years. After Ohio governor Frank Lausche threw out the first ball, Max Surkont pitched a three-hit shutout for the Braves' first victory in their Wisconsin reincarnation.

Following a snow-out at home on Tuesday, the Reds went to Chicago, lost a game there, and then floundered through seven weather cancellations and eight losses in fifteen days. Hornsby started out with Bell in center field, Greengrass in left, and, in right, a platoon arrangement involving Bob Marquis, Bob Borkowski, rookie Wally Post, and Willard Marshall. Early in May, however, he established the veteran, left-hand-hitting Marshall on a full-time basis. Platooning, he said, was "for the birds. I was never sold on it."[40] Meanwhile Marquis crashed into an outfield wall and badly injured his shoulder; early in July, Paul sold him to Portland of the Pacific Coast League.

With all the weather cancellations, Hornsby found himself with plenty of time to build on his unchallenged ranking as baseball's foremost lobby sitter. Greengrass remembered that he would readily converse about baseball with whoever happened along, even hotel bell captains; but if the subject changed—to the weather, politics, women, or anything else—he abruptly got up and left. One soggy afternoon in New York, as Hornsby waited to see whether there was any point in leaving for the Polo Grounds, he talked about why nobody hit .400 anymore. Today's players weren't willing to work to overcome their own weaknesses, too many of them guessed what a pitcher might throw instead of thinking about what *they* wanted to do, and nearly everybody was "home-run happy." "But I don't know," he said resignedly. "Players just don't have the same attitude today. They should love baseball. Where can you find any other business where you can get so much fun and still get paid for it?"[41]

The 1953 Cincinnati Reds erred less than any team in the National League except Brooklyn's champions, but otherwise they were reminiscent of Hornsby's 1930s Browns—plenty of punch, little speed, meager pitching. For the season, the Reds stole only twenty-two bases but totaled a franchise-record 166 home runs, with Kluszewski clouting forty (also a franchise record), followed by Bell with thirty, Greengrass with twenty, catcher Andy Seminick with nineteen, and Marshall with seventeen. Meanwhile Hornsby's pitchers gave up nearly 800 runs and ranked twelfth (of sixteen major-league teams) in earned run average. "I'd rather have old Grover Cleveland Alexander all looped up than my entire pitching staff," Hornsby said at one point.[42]

Yet what passed for pitching at Chicago and Pittsburgh was even worse, so that by June 8, when they defeated Brooklyn in the first of a four-game series at Ebbets Field, the Reds had won five straight to take over sixth place. His current ballclub not only was better than last year's

Browns, Hornsby announced, but consisted of "better men—and I mean men." The Browns had been "just heels, that's all."[43]

Three hammerings by the Dodgers followed that series-opening win, with the last, on Thursday afternoon, June 11, turning into a debacle. Right-hander Clarence "Bud" Podbielan took a 6–3 lead into the bottom of the eighth inning, then gave up a home run, double, and single before retiring his first batter. At that juncture, Hornsby made a rare trip to the mound to ask Podbielan if he wanted to come out; the pitcher shook his head and said it was his game to win or lose. After taking two strikes, second baseman Jim "Junior" Gilliam hit Podbielan's next pitch over the high right-field fence. After another out, two doubles and a single made the score 9–6, whereupon Hornsby finally waved Podbielan from the game.

When the Reds were retired in order to end it, Earl Lawson, a young reporter for the Cincinnati *Times-Star,* rushed into the visitors' dressing room. Lawson ("a sarcastic bastard," as Marquis remembered him) typified the new breed of sportswriter described by J. Roy Stockton: intrusive, impetuous, as willing to manufacture controversy as to discover it. Lawson had already had several sharp exchanges with Hornsby, and now, Greengrass recalled, he "got down in Hornsby's face" and wanted to know why Podbielan was left in so long. "You second-guessing son of a bitch—who else would I put in?" exploded Hornsby, and turned his back on the *Times-Star'*s representative.[44]

By Greengrass's account, Podbielan laughed off his eighth-inning collapse and held no hard feelings toward his manager, but writers in both New York and Cincinnati treated him as Hornsby's personal victim. Whatever joy the 12,265 fans at Ebbets Field gained from the Dodgers' rally, suggested the *New York Times'*s Joseph M. Sheehan, "was tempered by feelings of sympathy for Podbielan." To the *Daily News'*s Dick Young, "Hornsby resembled Nero sitting in the Coliseum watching lions chew up martyrs as he coldly sat by and watched Podbielan take a beating." The *Cincinnati Enquirer'*s Lou Smith believed Gabe Paul had already soured on Hornsby, and "today's game may lead to an early ouster." Lawson described the Reds players as believing that "given enough time, [Hornsby] will hang himself. The noose tightened considerably today."[45]

Before the next night's game, in Philadelphia, Hornsby told Lawson he was barred from the Reds' dressing room. The ban remained in force despite Lawson's appeals to Paul (who was traveling with the team) and bench-riding Grady Hatton, who assured the writer that "there's no way he could prohibit us from talking to you."[46] When the Reds returned home from an 8–6 road trip, Paul brought Hornsby and Lawson together, and Hornsby agreed to let Lawson back into the clubhouse for the first time in ten days. The Reds played good baseball on that home stand, and by winning a July 4 doubleheader at Milwaukee and taking four of seven games from the resurgent Braves, they improved their record to 34–39.

Then came five straight losses to Chicago and St. Louis, and again rumors of Hornsby's departure began to make the rounds. The Reds' record at the break for the All-Star Game—played at Crosley Field that year—was 37–46. That left them anchored in sixth place, seven and one-half games behind the fifth-place New York Giants. Lou Smith reported divided opinion on Hornsby among the visiting managers, executives, and writers in town for the game. Some gave him credit for the success of Kluszewski, Bell, and Greengrass; others thought that with the personnel he possessed, he ought to have his team in the first division.

Hornsby's estimate of George Lerchen—a first baseman just arrived from Tulsa whom Paul had personally scouted and brought up to the Reds—couldn't have helped his standing with Cincinnati's general manager. After watching Lerchen take a few cuts in batting practice, Hornsby sneered, "I can spit farther than you can hit." And while rookie Roy McMillan impressed people around the league with his virtuoso shortstop play, Hornsby downgraded the light-hitting youngster: "You can shake good fielders out of any tree."[47]

On Monday, July 27, the Cincinnati team traveled to Cooperstown, New York, to meet the Chicago White Sox in the exhibition game played annually in conjunction with the National Baseball Hall of

277

Fame's induction ceremonies. When Herman Wehmeier, a native Cincinnatian who'd been a thorough disappointment in his six years with the Reds, experienced trouble getting the ball over the plate in batting practice, Hornsby ordered him off the mound. An indignant Wehmeier wanted to know what was wrong. "You're wilder than a shit-house rat," explained Hornsby.[48]

Later, Hornsby congratulated new Hall of Fame inductees Dizzy Dean and Al Simmons, and posed with Ty Cobb, Cy Young, Connie Mack, and other baseball immortals. It was his first trip to Cooperstown since his own induction in 1942; it was also to be his last.

Three times that summer—twice on promotional occasions and once just because he was asked for help—Hornsby put his still-remarkable batting skills on display. As part of pregame activities for Main Street Businessmen's Association Night at Crosley Field, he drove several pitches from Waite Hoyt (now broadcasting Reds games on radio) to the base of the scoreboard in left center field; and on August 10, prior to an exhibition game in St. Louis with the Browns, he clouted a few more to the outfield's far reaches. Then, before a night game at the Polo Grounds, Giants shortstop Alvin Dark asked Hornsby for some batting tips, whereupon the Cincinnati manager grabbed one of Kluszewski's big bats and stepped to the plate. After calling where he would hit each ball delivered by the Giants' batting-practice pitcher, Hornsby proceeded to spray line drives left, center, and right, finishing his demonstration by driving the ball into the right-center-field stands. "That's all there is to it," he quipped as the tossed the bat away and turned to other concerns.[49]

In August the Reds lost seven straight games, including three to the usually hapless Pirates. When asked about Hornsby's future, Gabe Paul gave mixed signals. One day it was "Rogers Hornsby is our general, quote and unquote." Then again, "There's no hurry to discuss our plans for next year." At other times Paul just shrugged his shoulders and said nothing. Had Hornsby heard anything? "Not a word," said the manager late in August in New York. "But I'll continue to eat three squares a day regardless of where I am."[50]

The dwindling crowds at Crosley Field now regularly booed Hornsby, especially when runners were thrown out at home plate after he'd waved them home. Greengrass, who "loved the guy," nonetheless had to acknowledge that he was a "terrible third-base coach." Hornsby, thought Greengrass, didn't really study his players' all-around ability— whether, for example, they could actually run as fast as he thought they should.[51]

After losing a doubleheader in St. Louis on Labor Day, September 7, the Reds had dropped twenty-five of their last twenty-six games. "Even though I'm fifty-seven and big around the middle," said Hornsby, "I could hit better than some of my Reds have been doing lately."[52]

During the opener of that Labor Day set, Hornsby received a call on the dugout telephone, turned the team over to Buster Mills, and immediately left to catch a flight for Chicago. The caller from Chicago informed him that a short while earlier, Bernadette Harris had thrown herself from the third-floor window of the Fleetwood Hotel at 6029 Winthrop, and that in her purse was a note saying: "In case of accident, notify Rogers Hornsby."[53] Her purse also contained two newspaper pictures of Hornsby, a savings-account passbook showing cash deposits of $28,841 dating back to March 1952, and a driver's license bearing the name "Bernadette Ann Hornsby." Found in the apartment were a check for $1,000 as well as a blank check signed by Hornsby, a fur coat, a dozen or so pieces of jewelry, seven men's suits and two topcoats, a baseball jacket, and a plaque inscribed to Hornsby. Later it came out that, until ten days earlier, Harris had lived with Hornsby in the house in Cheviot, Ohio, but then, for reasons never disclosed, she'd returned to Chicago.

Attired in a double-breasted blue suit and silver necktie, Hornsby arrived at the Cook County morgue the next morning in the company of Jimmy Gallagher, the Cubs' general manager, and Gallagher's wife. "Visibly agitated" (as one reporter described him), he looked at the corpse of Bernadette Harris and said, "Oh—she must have fell on her face." Then Hornsby went to the coroner's inquest, where he described her as being his secretary and personal friend, someone who "wrote all my letters and took care of all my financial and personal business since 1945." But since the previous February, she'd been "highly nervous," convinced that she was going blind, even though "one doctor after another," including specialists at the renowned Mayo Clinic, found nothing wrong with her eyesight. Having recently seen a psychiatrist, she feared being institutionalized, although Hornsby had assured her that he wouldn't let that happen.[54]

Hornsby related that following a doubleheader in Chicago the previous Sunday (September 6), he, Harris, and the Gallaghers had dined together; afterward she saw him off at the train station when the Reds departed for St. Louis. "When I left," testified Hornsby, "she said 'I won't be able to see you again—I'm going blind.' " Asked whether he thought Harris was sufficiently depressed to commit suicide, Hornsby answered, "Yes, I think she was depressed that much."[55]

The coroner's jury quickly returned a verdict that Harris "committed suicide while temporarily insane due to despondency." Officials from the county Public Administrator's office then escorted Hornsby to the Uptown National Bank, where he opened her safety-deposit box. It contained $25,000 in fifty- and hundred-dollar bills as well as her will, which left all her possessions to him. When reporters asked whether he planned to attend the funeral services at Austin, Minnesota, Hornsby replied that it was necessary for him to remain in Chicago another couple of days "to get things straightened out."[56]

As the Gallaghers probably knew and others close to Hornsby guessed, for some time he'd been using Bernadette Harris to hide money from Jeannette Hornsby, who at any time might go back into court in St. Louis asking for an increase in her separate-maintenance allowance. According to Reds trainer Wayne Anderson, Hornsby's wife "was threatening to sue if he ever made a bank deposit." One of Anderson's duties was to guard a small black bag whenever Hornsby went to the dining car. "Keep an eye on it," Hornsby told him, "it holds all my money."[57]

Hornsby rejoined his ballclub at Crosley Field on September 11, in time to see Kluszewski hit his thirty-ninth homer off Philadelphia's

Robin Roberts to give Cincinnati a 6–5 victory. Five nights later Powel Crosley was on hand to watch the Reds lose to New York and fall three games behind the fifth-place Giants. Crosley wouldn't comment publicly on Hornsby's future; privately, he and Paul met with their manager, who wanted to know what the situation was. He would be notified in two days, they told him.

On Thursday morning, September 17, Paul called a news conference to announce that Hornsby wouldn't be rehired for 1954. "We have no criticism of the way Hornsby managed the club," said Paul. "We decided that perhaps another man could obtain better results with the team. We parted [with Hornsby] on the best of terms."[58] Buster Mills would be in charge over the final eight games of the season, but Mills wasn't being considered as Hornsby's permanent replacement.

By comparison with past Hornsby firings, this one was positively placid. "Regardless of what anyone else thinks," Hornsby told the press, "I believe I did the best job I could have done with this club. There are no hard feelings on my part. I wish the players and the club the best of luck." What would he do now? "I'm going back to Chicago and will make that my home while waiting for something else to show up in baseball."[59]

In Cincinnati, Lou Smith echoed what postmortemists on Hornsby's dismissals had been saying for decades: "Like most great players who become managers, Hornsby never learned to tolerate mediocrity. And that's fatal." Hornsby, Smith went on, was "a hostile man, lonesome and beyond the reach of sentiment." Ballplayers had changed; no longer would they "submit to ranting, hard-shell managers." The Chicago writer Ed Prell suggested that especially in light of Bernadette Harris's suicide, Crosley and Paul fired Hornsby largely out of public-relations considerations. Yet Prell was sorry to see Hornsby go, because he'd always been ideal for press people—honest to a fault and available "no farther away from a reporter's room than a chair in the hotel lobby." John P. Carmichael, Prell's Chicago colleague and Hornsby's acquaintance of twenty-five years, said simply, "He's as changeless as Gibraltar."[60]

Yet if Hornsby hadn't changed, baseball had—and he hadn't really adjusted either his attitudes toward ballplayers or his managing philosophy. The following January, Gabe Paul looked back on his experience with Hornsby and granted that no manager could have worked harder or cooperated better with the front office. Yet at one point, recalled Paul, he suggested to Hornsby that given the Reds' lack of pitching strength, maybe the club ought to hire "an old hand who could take over the pitchers and work with them." To that Hornsby responded (as quoted by Paul), "To hell with 'em. Make 'em learn the hard way." Paul became convinced that "the parade had passed Hornsby. His concept of managing was outmoded. He was still living in the days when the manager did everything. . . . he was hopelessly wedded to the past."[61]

The Reds finished sixth with a record of 68–86—a one-game improvement over 1952—but attracted 55,000 fewer fans to Crosley Field. Two days after the season ended, Paul announced the hiring of George "Birdie" Tebbetts, a former Tigers and Red Sox catcher who'd just managed Indianapolis to a fourth-place finish in the American Association.

At the Edgewater Beach Hotel, his new Chicago residence, Hornsby seemed cheerful, not worried about much of anything. Maybe he would reopen his baseball school, and, no, he wasn't mad at Paul or anybody else connected with the Reds. "They hired me and they can fire me." Had he been offered anything else in baseball? "Nah. Give 'em time. . . . I'd be interested in any honest work. I just want to keep workin'." At the upcoming World Series, "if anyone has a proposition, he'll know where to find me."[62]

The Reds still owed Hornsby a third of his $20,000, twelve-month manager's contract, and Bill Veeck would have to pay him a final $18,000 next year, so for the time being, he was doing all right financially. Though gray-haired and overweight, Hornsby was still, at fifty-seven, energetic, rosy-cheeked, proud of his perfect eyesight, and apparently in robust health. Even if he'd saved up enough to retire (which he hadn't), he wasn't ready to quit baseball. He never would be.

14

• • •

"I

Belong in

Baseball"

That December 1953, as he'd done so many times in the past, Rogers Hornsby attended the minor leagues' annual convention to hustle a job somewhere in Organized Baseball. At Atlanta, he renewed his acquaintance with Ty Cobb (and apparently patched over whatever resentments may have persisted from the 1952 *Life-Look* exchange), but he turned up not a single job prospect. One or two sportswriters speculated that George Weiss and Casey Stengel might find a place for Hornsby in the Yankees' organization, but when nothing happened on that front, Gabe Paul's judgment that the parade had passed Hornsby seemed confirmed.

Seemingly unrelated to Hornsby's firing, a report three months later out of the Yankees' spring-training camp at St. Petersburg, Florida, pointed up how far behind current trends he really was. While Stengel still oversaw on-field operations, he used his coaches for specialized instruction, Jim Turner working with pitchers, Bill Dickey with hitters and catchers, and Frank Crosetti with infielders. Already other major-league ballclubs had begun to copy the methods of the ultrasuccessful New Yorkers. In the decades ahead, management by committee—with the manager functioning essentially as committee chairman—would become the prevalent style in baseball command.

Although Hornsby would never again have a manager's job, he continued to find baseball-related work in one capacity or another. Late in 1953 he signed a contract with an outfit called National Productions, Inc., to produce a series of instructional films for television. Weekly fifteen-minute movies would be syndicated to local television stations, with Hornsby getting 50 percent of the syndication revenues. As things turned out, one fifteen-minute film—featuring Hornsby, Chicago White Sox outfielder Jim Busby, and an eleven-year-old boy—was made early in 1954 at Griffith Stadium in Washington, D.C. When it attacted few buyers, the entire project shut down.

For the rest of that year, Hornsby collected his last semimonthly checks from Bill Veeck, made a few hundred dollars doing occasional columns for the *Chicago Daily News,* and hatched plans for reviving his baseball school, dormant since 1951. Under a contract dated December 14, 1954, he agreed to pay his longtime sidekick Benny Meyer $360 per month "for faithful services performed as Secretary Treasurer and Field Instructor of the Rogers Hornsby Baseball College."[1] Again located at Hot Springs, the school operated from mid-February to April 1, 1955. Now, though, Hornsby faced competition from a number of other baseball schools scattered across the southern and southwestern states. Underestimating his costs, he still charged only $100 tuition plus room and board and, with fewer than 100 enrollees, barely broke even.

Back in Chicago—whether he was at Comiskey Park watching Marty Marion's contending White Sox or at Wrigley Field to see Stan Hack's struggling Cubs—Hornsby sounded off freely about what was wrong with today's game and players. One afternoon in September 1955, he and Clarence Rowland, who'd been in baseball even longer than Hornsby and was now one of three Cubs vice presidents, joined in criticizing the way contemporary managers used their men in platoons—another Yankees-influenced trend. Apropos of a recent

Yankees–White Sox game in which forty-one players appeared, Hornsby grumped that "it's getting daffier every year." If Miller Huggins had platooned him as a rookie, he might never have learned to hit; besides, "the ball has to come over the plate no matter which side the pitcher is throwin' it from." Platooning, Rowland added, "ruins the spirit of a player."[2]

The next year Hornsby denounced the growing tendency among managers to bring in a succession of relief pitchers, which meant that young hurlers never learned to "work out of jams." "Now," said Hornsby, "the average starting pitcher is just somebody who starts the game because somebody has to." Yet he also thought that because baseball was suffering from a general shortage of pitching talent, the ball itself ought to be deadened. That would not only help pitchers but cause "mediocre hitters" to "forget those long-distance swings and begin going for individual averages again. A dead ball would give you a more scientific game; more hit and run, more stealing, and more sacrificing."[3]

Hornsby's complaints and prescriptions still appeared in sportswriters' columns, even if his old-school way of looking at things appealed to fewer and fewer people inside baseball. At least where youngsters were concerned, he gained something of a platform—and more important, a steady, well-paying job at work he enjoyed—when, early in the spring of 1955, Chicago mayor Richard J. Daley appointed him director of the Mayor's Youth Foundation. Obtained mainly through the efforts of municipal judge Thomas Courtney (who, like Hornsby, lived at the Edgewater Beach Hotel), the appointment to the city payroll involved basically the same kind of work Hornsby had done from 1945 to 1949 for the *Chicago Daily News:* supervising an instructional program for boys on the city's recreational diamonds. A salary of $15,000 per year meant that he could discontinue the Hot Springs baseball school.

Hornsby almost drew too heavily on his store of goodwill with the Daley machine when he also signed to scout for the Cleveland Indians. When that news reached city hall, Daley decreed that his municipal employees would confine whatever scouting they did to spotting prospects for the Cubs and White Sox.

About 100,000 youngsters, representing virtually every racial and ethnic element in the city's population, enrolled in the program. Late in July 1956, Dorothy Stull of the weekly *Sports Illustrated* accompanied Hornsby to Horner Park on the North Side, where some 300 boys, ages eight to eleven, waited for him. Wearing sneakers and a baseball uniform with "Rogers Hornsby" on the front and "Mayor Daley's Youth Foundation" on the back, the sixty-year-old Hall of Famer "spoke to them in gentle and earnest tones of the art he loves and has given his life to: baseball." Stull found it hard to believe that "this man was the terrible-tempered Rogers Hornsby."[4]

"Now boys," she quoted Hornsby as telling his young charges, "Mayor Daley wants all you boys to know how to throw and hit and field the right way, and I'm going to show you how the big leaguers do it." He demonstrated throwing, infield play, and batting; hit fly balls to masses of youngsters; and patiently answered their questions—all except one. When a boy asked how to throw a softball, Hornsby replied curtly, "This is baseball. Next question."[5]

Later, assistants handed out copies of the Seven-Up Bottling Company's recently published composite edition of the seven how-to-play booklets Hornsby had written back in 1936. He lingered for another half hour or so, autographing books, gloves, and even the back of a girl's shirt. Then he drove Stull back to the Edgewater Beach, cursing his way through the traffic and explaining that he traveled about fifty miles a day to parks around the city. After precariously maneuvering his big Cadillac (a new yellow one) into the garage he rented alongside the hotel, he went up to his apartment, changed into street clothes, and allowed Stull to buy him lunch. As he picked up the menu, he brought out a pair of reading glasses. "My eyes aren't what they used to be," he admitted, "but I only use these things for reading. I can still play ball without them."[6]

Working his way through soup and a sandwich, Hornsby went over his troubles with club owners, the harmful effects of signing bonuses and platooning on young players, and the need to build confidence in professionals as much as in kids. "I love baseball," he said just before Stull said good-bye, "and I want to stay in it. I think I belong in baseball."[7]

Although he made passing reference to his son Bill (who as a player "didn't put out enough"), Hornsby talked no more to Stull about his personal life than he did to anybody else.[8] In fact, about six weeks earlier (June 1, 1956, to be exact), Mary Jeannette Pennington Hornsby, Bill's mother and Hornsby's wife of thirty-two years, died in St. Louis, where she'd continued to reside while Hornsby traversed the baseball map. The cause of her death wasn't made public, although acute alcoholism apparently had much to do with it. Hornsby didn't go to St. Louis for the funeral, and if the death of his long-estranged wife touched him at all, he gave no indication of it. Financially, of course, he would be considerably better off, inasmuch as he was relieved of the $400 per month he'd been sending her under the separate-maintenance order issued three years earlier.

He was also free to marry again. Sometime in 1956, he began seeing a Chicago woman named Marjorie Bernice Frederick Porter, a forty-nine-year-old widow who worked as a freelance bookkeeper. Marjorie Porter lived with her twenty-year-old daughter, Mary Beth, at 6121 North Hamilton Avenue, a little more than a mile west of Wrigley Field. On Sunday, January 27, 1957, Marjorie Porter and Rogers Hornsby were married at her apartment, which then became Hornsby's home as well.

A practicing Baptist, she wasn't much of a baseball fan and didn't approve of Hornsby's gambling. But to get out of the house, she occasionally accompanied him to the ballpark or racetrack (although she would never consent to bet). Elvin Tappe, who finally reached the majors in 1954 when the Cubs (on Hornsby's advice) drafted him from Kansas City, remembered Marjorie Hornsby as a vivacious, sweet-tempered person with whom Hornsby appeared to be content. "I think she gave him a good life in those later years," said Tappe.[9]

Hornsby's plentiful opinions on baseball subjects covered not only how the game on the field ought to be played but how baseball as sport and business ought to be run. In the summer of 1957 the Subcommittee on Monopoly Power of the Judiciary Committee, U.S. House of Representatives, chaired by Emmanuel Celler of New York, returned to the issue of Organized Baseball vis-à-vis the antitrust laws, on which Celler's subcommittee had first held hearings in 1951.

Again a parade of baseball celebrities past and present testified on such matters as the reserve clause, territorial rights, and minor-league operations. If the star of the 1951 hearings had been Ty Cobb, the most memorable witnesses this time were Casey Stengel and Bob Feller. But whereas Stengel entertained the subcommittee with his characteristic malapropisms and tortured syntax and contributed little of substance, Feller sternly compared ballplayers to "pawns" whom the owners treated "like children." Everybody else—from league presidents William Harridge and Warren Giles to players such as Ted Williams, Mickey Mantle, and Stan Musial—affirmed Commissioner Ford Frick's argument: Abrogation of the reserve clause and territorial rights would "result in the abolition of the professional game as we now know it."[10]

At the conclusion of fifteen days of testimony, the hearings had produced a substantial body of opinion and statistical data but, as later became evident, little inclination in Congress as a whole to alter Organized Baseball's antitrust exemption, which the U.S. Supreme Court had bestowed in 1922 in its Federal League decision.

Although Celler's subcommittee didn't solicit his views, Hornsby thought that his forty-three years as player, manager, coach, stockholder, executive, and even broadcaster entitled him to be heard. He sent chairman Celler a long letter that, while probably representing his wife's efforts in vocabulary and syntax, was a distinctly personal expression on a variety of issues: the reserve clause, farm systems, the draft, roster sizes, and radio and television broadcasting. Considerably more thoughtful than the oral testimony given before the subcommittee, Hornsby's letter elicited thanks from Celler for his "most cogent and provocative" comments. Acknowledging his "tremendous contribution to baseball," Celler promised that the letter would be placed in the records of the subcommittee and given "most careful attention indeed" by the Judiciary Committee as a whole.[11]

Hornsby agreed with baseball's officialdom (and most testifying players) that efforts to subject the sport to the antitrust laws and especially to abolish the reserve clause were "rash and irresponsible," but on several key issues he broke with baseball orthodoxy. Farm systems, he believed, should be done away with altogether, and no major-league club should control more than forty minor-leaguers at a time. After three years in professional ball, minor-leaguers should be up for grabs in an unrestricted draft, as opposed to the existing seven-year period (four years in the minors plus up to three farmings-out). Hornsby also favored cutting the May–September major-league roster limit from twenty-five to twenty-three, "to afford a greater spread of players for other cities, and undoubtedly . . . make for more interesting baseball games"—presumably by inhibiting platooning and relief pitching.[12]

In addition, Hornsby wanted to include umpires and minor-league players in the ten-year-old players' pension program—a suggestion the Major League Baseball Players Association wasn't then (and never would be) prepared to accept. Finally, to shore up the crumbling minors, he proposed reinstitution of the ban on major-league radio and television broadcasts beyond a fifty-mile radius, which the club owners had lifted in 1950 out of fear of antitrust legislation.

Obviously growing out of deep concern for the well-being of the thing he loved most, Hornsby's recommendations were soundly developed and, if implemented, would probably have worked a good effect on Organized Baseball's current ills. "I sincerely hope," he concluded, "that no act of any man will ever do anything detrimental to this American institution of baseball . . . and no effort on my part is too great as a contribution to its perpetuation."[13]

Aside from a column by the *New York Herald-Tribune's* Walter "Red" Smith, who characterized Hornsby's letter as "temperate and carefully thought out," his efforts to influence official thinking in Washington drew virtually no publicity.[14] Meanwhile, at home, his relations with city hall officialdom weren't good.

According to his friend Jack Ryan, the Daley organization was unhappy with Hornsby on various counts. Hornsby wasn't a registered Democrat, in fact wasn't registered as anything and apparently had never voted. Then, too, some of those around Daley—maybe even the mayor himself—appear to have harbored the same misgivings Sam Breadon had expressed to Grantland Rice back in 1946: that the circumstances of Hornsby's private life—his openly acknowledged fondness for gambling on the horses, his long separation from Jeannette Hornsby, Bernadette Harris's suicide—raised questions about his fitness to work with young people. Although Ryan no doubt exaggerated when he referred to Hornsby as "the [Democratic] party BLACK EYE in any election," his future as a city employee for the Mayor's Youth Foundation didn't look promising.[15]

At the end of 1957 another opportunity came along, perhaps just in time. Having worked about a week with the Cubs hitters at Mesa, Arizona, the previous February, Hornsby now received the offer of a full-time coaching job under Bob Scheffing (who'd succeeded Stan Hack a year earlier). Hornsby grabbed the chance, signed a contract for a few thousand dollars less than he'd been making with the city, and gladly said good-bye to the Daley organization.

Now, though, he found his fabled eyesight starting to fail. Early in January 1958 he underwent surgery to have a cataract removed from his left eye, and learned that he would have to wear spectacles full-time from then on. He dutifully acquired a pair, but he hated both the bother and the way they made him look; and after wearing the spectacles for about a month, he had himself fitted for contact lenses. Hornsby thus became one of the few Americans of his age using what, for most people, was still a new and exotic seeing aid.

Late in January he flew to St. Louis for the fiftieth anniversary dinner of the Baseball Writers Association of America. Although Dizzy Dean (now a popular baseball television personality) couldn't make it, twelve others were on hand to be honored as the all-time all-stars of the Cardinals and the long-lost Browns. When it was Hornsby's turn to speak, he looked out at the audience from behind his despised spectacles and looked back on his best years in baseball. Calling himself "the worst hitter ever to come to St. Louis" when he arrived in 1915, he said that he still considered the Missouri city his home. His greatest personal thrill had been winning the seventh game of the 1926 World Series for St. Louis. "I loved baseball," he went on, "and the . . . salary I earned made no difference, for I'd have played for nothing. Now, I wish some of these bonus players that are being signed today had the same attitude."[16]

By the end of February, outfitted with contact lenses, Hornsby was at Mesa's Rendezvous Park every morning to stand behind the batting cage and critique the Cubs at bat. Charlie Grimm, besides serving the ballclub as vice president, scout, and public-relations man, was also on hand to work with the infielders. Neither had much to say to the other.

People who knew Hornsby understood that, as Elvin Tappe put it, "he generally didn't care for colored players." Yet at Mesa he appeared to work effectively with the team's several black rookies and regulars, particularly Ernie Banks, whose 134 home runs over the past four seasons had made him the foremost power-hitting shortstop in the game's history. With Banks, Hornsby worked less on technique than on attitude, preaching confidence and determination as "the big thing . . . with anyone who becomes a success at anything."[17]

According to one report, though, several of the Cubs didn't agree with Hornsby's bunting instructions, which had them moving forward in the batter's box instead of squaring around and remaining stationary, as they'd been taught. When outfielder Chuck Tanner tried it Hornsby's way, he fouled the ball off his own mouth. As Tanner spat blood and cursed, Scheffing explained, "That's the same bunting technique that Branch Rickey taught and is used by everyone who ever played for him."[18]

Scheffing's club got off to a fine start, winning thirteen times in nineteen tries; at the break for the All-Star Game, the Cubs' 39–39 record was their best at that juncture in eleven years. The Baseball Writers Association commemorated the silver anniversary of the midsummer spectacle by announcing an all-time all-star team, selected by its membership. Consisting entirely of pre–World War II performers, the BBWAA team had Hornsby at second base, ahead of Eddie Collins, Frank Frisch, and Charlie Gehringer.[19]

By 1958, traveling in the major leagues—especially with National League teams—involved spending a lot of time aboard commercial airliners. Over the previous winter, the Giants had deserted Manhattan for San Francisco, while the Dodgers opened the 1958 season in the enormous and bizarrely configured Los Angeles Coliseum. The sixty-two-year-old Hornsby tired under the grind of transcontinental travel; Tappe remembered that swollen feet and legs—what Hornsby called gout—bothered him much of the time.

On the whole, though, Hornsby experienced a pleasant summer's return to the big time. He also seemed to derive increasing enjoyment from get-togethers with contemporaries for what old ballplayers called "fanning bees." At St. Louis, where the Cardinals' and Browns' all-time stars were brought back for more homage before an August night game, Hornsby, Dizzy Dean, Jesse Haines, Frank Frisch, and Ken Williams seconded each others' complaints about rookies' bonuses, a lack of dedication and endurance on the part of today's players, and various other shortcomings of baseball circa 1958. Looking over the spruced-up surroundings in old Sportsman's Park (which had become Busch Stadium under the ownership of beer baron August Busch), Hornsby lamented the mistake he made in not signing to manage the Cardinals in the fall of 1951. When he went with Bill Veeck, "that's where I booted one."[20]

The home-run craze, Hornsby remained convinced, had become the ruination of good hitting, something that "destroys the spirit of the club." Encouraged by club owners and glorified by sportswriters and fans, the slugger was now "the whole show. He can do no wrong." Asked about Ernie Banks, on his way to Most Valuable Player honors with a .313 batting average, forty-seven homers, and 129 runs batted in, Hornsby was quick to make an exception: "I hope Ernie gets a lot more homers. He's a fine ballplayer."[21]

However much Hornsby might preach his gospel, nearly all of Banks's teammates joined the slugging shortstop in swinging for the fences. While batting a middling .265 as a team and scoring only 709 runs, the Cubs knocked a franchise-record 182 homers and finished in fifth place, their best showing in six seasons. Philip K. Wrigley and associates rehired Scheffing, pitching coach Fred Fitzsimmons, third-base coach George Myatt, and player-coach Elvin Tappe. Hornsby's contract was also renewed for 1959, even though it could be argued that the Cubs players had mostly ignored his counsel. Wrigley, in singling out various people within the organization who'd contributed to the team's improvement, noticeably omitted Hornsby.

So the first week in February 1959 found Hornsby again stationed behind the batting cage at Mesa, working in the Cubs' rookie camp. Among his top prospects were Billy Williams, a sweet-swinging twenty-year-old up from Burlington (Three-I League), and Ron Santo, fresh out of high school and semipro baseball in Seattle, where Dave Kosher, the physically handicapped young man Hornsby befriended in 1951, had scouted him. Although Williams and Santo would be assigned to the Cubs' Texas League farm club at San Antonio for the coming season, Hornsby was convinced that both were "going to make it—you can see that already."[22]

Once the season began, Hornsby was in and out of Chicago, frequently traveling to scout and instruct players in the franchise's small farm system. Marjorie Hornsby accompanied him on one trip to San Antonio, where he had a chance to renew acquaintances with his grandchildren Ann and Rogers Hornsby III, now fifteen and eleven, respectively, who resided at San Antonio with their mother and stepfather, an air force officer named Dexter Martin.

Hornsby liked the grandson despite his declared preference for football over baseball, and Rogers III tagged after Hornsby around his hotel and accompanied him to the ballpark, with Hornsby never introducing him as Rogers Hornsby III, just as his grandson. When San Antonio manager Al "Rube" Walker told Hornsby he didn't want the kid on the field, Hornsby sent him to the outfield anyway and proceeded to hit fungoes in his direction for fifteen minutes or so.

As he'd done from time to time over the decades, Hornsby also made a stop in Austin to visit surviving relatives, walk through the family cemetery at Hornsby's Bend, and linger at the graves of his parents and two brothers. He may even have picked out the spot nearby where he, too, wanted to be buried.

Perhaps because Charlie Grimm disliked having him around Wrigley Field, Hornsby was free to take off for old-timers' events whenever he wanted. At Kansas City (where the Philadelphia Athletics relocated in 1955), he joined Ty Cobb, Jimmie Foxx, Paul Waner, Lefty Grove, and others in honoring Missourian Zack Wheat, recently inducted into the Baseball Hall of Fame. A few days later Hornsby wore a 1926-style Cardinals uniform in front of 53,000 people at Yankee Stadium, where the Yankees had turned their annual Old-timers Game into an extravaganza for NBC television's Saturday Game of the Week. After former President Herbert Hoover threw out the first ball, about forty ex-big-leaguers creaked their way through two innings. Hornsby sat it out.

The 1959 Chicago Cubs improved their previous season's record by two games (to 74–80) but again finished fifth. Even though Banks enjoyed another Most Valuable Player year, nearly everybody else slumped. Philip Wrigley, who'd taken an increasingly active role in Cubs affairs over the past decade, wasn't happy with the team's lack of progress under Scheffing or its lack of batting punch under Hornsby's tutelage, and Grimm and other front-office staff loyally agreed with Wrigley that changes had to be made. Hornsby didn't help his situation by appearing to contradict what his manager was doing. While Scheffing expressed satisfaction at being able to alternate left- and right-handed hitters in left field, at first base, and at catcher, Hornsby continued to tell anybody who would listen that platooning upset young players' timing at bat and afield, undermined their confidence, and turned potential stars into "humpty-dumpties."[23]

At season's end Wrigley announced that Scheffing was out, and that Grimm would again take over direction of the team on the field. Grimm kept player-coach Tappe but quickly fired Fitzsimmons and Myatt. Although Hornsby remained on the payroll, he found himself demoted to minor-league batting instructor. (In his third and last stint as Cubs manager, Grimm would last sixteen games into the 1960 season before going back upstairs, this time to switch places in the WGN radio booth with Lou Boudreau. Under Boudreau, the team fell to seventh place.)

Hornsby now faced more travel than ever, visiting Cubs farm clubs at Fort Worth; San Antonio; St. Cloud, Minnesota; Lancaster, Pennsylvania; and Morristown, Tennessee. Yet neither emotionally nor financially was he prepared to give up baseball. He qualified for a small monthly Social Security check, having paid into the system during his years with the *Chicago Daily News* and Mayor's Youth Foundation baseball programs. But he obdurately refused to apply for the pension, insisting that he wasn't about to take government handouts.

At the same time, he thought he was entitled to something from the players' pension fund, which required five years of service with a big-league club—either as player, manager, or coach—after April 1, 1947. When Hornsby inquired about his status, he was informed that although he had the necessary years of service dating from 1951, he didn't qualify for a pension because he was already fifty-five when he signed with the Browns, and nobody could enter the program past fifty-four. In effect, the pension contributions deducted from his big-league paychecks went for nothing; that, Hornsby wrote Sid Keener, "is an inflexible attitude to say the least."[24]

Once the 1960 season was over, the Hornsbys moved to a new apartment in a high-rise building at 5630 North Sheridan Road. Still devoting a major part of his life to gambling on horse races, Hornsby kept in regular contact with his bookmakers but also spent considerably more days at the tracks than in years past. It was about that time that Bill Hornsby—now married to Vida Kampe of St. Louis, the father of two, and the manager of a beer distributorship in Jackson, Tennessee— brought four-year-old Brad Hornsby to Chicago to meet his famous grandfather. After a period of distant contact at best, in recent years Rogers and Bill Hornsby had talked regularly by telephone and generally rebuilt their relationship. On that particular Chicago visit, three generations of Hornsbys spent a day at the Arlington Park Race Track on the northwest side of the city.[25]

Early in 1961, a freelance writer named Bill Surface contacted Hornsby about doing a piece on how major-league players and managers "cheated"—how they stretched, bent, and sometimes broke the rules. Surface worked under contract to the monthly magazine *True*, which appealed to a limited but loyal male readership attracted to stories of exploit and adventure. Surface, who'd never met Hornsby, went to the Hornsbys' North Sheridan Road residence and encountered what he later described as "a big man with a hard, ruddy face. Hard was the exact word for all of him—hard, narrowed eyes and thinning white hair, which he kept crew cut. . . . His handshake was brief but hard as the face and eyes."[26]

Surface and Hornsby put together an article—published in *True* the following August under the title "You've Got to Cheat to Win in Baseball"—for which Hornsby received a fee of $600.[27] They then agreed to extend their collaboration into a book that would incorporate the "Cheat" article, as well as Hornsby's reminiscences and opinions on the current state of baseball. Surface's subsequent experiences with Hornsby, as he told about them later, were mostly unpleasant.

For one thing, Hornsby insisted on narrating elliptically while he drove his Cadillac to, spent days at, and returned from the tracks. He was bitter about his treatment by baseball people, usually speaking with sarcasm, resentment, and remorse about his experiences in the sport. Once he even belittled Ernie Banks, who, in Hornsby's recollection, struck out twice against Milwaukee's Lew Burdette and returned to the dugout asking who the pitcher was. "If I was managing today," snarled Hornsby, "I'd beat the hell out of him. . . . All these kids in the stands know who's pitching, and here's a guy making $40,000 a year and ain't got the desire to look at the program."[28]

Usually arriving at the Arlington Park track about three hours before post time, Hornsby hung around the paddock area and grandstand, seeking tips from trainers and jockeys, listening to what other track habitués had to say, and generally demeaning himself for the sake of a little dubious information. At the end of one seven-hour day at Arlington, Hornsby had lost $474 on eight races. Although he'd eaten or drunk nothing since morning, he grabbed the next day's racing form, went to a telephone booth to call his bookie and learn that he'd won twenty-eight dollars on bets elsewhere, and prepared to head out to the local trotting races that night.

As rendered by Surface, Hornsby continually complained about all the "phonies" he'd had to deal with—in and out of baseball. That included the New York publishing firm of Coward-McCann, which brought out Hornsby and Surface's book in the spring of 1962. Fittingly entitled *My War with Baseball,* the book sold poorly, which caused Hornsby to seeth at the "New York Jews" who'd done little to push it. Surface pointed out that Hornsby hadn't been able to attend book-signing parties arranged by Coward-McCann in New York and Pittsburgh; besides, the firm's sales manager was Irish. "All those guys in New York is Jew," Hornsby insisted.[29]

When Surface and Hornsby began their collaboration, Hornsby already knew that the Cubs wouldn't rehire him for 1961. He quickly obtained a new job, though, and again he had Casey Stengel and George Weiss to thank. Rudely dumped following the Yankees' World Series loss to Pittsburgh the previous autumn, Stengel and Weiss signed as manager and general manager, respectively, of the inchoate New York Metropolitans—one of two new franchises being added to the National League for 1962. At their behest, the "Mets" hired Hornsby as a scout, mostly to watch National League teams in action at Wrigley Field and report on likely choices for the upcoming "expansion draft" of expendable players.[30]

That July, at the age of seventy-four, Ty Cobb died in an Atlanta hospital. Cobb was a multimillionaire, but outside of some Georgia relatives and a handful of baseball people, he possessed almost no real friends. Over the past decade, both Cobb and Hornsby had frequently and freely aired their discontents about the way baseball was being played and the shortcomings of today's players, managers, and club owners. The difference was that Cobb's blasts cost him nothing, whereas Hornsby, always trying to make a living in baseball, repeatedly rankled people whose goodwill he needed.

One way or another, Hornsby's name continued to get into the news. Early in December two attorneys filed suit in his behalf in U.S. district court in Chicago against the Seven-Up Bottling Company and two local Seven-Up distributors. Although the St. Louis–based company had distributed *7-Up Presents: How to Play Baseball, by Rogers Hornsby* for five years without any complaint on Hornsby's part, now he alleged copyright infringement, in that Seven-Up published its one-volume edition of his seven how-to-play booklets without his permission. Hornsby sued for a total of $1 million, asking a half million from Seven-Up in St. Louis and $250,000 each from the Chicago distributors.

With mediation and "tactful handling of the situation" on the part of his loyal St. Louis friend Sid Keener, Hornsby and Seven-Up reached some kind of settlement, although no terms were ever made public.[31] Whatever sum Hornsby may have been paid to drop his suit couldn't have been very large. Taken to trial, the litigation might have cost Seven-Up something in public relations; but given the fact that a few years earlier Hornsby had been freely handing out Seven-Up's edition of his how-to-play booklets, it's hard to imagine how he might have won his case.

With that litigation under way, Hornsby flew to New York for the annual dinner given by the local BBWAA chapter. Among the evening's awards to various baseball personages was a silver bat given to Hornsby, retroactively recognizing him as the National League's Most Valuable Player for 1924 and finally undoing Jack Ryder's dirty work.

Then Hornsby was off to St. Petersburg, Florida, for the New York Mets' first spring training, stopping off in Tennessee to visit with Bill and Vida Hornsby and his third- and fourth-born grandchildren—Brad, now almost six, and Terri Ann, nearly five. Besides a brand-new Mets cap and other baseball gear, Hornsby left behind his recently acquired silver bat, which his grandchildren proceeded to use like any other, oblivious to its significance (or collectible value).

While the Yankees shifted their spring operations to Fort Lauderdale, the Mets moved into St. Petersburg and occupied Miller Huggins Field and the Colonial Inn. Casey Stengel announced that Hornsby would be a full-fledged Mets coach, and George Weiss added that while Hornsby would be "principally a batting instructor," he would be with the team at home and on the road, as well as visit the organization's farm clubs. Almost sixty-six, still carrying about thirty or forty excess pounds, Hornsby nonetheless beat everybody onto the ballfield in the mornings and trailed everybody off in the late afternoons. But when he coached the pitchers on bunting technique, Stengel interrupted with "No, no. Don't move up—don't make that shift until he pitches." Although Stengel's interference probably embarrassed Hornsby, for once he kept his mouth shut and went along with what the boss wanted.[32]

When Robert Lipsyte of the *New York Times* sought out Hornsby one evening at the Colonial Inn, he found him ensconced in a chair in the corner of the lobby, "oblivious to the blare of the band in the night club a few feet away or the chatter from the television." Hornsby was lecturing half a dozen young Mets on the importance of learning the strike zone and avoiding cigarettes ("cuts down on your wind"), alcohol ("slows you up"), and movies ("might affect your batting eye"). "You've got to get to sleep by midnight," he admonished. "When I was a player, I went out with girls, that's human nature. But I always told myself that if you didn't get the pitch you want between 7 P.M. and midnight, forget it."[33]

"Baseball is my life," he told Lipsyte, "the only thing I know and can talk about. It's my only interest. . . . I'm not a good mixer. I get bored at parties and I bore other people. I don't like to get dressed up and go out." Just then a middle-aged woman wearing a tight skirt and low-cut blouse strolled by. "Look at that," Hornsby said disgustedly. "I think women should be on a pedestal. That lowers her." Reminded of his own checkered marital history, Hornsby opened up about his personal life more than he ever had—at least for the record. "My first wife," he said, "was too ritzy for me, and I was always a kind of lone wolf. . . . The trouble is, there are no perfect women. The fights— she'll want to go to a show, you want to stay home and rest your eyes." His present wife, though, was "a real church girl, a member of Eastern Star. . . . If I did everything she told me to do, I'd go to heaven."[34]

Hornsby didn't approve of men wearing short pants, either, especially for playing golf. "I don't think I'm old enough for golf," he snorted. "I'm used to other people chasing balls I've hit; damned if I'm going to run after a little ball myself." His particular relaxation always had been playing the horses. "But it was nobody's business but mine because when I got out there on the field there was nothing but baseball on my mind." When Lipsyte asked leadingly how he'd acquired such a tough reputation, Hornsby looked at him with eyes that were "very blue and very cold" and said, "Maybe because I'm not two-faced, because I'm sure no diplomat."[35]

Hornsby again made that clear before a Mets-Yankees game at St. Petersburg. A photographer wanted to get him together with the Yankees' Roger Maris, who'd hit sixty-one home runs the previous year to break Babe Ruth's single-season record. Maris's feat came in a season when the American League added expansion teams in Los Angeles and Washington, and he needed all of the new 162-game schedule to surpass the Babe. Hornsby was quoted as saying what many others believed: that the only thing Maris could do better than Ruth was run, and that Mickey Mantle, Maris's multitalented teammate, was a superior player. In *My War with Baseball,* which had just been published, Hornsby noted Maris's mediocre batting averages (only .269 in 1961) and dismissed him as a slugger who would "never have a big average. . . . He couldn't hit .400 if he added all his averages together."[36]

So when Hornsby picked up a bat and followed the photographer over to the Yankees' dugout, Maris turned his back and suddenly got very busy signing autographs at the field-box railing. Ignored and insulted, Hornsby stomped back across the field, grabbed a reporter, and sputtered, "What do you think of that bush leaguer, that swelled-up————, that————! He refused to pose with me. . . . He couldn't carry my bat. He didn't hit in two years what I hit in one."[37]

That evening, in the hotel lobby, Hornsby resumed his fulminations. Referring to the moody Maris's (usual) reluctance to sign autographs and his recently announced no-interview policy, Hornsby termed "unforgivable" such off-field behavior. "I just can't imagine anyone refusing to sign autographs"; good relations with the press were "basic for a ball player." Ruth and Cobb, despite their mutual animosity, had obligingly posed together whenever they were asked, but "that's the difference between a high-class fellow and a swelled-up guy."[38]

The next day Yankees manager Ralph Houk called a press conference to affirm that Maris was "A-1 to me and the players." As for Hornsby's comments, "I think it'll be swell if Mr. Hornsby takes care of his ball club and I'll take care of mine."[39]

That particular tempest had blown itself out by the time the Mets opened their home season at the refurbished Polo Grounds with a loss to Pittsburgh. They lost 119 other games in the National League's first year under the 162-game format. Whatever Hornsby may have accomplished with other teams to improve their hitting, he worked little effect on the inept Mets, who batted .240 and scored only 617 runs (while the opposition piled up 948). Yet close to a million fans paid to see an aggregation that was quickly rated with the worst ever. Late in July, more than 37,000 were on hand for a one-inning Old-timers Game between the 1951 New York Giants and Brooklyn Dodgers. Plaques were handed out to five former Giants and Dodgers who'd hit at least 200 home runs, including Hornsby.

As he'd done with the Cubs, Hornsby spent much of his time traveling between minor-league cities and towns where the Mets had established working agreements: Syracuse; Oklahoma City; Santa Barbara; Quincy, Illinois; and Auburn, New York. Late in July, at a reception at the Chicago Hilton before the next day's All-Star Game at Wrigley Field, Bill Surface found him "pale and tired" and complaining about how much he'd been on the road. And in not a single town, he moaned, had he found a racetrack.[40]

When they left the Hilton, Hornsby wouldn't hear of hiring a cab, insisting that they take the train to his apartment. On the way he said that he didn't expect to be with the Mets again in 1963 because "too much undermining" was going on within the organization. "This ought to be a nonstop train," he went on. "We'd go to Texas where the good people are. They have a small bunch of phonies down there, though;

won't let 'em have real horse-racing. . . . Won't be long, though. Texas is too good a state not to have racing."[41]

By the fall of 1962 Hornsby was pretty worn out, as well as troubled by blurred vision in his right eye. Told that he'd developed another cataract growth and again needed surgery, he entered Wesley Memorial Hospital, near the Chicago lakefront, on Monday, December 10. Ted Lyons, onetime White Sox pitching star and manager and a fellow Hall of Famer, entered Wesley Memorial at the same time for the same surgical procedure, and Lyons and Hornsby occupied rooms almost directly across the hall from each other. "We're an entry," quipped Hornsby in racetrack argot.[42]

Both mens' surgery proceeded routinely; Lyons went home on the fourteenth. On that same day, though, Hornsby developed cardiac fibrillation—what he called a "fibillin' heart"—and suffered a stroke that left him without feeling in his left arm and leg. His stepdaughter, Mary Beth, called Chicago sports broadcaster Jack Brickhouse to report that Hornsby wasn't doing well. Brickhouse rounded up fellow broadcasters Lou Boudreau and Harry Creighton as well as Jack Rosenberg, producer of WGN-TV's Cubs games, and the quartet visited Hornsby in his room. At one point Hornsby whispered to Rosenberg that he had something to tell him he'd never told anybody before, but he would wait until Rosenberg came back alone.

That was on Friday, January 4, 1963. That night Hornsby's temperature rose steadily and his breathing became irregular. Moved back into intensive care, he developed lung congestion and became semiconscious. The next morning, with his wife and stepdaughter at his bedside, he died of heart failure—technically, myocardial infarction.

News of his death jolted most of his acquaintances, who'd always considered him the picture of good health—clear-eyed, rosy-cheeked, and, despite his surplus poundage, still quick-stepped. He seemed to provide a model of clean living, having spent his whole life without tobacco or alcohol—and sound asleep an extraordinary amount of it. In fact, he'd been far from healthy. An autopsy revealed not only a heart attack some eleven hours before he died, but "hypertensive cardiovascular disease with [another] heart attack that dated back many years." One of his arteries was completely blocked. (Although none of his friends ever heard him complain of chest pains, it's likely the "gout" that had bothered him for years was actually a matter of poor circulation—the pooling of blood in his lower extremities.) The stroke he suffered, moreover, left "extensive damage of the right side of the brain."[43]

At the time of Hornsby's death, published research findings on the frequent correlation between high levels of cholesterol and the onset of cardiovascular disease were still only a few years old. Nearly all of his life, such high-cholesterol foods as whole milk, eggs, steak, and even ice cream (because of its high protein content) had been considered wholesome and strength-building. Hornsby urged aspiring young ballplayers to eat steak and drink lots of milk; he not only centered his own regular diet on those foods but indulged in rich desserts and ice-cream snacks with something akin to a passion. It's a plausible assumption that despite his renowned abstemiousness, Hornsby was a victim of his own lifestyle.

Among many obituaries and retrospective columns on Hornsby published over the ensuing weeks, two seemed especially apt. "Rogers Hornsby," said the *Sporting News,* "was tough, he was demanding. He was never schooled in the niceties of diplomacy. But it must be remembered that he . . . held baseball in such high esteem that he could not tolerate those who did not." And Red Smith observed that "he made hitting look easy . . . but he made everything else hard because to him baseball was not a game, it was a crusade."[44]

Hornsby's body lay overnight in Chicago at a mortuary on North Western Avenue, with services scheduled for the afternoon of January 8. Telegrams arrived from people around the country, including one from Hornsby's granddaughter Ann Rice, who wired from Vandenberg Air Force Base, California, that she couldn't be at the services because she and her husband, Richard, an air force lieutenant, were expecting their first child that month. George Weiss wired condolences on behalf of the Mets organization, adding that he'd been "personally honored to have

[Rogers Hornsby] as my friend," and Casey Stengel said, "Baseball has lost a great man."[45]

Mary Beth Porter told the press, "He didn't like flowers and his desire was that none be sent. He wanted any such money to go to the National Heart Fund instead."[46] Yet when the standing-room crowd of some 250 jammed the mortuary chapel, about a dozen floral arrangements, including one from the Mets shaped like a baseball diamond, decorated the altar. Among the notables in attendance were former American League president Will Harridge; former Pacific Coast League president and Cubs vice president Clarence Rowland; Lou Boudreau (now back in the WGN radio booth); Jack Brickhouse of WGN-TV; Hall of Fame director Sid Keener; and Hall of Fame members Gabby Hartnett, Ted Lyons, and Ray Schalk. Representatives of the Mets, Cardinals, and Reds were also on hand, but Elvin Tappe was the only active player who came.

Dr. August M. Hintz of North Shore Baptist Church kept the service mostly secular, as Hornsby would no doubt have wanted. Hintz quoted from Hornsby's playing record, read from his Hall of Fame plaque inscription, and then listed what he considered his outstanding qualities: "Determination to be honest and truthful at whatever the cost; dedication; hard work; spirit of fair play and sportsmanship; fundamental gentleness and kindness in helping youngsters." He also read from the Fifteenth Psalm: "Lord, who shall abide in thy tablernacle? who shall dwell in thy holy hill? / He that walketh uprightly, and worketh righteousness, and speaketh the truth in his heart."[47]

From Chicago, the remains were flown to Austin for interment at Hornsby's Bend. Besides his wife and stepdaughter, his son Bill and daughter-in-law Vida, his brother Everett, and his sister Margaret were present on Thursday, January 10, for a second memorial service at an Austin mortuary and then the graveside ceremony. So were a large number of other relatives and a substantial percentage of his 105 honorary pallbearers—Texans and Oklahomans whom Hornsby had known as ballplayers, managers, umpires, and sportswriters. The official pallbearers were all nephews and cousins.

First cousin Albert Hornsby, who probably knew him better than anybody among his Austin-area relatives, recalled his attendance at family reunions, where he would ask about absent kin, talk baseball, and play a little catch with youngsters. "He had a dry humor," said Albert, "but he never crowded in on anybody."[48]

On an overcast but warm midwinter day, Rogers Hornsby was laid to rest under bromeliad-festooned live oaks and cedars, in the cemetery near the Colorado River where hundreds of other Hornsbys were buried. The spot was only a few feet from the graves of his parents and brothers, and about 100 yards down a cactus- and mesquite-lined trail from where Reuben and Sarah Morrison Hornsby's cabin and stockade had stood 125 years before.

The monument subsequently erected was as unpretentious as the person it commemorated. Its inscription read simply "Rogers Hornsby, April 27, 1896–January 5, 1963." Except for the design of a ball held by small crossed bats above the name, the stone gave no suggestion that the man buried there had spent nearly half a century in the sport and business of baseball, and that he was one of the most extraordinary figures it would ever produce.

Epilogue

. . .

"What

Else Is

There?"

I t might have been predicted that Hornsby's complicated marital and parental history would produce some kind of postmortem unpleasantness. His will, which he apparently made before his third marriage in 1957, left his entire estate to Bill Hornsby. That consisted of savings estimated at no more than $25,000, plus an assortment of plaques, trophies, and other mementos. Rather than formally contest the will, Marjorie Hornsby and her attorney filed a dissent, which resulted in a subsequent court-ordered allocation to her of a portion of the estate. Besides an amount of cash, she appears to have retained Hornsby's 1926 World Series ring and various other valuables—a circumstance about which Bill Hornsby remained resentful. A little more than a week after Hornsby's death, Marjorie Hornsby took it upon herself to dispatch his Hall of Fame plaque to Dave Kosher in Seattle, together with a note that said: "My husband wanted you to have this." When local newspeople asked him to pose with the plaque, Kosher wouldn't accommodate them. "This is a great thing Mr. Hornsby did," he said. "I don't want to cheapen it."[1]

One way or another, a few items of Hornsby memorabilia ended up in the National Baseball Hall of Fame. In the summer of 1964 Bill Hornsby attended a brewers' convention at Binghamton, New York, then, accompanied by his wife and two children, drove to Cooperstown. The Hornsbys stayed two days, touring the Hall of Fame Museum and taking in other area sites. Bill Hornsby reminded local people that in 1946 he'd played for the nearby Oneonta Red Sox.

Bill Hornsby continued in the beer business in Tennessee, operating in partnership with Johnny Beazely, pitching star of the Cardinals' 1942 World Series victory over the Yankees. He died in Nashville in 1984 at age fifty-nine, following a stroke. Rogers Hornsby's first wife outlived not only her first husband, Rogers Hornsby Jr., Jeannette Pennington Hornsby, and Bill Hornsby, but two subsequent husbands as well as Marjorie Hornsby. Marjorie Hornsby died in 1970 at New Port Richey, Florida, but Sarah Elizabeth Martin Hornsby Finley Hayden survived until 1978, when she died at Denison, Texas, her hometown. Hornsby's two pairs of grandchildren went separate ways, having only the vaguest knowledge of their half-cousins until the early 1990s. Contacts by various people seeking permission to use Hornsby's name and images on T-shirts and other items of merchandise finally made them aware of each others' existence.

Neither Hornsby's survivors nor other people who liked and admired him were pleased by Bill Surface's article titled "The Last Days of Rogers Hornsby," which appeared in the popular weekly magazine *Saturday Evening Post* about five months after Hornsby's death.[2] Based on his experiences with Hornsby in Chicago during the preparation of magazine pieces and the book *My War with Baseball,* Surface's *Saturday Evening Post* article, in both timing and content, was remarkably reminiscent of another article published late in 1961 by Al Stump, who ghostwrote Ty Cobb's autobiography.[3] Like Stump's, Surface's article appeared about six months after its subject died. As Stump did with Cobb, Surface portrayed Hornsby as selfish, mean-spirited, and bigoted. (In Surface's rendition, Hornsby was also stingy—about everything but his horseplaying.)

No doubt what both Stump and Surface reported was largely accurate. As products of their times and region, Cobb and Hornsby preferred not to associate with "colored people," although unlike Cobb, Hornsby kept working in baseball and thus had to adjust to increasing contact with black ballplayers. Like most of their countrymen, both Cobb and Hornsby engaged in offhanded, generalized slurs against various racial, ethnic, and religious groups. Such remarks looked bad when quoted in print, but they shouldn't have shocked anybody.

Surface's depiction of Hornsby as anti-Semitic especially irritated Zeke Handler, Hornsby's friend ("of full Hebraic extraction," as Handler put it) from the early 1940s, when they both worked for the Fort Worth Cats. "What few teeth I have remaining almost fell out" was the way Handler described his reaction to Surface's piece. Admitting that Hornsby was "cold, blunt," and prone to "fly off the handle" if displeased about something, Handler nonetheless recalled Hornsby's considerate behavior toward his daughter Golda and maintained that "behind his frigid exterior . . . there at times flowed the milk of human kindness."[4] Handler might also have noted that besides himself, Hornsby maintained long and warm acquaintances with other Jewish people, such as George Weiss, Jack Rosenberg, and Dave Kosher. Had Hornsby remarked (as he probably did on occasion) that some of his best friends were Jews, it would have sounded as inane coming from him as it did from anybody else, but in his case it would have been true.

Hornsby, wrote the Boston columnist Austin Lake shortly after his death, "was as addicted to the truth as a drunk was to his bottle."[5] A cynic might have added that he was at least as addicted to horseplaying as he was to the truth. To the end, Hornsby remained a habitual and unregenerate better on the races, as well as an unapologetic one. And for all his insistence that his gambling affected nobody but himself, it obviously caused him a lot of trouble inside and outside baseball. Yet by 1950, when Hornsby finally got back into Organized Baseball, a more permissive climate prevailed in both that sport and the general society, and his gambling history had become more an element in his persona than a problem for club owners and baseball's officialdom.

Even so, to the end of his life, he continued to bet as much and as often as he could—and to lose more often than he won.

Little is to be gained, it would seem, from excursions into the realm of psychoanalysis, with its theory that gamblers are actually to be understood as masochists, driven by an unconscious wish to lose. Nor is it necessary to label Hornsby's penchant for playing the horses in clinical terms as "compulsive," "addictive," or whatever. That it was excessive seems plain enough; even so, as one specialist in the psychology of gambling has noted, "Excess is not absolute, but is personally and socially defined." While Hornsby may have experienced some ambivalence about the consequences of his gambling, he clearly enjoyed it and didn't care to stop. If he really needed to gamble, it was a matter of needing to do something that gave him pleasure, even if it hurt his pocketbook.[6]

Other psychologists have observed that habitual gamblers tend to be risk takers (which of course is basic to success in competitive athletics), as well as focused on the present at the expense of the future. Moreover, such people have a limited range of interests and need to fill "non-alive" time, so that the suspense of having money riding on an unpredictable outcome imparts "a sense of really living because mind and body are *stimulated* and become 'filled with life.' "[7] While Hornsby spent much of his time lobby sitting, frequently that apparent idleness was also a matter of waiting out race results.

Still other researchers have described excessive gamblers as people "who are able to get along without the good will of others to a much greater extent than is usual." Thus (like Hornsby) they "feel themselves to be, and are, 'lone wolves.' " Such a "the-hell-with-the-neighbors" attitude can be a source of strength, in that it "frees them from much anxious preoccupation with the opinion of casual strangers or of members of the family." Yet the same lone-wolf independence can make gamblers resist, avoid, and lie to people trying to meet them halfway.[8]

So why did Hornsby gamble so much, for more than two-thirds of his life? The commonsense answer would be that he did it for the same reason he stayed as close to baseball as he possibly could: he enjoyed both betting on the horses and being involved in baseball; both gave him more excitement and pleasure than he could gain from anything else. For Hornsby, moreover, playing the horses brought satisfaction enough in itself; his gambling didn't need to be—and usually wasn't—a social event. Up to the last few years of his life, he did nearly all his betting offtrack with bookmakers. Unlike John McGraw, for example, Hornsby didn't enjoy the ambience of the track—didn't enjoy crowds and the camaraderie of cronies, touts, trainers, and jockeys as McGraw did. Hornsby's gambling was usually a private matter, a transaction between himself and his bookmaker and nobody else's business. Conversely, he viewed dice and card games with contempt, and even if casinos were readily accessible (as during his two stays in Mexico), he wasn't interested.

For all his ups and downs, Rogers Hornsby never indicated any basic dissatisfaction with the structure and pattern of his life. He hated parties and nightclubs, generally avoided movies and stage productions, and insisted on an early bedtime. Inasmuch as he wasn't especially handsome, one might suppose that women would have found him uninteresting, even downright boring. Yet he never seemed to have any difficulty finding attractive women to love him and share his life, even though three of his four long-term relationships (with two wives and what people still called a "mistress") ended unhappily.

Hornsby loved baseball as few professional ballplayers have—or at least as few have been willing to affirm so frequently and unambiguously. Although he was nothing extraordinary afield, nobody doubted his greatness when he had a bat in his hands. He knew the strike zone, hit the ball where it was pitched and to all fields, and frequently hit with power. If not the foremost pure hitter who ever lived, he won almost universal recognition as the best who'd ever swung from the right side of the plate. That particular tribute—accorded at the peak of his playing career in the 1920s—remained with him for the rest of his life. Whatever else might be said about Hornsby, wrote John B. Sheridan in 1928, he possessed two redeeming qualities: "He can hit the ball better than any right-handed hitter I have ever seen . . . and he has courage, intestines, 'guts'—if you will. For these, I love him."[9]

For a later generation of ballplayers, Hornsby's reputation as baseball's greatest right-handed hitter carried little weight. Nor did it for Bill Veeck, who remarked not long before Hornsby's death: "I always felt sorry for Rog. He goes from job to job in baseball, his lifetime batting average sitting upon his chest like a medal, and he is a stranger among his own kind."[10]

"I'm kind of cold-blooded," Hornsby told Robert Lipsyte during spring training in 1962 with the New York Mets. "When I put on the uniform, that's it. I'm out there to play to win and that's it." For Hornsby, baseball was not only the best kind of athletic competition in existence; being a professional ballplayer was absolutely the best way to make a living. "Baseball," he once said, "is the one and only bona fide American game . . . and it should come first." On another occasion he dismissed "any physically able boy who doesn't play baseball" as being "*not,* in my opinion, an American. I think it's just as important to learn to pitch, catch and hit a baseball as it is to learn history or the ABC's. Baseball should be a requirement in school."[11]

As a manager in the minor leagues, Hornsby handled both youngsters and veterans effectively and usually with success, especially at Beaumont in 1950 and Seattle the following year. His one great achievement in the majors was to lead the St. Louis Cardinals to a world's championship when he was only thirty years old. Otherwise his experiences managing big-league clubs ranged from persistent frustration (Cubs, 1931–32) to persistent gloom (Braves, 1928; Browns, 1933–37) to open acrimony (Browns, 1952) to relentless mediocrity (Reds, 1952–53).

To the end, Hornsby was respected as a solid, no-nonsense baseball man, but his methods changed little after 1925, when Sam Breadon named him to pilot the Cardinals. He reached the majors at a time when managers usually went with set lineups and pitchers were expected to finish what they started. In 1915, the sixteen National and American League pitching staffs completed 1,343 games; ten years later—despite the post-1920 hitting surge—pitchers still completed 1,209 games. But by 1952, when Hornsby returned to the majors as the Browns' manager, big-league starters finished only 949 games; by 1962, twenty pitching staffs could manage only 844 complete games.

Over the years, Hornsby accepted neither the trend toward platooning nor the parallel trend toward the use of relief-pitching specialists. Whereas the 1926 Cardinals won everything with only eight pitchers and a four-man rotation, by the early 1950s, ten- and eleven-man staffs and five- and even six-man rotations were the rule. À la Casey Stengel, managers increasingly juggled their lineups, often platooning at five or six positions.

Managing, as Hornsby saw it, had less to do with strategy than with leadership. It came down to getting everybody to want to win as much as he did, then putting his best eight men in the regular lineup and sending his best available pitcher to the mound. If his starter couldn't do the job, it was pointless to talk about it; just wave him out and somebody else in. By the 1950s, many of his peers thought they needed pitching coaches, but Hornsby continued to believe that a man learned to pitch by pitching. A pitcher didn't need a lot of fancy stuff, either—just a good fastball and curve and the ability to throw both where and when he needed to. Hornsby dismissed the slider, which came into widespread use in the 1950s, as no more than a "nickel curve," observing that nonbreaking sliders often ended up in the outfield seats.

So for Hornsby baseball wasn't really complicated, except that managers made it that way by trying to control everything their players did. Whether Hornsby's kind of baseball made for a better or worse game on the field could be a matter for endless argument, arraying those who knew baseball as it once was against those who liked what it had become.

Although he disdained specialized pitching instruction, Hornsby was confident that he could teach men to become better hitters. Once he quit playing, his batting renown translated into a reputation for knowing more about how to hit than anybody alive, and from the 1930s on, he worked with numerous players in the majors and minors. Some, such as Beau Bell and Jim Greengrass, acknowledged that he helped them a great deal. Others—from the cocky, marvelously talented young Ted Williams to the struggling, confused Pat Seerey—either didn't need or couldn't use Hornsby's plate counsel. His efforts with the 1962 New York Mets obviously did little good.

"To know and to like Hornsby and be liked by him," observed the St. Louis baseball writer Bob Broeg some years after Hornsby died, "was to understand him, make allowances for his shortcomings and appreciate his baseball skills, his earnestness and his interest in children. Hard-boiled Hornsby was a pushover for kids."[12] That seems a fair estimate. Although he was a rotten father to his firstborn son and, during one period, had little to do with his second, his four grandchildren would remember him as warmhearted, solicitous, and generous. And while he was often ill-tempered and brutally blunt in his dealings with adults, in working with tens of thousands of youths in his Hot Springs and Chicago baseball programs, he was characteristically patient, forbearing, and anxious to get them to love the game as he did.

If greatness is to be measured by whether one adds to the sum total of human happiness, Rogers Hornsby would hardly qualify. But he was a truly great figure in baseball, and it might be assumed that as player, manager, and teacher of young people, he may have added to the sum total of human enjoyment. Extraordinarily narrow-minded, he cared for little besides baseball—and what horse looked good on a given day.

Whatever else might be said of Hornsby (and much was said, good and bad), nobody ever accused him of being what he sneeringly called a "yes man." Like his gambling, his candor cost him dearly in both personal and professional terms. Tough, obstinate, he was often aggravated and just as often aggravating. He made his way through a complicated world with a basically uncomplicated attitude. Once asked what he'd gotten out of his life, he summed it up this way: "I wore a big-league uniform and I had the best equipment and I traveled in style and could play ball every day. What else is there?"[13]

Notes

• • •

Prologue: Beaumont, Texas, Summer 1950

1. This account of the episode derives from my own recollection as one of those present that night.

2. *Sporting News,* February 2, 1928, p. 4; Franklin C. Lane, "The Last of the Field Leaders," *Baseball Magazine* 24 (July 1931), p. 343; Travis Jackson, interview by author, Waldo, Arkansas, December 3, 1985; Steve Smart, "Les Tietje," *National Pastime* 13 (1993), p. 82.

3. George "Specs" Toporcer, "The Greatest Hitter of All Time," *Baseball Bluebook* 7 (May 1953), p. 72; *Chicago Tribune,* December 12, 1930, p. 24.

4. San Antonio *Light,* April 12, 1950, p. 12; Boston *Record-American,* January 8, 1963, p. 46; Rogers Hornsby and Bill Surface, *My War with Baseball* (New York: Coward-McCann, 1962), pp. 14–15.

5. *Sporting News,* March 17, 1927, p. 5.

6. *Cincinnati Enquirer,* Aug. 13, 1953, p. 27; Rogers Hornsby III, interview by author, Denison, Texas, December 5, 1992.

7. *St. Louis Post-Dispatch,* April 15, 1943, p. 2D.

8. Hornsby and Surface, *My War with Baseball,* p. 15.

9. Arthur Daley, *Kings of the Diamond* (New York: Putnam's, 1962), p. 208.

10. John Dos Passos, *The Big Money* (1936; paperback ed., New York: New American Library, 1969), p. 117.

11. Marshall Smelser, *The Life That Ruth Built: A Biography* (1975; reprint, Lincoln: University of Nebraska Press, 1993), p. xi.

1. Stockyards Boy

1. Rogers Hornsby, *My Kind of Baseball*, ed. J. Roy Stockton (New York: David McKay, 1953), p. 29.

2. *Sporting News*, January 29, 1942, p. 2.

3. J. Roy Stockton, "Rogers Hornsby," *St. Louis Post-Dispatch Sunday Magazine*, January 3, 1926, p. 3.

4. Ibid.

5. Organized Baseball, the pyramidal structure in place since the 1880s, consisted of the two major leagues and the officially recognized minor leagues, of which there were twenty-four at the start of the 1914 season.

6. Lee Allen and Tom Meany, *Kings of the Diamond: The Immortals in Baseball's Hall of Fame* (New York: Putnam's, 1965), p. 124.

7. *Sporting News*, January 19, 1963, p. 11.

8. Rogers Hornsby and Bill Surface, *My War with Baseball* (New York: Coward-McCann, 1962), p. 37; *Sporting News*, November 26, 1947, p. 7.

9. The Western Association's top 1915 batting average, compiled by John Robinson of Muskogee, was .323.

10. *Sporting News*, September 9, 1915, p. 3.

11. Ibid.

2. Making It

1. *Sporting News*, September 9, 1915, p. 5.

2. The other all-wooden facility in 1915 was the Chicago Cubs' West Side Park, which the Cubs vacated the next year for Federal League Park, the future Wrigley Field on the North Side.

3. *Sporting News*, December 25, 1941, p. 1; September 30, 1926, p. 4.

4. Ibid., September 30, 1926, p. 4.

5. Ibid., June 14, 1928, p. 7.

6. After Hornsby became a great player, sportwriters manufactured a fable out of his double off Alexander, to wit: Bill Killefer, now in his sixth season in the majors and Alexander's favorite catcher, asked Alexander to "groove one"

for the rookie, whose family had befriended him in Texas. Alexander complied; Hornsby hit the ball against the left-field wall. In fact, Killefer sat out that game (September 19, 1915) in favor of Ed Burns, and with Alexander winning by only 4–2, it seems highly unlikely that he had occasion to ease up on anybody. Yet both Alexander and Hornsby repeatedly told the story in later years.

7. Later told in several versions, often by Hornsby himself, the incident was first reported in the spring of 1916. The above quotation is from *St. Louis Post-Dispatch,* April 7, 1916, p. 24.

8. Rogers Hornsby and Bill Surface, *My War with Baseball* (New York: Coward-McCann, 1962), p. 38; *St. Louis Post-Dispatch Sunday Magazine,* January 3, 1926, p. 3.

9. Frustrated in their efforts to acquire the Cardinals, the Baltimore group then brought suit in the federal courts, on the grounds that Organized Baseball was a monopoly operating in restraint of interstate commerce. In 1922 the U.S. Supreme Court handed down its historic ruling in the so-called Federal League case, exempting Organized Baseball from federal antitrust laws.

10. *St. Louis Post-Dispatch Sunday Magazine,* January 3, 1926, p. 3; *Sporting News,* March 30, 1916, p. 2; *St. Louis Post-Dispatch,* March 14, 1916, p. 17.

11. *Sporting News,* March 14, 1916, p. 17; March 15, 1916, p. 11; March 18, 1916, p. 6; March 30, 1916, p. 2; June 14, 1928, p. 7.

12. *St. Louis Post-Dispatch,* March 6, 1916, p. 16.

13. Ibid., April 11, 1916, p. 19.

14. Ibid., April 7, 1916, p. 23; April 10, 1916, p. 10.

15. *Sporting News,* May 11, 1916, p. 18.

16. *St. Louis Post-Dispatch,* June 29, 1916, p. 18.

17. Ward Mason, "The Star of the 1916 Recruits," *Baseball Magazine* 10 (October 1916), p. 48.

18. *Sporting News,* July 16, 1916, p. 3; *St. Louis Post-Dispatch,* July 16, 1916, p. 28; August 8, 1916, p. 28.

19. *St. Louis Post-Dispatch,* March 16, 1917, p. 11.

3. Toward Stardom

1. Branch Rickey to August Herrmann, May 15, 1917, Branch Rickey Collection, National Baseball Library, Cooperstown, New York.

2. *St. Louis Post-Dispatch,* June 29, 1917, p. 16.

3. *Sporting News,* August 16, 1917, p. 2.

4. *St. Louis Post-Dispatch,* December 6, 1917, p. 29; January 2, 1918, p. 2D.

5. Ibid., January 5, 1918, p. 8.

6. Ibid., March 1, 1918, p. 18.

7. Ibid., March 14, 1918, p. 20.

8. Actually Hendricks had played briefly in the majors in 1902–3, with New York and Chicago in the National League and Washington in the American League.

9. At that time, the National Association of Professional Baseball Clubs, the overall governing authority for the minor leagues, classified the minors according to population as AA, A, B, C, and D circuits. After World War II, the new designations became AAA, AA, A, B, C, and D. Since 1963, minors have been grouped as AAA, AA, A, and Rookie circuits.

10. *St. Louis Post-Dispatch,* July 6, 1918, p. 16.

11. Ibid., July 16, 1918, p. 18.

12. Ibid., July 17, 1918, p. 18.

13. *Sporting News,* September 5, 1918, p. 6.

14. *Chicago Daily News,* undated clipping [1966], in Rogers Hornsby Collection, National Baseball Library, Cooperstown, New York.

15. *Sporting News,* September 5, 1918, p. 2.

16. *Sporting News,* September 12, 1918, p. 5.

17. Ibid., December 17, 1918, p. 24.

18. Ibid., January 1, 1919.

19. Quoted in Robert Gregory, *Diz: Dizzy Dean and Baseball during the Great Depression* (New York: Viking, 1992), p. 82.

20. *Frank G. Rowe vs. Rogers Hornsby,* October term, 1919, transcript in Clerk of the Circuit Court Records, City of St. Louis, Civil Courts Building, St. Louis, Missouri.

21. Ibid.

22. Quoted in Murray Polner, *Branch Rickey* (New York: Atheneum, 1982), p. 80.

23. Arthur Mann, *Branch Rickey: American in Action* (Boston: Houghton Mifflin, 1957), p. 101.

24. *St. Louis Post-Dispatch,* December 12, 1919, p. 30; January 30, 1920, p. 30.

4. Best in His League

1. *Sporting News,* May 20, 1920, p. 4; June 10, 1920, p. 1.

2. *St. Louis Post-Dispatch,* November 1, 1920, p. 15; November 16, 1920, p. 18.

3. The National Commission, created as part of a peace settlement between the National and American Leagues, consisted of the two league presidents plus a third member, who was elected by the owners and served as its chairman. By the fall of 1920 the commission had no chairman, the owners having refused to reelect Garry Herrmann to the position. Two years earlier, National League president John Tener—alienated by contrary judgments on player disputes voted by the other two commission members (including the voiding of Pittsburgh's claim on George Sisler)—had resigned in disgust. John Heydler, longtime secretary to the National League, eventually succeeded him. Ban Johnson, founder of the American League and its president for twenty-six years (1901–27), was the only surviving member of the original National Commission, but Johnson faced powerful opposition from several club owners in his own league.

4. *Sporting News,* June 1, 1949, p. 14.

5. *St. Louis Post-Dispatch,* April 11, 1921, p. 17.

6. Branch Rickey, *The American Diamond: A Documentary of the Game of Baseball* (New York: Simon and Schuster, 1965), p. 49; George Toporcer, "The Greatest Hitter of All Time," *Baseball Bluebook* 7 (May 1953), p. 72.

7. *St. Louis Post-Dispatch,* August 14, 1921, p. 11.

8. Before 1911, Spalding's baseball had a solid rubber core.

9. *Sporting News,* October 13, 1921, p. 1.

10. *St. Louis Post-Dispatch,* December 31, 1921, p. 8.

11. Ibid., March 3, 1922, p. 20.

12. Ibid., March 16, 1922, p. 30.

13. Ibid., August 9, 1922, p. 18.

14. *Sporting News,* June 1, 1922, p. 1.

15. In 1897 Willie Keeler of the Baltimore Orioles in the old National League compiled a forty-four-game hitting streak, and in 1911 Ty Cobb hit safely in forty games. Two days before Hornsby's streak came to an end, George Sisler broke Cobb's American League record.

16. *St. Louis Post-Dispatch,* August 9, 1922, p. 18.

5. Troubles

1. George H. Williams to Branch Rickey, May 29, 1923, Branch Rickey Papers, Library of Congress, Washington, D.C.

2. *Sarah E. Hornsby vs. Rogers Hornsby,* June term, 1923, transcript in Clerk of the Circuit Court Records, City of St. Louis, Civil Courts Building, St. Louis, Missouri.

3. *St. Louis Post-Dispatch,* June 23, 1923, p. 3. Hornsby's letter and much other specific material relating to both his and Jeannette Pennington Hine's marital difficulties were copiously reported in the *Post-Dispatch,* St. Louis's leading afternoon newspaper. A Pulitzer-chain daily, the *Post-Dispatch* combined reformist agitations with detailed coverage of celebrity scandal.

4. Ibid.

5. *St. Louis Post-Dispatch,* May 4, 1923, p. 25.

6. Ibid., June 14, 1923, p. 3.

7. Ibid., June 23, 1923, p. 3.

8. Ibid., June 13, 1923, p. 3.

9. Ibid., June 20, 1923, p. 20.

10. As things turned out, Stuart's feat wasn't the start of anything extraordinary. He won eighteen more games over that and two more seasons, then dropped to the minors.

11. *St. Louis Post-Dispatch,* September 11, 1923, p. 25; *Sporting News,* October 11, 1923, p. 4.

12. *Sporting News,* December 13, 1923, p. 1. Late in 1923 Ainsmith finally got his money from the Cardinals, but only after appealing to Commissioner Landis.

13. Ibid., September 20, 1923, p. 2; *St. Louis Post-Dispatch,* September 30, 1923, p. 28; September 1, 1923, p. 18.

14. *St. Louis Post-Dispatch,* September 27, 1923, p. 29; September 30, 1923, p. 28; Arthur Mann, *Branch Rickey: American in Action* (Boston: Houghton Mifflin, 1957), p. 124.

15. *Frank J. Quinn vs. Rogers Hornsby,* February term, 1927, transcript in Clerk of the Circuit Courts Records, City of St. Louis, Civil Courts Building, St. Louis, Missouri.

16. *St. Louis Post-Dispatch,* September 28, 1923, p. 37.

17. Ibid.

18. Quoted in Marshall Smelser, *The Life That Ruth Built: A Biography* (1975; reprint, Lincoln: University Nebraska Press, 1993), p. 317.

19. *St. Louis Post-Dispatch,* October 26, 1923, p. 50.

20. Ibid., November 1, 1923, p. 33.

21. Ibid., November 12, 1923, p. 27; December 22, 1923, p. 12; Charles C. Alexander, *John McGraw* (New York: Viking, 1988), p. 253. Including Charles Stoneham's promise to pay an additional $50,000 if the Giants won the 1920 pennant (which they didn't do), the bid for Hornsby had actually been $350,000.

22. *St. Louis Post-Dispatch,* December 14, 1923, p. 48; December 25, 1923, p. 10.

23. Ibid., February 22, 1924, p. 30.

24. *Quinn vs. Hornsby,* p. 6.

6. .424—and Cardinals Manager

1. Rogers Hornsby and Bill Surface, *My War with Baseball* (New York: Coward-McCann, 1962), p. 42.

2. Keeler's 1897 average, while a remarkable feat, was compiled at a time when the pitchers were still adjusting to the lengthening of the distance to home plate by five and one-half feet—a rule change that went into effect with the 1893 season.

3. *St. Louis Post-Dispatch,* August 24, 1924, p. 48.

4. Ibid., October 16, 1924, p. 31; February 8, 1925, pt. 2, p. 1.

5. The American League had authorized such an award for the past two years, but no such National League's Most Valuable Player selection had been made before 1924.

6. *Sporting News,* December 11, 1924, p. 1; February 16, 1974, p. 30.

7. *St. Louis Post-Dispatch,* December 2, 1924, p. 30; December 3, 1924, p. 30.

8. *Sporting News,* July 24, 1924, p. 5.

9. Before 1901 in the National League and 1903 in the American League, foul strikes weren't counted as strikes except on attempted bunts.

10. *Sporting News,* March 30, 1922, p. 4; April 29, 1926, p. 4; June 10, 1926, p. 4.

11. Charles C. Alexander, *John McGraw* (New York: Viking, 1988), p. 65; *Athletic Journal,* quoted in *Sporting News,* April 12, 1928, p. 4.

12. Hornsby and Surface, *My War with Baseball,* p. 79; J. Roy Stockton, "Rogers Hornsby," *St. Louis Post-Dispatch Sunday Magazine,* January 3, 1926, p. 3.

13. Stockton, "Rogers Hornsby," p. 3.; *Sporting News,* August 6, 1942, p. 13.

14. *St. Louis Post-Dispatch,* August 22, 1926, p. 28; Boston *Record-American,* January 8, 1963, p. 28.

15. Ernest J. Lanigan typescript, Rogers Hornsby Collection, National Baseball Library, Cooperstown, New York.

16. Donald Honig and Laurence Ritter, *Baseball: When the Grass Was Real* (New York: Coward, McCann, and Geoghegan, 1975), p. 179.

17. George Toporcer, "The Greatest Hitter of All Time," *Baseball Bluebook* 7 (May 1953), p. 71.

18. Chicago *American,* January 8, 1963, p. 16; *Boston Globe,* July 15, 1969, p. 25; *Sporting News,* October 5, 1944, p. 9.

19. Branch Rickey, *The American Diamond: A Documentary of the Game of Baseball* (New York: Simon and Schuster, 1965), p. 49; Travis Jackson, interview by author, Waldo, Arkansas, December 3, 1985.

20. Elwood "Woody" English, interview by author, Newark, Ohio, September 10, 1991.

21. *Sporting News,* January 17, 1962, p. 1.

22. *St. Louis Post-Dispatch,* November 3, 1925, p. 23.

23. *New York Times,* May 6, 1943, p. 27.

24. *St. Louis Post-Dispatch,* November 9, 1925, p. 67.

25. *Sporting News,* October 31, 1951, p. 10; January 31, 1962, p. 23.

26. Toporcer, "Greatest Hitter of All Time," p. 72; Frank Graham, *McGraw of the Giants* (New York: Putnam's, 1944), 216.

27. St. Louis *Globe-Democrat,* February 11, 1925, p. 3.

28. Hornsby and Surface, *My War with Baseball,* p. 42.

29. *St. Louis Post-Dispatch,* April 14, 1925, p. 25.

30. *Sporting News,* June 4, 1925, p. 1.

31. Ibid., June 1, 1949, p. 14; June 6, 1947, p. 3; Hornsby and Surface, *My War with Baseball,* p. 43. Of the various accounts of the events surrounding Rickey's firing and Hornsby's hiring, my judgment is that the sources cited above are the most generally reliable.

32. *St. Louis Post-Dispatch,* May 30, 1925, p. 1; May 31, 1925, p. 68.

33. Arthur Mann, *Branch Rickey: American in Action* (Boston: Houghton Mifflin, 1957), pp. 133, 135.

34. *Sporting News,* November 11, 1926, p. 5.

35. Franklin C. Lane, "Hornsby's Winning System," *Baseball Magazine* 20 (November 1926), p. 540.

36. *St. Louis Post-Dispatch,* June 1, 1925, p. 20.

37. Ibid., June 11, 1925, p. 20.

38. *Sporting News,* November 1, 1961, p. 20.

39. *St. Louis Post-Dispatch,* September 28, 1925, p. 23.

7. The Summit

1. Otto Williams, a onetime major-league infielder who'd been in professional baseball nearly thirty years, was hired as Hornsby's second coach.

2. *St. Louis Post-Dispatch,* November 3, 1925, p. 27.

3. *Sporting News,* March 11, 1926, p. 3; *St. Louis Post-Dispatch,* March 21, 1926, p. 26.

4. *Sporting News,* April 25, 1956, p. 6.

5. *St. Louis Post-Dispatch,* March 21, 1926, p. 26.

6. *Detroit News,* April 27, 1937, p. 28.

7. *St. Louis Post-Dispatch,* May 18, 1926, p. 26.

8. Ibid., June 24, 1926, p. 26; *Sporting News,* July 1, 1926, p. 1.

9. *St. Louis Post-Dispatch,* July 20, 1926, p. 21.

10. Wecke's recollection as reported by Bob Broeg, telephone conversation with author, August 8, 1992.

11. Rogers Hornsby and Bill Surface, *My War with Baseball* (New York: Coward-McCann, 1962), p. 106; Arthur Mann, *Branch Rickey: American in Action* (Boston: Houghton Mifflin, 1957), p. 143; *Sporting News,* June 11, 1949, p. 4.

12. *St. Louis Post-Dispatch,* September 14, 1926, p. 32.

13. Lawrence Ritter, *The Glory of Their Times,* rev. ed. (New York: William Morrow, 1984), pp. 254–55.

14. *St. Louis Post-Dispatch,* October 3, 1926, p. 85.

15. Ibid., September 30, 1926, p. 38.

16. *Sporting News,* October 25, 1961, p. 10.

17. *St. Louis Post-Dispatch,* October 11, 1926, pt. 3, p. 19.

18. Ibid.; *Sporting News,* November 11, 1961, p. 11.

19. *St. Louis Post-Dispatch,* October 17, 1926, p. 5S.

20. Ibid.

21. Ibid., pt. 3, p. 19. For the above account of Alexander's seventh-game heroics, I've relied on the contemporary recollections of Hornsby, Alexander, and others, as opposed to a large number of later renditions by the same people, as well as by journalists and historians. Because they have a particularly truthful ring, I've also taken Flint Rhem's 1961 recollections at face value.

22. *St. Louis Post-Dispatch,* October 11, 1926, p. 3.

23. Associated Press dispatch, Austin, Texas, October 13 [1926], in Rogers Hornsby Collection, National Baseball Library, Cooperstown, New York.

8. Touring the National League

1. *St. Louis Post-Dispatch,* November 10, 1926, p. 26.

2. Ibid., December 12, 1926, p. 1.

3. Ibid., October 10, 1926, p. 26.

4. Ibid., December 2, 1926, p. 28; December 6, 1926, p. 24; December 7, 1926, p. 24.

5. *Sporting News,* June 11, 1949, p. 14; Arthur Mann, *Branch Rickey: American in Action* (Boston: Houghton Mifflin, 1957), p. 148.

6. Franklin C. Lane, "The Amazing Hornsby Deal," *Baseball Magazine* 21 (March 1928), p. 436; Bob Broeg, telephone conversation with author, August 5, 1992.

7. Frank Graham, *McGraw of the Giants* (New York: Putnam's, 1944), p. 213.

8. *St. Louis Post-Dispatch,* December 20, 1926, p. 34; December 23, 1926, p. 35; *Sporting News,* December 23, 1926, p. 1; Rogers Hornsby and Bill Surface, *My War with Baseball* (New York: Coward-McCann, 1962), p. 29.

9. *St. Louis Post-Dispatch,* December 21, 1926, p. 35.

10. Ibid., January 8, 1927, p. 6; January 9, 1927, p. 1S.

11. Ibid., February 2, 1927, p. 28.

12. Graham, *McGraw of the Giants,* p. 213.

13. *New York Times,* September 18, 1953, p. 31.

14. *Sporting News,* March 31, 1927, p. 1; *New York Times,* March 6, 1927, p. 19. Stoneham was referring to earlier National League practices whereby club owners gained controlling interests in more than one franchise. He ignored the fact that going back to 1890, stockholders in the Boston National League franchise had held stock in the Giants, and that Yankees owner Jacob Ruppert held the mortgage on Fenway Park, home of the Boston Red Sox, as a consequence of the deal that brought Babe Ruth to New York after the 1919 season.

15. Graham, *McGraw of the Giants,* p. 216.

16. John H. Heydler to All Club Presidents, April 11, 1927, Rogers Hornsby Collection, National Baseball Library, Cooperstown, New York.

17. Transcript of telephone conversations, John A. Heydler with Rogers Hornsby and William F. Fahey, April 6, 1927, ibid.

18. Red Smith column in *New York Herald-Tribune,* undated, ibid.

19. Undated typescript, Hornsby Collection, National Baseball Library.

20. *New York Times,* April 11, 1927, sec. 10, p. 1; John A. Heydler to Kenesaw M. Landis, April 9, 1927; Heydler to J. G. Taylor Spink, April 15, 1927, Hornsby Collection, National Baseball Library.

21. *St. Louis Post-Dispatch,* January 14, 1927, p. 34; January 22, 1927, p. 30.

22. *Sporting News,* February 18, 1978, p. 6.

23. Weekly issues of the *Sporting News* during the 1927 season carried Wilson's and Spalding's advertisements for the two gloves.

24. *St. Louis Post-Dispatch,* June 15, 1927, p. 17.

25. Ibid., p. 18; *Sporting News,* June 23, 1927, p. 1.

26. Hornsby and Surface, *My War with Baseball,* p. 30.

27. *New York Times,* January 11, 1928, p. 32.

28. *Sporting News,* June 8, 1949, p. 15.

29. *St. Louis Post-Dispatch,* November 1, 1928, p. 5.

30. *New York Times,* January 13, 1928, p. 18.

31. Ibid., October 30, 1927, p. 1.

32. *St. Louis Post-Dispatch,* December 19, 1927, p. 11; December 20, 1927, p. 3.

33. Ibid.

34. Ibid., December 22, 1927, p. 4.

35. Ibid., January 11, 1928, p. 4.

36. *New York Times,* January 11, 1928, p. 1.

37. Universal Service dispatch from *New York Daily Mirror,* January 30, 1928, Hornsby Collection, National Baseball Library; *St. Louis Post-Dispatch,* January 12, 1928, p. 24.

38. Charles C. Alexander, *John McGraw* (New York: Viking, 1988), p. 281; *St. Louis Post-Dispatch,* January 13, 1928, p. 32.

39. Quoted in Arthur Daley column, *New York Times,* September 18, 1953, p. 31.

40. *St. Louis Post-Dispatch,* January 12, 1928, p. 24.

41. *New York Times,* January 14, 1928, p. 9.

42. *St. Louis Post-Dispatch,* February 20, 1928, p. 18.

43. After one February visit, Barto prescribed (and himself sold to the Hornsbys) a bottle of whiskey.

44. In 1947 Coffee Pot Park, used by the St. Louis Cardinals since 1938, would be renamed Al Lang Field, after the onetime Pittsburgher who persuaded big-league teams to begin training at St. Petersburg. Crescent Lake Park, where the Yankees trained from 1925 to 1961, was named for Miller Huggins after his death in 1929 (and was later called Stengel-Huggins Field).

45. Quoted in Daniel Okrent and Harris Lewine, eds., *The Ultimate Baseball Book* (Boston: Houghton Mifflin, 1982), p. 151.

46. *New York Times,* May 24, 1928, p. 23.

47. *Boston Traveler,* May 23, 1931, p. 16.

48. Ibid. As of the 1926 season, sacrifice flies were recorded on a fly ball on which a runner advanced to any base.

49. Fred Lieb, *Baseball as I Have Known It* (New York: Tempo-Grosset and Dunlap, 1977), p. 54.

50. *Sporting News,* June 7, 1928, p. 3.

51. Ibid., October 25, 1928, p. 1.

52. *Chicago Tribune,* November 8, 1928, p. 23.

53. *Sporting News,* December 27, 1928, p. 3.

9. "Enough of Second-Guessers"

1. Elwood "Woody" English, interview by author, Newark, Ohio, September 10, 1991.

2. *Sporting News,* January 1, 1933, p. 8.

3. Rogers Hornsby and Bill Surface, *My War with Baseball* (New York: Coward-McCann, 1962), p. 48.

4. Wrigley Field wouldn't acquire its characteristic ivy-covered outfield walls until after the original bleachers were replaced by new outfield stands following the 1937 season.

5. *Sporting News,* January 9, 1930, pp. 2–3.

6. *Chicago Tribune,* October 10, 1929, p. 16.

7. Ibid., October 13, 1929, p. 1.

8. Ibid.

9. Ibid., p. 28.

10. Franklin C. Lane, "Rogers Hornsby Springs a New Sensation," *Baseball Magazine* 27 (September 1933), pp. 443–444. The famed sports journalist Grantland Rice, who also liked to wager on horses and also lost money in the Crash, once figured his odds at 1–5 in the market, 1–10 at the track, concluding that both were "no good as sound investments." Grantland Rice, *The Tumult and the Shouting: My Life in Sport* (New York: A. S. Barnes, 1954), p. 280.

11. *Chicago Daily News,* January 7, 1963, p. 22.

12. *Chicago Tribune,* April 8, 1930, p. 19.

13. *Sporting News,* May 22, 1930, p. 4; Charles C. Alexander, *John McGraw* (New York: Viking, 1988), p. 294.

14. *Chicago Tribune,* July 17, 1930, p. 19.

15. Clipping from *Sacramento Bee* (1991), Rogers Hornsby Collection, *Sporting News* Archives, St. Louis, Missouri.

16. *Chicago Tribune,* September 23, 1930, p. 1.

17. *Sporting News,* October 2, 1930, p. 2.

18. *Chicago Tribune,* January 11, 1931, pt. 2, p. 2.

19. *Sporting News,* March 12, 1931, p. 1; Paul Mickelson column [February 1931], unidentified clipping, Hornsby Collection, *Sporting News* Archives.

20. Grimm quoted in William B. Mead, *Two Spectacular Seasons: 1930, the Year*

the Hitters Ran Wild; 1968, the Year the Pitchers Took Over (New York: Macmillan, 1990), p. 113; English interview.

21. *Chicago Daily News,* undated John P. Carmichael column [1937], Hornsby Collection, *Sporting News* Archives.

22. *Sporting News,* April 2, 1931, p. 1.

23. *Chicago Tribune,* July 1, 1931, p. 25; *New York World-Telegram,* July 2, 1931, p. 32.

24. Hornsby did use Wilson as a pinch hitter in the ninth inning; Wilson fouled out.

25. *Chicago Tribune,* September 7, 1931, p. 30.

26. Ibid., September 6, 1931, p. 17.

27. Gabby Hartnett prompted a reprimand from Commissioner Landis because, before that particular charity game at Comiskey Park, he was photographed leaning over a box-seat railing, signing a scorecard for Al Capone's son, and talking with Capone, state representative Roland Libonati, Jack "Machine Gun" McGurn, and two of Capone's bodyguards. At that time Capone was awaiting trial for income-tax fraud.

28. *Chicago Tribune,* December 10, 1931, p. 25.

29. *Sporting News,* February 4, 1932, p. 2.

30. Quoted in Robert Gregory, *Diz: Dizzy Dean and Baseball During the Great Depression* (New York: Viking, 1992), p. 346.

31. John P. Carmichael in *Sporting News,* September 30, 1953, p. 12.

32. *Sporting News,* June 9, 1932, p. 2.

33. *Chicago Tribune,* July 7, 1932, p. 1. Violet Valli's legal name was Violet Popovich.

34. The Violet Valli saga continued for some months. In August the prosecutor's office eventually dropped its charges against her, and she began appearing at a local burlesque theater. Subsequently police arrested a Chicago man for stealing letters from Jurges to Valli and trying to extort money from Jurges and Cuyler. Woody English remembered an incident the following winter at a North Side bowling alley, when Valli came in and Jurges, English, and several other Cubs scrambled to get out of the place. English interview.

35. *Sporting News,* August 13, 1932, p. 1.

36. *St. Louis Post-Dispatch,* January 14, 1933, p. 15; *Chicago Tribune,* August 3, 1932, p. 1.

37. *Chicago Tribune,* August 3, 1932, p. 1.

38. Ibid., August 4, 1932, p. 15.

39. *Sporting News,* August 11, 1932, p. 1; *Chicago Tribune,* August 3, 1932, p. 17; August 4, 1932, p. 15.

40. *Chicago Tribune,* August 12, 1932, p. 19; August 13, 1932, p. 19.

41. Ibid., August 14, 1932, pt. 2, p. 1.

42. Ibid., pt. 2, p. 2.

43. Ibid.; *Sporting News,* August 25, 1932, p. 5.

44. *Sporting News,* August 25, 1932, p. 5.

45. J. G. Taylor Spink, *Judge Landis and Twenty-Five Years of Baseball* (1947; reprint, St. Louis: Sporting News Publishing, 1974), p. 209; *Sporting News,* August 25, 1932, p. 4.

46. *Sporting News,* September 29, 1932, p. 1.

47. *Chicago Tribune,* October 15, 1932, p. 21.

48. *Sporting News,* October 20, 1932, p. 5.

49. Franklin C. Lane, "The Passing of Rogers Hornsby," *Baseball Magazine* 25 (October 1932), p. 519.

10. Browns Blues

1. *St. Louis Post-Dispatch,* October 25, 1932, p. 20.

2. Ibid., p. 2.

3. Ibid., pp. 1–2; *Sporting News,* October 27, 1932, p. 1.

4. *Sporting News,* December 29, 1932, p. 3.

5. *St. Louis Post-Dispatch,* March 8, 1933, p. 4B.

6. *Sporting News,* April 27, 1933, p. 1.

7. *St. Louis Post-Dispatch,* July 26, 1933, p. 2B.

8. *Sporting News,* October 26, 1933, p. 6.

9. *St. Louis Post-Dispatch,* July 25, 1933, pp. 1–2.

10. *Chicago Tribune,* August 1, 1930, p. 17.

11. *Sporting News,* February 11, 1932, p. 7; August 3, 1933, p. 4; *New York Times,* September 18, 1953, p. 23.

12. *St. Louis Post-Dispatch,* July 27, 1933, p. 2B; July 28, 1933, spts., p. 1.

13. *Sporting News,* August 10, 1933, p. 2; *St. Louis Post-Dispatch,* August 16, 1933, p. 1B.

14. *St. Louis Post-Dispatch,* August 13, 1933, pt. 6, pp. 1–2.

15. Rogers Hornsby, *My Kind of Baseball,* ed. J. Roy Stockton (New York: David McKay, 1953), pp. 119–120; Bob Broeg, telephone conversation with author, August 5, 1992. Broeg, who would go on to a distinguished career in sports journalism in St. Louis, was a teenage spectator at Sportsman's Park that afternoon.

16. The San Antonio Missions, the Browns' Texas League farm, outdrew the parent club by about 20,000!

17. Ball's death followed by seventeen days that of William H. Veeck, who succumbed to leukemia in Chicago.

18. *Sporting News,* May 29, 1957, p. 28.

19. *St. Louis Post-Dispatch,* February 8, 1934, p. 2B.

20. Ollie Bejma, interview by author, South Bend, Indiana, September 12, 1991.

21. *New York Herald-Tribune,* May 1, 1934, p. 22.

22. *St. Louis Post-Dispatch,* June 5, 1934, p. 3B; June 19, 1934, p. 2B; July 27, 1934, p. 26.

23. Several decades afterward, Charles L. Connor remembered that Hornsby was a client of his father, a well-known St. Louis bookmaker. One day at Sportsman's Park, apparently out of concern for how it might look to Commissioner Landis, Hornsby ignored the elder Connor's request that he come to the field-box railing and shake his son's hand.

24. *St. Louis Post-Dispatch,* August 23, 1934, p. 16.

25. Of course Ruth didn't retire, as he was expected to. Released by the Yankees, he signed in the off-season with the Boston Braves as player and "assistant manager." He lasted for twenty-eight games in 1935, then gave up for good.

26. *St. Louis Post-Dispatch,* December 22, 1934, p. 1B.

27. Thus Barr got his start in umpiring pedagogy. Subsequently he would found his own school for umpires in Florida and go on to make it the most renowed institution of its kind.

28. *St. Louis Post-Dispatch,* March 7, 1935, p. 4B.

29. Ibid., May 1, 1935, p. 1B.

30. *Sporting News,* May 30, 1935, p. 2.

31. *New York Herald-Tribune,* July 19, 1935, p. 14; *St. Louis Post-Dispatch,* July 21, 1935, p. 2B.

32. *New York Herald-Tribune,* September 17, 1935, p. 15; *St. Louis Post-Dispatch,* September 5, 1935, p. 1B. Hornsby gave another and partly erroneous version of his run-in with Dick "Kauffman" in Rogers Hornsby and Bill Surface, *My War with Baseball* (New York: Coward-McCann, 1962), pp. 18–19.

33. *New York Herald-Tribune,* September 17, 1935, p. 15.

34. *Sporting News,* September 12, 1935, p. 3.

35. Quoted in ibid., October 31, 1935, p. 5.

36. The Crawfords defeated the Cubans in a six-game championship series, the Crawfords and Cubans having won the first and second halves, respec-

tively, of the Negro National League season. Split-season play was a character-istic feature of Negro-league baseball.

37. *Sporting News,* November 7, 1935, p. 8. As good as the 1935 Pittsburgh Crawfords were, they may have been even better the next year, when Leroy "Satchel" Paige rejoined them. Early in the 1935 season, Paige had left the Crawfords to pitch for an integrated semipro team based at Fargo, North Dakota. That October, while the Crawfords battled the American All-Stars in Mexico City, Satchel Paige's All-Stars played in California against Dizzy Dean's All-Stars, who consisted mostly of past and present Pacific Coast Leaguers. Paige's team included such Negro league standouts as Norman "Turkey" Stearns, George "Mule" Suttles, Raleigh "Biz" Mackey, and Chet Brewer.

38. *Sporting News,* November 7, 1935, p. 8.

39. *St. Louis Post-Dispatch,* November 11, 1935, p. 3E; January 30, 1936, p. 2B.

40. Minutes of proceedings, notation for January 31, 1936, *Quinn vs. Hornsby,* transcript in Clerk of the Court Records, Circuit Court, City of St. Louis, Civil Courts Building, St. Louis, Missouri.

41. *St. Louis Post-Dispatch,* February 18, 1936, p. 2B; January 7, 1936, p. 3B.

42. Ibid., March 11, 1936, spts. sec., p. 7; March 26, 1936, spts. sec., p. 1.

43. Ibid., May 11, 1936, p. 1B.

44. Ibid., June 10, 1936, p. 2B; *Sporting News,* July 9, 1936, p. 3.

45. Steve Smart, "Les Tietje," *National Pastime* 13 (1993), p. 82.

46. *Sporting News,* May 7, 1936, p. 3.

47. Crowds for Browns home games tailed off badly over the last six weeks of the season, so that their final 1936 attendance still fell short of 100,000.

48. *Sporting News,* August 20, 1936, p. 1.

49. *St. Louis Post-Dispatch,* October 28, 1936, p. 2B.

50. Ibid., November 15, 1936, p. 3B.

51. *Sporting News,* October 15, 1936, p. 2.

52. The title "general manager" itself was new to baseball. Before the 1930s, people working under club presidents were usually called "business managers," if such a position existed at all.

53. *Sporting News,* November 19, 1936, p. 1; *St. Louis Post-Dispatch,* November 15, 1936, pp. 1B, 3B.

54. *St. Louis Post-Dispatch,* November 11, 1936, p. 3B.

55. Ibid., January 18, 1937, p. 1B.

56. Shevlin quoted in *Sporting News,* March 18, 1937, p. 3; Hornsby in *St. Louis Post-Dispatch,* March 8, 1937, p. 2B.

57. *St. Louis Post-Dispatch,* March 8, 1937, p. 2B.

58. Ibid., March 17, 1937, p. 2B; March 24, 1937, p. 2B.

59. Ibid., March 29, 1937, p. 3B.

60. Ibid., April 13, 1937, p. 2B.

61. *Sporting News,* May 6, 1937, p. 1.

62. *St. Louis Post-Dispatch,* June 24, 1937, p. 3C; July 3, 1937, p. 2B; July 4, 1937, p. 1B.

63. Smart, "Les Tietje," p. 82.

64. John P. Carmichael column, *Chicago Daily News,* undated [spring 1962], Hornsby Collection, *Sporting News* Archives, St. Louis, Missouri. According to what Carmichael wrote that Hornsby had told him, with the track again muddy a few days later, Quince King ran again, this time at 8–1 odds to win. Hornsby "bet $3000 across for myself and $300 for the boy," and won an additional $24,000. Ibid. Hornsby himself gave a different account of his 1937 betting coup in *My Kind of Baseball,* pp. 116–118.

65. Hornsby and Surface, *My War with Baseball,* pp. 26–27; Hornsby, *My Kind of Baseball,* pp. 118–119.

66. *Sporting News,* July 29, 1937, p. 1; *St. Louis Post-Dispatch,* July 21, 1937, p. 1B; San Francisco *Call-Tribune,* June [?] 1951, clipping in Hornsby Collection, *Sporting News* Archives.

67. *Sporting News,* July 29, 1937, p. 1; *St. Louis Post-Dispatch,* July 22, 1937, p. 1B.

68. *Sporting News,* July 29, 1937, p. 2.

69. *St. Louis Post-Dispatch,* July 24, 1937, p. 2B.

70. *Sporting News,* July 29, 1937, p. 2.

11. Vagabond Years

1. Figuring ratios between money values past and present is always inexact, but a conservative estimate would put Hornsby's earnings in the 1920s–30s at roughly $6–7 million in 1990s dollars.

2. *St. Louis Post-Dispatch,* July 29, 1937, p. 2.

3. For career purposes, of course, his batting records in part-time duty with the Browns in 1933–37 also figure in.

4. Hornsby wasn't unfamiliar with airplane travel. Over one off-season, when he and Jeannette still had the farm outside St. Louis, he took a few flying lessons at neighboring Lambert Field.

5. Their usual wretched pitching doomed the Browns, even though they registered the second-highest team batting average in the American League

(.285), with Sammy West batting .328, Joe Vosmik .325, Ethan Allen .316, Beau Bell .340 (with 117 runs batted in), and Harlond Clift .306 (with twenty-nine homers and 118 runs batted in).

6. *Sporting News,* October 31, 1951, p. 10.

7. Ibid., January 20, 1938, p. 8.

8. Ibid., March 24, 1938, p. 10.

9. *Chicago Sun-Times,* January 8, 1963, p. 68.

10. *Sporting News,* April 21, 1938, p. 8.

11. Ibid., May 5, 1938, p. 7.

12. The Texas League and Southern Association would be classified AA in the post–World War II period.

13. *Sporting News,* July 21, 1938, p. 8.

14. Under Cuyler, the Lookouts would go on to win the 1939 Southern Association pennant.

15. Unidentified clipping in Rogers Hornsby Collection, *Sporting News* Archives, St. Louis, Missouri.

16. Rogers Hornsby, as told to Dick Farrington, " 'Me an Underminer? Not on Your Life,' Says Hornsby," *Sporting News,* December 29, 1938, p. 3.

17. Ibid., January 5, 1939, p. 5; February 23, 1939, p. 6; March 10, 1939, p. 9.

18. Ibid., August 1, 1940, p. 1.

19. Ibid., June 26, 1941, p. 3. Under Homer Peel, Oklahoma City finished sixth in 1941, with a record of 69–85.

20. Ibid., November 27, 1941, p. 6.

21. Ibid., December 11, 1941, p. 12.

22. Ibid., January 8, 1942, p. 1.

23. Ibid., January 29, 1942, p. 2; *St. Louis Post-Dispatch,* January 20, 1942, p. 3B.

24. *Sporting News,* January 29, 1942, p. 2.

25. Zeke Handler letter [June 1963], Rogers Hornsby Collection, *Sporting News* Archives.

26. *Sporting News,* July 23, 1942, p. 9.

27. Ibid., March 4, 1943, p. 10.

28. *Sporting News,* February 3, 1944, p. 6; Rochester *Democrat-Chronicle,* January 6, 1963, p. 2C.

29. Rogers Hornsby and Bill Surface, *My War with Baseball* (New York: Coward-McCann, 1962), p. 52.

30. *Sporting News,* May 25, 1944, p. 6.

31. Ibid.

32. Ibid., August 30, 1945, p. 9.
33. *Cincinnati Enquirer,* September 9, 1953, p. 1.
34. *Sporting News,* February 38, 1946, p. 2.
35. The Branch Rickey Papers, Library of Congress, Washington, D.C., contain an announcment of commencement exercises at Denison High School on June 4, 1937, sent to Rickey by Rogers Hornsby Jr. No such item can be found in the Hornsby collections at either the National Baseball Library, Cooperstown, New York, or the *Sporting News* Archives, St. Louis, Missouri.
36. *Sporting News,* August 20, 1952, p. 10.
37. Quoted in Rogers Hornsby, *My Kind of Baseball,* ed. J. Roy Stockton (New York: David McKay, 1953), p. 12.
38. *Sporting News,* July 23, 1947, p. 7.
39. Ibid., November 26, 1947, p. 15; *Cleveland News,* undated McAuley column [1952], Hornsby Collection, *Sporting News* Archives.
40. *Sporting News,* November 26, 1947, p. 15.
41. See, for example, ibid., November 12, 1947, p. 12.
42. Bill McKechnie, the fifth pennant-winning St. Louis manager (1928), was absent.
43. *Sporting News,* February 23, 1949, p. 8.
44. *Atlanta Constitution,* December 24, 1949, p. 14.
45. Ann Hornsby Rice, interview by author, McLean, Virginia, March 24, 1993.

12. Making It Back

1. Following World War II, the governing National Association designated the top three minor leagues (International and Pacific Coast Leagues and American Association) as Class AAA and the Texas League and Southern Association as Class AA.
2. *Sporting News,* February 15, 1950, p. 1.
3. Ibid., March 31, 1950, p. 33.
4. Keith Thomas, interview by author, Rocky Mount, North Carolina, May 26, 1992.
5. Black players had already appeared with big-league teams in exhibition games in several Texas League cities. In Beaumont, for example, Robinson drew an overflow crowd with the Dodgers in March 1949, and Sam Jethroe appeared with the Boston Braves a year later. But it would be 1952 before pitcher-outfielder Dave Hoskins, assigned to Dallas by the Cleveland Indians, broke the color line in a regular-season Texas League game.

6. Elvin Tappe, interview by author, Quincy, Illinois, June 18, 1992.

7. Tappe interview; Bob Marquis, interview by author, Beaumont, Texas, December 13, 1992.

8. *Dallas Morning News,* March 14, 1950, p. 27; *Sporting News,* May 17, 1950, p. 30.

9. Rogers Hornsby, *My Kind of Baseball,* ed. J. Roy Stockton (New York: David McKay, 1953), p. 25; *Beaumont Enterprise,* June 19, 1952, p. 24.

10. One of Branch Rickey's major additions to the extensive Brooklyn farm system he built during the mid- and late-1940s was Fort Worth, through which moved a steady stream of the Dodgers' prime prospects.

11. Something I personally glimpsed several times, inasmuch as the tavern was next door to the barber shop where my father and I got our haircuts. Bob Marquis and Clarence Beers, two of Hornsby's players in 1950, affirm that he bet regularly that summer. Marquis interview; Clarence Beers, interview by author, Houston, Texas, December 11, 1992.

12. Thomas interview.

13. Ibid.; *Sporting News,* August 23, 1950, p. 33; *St. Louis Globe-Democrat,* August 14, 1950, p. 32.

14. One of my most vivid memories from that summer is of a night in Beaumont when the Roughnecks gave Grimm's pitchers a particularly severe battering. As Grimm trudged repeatedly from the third-base visitors' dugout to the mound and back, Hornsby, occupying the third-base coaching box, would turn toward left field and literally shake with laughter.

15. Beers interview.

16. *Sporting News,* August 23, 1950, p. 33.

17. *Beaumont Enterprise,* June 19, 1952, p. 16.

18. *Sporting News,* August 20, 1952, p. 10; Jack Brickhouse, interview by author, Peoria, Illinois, April 27, 1990.

19. Hornsby succeeded fellow Texan Paul Richards, who, despite Seattle's sixth-place finish in 1950, had moved up to manage the Chicago White Sox.

20. For the last three weeks of the Puerto Rican winter season, Ponce played under the direction of Benny Huffman, a Ray Doan baseball school graduate who'd backed up Rollie Hemsley on the 1937 St. Louis Browns and, as he knocked around the minor leagues in the following years, maintained contact with his onetime manager.

21. While McDougald made the Yankees roster that spring, Courtney, Marquis, and Nevel were all assigned to Kansas City, New York's American Association farm club.

22. Ibid., May 16, 1951, p. 21.

23. From 1946 through 1950, Oklahoma City was a Cleveland Indians farm club.

24. *Sporting News,* January 19, 1963, p. 34.

25. *Sporting News,* May 16, 1951, p. 30; *Seattle Times,* June 15, 1952, p. 28.

26. Harold Brown, interview by author, Greensboro, North Carolina, May 27, 1992.

27. Brown did remember, though, that a woman visited him in Seattle that season. He didn't know who she was; undoubtedly it was Bernadette Harris.

28. *Sporting News,* June 13, 1951, p. 27.

29. Undated *Cleveland News* column by Ed McAuley [April 1952], in Rogers Hornsby Collection, *Sporting News* Archives, St. Louis, Missouri.

30. *Sporting News,* September 12, 1951, p. 27.

31. Ibid., September 19, 1951, p. 21.

32. *San Francisco Examiner,* September 29, 1951, p. 28.

33. Hornsby, *My Kind of Baseball,* p. 168.

13. "As Changeless as Gibraltar"

1. Bill Veeck and Ed Linn, *Veeck—as in Wreck* (New York: Putnam's, 1962), p. 229.

2. *Sporting News,* October 17, 1951, p. 5; *St. Louis Post-Dispatch,* October 30, 1951, p. 1C.

3. *Sporting News,* October 17, 1951, p. 14.

4. Ibid.

5. Ibid., October 17, 1951, p. 14; December 26, 1951, p. 9.

6. Ibid., March 3, 1952, p. 15.

7. *St. Louis Post-Dispatch,* February 22, 1952, p. IC; February 24, 1952, p. 2C.

8. Ibid., February 28, 1952, p. 1C; March 29, 1952, p. 4B. Late in February 1952, I accompanied my father to St. Louis for the annual convention of the American Association of School Administrators, which met in conjunction with the National Education Association. One afternoon we took a streetcar out to cold and dreary Sportsman's Park. Wandering unhindered inside the ballpark (as one could do in that less security-conscious time), we encountered tall, husky, bespectacled Bill DeWitt, who greeted us with utmost cordiality and showed particular interest in our opinions of Hornsby, whom we'd watched at Beaumont two years earlier. DeWitt never mentioned his own earlier experiences with Hornsby in St. Louis, either with the Cardinals as Branch Rickey's assistant or with the Browns as number-two man to Donald Barnes.

9. Milton Richman column, undated [June 1952], Rogers Hornsby Collection, *Sporting News* Archives, St. Louis, Missouri.

10. Ned Garver, interview by author, Ney, Ohio, September 11, 1991.

11. Richman column [June 1952]. As was the case everywhere else in Texas, Corpus Christi was still a wholly segregated town (which in that particular locale affected not only black-white relations but, selectively, Anglo-Hispanic contacts). In Corpus Christi and other Texas cities where the Browns played, Paige stayed at all-black hotels or rooming houses in areas where, typically, white cabdrivers were reluctant to venture. (It might be noted, though, that if anybody knew how to deal with such situations, it should have been Paige, who pitched just about everywhere in the United States and encountered American racial mores in all their variants.)

12. Among those who occupied less than half the capacity of Beaumont's Stuart Stadium on the afternoon of Wednesday, April 2, 1952, were my mother, father, and myself.

13. Rogers Hornsby, *My Kind of Baseball*, ed. J. Roy Stockton (New York: David McKay, 1953), p. 171.

14. Bob Broeg, interview by author, St. Louis, Missouri, June 17, 1992; *Sporting News*, April 30, 1952, p. 1; June 18, 1952, p. 10.

15. *Sporting News*, June 4, 1952, p. 13.

16. Hugh Trader Jr., column in *Baltimore News-Post*, April 10, 1954, in Hornsby Collection, *Sporting News* Archives.

17. *St. Louis Post-Dispatch*, June 10, 1952, p. 1.

18. *Sporting News*, June 18, 1952, pp. 1, 3.

19. Ibid., June 25, 1952, p. 10.

20. Ibid., p. 3; *St. Louis Post-Dispatch*, June 11, 1952, p. 3C; Garver interview.

21. *St. Louis Post-Dispatch*, June 11, 1952, p. 3C.

22. Ibid., p. 1.

23. Ibid., pp. 1, 3.

24. Ibid., June 18, 1952, p. 12.

25. Ty Cobb, "They Don't Play Baseball Anymore," *Life* 32 (March 17, 1952), p. 147; Charles C. Alexander, *Ty Cobb* (New York: Oxford University Press, 1984), pp. 224–225.

26. Rogers Hornsby and Tim Cohane, "It's Still Baseball, Ty Cobb!" *Look* 16 (June 12, 1952), pp. 55–56ff. On the page immediate following Hornsby's piece in the June 12, 1952, issue of *Look* was a suddenly irrelevant picture story on Hornsby and his players, entitled "Under Hornsby and Veeck the Browns Have Ideas." Cobb's telegram, to Don Donaghey, June 13, 1952, is in

the Rogers Hornsby Collection, National Baseball Library, Cooperstown, New York.

27. *Sporting News,* June 18, 1952, p. 6; Milton Richman column, *Chicago Daily News,* undated, in Hornsby Collection, *Sporting News* Archives.

28. *Sporting News,* August 6, 1952, p. 1.

29. Ibid., p. 10.

30. Quoted in Hornsby, *My Kind of Baseball,* pp. 183–84. Paul elaborated on his estimate of Hornsby in "Who Says Hornsby's Too Tough?" *Sport* 8 (July 1953), pp. 20–21f.

31. Jim Greengrass, telephone conversation with author, July 17, 1992.

32. *Cincinnati Enquirer,* July 29, 1952, p. 1; August 6, 1952, p. 13.

33. Greengrass conversation.

34. Meanwhile the St. Louis Browns more than doubled their home attendance, played somewhat poorer ball under Marty Marion than under Hornsby, and finished in seventh place with a 64–90 record. Satchel Paige won twelve games and saved ten others, while Clint Courtney batted .286 and gained American League Rookie of the Year honors. By season's end, though, Jim Rivera and Leo Thomas were with the White Sox, George Schmees was with Boston, and Ned Garver was with Detroit, where he now complained that Bill Veeck had insisted he pitch with a sore arm.

35. *Sporting News,* January 14, 1953, p. 14.

36. Hornsby, *My Kind of Baseball,* pp. 172, 185.

37. *Sporting News,* March 11, 1953, p. 5; *Cincinnati Enquirer,* March 1, 1953, p. 29.

38. *Cincinnati Enquirer,* March 18, 1953, p. 16.

39. One of several concessions major-league players won from club owners in the immediate post–World War II years was the right to have such a player representative on each team, elected by team members.

40. *Cincinnati Enquirer,* May 4, 1953, p. 24.

41. Ibid., May 6, 1953, p. 34.

42. Earl Lawson, *Cincinnati Seasons: My 34 Years with the Reds* (South Bend, Ind.: Diamond Communications, 1987), p. 97.

43. Unidentified clipping [May 2, 1953], in Hornsby Collection, *Sporting News* Archives.

44. Marquis interview; Greengrass conversation; *Cincinnati Enquirer,* June 12, 1953, p. 28; Lawson, *Cincinnati Seasons,* pp. 101–102. Although Lawson's book is useful for particular aspects of the 1953 season, its venomously anti-Hornsby bias—and occasional factual mistakes—have caused me to use it with extreme caution.

N O T E S

45. Lawson, *Cincinnati Seasons*, p. 102; *New York Times*, June 12, 1953, p. 20; *Cincinnati Enquirer*, June 12, 1953, p. 28.

46. Lawson, *Cincinnati Seasons*, p. 101. According to Lawson, Hatton went to Gabe Paul to complain about Hornsby's practice of urinating in the clubhouse shower. Like most anecdotes, that one has enlarged in the retelling, so that by the time they published *The Cincinnati Game* in 1988, Lonnie Wheeler and John Baskin's version had become: "one day . . . the losing [Reds] pitcher found himself showering beside his crusty manager. Busy lathering his head, Hornsby was casually urinating on the leg of the pitcher, who suddenly leapt from the shower, dressed, and registered a complaint with general manager Gabe Paul" (Wilmington, Ohio: Orange Frazer Press, p. 124).

Given reports by various men who played for Hornsby on various teams (including the Reds) that he never showered at the ballpark, the urination story—in whatever form it's told—seems highly improbable.

47. *Sporting News*, July 22, 1953, p. 8; Lawson, *Cincinnati Seasons*, p. 100.

48. Lawson, *Cincinnati Seasons*, p. 99.

49. Greengrass conversation.

50. *Cincinnati Enquirer*, August 10, 1953, p. 19; August 29, 1953, p. 13; *Sporting News*, August 26, 1953, p. 15.

51. Greengrass conversation.

52. *Sporting News*, September 16, 1953, p. 4.

53. *Cincinnati Enquirer*, September 8, 1953, p. 1.

54. Ibid., September 8, 1953, p. 1; September 9, 1953, p. 1; *Sporting News*, September 16, 1953, p. 2.

55. *Cincinnati Enquirer*, September 9, 1953, p. 1; *Chicago Tribune*, September 9, 1953, p. 1.

56. *Cincinnati Enquirer*, September 9, 1953, p. 1.

57. *Sacramento Bee*, undated clipping [1991], in Hornsby Collection, *Sporting News* Archives.

58. *Cincinnati Enquirer*, September 18, 1953, p. 33; *Sporting News*, September 23, 1953, p. 25.

59. *Sporting News*, September 23, 1953, p. 4; *Cincinnati Enquirer*, September 18, 1953, p. 33.

60. *Cincinnati Enquirer*, September 18, 1953, p. 33; *Sporting News*, September 23, 1953, pp. 12, 25.

61. *Sporting News*, January 27, 1954, p. 14. Jim Greengrass agreed that Hornsby wasn't good with pitchers, didn't really understand their uniqueness as ballplayers, and probably didn't like pitchers as a breed. Greengrass conversation.

337

62. *Cincinnati Enquirer,* September 19, 1953, p. 17; September 26, 1953, p. 17; *Sporting News,* September 30, 1953, p. 25.

14. "I Belong in Baseball"

1. Copy of contract in Rogers Hornsby Collection, National Baseball Library, Cooperstown, New York.

2. *Sporting News,* September 21, 1955, p. 4.

3. Ibid., June 20, 1956, p. 15; July 4, 1956, p. 16.

4. Dorothy Stull, "Conversation Piece: Rogers Hornsby," *Sports Illustrated* 6 (September 10, 1956), p. 32.

5. Ibid.

6. Ibid., p. 64.

7. Ibid.

8. Ibid.

9. Elvin Tappe, interview by author, Quincy, Illinois, June 18, 1992.

10. Stephen R. Lowe, *The Kid on the Sandlot: Congress and Professional Sports, 1910–1992* (Bowling Green: Bowling Green State University Popular Press, 1995), p. 31.

11. Emmanuel Celler to Rogers Hornsby, August 14, 1957, Hornsby Collection, National Baseball Library.

12. Rogers Hornsby to Hon. Emanuel [*sic*] Celler, August 9, 1957, ibid.

13. Ibid. The text of Hornsby's letter to Representative Celler may also be found in House of Representatives, Committee on the Judiciary, *Organized Professional Team Sports: Hearings,* 85th Cong., 1st sess. (1957), p. 3148.

14. Red Smith column in *New York Herald-Tribune,* Hornsby Collection, *Sporting News* Archives St. Louis, Missouri.

15. Jack Ryan piece for *Sporting News* [unpublished], February 1956, typescript in Rogers Hornsby Collection, *Sporting News* Archives, St. Louis, Missouri.

16. *Sporting News,* January 29, 1958, p. 19.

17. Tappe interview; *Sporting News,* March 12, 1958, p. 6.

18. *Sporting News,* April 23, 1958, p. 5.

19. The rest of the BBWAA all-time team consisted of Ty Cobb, Tris Speaker, and Babe Ruth as outfielders; Harold "Pie" Traynor, Honus Wagner, and Lou Gehrig in the infield; Bill Dickey as catcher; Walter Johnson, Lefty Grove, Christy Mathewson, and Carl Hubbell as pitchers; and John McGraw as manager.

20. *Sporting News,* August 27, 1958, p. 4.

21. Ibid., September 3, 1958, p. 2.

22. Ibid., March 25, 1959, p. 15.

23. Ibid., August 5, 1959, p. 2.

24. Rogers Hornsby to Sid C. Keener, undated [1962], Hornsby Collection, National Baseball Library.

25. Brad H. Hornsby, interview by author, Murfreesboro, Tennessee, June 23, 1993, and telephone conversation, March 18, 1994.

26. Bill Surface, "The Last Days of Rogers Hornsby," *Saturday Evening Post* 236 (June 15, 1963), p. 72.

27. Rogers Hornsby and Bill Surface, "You've Got to Cheat to Win in Baseball," *True* 14 (August 1961), pp. 59–60ff.

28. Surface, "Last Days of Rogers Hornsby," p. 76.

29. Ibid., p. 76.

30. The National League's decision to expand to a ten-club league for 1962, like that of the American League for 1961, resulted directly from the threat posed by Branch Rickey's Continental League project to move into choice territories such as New York, Houston, Los Angeles, and Minneapolis–St. Paul. Thus, unintentionally and indirectly, Rickey again had a role in Hornsby's reemployment.

31. Rogers Hornsby to Sid C. Keener [undated], Hornsby Collection, National Baseball Library.

32. *Sporting News,* January 31, 1962, p. 23; February 28, 1962, p. 24.

33. Robert Lipsyte, "Rajah's Return," *New York Times Magazine,* April 29, 1962, p. 33; Lipsyte column, *New York Times,* June 16, 1969, p. 64.

34. *New York Times,* June 16, 1969, p. 64. Eastern Star is the women's auxiliary of the Masonic Order. By "my first wife," it's not entirely clear whether Hornsby meant Sarah Martin Hornsby or Jeannette Pennington Hornsby, although from his context of his remarks it would appear he was actually talking about his *second* wife, Jeannette.

35. Lipsyte, "Rajah's Return," pp. 32, 36.

36. Rogers Hornsby and Bill Surface, *My War with Baseball* (New York: Coward-McCann, 1962), p. 86. Hornsby's views on sluggers versus hitters were also aired in Rogers Hornsby and Bill Surface, "What Home-Run Fever Is Doing to Baseball," *This Week Magazine,* March 25, 1962, pp. 12ff.

37. *Sporting News,* April 4, 1962, p. 11.

38. Ibid.

39. Ibid.

40. Surface, "Last Days of Rogers Hornsby," p. 76. That was the last year in a four-year stretch in which, to fatten the players' pension fund, two All-Star Games were played each summer.

41. Ibid.
42. Ibid. An "entry" is a two-horse betting combination.
43. Frederick Stenn, M.D., to Marjorie Hornsby, January 14, 1963, Hornsby Collection, National Baseball Library.
44. *Sporting News,* January 19, 1963, p. 10; Red Smith undated *New York Herald-Tribune* column, Hornsby Collection, *Sporting News* Archives.
45. Telegrams, Mrs. Richard J. Rice, George M. Weiss, and Casey Stengel to Mrs. Rogers Hornsby, January 5, January 7, 1963, Hornsby Collection, National Baseball Library.
46. *New York Times,* January 7, 1963, p. 8.
47. Associated Press release, January 9, 1963, Hornsby Collection, *Sporting News* Archives.
48. Austin *American* [January 9, 1963], clipping in Hornsby Family Collection, Austin History Center, Austin, Texas.

Epilogue: "What Else Is There?"

1. Hy Zimmerman column in *Seattle Post-Intelligencer* [undated], clipping in Rogers Hornsby Collection, *Sporting News* Archives, St. Louis, Missouri.
2. Bill Surface, "The Last Days of Rogers Hornsby," *Saturday Evening Post* 506 (June 15, 1963), pp. 72ff.
3. Al Stump, "Ty Cobb's Wild Ten-Month Fight to Live," *True* 14 (December 1961), pp. 38–41ff; reprinted in Charles Einstein, ed., *The Baseball Reader* (New York: Lippincott and Crowell, 1980), pp. 282–300.
4. Zeke Handler to *Sporting News* [unpublished], June 1963, Rogers Hornsby Collection, *Sporting News* Archives, St. Louis, Missouri.
5. Boston *Record-American,* January 8, 1963, p. 17.
6. Jim Orford, *Excessive Appetites: A Psychological View of Addictions* (New York: Wiley, 1985), pp. 37, 43, 321; Tomas Martinez, *The Gambling Scene: Why People Gamble* (Springfield, Ill.: C. C. Thomas, 1983), p. 69. One of the more influential examples of the psychoanalytical school is Edmund Bergler, *The Psychology of Gambling* (1957; reprint, New York: International University Press, 1970).
7. Martinez, *Gambling Scene,* p. 64 (italics in original); Cecil Peck, "Risk-Taking and Compulsive Gambling," *American Psychologist* 41 (April 1986), pp. 461–465.
8. Charlotte Olmsted, *Heads I Win; Tails You Lose* (New York: Macmillan, 1962), p. 202.
9. *Sporting News,* February 9, 1928, p. 4.

10. Bill Veeck and Ed Linn, *Veeck—as in Wreck* (New York: Putnam's, 1962), p. 240.

11. Robert Lipsyte, "Rajah's Return," *New York Times Magazine,* April 29, 1962, p. 36; *Sporting News,* June 21, 1951, p. 14; Rogers Hornsby and Bill Surface, *My War with Baseball* (New York: Coward-McCann, 1962), p. 207. Italics in original.

12. *Sporting News,* February 22, 1969, p. 24.

13. Ibid., January 19, 1963, p. 12.

Bibliography

• • •

Archival Resources

Rogers Hornsby Collection, National Baseball Library, Cooperstown, New York.

Rogers Hornsby Collection, *Sporting News* Archives, St. Louis, Missouri.

Hornsby Family Genealogy, in possession of Brad H. Hornsby, Murfreesboro, Tennessee.

Hornsby Family Records, Austin History Center, Austin, Texas.

Joe McCarthy Collection, National Baseball Library, Cooperstown, New York.

Branch Rickey Collection, National Baseball Library, Cooperstown, New York.

Branch Rickey Papers, Library of Congress, Washington, D.C.

Runnels County Deed Records, County Clerk's Office, Ballinger, Texas.

Clerk of the Circuit Court Records, City of St. Louis, 1919–35, Civil Courts Building, St. Louis, Missouri.

Government Documents

U.S. Congress. House of Representatives. Committee on the Judiciary. *Organized Professional Team Sports.* Hearings, 85th Cong., 1st sess. (1957).

Newspapers

Atlanta Constitution, 1949.

Austin (Tex.) *American,* 1963.

Beaumont Enterprise, 1950–52.

Boston Globe, 1969.

Boston *Record-American,* 1963.

Boston Traveler, 1931.

Chicago *American,* 1963.

Chicago Daily News, 1930–32, 1945–63, 1966.

Chicago *Sun-Times,* 1963.

Chicago Tribune, 1928–33, 1946–63.

Cincinnati Enquirer, 1952–54.

Cleveland News, 1947.

Cleveland *Plain Dealer,* 1935, 1947.

Cleveland Press, 1947.

Detroit News, 1937.

LaSalle (Ind.)-Peru (Ind.)-Oglesby (Ill.) *Daily Post-Tribune,* 1946.

New York *Daily Mirror,* 1928.

New York Herald-Tribune, 1934–35.

New York Times, 1926–69.

New York *World-Telegram,* 1931.

Rochester (N.Y.) *Democrat-Chronicle,* 1963.

Sacramento Bee, 1990.

San Antonio Express, 1950.

San Antonio Light, 1950.

San Francisco *Call-Tribune,* 1951.

San Francisco Examiner, 1951.

Seattle Times, 1952.

Sporting News, 1914–94.

St. Louis *Globe-Democrat,* 1925.

St. Louis Post-Dispatch, 1915–37, 1942–43, 1951–63.

Personal Communications

Beers, Clarence. Interview. Houston, Texas, December 11, 1992.

Bejma, Aloys "Ollie." Interview. South Bend, Indiana, September 12, 1991.

Bejma, Clara. Interview. South Bend, Indiana, September 12, 1991.

Brickhouse, Jack. Interview. Peoria, Illinois, April 27, 1990.

Broeg, Bob. Interview. St. Louis, Missouri, June 17, 1992. Telephone conversations. August 5 and 8, 1992.

Brown, Harold "Skinny." Interview. Greensboro, North Carolina, May 27, 1992.

English, Elwood "Woody." Interview. Newark, Ohio, September 10, 1991.

Garver, Ned. Interview. Ney, Ohio, September 11, 1991.

Greengrass, Jim. Telephone conversation. July 17, 1992.

Hornsby, Brad H. Interview. Murfreesboro, Tennessee, June 23, 1993. Telephone conversation. March 18, 1994.

Hornsby, Rogers, III. Interview. Denison, Texas, December 5, 1992.

Jackson, Travis. Interview. Waldo, Arkansas, December 3, 1985.

Marquis, Bob. Interview. Beaumont, Texas, December 13, 1992.

Rice, Ann Hornsby. Interview. McLean, Virginia, March 24, 1993.

Rosenberg, Jack. Telephone conversation. July 24, 1992.

Tappe, Elvin. Interview. Quincy, Illinois, June 18, 1992.

Thomas, Keith. Interview. Rocky Mount, North Carolina, May 26, 1992.

Books

Alexander, Charles C. *John McGraw*. New York: Viking, 1988.

————. *The Ku Klux Klan in the Southwest*. Lexington: University of Kentucky Press, 1965.

————. *Our Game: An American Baseball History*. New York: Henry Holt, 1991.

————. *Ty Cobb*. New York: Oxford University Press, 1984.

Allen, Lee. *Cooperstown Corner: Columns from the Sporting News, 1962–1969*. Cooperstown: Society for American Baseball Research, 1990.

————. *The National League Story*. New York: Hill and Wang, 1961.

Allen, Lee, and Tom Meany. *Kings of the Diamond: The Immortals in Baseball's Hall of Fame*. New York: Putnam's, 1965.

Astor, Gerald. *The Baseball Hall of Fame Fiftieth Anniversary Book*. New York: Prentice-Hall, 1988.

The Baseball Encyclopedia. 9th ed. New York: Macmillan, 1993.

Benson, Michael. *Ballparks of North America.* Wilmington: McFarland, 1989.

Bergler, Edmund. *The Psychology of Gambling.* 1957. Reprint, New York: International University Press, 1970.

Broeg, Bob, and William M. Miller. *Baseball from a Different Angle.* South Bend: Diamond Communications, 1988.

Brown, Warren. *The Chicago Cubs.* New York: Putnam's, 1946.

Burk, Robert F. *Never Just a Game: Players, Owners, and American Baseball to 1920.* Chapel Hill: University of North Carolina Press, 1994.

Carmichael, John P., ed. *My Greatest Day in Baseball.* New York: A. S. Barnes, 1946.

Carroll, H. Bailey, and Eldon S. Banda, eds. *The Handbook of Texas.* 3 vols. Austin: Texas State Historical Association, 1952, 1976.

Carter, Craig. *Daguerreotypes.* 8th ed. St. Louis: Sporting News Publishing, 1990.

Cobb, Ty, and Al Stump. *My Life in Baseball: The True Record.* 1961. Reprint, Lincoln: University of Nebraska Press, 1993.

Creamer, Robert. *Babe: The Legend Comes to Life.* New York: Simon and Schuster, 1974.

————. *Stengel: His Life and Times.* New York: Simon and Schuster, 1984.

Curran, William. *Big Sticks: The Batting Revolution of the Twenties.* New York: William Morrow, 1990.

————. *Mitts: A Celebration of Fielding.* New York: William Morrow, 1985.

Daley, Arthur. *Kings of the Diamond.* New York: Putnam's, 1962.

Dickey, Glenn. *The History of American League Baseball since 1901.* New York: Stein and Day, 1980.

————. *The History of National League Baseball since 1876.* New York: Stein and Day, 1982.

Einstein, Charles, ed. *The Baseball Reader.* New York: Lippincott and Crowell, 1980.

Enright, Jim. *The Chicago Cubs.* New York: Macmillan, 1975.

Eskenazi, Gerald. *Bill Veeck: A Baseball Legend.* New York: McGraw-Hill, 1988.

Falkner, David. *Nine Sides of the Diamond.* New York: Random House, 1990.

Gorman, Bill. *The Story of Jimmie Foxx: Baseball's Forgotten Slugger.* New York: Bill Goff, 1990.

Graham, Frank. *McGraw of the Giants.* New York: Putnam's, 1944.

————. *The New York Giants.* New York: Putnam's, 1952.

Gregory, Robert. *Diz: Dizzy Dean and Baseball during the Great Depression.* New York: Viking, 1992.

Honig, Donald, and Lawrence Ritter. *Baseball: When the Grass Was Real.* New York: Coward, McCann, and Geoghegan, 1975.

Hornsby, Rogers. *My Kind of Baseball.* Ed. J. Roy Stockton. New York: David McKay, 1953.

Hornsby, Rogers, and Bill Surface. *My War with Baseball.* New York: Coward-McCann, 1962.

Johnson, Lloyd, and Miles Wolff, eds. *The Encyclopedia of Minor League Baseball.* Durham: Baseball America, 1993.

Knight, Oliver. *Fort Worth: Outpost on the Trinity.* Norman: University of Oklahoma Press, 1953.

Lawson, Earl. *Cincinnati Seasons: My 34 Years with the Reds.* South Bend, Ind.: Diamond Communications, 1987.

Lieb, Fred. *The Baltimore Orioles.* New York: Putnam's, 1955.

————. *Baseball as I Have Known It.* New York: Tempo-Grosset and Dunlap, 1977.

————. *The Baseball Story.* New York: Putnam's, 1950.

————. *The St. Louis Cardinals.* New York: Putnam's, 1944.

————. *The Story of the World Series.* New York: Putnam's, 1965.

Lipsitz, George. *The Sidewalks of St. Louis: Places, People, and Politics in an American City.* Columbia: University of Missouri Press, 1991.

Lowe, Stephen R. *The Kid on the Sandlot: Congress and Professional Sports, 1910–1992.* Bowling Green: Bowling Green State University Popular Press, 1995.

Lowry, Philip J. *Green Cathedrals.* Cooperstown: Society for American Baseball Research, 1986.

Mann, Arthur. *Branch Rickey: American in Action.* Boston: Houghton Mifflin, 1957.

Martinez, Tomas. *The Gambling Scene: Why People Gamble.* Springfield, Ill.: C. C. Thomas, 1983.

Mead, William B. *Two Spectacular Seasons.* New York: Macmillan, 1990.

Meany, Tom. *Baseball's Greatest Pitchers.* New York: A. S. Barnes, 1952.

Murdock, Eugene C. *Ban Johnson: Czar of Baseball.* Westport: Greenwood Press, 1982.

————. *Baseball between the Wars: Memoirs of the Game by the Men Who Played It.* Westport: Meckler, 1992.

————. *Baseball Players and Their Lives: Oral Histories of the Game, 1920–1948.* Westport: Meckler, 1991.

Okonnen, Marc. *The Federal League: Baseball's Third Major League, 1914–1915.* Cooperstown: Society for American Baseball Research, 1989.

Okrent, Daniel, and Harris Lewine, eds. *The Ultimate Baseball Book.* Boston: Houghton Mifflin, 1982.

Olmsted, Charlotte. *Heads I Win; Tails You Lose.* New York: Macmillan, 1962.

O'Neal, Bill. *The International League.* Austin: Eakin, 1992.

————. *The Pacific Coast League.* Austin: Eakin, 1990.

————. *The Texas League.* Austin: Eakin, 1987.

Orford, Jim. *Excessive Appetites: A Psychological View of Addictions.* New York: Wiley, 1985.

Pate, J'Nell L. *Livestock Legacy: The Fort Worth Stockyards, 1887–1987.* College Station: Texas A & M University Press, 1988.

Peterson, Robert. *Only the Ball Was White.* 1970. Reprint, New York: McGraw-Hill, 1984.

Polner, Murray. *Branch Rickey.* New York: Atheneum, 1982.

Porter, David L. *Biographical Dictionary of American Sports: Baseball.* Westport: Greenwood Press, 1987.

Ribowsky, Mark. *Don't Look Back: Satchel Paige in the Shadows of Baseball.* New York: Simon and Schuster, 1994.

Rice, Grantland. *The Tumult and the Shouting: My Life in Sport.* New York: A. S. Barnes, 1954.

Rickey, Branch. *The American Diamond: A Documentary of the Game of Baseball.* New York: Simon and Schuster, 1965.

Riess, Steven A. *Touching Base: Professional Baseball and American Culture during the Progressive Era.* Westport: Greenwood Press, 1980.

Ritter, Lawrence. *The Glory of Their Times.* Rev. ed. New York: William Morrow, 1984.

————. *Lost Ballparks: A Celebration of Baseball's Legendary Fields.* New York: Viking, 1992.

Ritter, Lawrence, and Donald Honig. *The Image of Their Greatness.* New York: Crown, 1979.

Rosenthal, Harold. *The Ten Best Years of Baseball: An Informal History of the Fifties.* New York: Van Nostrand Reinhold, 1981.

Rudwick, Elliott M. *Race Riot at East St. Louis, July 2, 1917.* Carbondale: Southern Illinois University Press, 1964.

Seidel, Michael. *Ted Williams: A Baseball Life.* Chicago: Contemporary Books, 1991.

Seymour, Harold. *Baseball: The Golden Age.* New York: Oxford University Press, 1971.

Smelser, Marshall. *The Life That Ruth Built: A Biography.* 1975. Reprint, Lincoln: University of Nebraska Press, 1993.

Smith, Curt. *America's Dizzy Dean.* St. Louis: Bethany Press, 1978.

————. *Voices of the Game.* Rev. ed. New York: Simon and Schuster, 1992.

Spink, J. G. Taylor. *Judge Landis and Twenty-Five Years of Baseball.* 1947. Reprint, St. Louis: Sporting News Publishing, 1974.

Staten, Vince. *Ol' Diz: A Biography of Dizzy Dean.* New York: HarperCollins, 1992.

Veeck, William Jr., and Ed Linn. *Veeck—as in Wreck.* New York: Putnam's, 1962.

Voight, David Q. *American Baseball.* 3 vols. Norman: University of Oklahoma Press; State College: Penn State University Press, 1966–84.

————. *Baseball: An Illustrated History.* State College: Penn State University Press, 1987.

Ward, Geoffrey C., et al. *Baseball: An Illustrated History.* New York: Knopf, 1994.

Wheeler, Lonnie, and John Baskin. *The Cincinnati Game.* Wilmington, Ohio: Orange Frazer Press, 1988.

Articles

Alexander, Charles C. "The Tempestuous Texan: Rogers Hornsby." *Legacies* 2 (spring 1990), pp. 29–35.

Bennett, Joseph E. "The Hornsby Years." *Texas Mason* 2 (spring 1993), pp. 12–17.

Breit, Harvey. "Mister Baseball Starts His Second Career." *New York Times Magazine,* May 11, 1952, pp. 15f.

Brown, William E. Jr. "Sunday Baseball Comes to Boston." *National Pastime* 14 (1994), pp. 83–85.

Cobb, Ty. "They Don't Play Baseball Any More." *Life* 32 (March 17, 1952), pp. 136–138f.

————. "Tricks That Won Me Ball Games." *Life* 32 (March 24, 1952), pp. 63–64f.

Colver, J. Newton. "Hornsby the Greatest Batter of All Time." *Baseball Magazine* 20 (October 1927), pp. 507–508ff.

Gershman, Michael. "Wooden Weapons." *Sports Heritage* 1 (July–August 1987), pp. 25–32.

Gietschier, Steven P. "Bill Veeck: Indian Chief." *Timeline* 7 (April–May 1990), pp. 28–39.

————. "The Short, Sweet Indian Summer of Satchel Paige." *Timeline* 6 (April–May 1989), pp. 44–53.

BIBLIOGRAPHY

Gould, James M. "How Rogers Hornsby Was Chosen the Most Valuable Player." *Baseball Magazine* 19 (January 1926), pp. 361–362.

Graff, Henry F. "Hornsby, Rogers." In John A. Garraty, ed., *The Dictionary of American Biography: Supplement Seven,* pp. 364–366. New York: Scribner's, 1981.

"The Great Hornsby Mystery: Was Rajah Too Ambitious?" *Literary Digest* 96 (February 25, 1928), pp. 57–60.

"Hard-Boiled Hornsby Starts in on the Browns." *Life* 32 (March 31, 1952), pp. 84–86.

Hornsby, Rogers. "How to Get Fired." *Look* 17 (July 14, 1953), pp. 76–81.

Hornsby, Rogers, and Tim Cohane. "It's Still Baseball, Ty Cobb!" *Look* 16 (June 17, 1952), pp. 55–64.

Hornsby, Rogers, and Kyle Crichton. "Here's What I Mean." *Collier's* 102 (July 16, 1938), pp. 20f.

Hornsby, Rogers, and Bill Surface. "You've Got to Cheat to Win in Baseball." *True* 14 (August 1961), pp. 59–60ff.

———. "What Home-Run Fever Is Doing to Baseball." *This Week Magazine,* March 25, 1962, pp. 12ff.

"Hornsby Out." *Time* 30 (August 2, 1937), p. 35.

"Hornsby's Bend." *Texas Public Employee* 23 (August–September 1968), pp. 10–11f., 10–13.

Lane, Franklin C. "The Amazing Hornsby Deal." *Baseball Magazine* 21 (March 1928), pp. 435–436f.

———. "The Greatest Player in the National League." *Baseball Magazine* 23 (May 1930), pp. 535–536f.

———. "Hornsby Moves On." *Baseball Magazine* 22 (January 1929), pp. 343f.

———. "Hornsby's Winning System." *Baseball Magazine* 19 (November 1926), pp. 540–541f.

———. "How Rogers Hornsby and Frank Frisch Compare." *Baseball Magazine* 20 (June 1927), pp. 291–293f.

———. "The Last of the Field Leaders." *Baseball Magazine* 24 (July 1931), pp. 343–344.

———. "The Passing of Rogers Hornsby." *Baseball Magazine* 25 (October 1932), pp. 487–488f.

———. "Rogers Hornsby: A $250,000 Star." *Baseball Magazine* 14 (April 1921), pp. 507–510f.

Lipsyte, Robert. "Rajah's Return." *New York Times Magazine,* April 29, 1962, pp. 36ff.

BIBLIOGRAPHY

"Lively Controversy over the Lively Ball." *Literary Digest* 103 (October 5, 1929), pp. 78–81.

Macht, Norman. "Woody English Insists—The Babe Didn't Point." *Baseball Research Journal* 20 (1991), pp. 67–68.

Mason, Ward. "The Star of the 1916 Recruits." *Baseball Magazine* 9 (October 1916), pp. 45–48.

Meany, Tom. "Browns Stop Singin' the Blues." *Collier's* 129 (June 12, 1952), pp. 16–17ff.

"New Job, Old Attitude." *Newsweek* 38 (October 22, 1951), p. 91.

Paul, Gabe. "Who Says Hornsby's Too Tough?" *Sport* 8 (July 1953), pp. 20–21f.

Peck, Cecil. "Risk-Taking and Compulsive Gambling," *American Psychologist* 41 (April 1986), pp. 461–465.

Price, Bill. "Braves Field." *Baseball Research Journal* 7 (1978), pp. 1–6.

"Rajah Deposed." *Time* 59 (June 23, 1952), p. 57.

"Sad Decline of Base-Thievery in Baseball." *Literary Digest* 82 (August 2, 1924), pp. 52–53.

Shutt, Timothy Baker. "Year of the Booming Bat." *Sports History* 1 (September 1987), pp. 26–33.

Smart, Steve. "Les Tietje." *National Pastime* 13 (1993), pp. 81–83.

Stockton, J. Roy. "Can the Rajah Rejuvenate the Browns?" *Saturday Evening Post* 224 (February 9, 1952), p. 30f.

Stull, Dorothy. "Conversation Piece: Rogers Hornsby." *Sports Illustrated* 6 (September 10, 1956), pp. 32–34f.

Stump, Al. "Ty Cobb's Wild Ten-Month Fight to Live." *True* 14 (December 1961), pp. 38–41ff; reprinted in Charles Einstein, ed., *The Baseball Reader*, pp. 282–300. New York: Lippincott and Crowell, 1980.

Surface, Bill. "The Last Days of Rogers Hornsby." *Saturday Evening Post* 236 (June 15, 1963), p. 72ff.

Toporcer, George. "The Greatest Hitter of All Time." *Baseball Bluebook* 7 (May 1953), pp. 66–73.

"Under Hornsby and Veeck the Browns Have Ideas." *Look* 16 (June 12, 1952), pp. 67–68f.

Vaughn, Gerald F. "Jorge Pasquel and the Evolution of the Mexican League." *National Pastime* 12 (1992), pp. 9–13.

"Where the Consistent Hitter Wins Out: Interview with Rogers Hornsby." *Baseball Magazine* 19 (September 1926), pp. 438f.

Index

• • •